PROBLEMS IN AFRICAN HISTORY

Problems in African History

The Precolonial Centuries

THIRD UPDATED EDITION

Edited by

ROBERT O. COLLINS

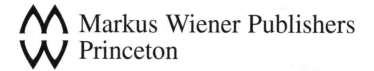 Markus Wiener Publishers
Princeton

Fifth printing, 2010.

For information write to:
Markus Wiener Publishers, Inc.
231 Nassau St., Princeton, NJ 08542
www.markuswiener.com

Map design: David Lanter, Michael Figueroa, Benjamin Arnel Tilentino, Stephen Kirin, Marina Carmen Smith, Lupe Herrera, and Steve Sanderson of the Digital Computer Cartographic Laboratory of UCSB

Book design: Cheryl Mirkin

Library of Congress Cataloguing-in-Publication Data
Problems in African History : the precolonial centuries /
edited by Robert O. Collins.
    Updated ed.
    Includes bibliographical references and index.
    ISBN-13: 978-1-55876-360-9 (alk. paper)
    ISBN-10: 1-55876-360-0 (alk. paper)
    1. Africa—History—To 1884. I. Collins, Robert O., 1933–
DT20.P76 2004
960'.2—dc22   2004057995

Markus Wiener Publishers books are printed in the United States of America on acid-free paper, and meet the guidelines for permanence and durability of the Committee on Production Guidelines for Book Longevity of the Council on Library Resources.

Dedication

*To my former students at the University of California,
Santa Barbara, in Seminar 201,* Problems in African History,
*who have digested, discussed, disagreed, and distilled
over a quarter of a century the abundance of new learning
which has made the "dark continent" light.*

Contents

Preface

This collection of problems in precolonial African history is the product of some of the issues central to understanding the African past that have been digested, discussed, disagreed, and distilled for nearly forty years in my seminar on precolonial Africa. In the last half century the information available for scholars and students about the history of precolonial Afirca has become more abundant and insightful than anyone would have believed in 1960, the year of African independence. The proliferation of monographs and journals spawned by the intellectual enthusiasm, let alone the romance and magnetism of the unknown, has resolved certain issues which were "problems" a generation ago, but at the same time new "problems" have been brought to the attention of scholars that deserve the same scrutiny as those for which there is now a common consensus.

The present revised volume of problems, like its predecessors first published in 1968 and then revised to introduce new problems in 1993, is the continuing distillation in my graduate seminar of the old problems of precolonial Africa and the challenge of the new that have emerged out of our ever-growing understanding of the African past. This revised edition does not introduce any new problems to those in the 1993 edition, but after yet another decade I would be remiss not to include the popular controversy precipitated by the publication of Martin Bernal's *Black Athena: The Afroasiatic Roots of Classical Civilization* in the first problem, "Africa and Egypt." In Problem VI, "Slavery in Africa," I have made an effort to bring a greater balance in understanding the African overseas slave trade by including a discussion of the Asiatic slave trade. Long ignored by scholars obsessed with the trans-Atlantic slave trade, that of Asia has now become a subject of serious study to account for the passage to Asia for over a thousand years of approximately the same number of Africans forced across the Atlantic in less than four hundred. Space, of course, limits the amount of material devoted to each problem, but the selections that follow are those determined not only by myself but by my students through time as the best representatives of the central issues in the African past before the coming of the Europeans.

There are many to whom I owe a debt of gratitude for their ideas and assistance that have enormously improved the presentation of the problems. John O. Hunwick, Professor of History at Northwestern University, was most helpful in conceptualizing the problem of Islam in Africa, and for his wise suggestions as to selections that present the dilemmas and contradictions that arise in an African society confronted by Islam. There is one group that deserves special recognition under the leadership of Proessor David Lanter of the Department of

Geography at the University of California Santa Barbara, and Director of the Digital Computer Cartographic Laboratory at UCSB. Michael Figueroa supervised a team led by Benjamin Arnel Tilentino, Stephen Kirin, Marina Carmen Smith, Lupe Herrera, and Steve Sanderson who produced maps of the highest quality on their friendly computers.

My thanks also go to the following authors for granting permission to reprint their works or portions thereof. Unfortunately, Edith R. Sanders, Sir Harry Johnston, Malcolm Guthrie, Walter Rodney, and Cheikh Anta Diop have died, but their works are perhaps their finest testimonial. Fortunately all the other authors appear to be alive and well and continue to contribute to Africa's past. In order of appearance in the volume they are: Merrick Posnansky, Raymond Mauny, Martin Bernal, Guy MacLean Rogers, Joseph Greenberg, Colin Flight, Thomas Spear, J. D. Omer-Cooper, C. C. Wrigley, Jan Vansina, Thomas Reefe, D. N. Beech, G. I. Jones, Mervyn Hiskett, M. G. Smith, M. L. Juniad, Peter Waterman, John Thornton, Calude Meillassoux, Martin Klein, George Brooks, Iris Berger, Nakanyike Musisi, Oyeronke Oyewumi, J. D. Fage, Suzanne Meirs, Igor Kopytoff, and Paul Lovejoy.

I am grateful to the editors of the following periodicals who have authorized me to reprint passages from their articles: *The Uganda Journal, The Journal of African History, Bulletin de l'Institut d'Afrique Noire, International Journal of American Linguistics,* and *History in Africa.* Finally I wish to acknowledge the kindness of the following publishing firms which permitted me to include passages from books bearing their imprint: George Routledge & Sons Ltd., Cambridge University Press, Free Association Books, Lawrence Hill and Co., Longman Group Ltd., Oxford University Press, University of Wisconsin Press, University of California Press, Holmes and Meier Publishers, the Hamdard Foundation, Afrika-Studiecentrum, Stanford University Press, University of Chicago Press, University of North Carolina Press, and the Pergamon Press.

All but the most necessary footnotes have been eliminated by permission from the selections that follow.

ROC
Santa Barbara, California

Introduction

The study of a peoples' history usually begins with the writings of their historians. For must students this is also the end of their studies. For a few it is but the beginning, the starting point of their own explorations into the source materials bequeathed to them by earlier generations and with which they will fashion their interpretations from within their own culture, education, and intellectual baggage. In the search for the past the historian has two principal tasks. First, the facts must be obtained. Second, they must be interpreted. To do the one without the other reduces the historian to a *griot,* a hagiographer, or a teller of tales more for amusement than education. From ancient times history has always been part of both, but in our modern age previous generations of historians under the impact of science and later social science have set out not only to collect the facts but to interpret them within the context of their own methodology. The range of understanding the past extends from the olympian confidence of Lord Acton's belief in "ultimate history" to the modernists who appear to believe that all that has gone before is a matter of cultural irrelevancy.

The sensible scholars are content if not resigned to the appearance of new interpretations by subsequent generations, no matter how unsound, and only a few still cling to the fading hope of writing definitive history. Nevertheless, the task of the historian has not changed since Herodotus. Facts must be collected and analyzed in the context of an individual's own methodology. Traditionally, facts are found in the written word and are gleaned from chronicles, accounts, narratives, diaries, and documents preserved through the ages. In the nineteenth century historians made a fetish of facts that led, not unnaturally, to a passionate belief that documents, and only documents, can provide the bricks and mortar by which the scholar could reconstruct the past. "The reverent historian approached them [documents] with bowed head and spoke of them in awed tones. If you find it in the documents, it is so."[1]

Today historians still hold to much of the nineteenth century faith in documents; and although they have become more skeptical and critical of their use and reluctantly acknowledge that no definitive interpretation can be derived from any given set of facts, they continue, in the main, to assert that history can only be written from a legacy of words. When the historian writes of the past of literate peoples, perhaps the dependence on documents is justifiable. Unfortunately, this same reliance upon documents, indeed the insistence upon them, has led to a disregard for the past of nonliterate socie-

---

[1]Carr, Edward Hallet, *What is History?* (New York: Vintage, 1961), p. 15.

ties. If a people have left no written records, no documents, no archives, too often the historian assumes that they have no history worth writing. From this position, it is but a short step to the arrogant denial of a peoples' past. Few historians would go that far, not however from any appreciation of a nonliterate society, but from a contentment to rummage through archives and blissfully ignore the history of continents and cultures whose past can conveniently be relegated to an inaccurate footnote.

Such would undoubtedly have remained the position of the history of Africa—at best a codicil to European colonial history, at worst a tale of barbarism not worth remembering—had not the demand of independent Africa and the scholarly research of those not committed to the colonial epoch stimulated the search for it. Even before independence a few historians recognized that Africa had a past and, spurred on by their own interest, sought to find it. In the past generation the number of historians of Africa of every ethnic group has increased to meet the demand of the African people for their own history as well as to satisfy the curiosity of non-Africans about this "new found land" and its inhabitants, Stanley's "Dark Continent." At first the historians of Africa approached its past in the traditional manner, utilizing the methods and techniques refined in the writing of histories of literate societies. Invariably such skills were confined to the examination and interpretation of documents. To the historian of Africa this traditional methodology was not entirely satisfactory. To be sure, there are many documents about the African past both in and outside Africa, but for the most part they are the products of colonial rule or non-African travelers, merchants, and missionaries. This vast body of documentary evidence has and will provide many facts about Africa and the Africans, but even the most ethnocentric historian must sense, even if s/he does not know, that a satisfactory rendering of the African past cannot rely alone on the observations and records of aliens. The dearth of indigenous documentary source materials has clearly discouraged the historian of Africa and probably accounts for the tardy interest in the African past by historians trained in the Western tradition of historiography. Rejected by the limited techniques of his or her own profession, the historian of Africa has turned increasingly to the skills of the natural scientists and social scientists to provide the tools to seek out the history of nonliterate peoples. It is extremely doubtful whether any historian can hope to acquire a competency in the many disciplines now employed to uncover the African past, but if the variety of techniques are beyond human capacity to master, at least the historian of Africa can acquire proficiency in a few and a working acquaintance of the many. If the demands of African history are great, the rewards of exploring an uncharted past are even greater.

"Imagine that Caesar arrived in Gaul and landed in Britain in 1880, a mere century ago, and that your known history began then. You were not

Roman, your language was not Latin, and most of your cherished customs had no historical justification. Your cultural identity was amputated from its past. Would you not feel somewhat incomplete, somewhat mutilated? Would you not wonder what your cultural heritage was before Caesar?...It is no consolation to be told by others that, because there are no written sources, no past can be recovered, as if living traces of that past were not part and parcel of daily life."[1]

The archaeologist has already provided valuable information about the African past. In the future he shall undoubtedly supply even more if provided with the peace and resources which that discipline requires. Fascinated by the lands of the Fertile Crescent or the ruins of dynastic Egypt, archaeologists have expended great energy and thought uncovering the remnants of the cultures of the Middle East and the Nile Valley while to some extent ignoring the rest of Africa. Nevertheless the archaeologist remains virtually the only source of information for the cultures of Africa's ancient inhabitants. With the remarkable excavations of L. S. B. Leakey and his wife Mary at Olduvai Gorge, archaeology revealed the beginning of human history in the region. Its continual evolution was made evident through the further work of Richard Leakey at Lake Turkana and of Professor Johnson among the australopithecines in Ethiopia, not only by uncovering skeletal remains but by analyzing the ruins and patterns of architecture and technology of the evolving cultures up to and including the Age of Iron. Africa has many ruins—Kush, Zimbabwe, Gao, Ngazargamu, Darfur, and Kilwa are among the best known —where excavations have uncovered weapons, tools and pottery, and carbon-14 dating has provided an approximate chronology to accompany the cultural findings. Countless sites are still to be investigated and much remains to be done, but the outlines of ancient Africa have been largely reconstructed by the archaeologist from the facts uncovered and the interpretations of them.

One of the most important and most neglected sources of historical inquiry for the African past has been botanical science. The botanist has provided evidence and understanding of the development and spread of food production that have played such an important role in the evolution of African cultures. Despite the relative dearth of African archaeological remains, there is widespread agreement that crucial cereal crops, sorghum (dura), millets, and rice, are indigenous to Africa and without them the Africans, particularly the Bantu

---

[1] Jan Vansina, *Paths in the Rainforest: Toward a History of Political Tradition in Equatorial Africa* (Madison: University of Wisconsin Press, 1990), p. xi.

peoples, could not have prospered and migrated throughout the continent. All of these crops were cultivated in the savanna plains or river deltas and were the principal foods until the introduction by the Portuguese of maize (corn) and manioc (cassava) from the New World in the fifteenth century. Maize replaced sorghum and the millets as the principal cereal crop while manioc replaced the yam as the principal food crop of the tropical rainforest. Of particular significance was the introduction of the banana from Southeast Asia. It remains unclear as to when the banana first reached the eastern African coast, but there is a sliver of evidence that it was being cultivated in 525 CE at Adulis on the Red Sea. The banana requires relatively little care, yielding massive amounts of edible fruit annually, and remains unaffected by the dry season. It became the staple foodstuff for the expansion of the Bantu on the Lake Plateau of equatorial Africa. Although it remains to be seen whether further botanical research can resolve the conflicting theories regarding the spread of the banana, the assistance of the botanist will continue to contribute to the unraveling of the African past.

Although few historians are acquainted with the intricacies of linguistics, historians in recent years have turned increasingly to linguistic scholarship for information about the relationships and movements of African peoples. Not infrequently, the historians have demanded more than linguistic research warrants and occasionally they have gone further by inferring from linguistic evidence, which they often do not fully understand, conclusions that linguistic scholars themselves are hesitant to accept. Nevertheless, linguistic techniques have provided and will continue to provide tools for the historian that unlock the complexities of the African past, particularly the relationsip of the Bantu languages to those of West Africa. Such relationships between languages with similar characteristics are critical determinants in deciphering the diffusion and migration of Africans, just as the study of the reconstructed ancestral language can often reveal information about the origin of those African speakers and their cultures.

Ethnography, the study of contemporary cultures, has proved an invaluable tool for the historians of Africa. At one time or another every historian of Africa has turned to the descriptions of anthropologists in order to seek understanding of a contemporary culture, for no historian can write of a people's past without knowing something of their present. Moreover, during field work the anthropologist invariably collects information about the past that the historian can utilize, not only to help piece together the history of a particular people, but also to place them in the wider framework of regional or continental history. This is an important distinction, for the investigations of anthropologists in Africa have become for the historian more primary documents than commentaries on contemporary cultures. No cultures are static; they are constantly in a state of change over time. Consequently, anthropological studies undertaken a half century ago frequently have little relevance to that society today. Many Africans have charged the anthropologist as a cultural imperialist, enshrining the ways of a society that may no longer exist or which has changed. There is much truth in that accusation, but it is also unfair, particularly for the historian. If the historian of Africa is probing the past of a peoples fifty years ago, a century, or perhaps more, it is the original documentation written by the anthropologists of those years that provides indispensable information, which otherwise must be reconstructed by complex and suspicious oral traditions or alien documentation of traders, missionaries, or administrators many of whom were not that concerned with the cultural life of the people among whom they lived. Any historian of any sense knows that the anthropological texts may not provide any relevance to an African society of today, but they are the gold mines of the past.

The use of oral traditions to write African history has long been recognized, fully utilized, and abused. In the decades of the 1960s and 1970s the methodology of oral traditions achieved a popularity that, in its enthusiasm, could threaten to brush aside its limitations. Expansive schemes for the collection of oral data have been proposed for nearly a generation with, as one would expect, some astounding insights and analyses as well as those that fall into the category of historical mythology. To their credit the advocates of the use of oral traditions are the first to point out that there are inherent dangers in their use without careful adherence to methods of collection, transmission, rigorous use, and corroboration. They must be examined within the cultural framework of the society, which presupposes a wide knowledge of the people whose traditions are being transcribed. Then the traditions themselves must be analyzed for their authenticity both by external and internal methods of verification. Once the evidence has been collected and its reliability ascertained, the historian must synthesize the data into a meaningful and interpretive account. At this point many pitfalls await the historian, not least among them transferring the relative chronology of age set lists (boys of similar ages initiated into manhood at a singular ceremony) or, at best, generations into the absolute chronology of the historian. Finally, the availability of traditions will vary widely from one African society to another, and the very abundance or dearth will in turn condition their use as evidence. Generally, among sedentary peoples with state systems the traditions passed down from one generation to another will form a larger and more reliable body of documentation than the scattered remembrances of nomadic or seminomadic peoples. Nevertheless, in spite of such limitations and reservations, oral traditions will continue to furnish valuable knowledge of the African past that, when synthesized with sensitivity, will make possible the writing of history hitherto unapproachable through the more customary sources open to the historian.

Finally, the use of documentary evidence itself supplies the basic materials from which most of the history of Africa is written today, and this is not expected to change. Any attempt to discuss the techniques and methods for the analysis of written records would be presumptuous here, for even the beginning student of history is exposed to a plethora of problem books, published collections, and documents and readers from which the student is required to learn how to interpret written evidence. In more advanced history courses, such investigations frequently attain a high level of sophistication; whatever may be the faults of the professional historian, the techniques of document examination are not usually among them. Nevertheless, the very provincialism of Western historians and their absorption with American or European history have frequently led them to believe that Africa is an archival wasteland. Nothing could be further from the truth. Most of the former colonial territories possess archives. Some are staffed by trained archivists and contain records extending back beyond the period of actual colonial rule. The independent African states have sought to expand and modernize these services usually under difficult conditions. Moreover, the district and provincial headquarters outside the capital invariably have extensive and valuable records pertaining to local history, despite their having been severely damaged by local conflicts. The archives of Africa never cease to surprise alien scholars with the richness of their documentation. Beyond Africa, in Europe and America, there are, of course, the well-known archives of colonial ministries, missionary organizations, and philanthropic groups as well as those of learned societies and commercial firms. Together they form an immense body of source materials for the study of the African past. Although historians of Africa are generally well acquainted with these repositories, the exploration of the archives like the writing of African history itself is now in the beginnings of an age of maturation.

TOPOGRAPHIC MAP OF AFRICA

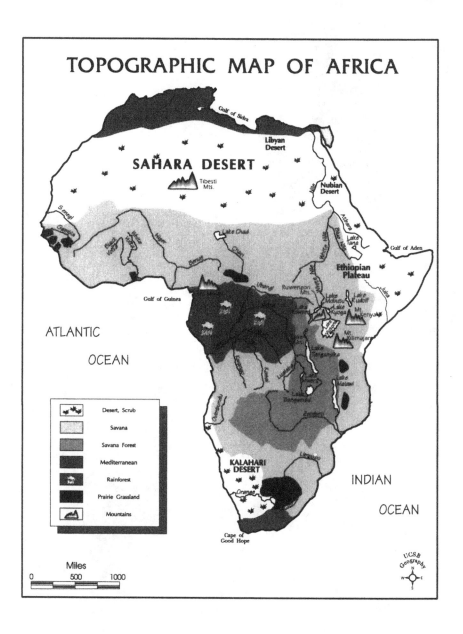

Gulf of Sidra

Libyan Desert

SAHARA DESERT

Tibesti Mts.

Nubian Desert

Senegal

Gambia

Niger

Lake Chad

Benue

Lake Tana

Gulf of Aden

Ethiopian Plateau

Gulf of Guinea

Ruwenzori Mts.

Lake Mobutu

Lake Rudolf

Mt. Kenya

ATLANTIC

OCEAN

Lake Victoria

Mt. Kilimanjaro

Lake Tanganyika

Lake Bangweulu

Lake Malawi

Zambezi

INDIAN

OCEAN

	Desert, Scrub
	Savana
	Savana Forest
	Mediterranean
	Rainforest
	Prairie Grassland
	Mountains

KALAHARI DESERT

Orange

Limpopo

Cape of Good Hope

Miles

0   500   1000

UCSB Geography

N
W—◇—E
S

PROBLEM I
AFRICA AND EGYPT

Although many millennia have elapsed in the evolution of the relationship between dynastic Egypt and African civilizations, scholars have long sought to determine to what extent Africa has borrowed from the culture of Pharaonic Egypt, or more controversially what characteristics Africa has contributed to the growth of Egyptian, Grecian, Roman, and the civilizations of the West. The problem is tantalizing in its geographical, historical, and intellectual sweep, frequently charged with the emotional intensity of identification from those individuals of African descent who seek their claim of cultural affirmation in a disputable Egyptian origin. This is not an academic dissimulation to be argued among the scholastics protected by the ivy-covered walls of academe, but one that strikes at the basic beginnings of cultural orientation, charged with all the emotional rhetoric of racism and the pietistic claims of certitude. The relationship of Africa and Egypt is as old as Herodotus: "Sesostris alone of all Egyptian kings ruled over Ethiopia."[1]

As European explorers, missionaries, and merchants gradually made their way into the interior of the African continent during the nineteenth century, they were astonished and perplexed to encounter states and kingdoms that appeared to contradict the European image of "Darkest Africa." In fact the darkness was the appalling ignorance of Africa and the Africans by supposedly educated and enlightened Europeans. Besides new and exotic cultures, the European incomers were puzzled to discover that the Africans were perfectly capable of organizing their societies within an accepted system of governance. Much of this European skepticism was deeply rooted in the nineteenth-century confirmation by social Darwinists that indeed human evolution had resulted in civilized and primitive, superior and inferior peoples. This dichotomy appeared all the more obvious by the enormous technical disparity between European and African societies that reinforced nineteenth-century ideas of racial inferiority of blacks forged during the centuries of the

---

[1]*The Histories of Herodotus of Halicarnassus*, vol. 1, translated by Harvey Carter (New York: The Heritage Press, 1958), p. 131.

trans-Atlantic slave trade. During the early decades of the twentieth century, Europeans simply refused to accept the idea that black Africans were capable of creating state systems. Scholars, led by E. G. Seligman, the first professor of Ethnology in the University of London, proposed that the political skills of black Africans were clearly learned or borrowed from wandering bands of white Caucasians. The Hamitic Myth was born.[2]

Seligman and others soon expanded their original idea that many African customs were borrowed from dynastic Egypt into a larger theory of "an older wide-flung Hamitic complex," the belief in a race of tall, lean, light-skinned people who originally came from Egypt or southwest Asia and later migrated throughout Africa spreading the superior political and cultural ideas that were inherent in their blood. This "Hamitic hypothesis" inferred that Africa was a primitive wilderness inhabited by peoples who were civilized by the superior, Caucasian migrating Hamites. Consequently, the degree of political and cultural evolution of the African depended upon the milliliters of Hamitic blood carried in their veins. Writing well before Seligman, Sir Harry Johnston in his linguistic studies of the Bantu (see Problem II) observed, or so he thought, a physical similarity between the ancient Hamitic Egyptians and the ruling caste of every Bantu African, implying what later became explicit, that even the political development of African peoples was the product of intermixture with a superior, presumably Hamitic, race.[3]

The Hamitic hypothesis remains as pervasive as it is discredited. Edith R. Sanders argues that not only were there no white Hamites, but those who might have been in Biblical mythology were not the inferior subservient Africans of Noah, who most certainly does not need to have sons of racial differentiation at the time of the great flood. By the sixth century C.E., the oral traditions of the Hebraic community had determined that the descendants of Ham were black, sinful, and degenerate, which later helped to assuage Christian doubts as to the morality of slavery. This idyllic mythology was rudely disturbed by the French invasion of Egypt in 1798, when scholars accompanying the army confirmed that the roots of Western civilization were deeper than those of Athens or Rome and were African Egyptian, a proposition hardly acceptable to the revolutionaries of France despite the intellectual universality of the eighteenth-century Enlightenment.

If Sanders cites biblical texts to change the leopard's spots, Merrick Posnansky brings to bear the heavy artillery of archaeology to argue that kingship in Uganda came from Uganda and not dynastic Egypt. In discussing the relationship between Pharaonic Egypt and Uganda, particularly the interlacustrine kingdoms, Professor Posnansky can find little or no evidence from archaeological sites to link any direct

---

[2]For a summarization of the Hamitic hypothesis, see Professor C. G. Seligman, "Some Aspects of the Hamitic Problem," in the *Journal of the Royal Anthropological Institute*, London, The Institute, vol. XLIII, 1913, pp. 665–7.

[3]See: Presidential Address to the Anthropological Section, *Reports of the British Association for the Advancement of Science* (Manchester, 1915), pp. 11–12.

Egyptian influence in tropical Africa. He asserts that such theories have been based on very inadequate information. Indeed, he argues with his accustomed precision that a great deal of firm evidence exists to indicate the independent development of cultures. While recognizing the similarities between certain dynastic Egyptian and interlacustrine cultures, he argues that:

> With large gaps in the evidence available it is premature to accept any single hypothesis to explain either direct links between Uganda and other cultural areas, such as Ethiopia or Meroe, or the role of the Nile Valley civilizations in the diffusion of political ideas and institutions.[4]

The French savants who accompanied Napoleon's military expedition to Egypt founded not only the modern study of Egyptology but also the perplexing relationship between ancient Egypt and Africa. From that time forth the arguments have opened the floodgates of intellectual inquiry and emotional passion as to whether the dynastic Egyptians were blacks who made significant contributions to the Western world, while Napoleon's scholars were converting Hamites into Caucasians whose mission was to bring civilization to Africa. One of the most significant protagonists in this "Great Debate" thought otherwise. The late Cheikh Anta Diop from Senegal argued forcefully that the Egyptians were neither Hamites nor Caucasians dispensing civilization to Africans but in fact were themselves black Africans.

Cheikh Anta Diop asked, "What were the Egyptians?" He insists that the available evidence clearly demonstrates that the Egyptians were black, and as the ancestors of the Africans living throughout the continent today, they were the first to devise the disciplines of mathematics, science, religion (Divine Kingship), agriculture, and medicine, ironically using the very evidence of his most ideological adversary, Professor C. G. Seligman. Diop's hypothesis has been extremely influential in the revival of the African past and in the formation of an African-based school of scholarship that emphasizes the role of Africa in Egypt.

Raymond Mauny has critically examined some of the principal proofs employed by Diop to support his thesis and rejects them. Although more than willing to admit that there were certainly Africans in ancient Egypt, a matter about which there is virtually no dispute, Professor Mauny denies that the Egyptians were the ancestors of the inhabitants of the present population of West Africa. Rather, Egypt to Mauny was a melting pot of many ethnic groups from Asia as well as Africa, and to credit dynastic Egyptian civilization to any one particular group is blatant racism. Mauny cannot accept the degrading practical and intellectual need for Africans to require the diffusion of political, economic, or social ideas from the Hamites or the Egyptians. Nor does he see the necessity for the refugees by the Nile from the deser-

---

[4]Merrick Posnansky, "Kingship, Archaeology, and Historical Myth," Presidential address, 19 January 1966, in *Uganda Journal*, 30, no. 1 (Kampala, Uganda: the Uganda society, 1966), pp. 1–12.

tification of the Sahara to seek civilization from those of the Sahel, the grasslands south of the desert. Increasingly, scholars like Mauny are reluctant to accept the direct transfer of ideas and institutions uncritically from one culture to another and today place greater emphasis on the independent development of institutions hitherto assumed to have been borrowed.

A year after the death of Cheikh Anta Diop in 1986 Martin Bernal published *Black Athena: The Afroasiatic Roots of Classical Civilization*, in which he argued persuasively that the evolution of western civilization from Greece was a complex interaction between Greece and the Afroasiatic cultures of much greater antiquity, particularly dynastic Egypt. He argued that the ancestors of the classical Greeks were civilized by Egyptian and Phoenician colonization and the later Greeks regularly studied in Egypt. Until the eighteenth century European Enlightenment, Egypt was still regarded as the source of learning that included that of the classical Greeks. Thereafter the age of reason opposed Egyptian philosophical thought in favor of Greek artistic perfection and the development of Eurocentric racism. Thus the ancient dark-skinned African Egyptians, *Black Athena*, lost their heritage as the precursors of western civilization to the classical Greeks.[5]

The publication of *Black Athena* in 1987 produced a storm of controversy that was swept up in the popular media, emotionally discussed in the public forum, and fiercely defended by Martin Bernal and his supporters when his arguments were attacked by the legion of classical scholars that resulted in the publication of *Black Athena Revisited* in 1996 in which Guy MacLean Rogers summed up the arguments for the Greeks in his *Quo Vadis*.[6]

By the beginning of the twenty-first century the two opposing sides have more or less declared an armistice. On the one hand classical scholars can no longer discount the importance of the influence of Egypt and the Near East on Greek civilization. On the other hand the dynastic Egyptians are most certainly in Africa but not the culmination of the unique development of African societies and states in sub-Saharan Africa.[7]

---

[5]Jacques Berkinerblau, *Heresy in the University: The Black Athena Controversy and the Responsibilities of American Intellectuals* (New Brunswick: Rutgers University Press, 1999).

[6]See also: Mary Lefkowitz, *Not Out of Africa: How Afrocentrism Became an Excuse to Teach Myth as History* (New York: Basic Books, 1996).

[7]See also: Martin Bernal's rebuttal to Lefkowitz and Rogers: Martin Bernal, *Black Athena Writes Back* (Chapel Hill, N.C.: Duke University Press, 2001).

The Hamitic Hypothesis: Its Origin in Time

BY EDITH R. SANDERS[8]

The Hamitic hypothesis is well-known to students of Africa. It states that everything of value ever found in Africa was brought there by the Hamites, allegedly a branch of the Caucasian race.

On closer examination of the history of the idea, there emerges a previous elaborate Hamitic theory, in which the Hamites are believed to be Negroes. It becomes clear then that the hypothesis is symptomatic of the nature of race relations, that it has changed its content if not its nomenclature through time, and that it has become a problem of epistemology.

In the beginning there was the Bible. The word "Ham" appears there for the first time in Genesis, chapter five. Noah cursed Ham, his youngest son, and said:

> Cursed be Canaan;
> A servant of servants shall he be
> unto his brethren.
> And he said, Blessed be Jehovah, the God of
> Shem; And let Canaan be his servant. God enlarge
> Japhet, And let him dwell in the tent of Shem
> And let Canaan be his servant.

Then follows an enumeration of the sons of Noah: Shem, Ham, Japhet, and their sons who were born to them after the flood. The Bible makes no mention of racial differences among the ancestors of mankind. It is much later that an idea of race appears with reference to the sons of Noah; it concerns the descendants of Ham. The Babylonian Talmud, a collection of oral traditions of the Jews, appeared in the sixth century AD; it states that the descendants of Ham are cursed by being black, and depicts Ham as a sinful man and his progeny as degenerates. Thus, early tradition identified

---

[8]Edith R. Sanders (1922–1990) received her Ph.D. in anthropology from Columbia University in 1968. She taught at Fairleigh Dickinson University in New Jersey and then at Fordham University in New York City. Among her publications are: *Anthropology, Hamlet,* and *History* published in 1987; *Diogenes,* in 1977; and *The Hamitic Hypothesis; Its Origin and Function in Time Perspective,* in 1969, from *Journal of African History,* 10, no. 4 (Cambridge: Cambridge University Press), pp. 521–532.

the Hamites with Negroes and endowed them with both certain physiognomical attributes and an undesirable character. This notion persisted in the Middle Ages, when fanciful rabbinical expansions of the Genesis stories were still being made. Ham, some of them said, was supposed to have emasculated Noah, who cursed him thus:

> Now I cannot beget the fourth son whose children I would have ordered to serve you and your brothers! Therefore it must be Canaan, your firstborn, whom they enslave. And since you have disabled me . . . doing ugly things in blackness of night, Canaan's children shall be borne ugly and black! Moreover, because you twisted your head around to see my nakedness, your grandchildren's hair shall be twisted into kinks, and their eyes red; again because your lips jested at my misfortune, theirs shall swell; and because you neglected my nakedness, they shall go naked, and their male members shall be shamefully elongated! Men of this race are called Negroes, their forefather Canaan commanded them to love theft and fornication, to be banded together in hatred of their masters and never to tell the truth.

Scholars who study the Hebrew myths of the Genesis claim that these oral traditions grew out of a need of the Israelites to rationalize their subjugation of Canaan, a historical fact validated by the myth of Noah's curse. Talmudic or Midrashic explanations of the myth of Ham were well known to Jewish writers in the Middle Ages, as seen in this description by Benjamin of Tudela, a twelfth-century merchant and traveller south of Aswan:

> There is a people . . . who, like animals, eat of the herbs that grow on the banks of the Nile and in their fields. They go about naked and have not the intelligence of ordinary men. They cohabit with their sisters and anyone they can find . . . they are taken as slaves and sold in Egypt and neighbouring countries. These sons of Ham are black slaves.

Ideas have a way of being accepted when they become useful as a rationalization of an economic fact of life. As Graves and Patai put it, "That Negroes are doomed to serve men of lighter color was a view gratefully borrowed by Christians in the Middle Ages; a severe shortage of cheap manual labor caused by the plague made the reinstitution of slavery attractive."

The notion of the Negro-Hamite was generally accepted by the year 1600. In one of the earliest postmedieval references found, Leo Africanus, the great Arab traveller and onetime protege of Pope Leo X, wrote about Negro Africans as being descended from Ham. His translator, the Englishman John Pory, followed the text with his own commentary in which he stressed the punishment suffered by Ham's descendants, thus reinforcing the myth in modern times.

Some seventeenth-century writers acquaint us with notions current in their time by citing European authors, known or unknown today, who wrote, directly or indirectly, about the low position of Negro-Hamites in the world. This was further strengthened by European travellers who went to Africa for reasons of trade or curiosity. Concurrently, there existed another point of view, in which the term "Hamite" denoted a sinner of some sort, not necessarily a Negro, although the characteristics of the Hamite were the same negative ones variously attributed to the Negro.

The idea of a Negro-Hamite was not universally accepted. Some individuals believed that the blackness of the Negro was caused by the soil on which he lived together with the extreme heat of the sun. Others doubted that either the climate theory or the efficacy of Noah's curse were responsible for the Negro's physiognomy, but reasoned that "their colour and wool are innate or seminal, from their first beginning. . . ."

By and large, however, the Negro was seen as a descendant of Ham, bearing the stigma of Noah's curse. This view was compatible with the various interests extant at that time. On the one hand, it allowed exploitation of the Negro for economic gain to remain undisturbed by any Christian doubts as to the moral issues involved. "A servant of servants shall he be" clearly meant that the Negro was preordained for slavery. Neither individual nor collective guilt was to be borne for a state of the world created by the Almighty. On the other hand, Christian cosmology could remain at peace, because identifying the Negro as a Hamite—thus as a brother—kept him in the family of man in accordance with the biblical story of the creation of mankind.

The eighteenth century saw an efflorescence of scientific inquiry, which directed its efforts to the understanding of man's place in the world. Modern science had developed a century earlier and had attempted to establish order in the universe; the nature of man, however, was not part of scientific investigation, but remained in the province of theology. This state of affairs became unsatisfactory to the later scholars, namely the philosophers of the Enlightenment, who tried to apply scientific methods to the study of man and whose theories as to the origin of the race often came into direct conflict with the Scriptures.

The Negro's place in nature was the subject of great debate at that time. One of the crucial issues of this debate was the question of unity in mankind, or monogenism, as opposed to the separate creation of races of polygenism. The concept of the Negro-Hamite was steadily losing ground because theological interpretation of the peopling of the world did not satisfy the men of the Enlightenment. The myth was now kept alive mainly by the clergy, who tried to keep their hold on the laity by discrediting the savants as infidels.

The polygenist theories led to a widespread belief that the Negro was subhuman and at the same time de-emphasized his relationship to the accursed Ham. The monogenist theories attempted to explain Negro physical characteristics by natural rather than mythical causes. The conservative theologians still clung to the now classic exegesis of the Old Testament and discouraged any attempt at a different interpretation. At the end of the eighteenth century, many famous men espoused and popularized one or two views regarding the Negro. One was that he was the result of "degeneration" due to various environmental conditions. The other and more frequent view was that he was a separate creation, subhuman in character.

The Western world, which was growing increasingly rich on the institution of slavery, grew increasingly reluctant to look at the Negro slave and see him as a brother under the skin. Some writers feel that the image of the Negro deteriorated in direct proportion to his value as a commodity, and the proudly rational and scientific white man was impatient to find some definitive proof for the exclusion of the Negro from the family of man and for ultimate denial of common ancestry.

The catalyst which made this possible was an historical event, namely Napoleon's invasion of Egypt in 1798. Because Napoleon shared the passion for science and antiquities that was the hallmark of the Enlightenment, he invited archaeologists and other scientists to join him. The experts who had accompanied him discovered treasures that led them to found the new science of Egyptology and an institute on Egyptian soil. These discoveries were to revolutionize history's view of the Egyptian and lay the basis for a new Hamitic myth.

Napoleon's scientists made the revolutionary discovery that the beginnings of Western civilization were earlier than the civilizations of the Romans and the Greeks. Mysterious monuments, evidences of the beginnings of science, art, and well-preserved mummies were uncovered. Attention was drawn to the population that lived among these ancient splendours and was presumably descended from the people who had created them. It was a well-mixed population, such as it is at the present time, with physical types running from light to black and with many physiognomical variations. The French scholars came to the conclusion that the Egyptians were Negroids. Denon, one of Napoleon's original expedition, describes them as such, ". . . a broad and flat nose, very short, a large flattened mouth . . . thick lips, etc."

The view that the Egyptians were "Negroid" and highly civilized apparently existed before the French expedition to Egypt. Count Volney, a French traveller to the Middle East, spent four years in Egypt and Syria and wrote in a well-known book:

How are we astonished . . . when we reflect that to the race of negroes, at present our slaves, and the objects of our contempt, we owe our arts, sciences . . . when we recollect that, in the midst of these nations, who call themselves the friends of liberty and humanity, the most barbarous of slaveries is justified; and that it is even a problem whether the understandings of negroes be of the same species with that of white men!

In spite of the deserved respect which Volney enjoyed, his opinions on this subject were not accepted.

Nevertheless, the Egyptian expedition made it impossible to hide that seeming paradox of a population of Negroids who were, once upon a time, originators of the oldest civilization of the West. The conflicting ideologies which existed in the West made it difficult for the various proponents of these ideologies to deal with the notion as it stood. Such a notion upset the main existing tenets; it could not be internalized by those individuals on both sides of the Atlantic who were convinced of the innate inferiority of the Negro, nor by those who adhered to the biblical explanation of the origin of races. To the latter such an idea was blasphemous, as Noah's curse condemned the Hamites to misery and precluded high original achievement.

Egypt became the focus of great interest among the scientists as well as among the lay public. The fruits of this interest were not long in coming. A few short years after the Egyptian expedition, there appeared a large number of publications dealing with Egypt and Egyptians. Many of these works seemed to have had as their main purpose an attempt to prove in some way that the Egyptians were not Negroes. The arguments which follow brought forth the questions of language, migration, ancient writers, and the existence of mummies. The polygenist theories of race postulated that as each race was created separately, so it was endowed with its own language. Because the Coptic language was clearly related to Arabic, it was convenient to draw the conclusion that the nations who spoke related languages must have proceeded from one parental stock. Since the Ethiopians, Nubians, and other allied peoples were declared not to be Negro by European travellers, the Egyptians could not be said to be of African (Negro) race, as all of these peoples were colonists from Syria or Arabia Felix. Since ancient writers were silent on the subject of the Negroid physiognomy of the Egyptians, it was understood that in effect Egyptians were not Negroid, as such a fact would have startled the ancients into a detailed description. Herodotus himself, ran the argument, described them in comparative not absolute terms. Thus "black and woolly haired" meant black as compared to the Greeks and woolly haired as compared to the Greeks. Some said that the existence of the mummies itself constitute sufficient proof that these people were non-Negro; to W. G. Browne the . . . prescience of that people concerning errors into which posterity might fall, exhibits irrefutable proof of their features and of the colour of their skin . . . clearly implying, therefore, that the ancient Egyptians knew they could be mistaken for Negroes, and so left their bodies in evidence to refute such an allegation.

Browne insisted that the Egyptians were white. Although he himself did not call them "Hamites," he paved the way for his successors who were to identify the Egyptians as such.

Modern times showed their influence on theological writings as well. The new Hamitic concept made its appearance quite early in the nineteenth century, spearheaded by the clergy. If the Negro was a descendant of Ham, and Ham was cursed, how could he be the creator of a great civilization? It follows logically that the theologians had to take another look, both at the Bible and at its explanation of the origin of the races of man. The veracity of the Scriptures obviously could not be denied. New interpretations of the meaning of Scriptures were offered. Egyptians, it was now remembered, were descendants of Mizraim, a son of Ham. Noah had only cursed Canaan-son-of-Ham, so that it was Canaan and his progeny alone who suffered the malediction. Ham, his other sons, and their children were not included in the curse.

For example, the Reverend M. Russell took up the issue of the Hamites and the Egyptians:

> In the sacred writings of the Hebrews it [Egypt] is called Mizraim
> . . . the name which is applied to Egypt by the Arabs of the
> present day. The Copts retain the native word "Chemia" which
> perhaps has some relation to Cham, the son of Noah; or as Plu-
> tarch insinuates, may only denote that darkness of colour which
> appears in a rich soil or in the human eye.

He admits that there is a peculiarity of feature common to all the Copts, but asserts that neither in countenance nor personal form is there any resemblance to the Negro.

He and other scholars re-read the Book of Genesis focusing on the genealogy of the three ancestors of mankind, and especially Ham. The histories of the sons of Ham were discussed, particularly those of Cush and Mizraim. The question was raised then whether it was Ham who had been cursed after all, or was it only Canaan? It was indeed Canaan who was cursed, but the rest of the progeny of Ham went on to prosper.

So it came to pass that the Egyptians emerged as Hamites, Caucasoid, uncursed and capable of high civilization. This view became widely accepted and it is reflected in the theological literature of that era. A survey of Biblical dictionaries of the period is quite revealing as to the wide acceptance of the new Hamites. *Cyclopedia of Biblical Literature,* published in 1846 by John Kitto, D.D., F.S.A., has a long article under the name *Ham.* It is stressed that the curse of Noah is directed only against Canaan. The general opinion is stated that all southern nations derive from Ham. However, the article admits difficulties in tracing the history of the most important Hamitic nations—the Cushites, the Phoenicians, and the Egyptians—due to their great intermixture with foreign peoples. Thus, the early decades of the nineteenth century greeted a new Hamitic myth, this time with a Caucasoid protagonist. At the same time the scientific bases of the new Hamitic myth were being devised and, allegedly, substantiated.

Perhaps because slavery was both still legal and profitable in the United States, and because it was deemed necessary and right to protect it, there arose an American school of anthropology which attempted to prove scientifically that the Egyptian was a Caucasian, far removed from the inferior Negro. As Mannheim said, each intellectual stand is functionally dependent on the "differentiated social group reality standing behind it." Such workers as Dr. Morton, assisted in various ways by Josiah Nott and George Gliddon, collected, measured, interpreted and described the human crania. The comparative studies made of these crania led Morton to believe that the Egyptian osteological formation was Caucasian, and that it was a race indigenous to the Nile Valley. He also postulated fixity of species, considering it a primordial organic form, permanent through time. Nott and Gliddon, who acted as Morton's apostles, also bolstered his interpretation by explaining the Negroid admixture of the Egyptians as being a population which descended from numerous Negro slaves kept by Egyptians in ancient days. These theories attempted to include the Egyptians in the branch of the Caucasoid race, to explain their accomplishments on the basis of innate racial superiority, and to exclude the Negro from any possibility of achievement by restating his alleged inferiority and his position of "natural slave." The conclusions of American scholars found a receptive audience in Europe, where craniology was considered to yield positive and meaningful data, a point of view expressed by two scientists of world renown, the Drs. Retzius of Sweden and Broca of France. The intellectual vogue of the day was the stress on "facts," not abstract theories, in all disciplines. Craniology provided a seemingly concrete "fact," thus fitting in neatly with the prevailing academic attitudes. Again, there was no complete consensus among anthropologists. The most prominent opponent of the American school of anthropology was James Prichard of England, who was not convinced that the Egyptians belonged to the Caucasian race.

The science of philology added weight to the new Hamitic theory. This young science was developing at a time when language and race were considered to be inextricably bound together, an approach which lent itself to polygenist theories. Bunsen, a philologist and an Egyptologist, reported two branches of cognate languages, the Semitic and what he called the Iranian. Khamitic or Egyptian he postulated to be anterior to Semitic and antediluvian. Here was irrefutable proof, it seemed, that the Hamitic language belonged to the Caucasoid peoples, and it was eagerly adopted by scholars and theologians. The new Hamitic myth was gaining momentum.

The late nineteenth century provided two new ideologies which utilized and expanded the concept of the Caucasoid Hamite: colonialism and modern racism. Both shaped the European attitude to Africa and Africans. The travellers found a variety of physical types in Africa, and their ethnocentrism made them value those who looked more like themselves. These were declared to be Hamitic, or of Hamitic descent, and endowed with the myth of superior achievements and considerable beneficial influence on their Negro brothers. John Hanning Speke was seminal to the Hamitic hypothesis which we know today. Upon discovery of the kingdom of Buganda with its complex political organization, he attributed its "barbaric civilization" to a nomadic pastoralist race related to the Hamitic Galla, thus setting the tone for the interpreters to come. The Hamites were designated as early culture-bearers in Africa owing to the natural superiority of intellect and character of all Caucasoids. Such a viewpoint had dual merit for European purposes: it maintained the image of the Negro as an inferior being, and it pointed to the alleged fact that development could come to him only by mediation of the white race. It also implied a self-appointed duty of the "higher" races to civilize the "lower" ones, a notion which was eventually formulated as "the white man's burden." At this point in time, the Hamite found himself in an ambiguous position. On the one hand he was considered to be Caucasoid, that is superior. On the other hand he was a native, part of the "burden," a man to benefit from European civilization. Here the Teutonic theory of race showed its adaptability. Having devised a hierarchy within the Caucasian race, the builders of the theory placed the Teutonic Anglo-Saxon on top of the ladder with the Slavs on the lowest rung. But an even lower position could always be added, and the Hamites filled the space admirably. Politics and race theories seemed natural allies; they provided a seemingly cogent ideological framework for colonial expansion and exploitation.

The beginning of the twentieth century saw the Caucasoid-Hamite solidly established. Science supplanted theology as the alpha and omega of truth. Racial "scientific" classifications, which had to face the physical diversity of the various "Hamites," established a separate Hamitic *branch* of the Caucasian race, closely following the creation of a linguistic entity called a *family* of Hamitic languages. Linguistic typologies were based on racial types and racial classifications on linguistic definitions. The confusion surrounding the "Hamite" was steadily compounded as the terms of reference became increasingly overlapping and vague. The racial classification of "Hamites" encompassed a great variety of types from fair-skinned, blonde, blue-eyed (Berbers) to black (Ethiopians). Two early racial typologies were devised by Sergi and Brinton. Sergi called certain populations Hamitic chiefly on the basis of their linguistic characteristics. Among these were the inhabitants of the Sahara, the Berbers and even such people "who have wholly, or partially, lost their language," like the Egyptians, Watusi and Masi. They were divided into the Eastern branch, and the Northern branch. The Eastern branch included the ancient and modern Egyptians (excluding the Arabs), Nubians, Bejas, Abyssinians, Gallas, Danakil, Somali, Masai and Watusi (or Wa-huma). The Northern branch included the Berbers, Tebus, Fulbes (Fulani) and the Gaunches of the Canaries. Brinton denoted Lybians, Egyptians, and the East African groups as Hamitic, and remarked that each of these groups is distinguished by physical and linguistic differences. He went on to state that "the physical appearance of the Libyan peoples distinctly marks them as members of the white race, often of uncommonly pure blood. As the race elsewhere, they present the blonde and brunette type, the latter predominant, but the former extremely well marked." Because Brinton also considered the Iberians to be Hamites, and not Basques, his description of the Libyans seems to imply that the Libyans are a sort of halfway house of the "Hamitic" race, because they combine elements of the blonde Hamites (of Europe) and the brunette Hamites (of East Africa). This reasoning appears to be no more logical than that of Sergi, who first bases a racial group on its linguistic characteristics and then includes in it people who have "wholly or partially" lost the language!

Linguistic classifications were based on geography, racial characteristics, and occupation, rather than on rigorous methodology pertaining solely to language. Grammatical gender became the main diagnostic of the so-called Hamitic languages. Although grammatical gender exists in many unrelated languages of the world, it was not found in the languages of the "true" Negro (racial category again). Thus linguistic typologies had racial bases just as racial typologies were based on linguistics.

Because the Hamites discovered in Africa south of the Sahara were described as pastoralists and the traditional occupation of the Negro was supposedly agriculture, pastoralism and all its attributes became endowed with an aura of superiority of culture, giving the Hamite a third dimension: cultural identity.

The historians who began to compile histories of Africa wrote with an often unconscious racial bias, and accepted the dicta of the discoverers of that continent as indisputable proven facts and presented them as historical explanations of the African past.

Much of anthropology gave its support to the Hamitic myth. Seligman found a cultural substratum of supposedly great influence in Africa. In 1930 he published his famous *Races of Africa,* which went through several editions and which was reprinted in 1966 still basically unchanged. He refined the Sergi-devised classifications of Hamitic peoples, adding the category of Nilotes or "half-Hamites." Every trace and/or sign of what is usually termed "civilized" in Africa was attributed to alien, mainly Hamitic, origin. In such a way, ironworking was supposed to have been introduced to the Negroes by pastoral Hamites, along with complex political institutions, irrigation and age-grade systems. Archaeological findings of any magnitude were also ascribed to outside influences and kept the Negro African out of his own culture history. In the eyes of the world the Negro stood stripped of any intellectual or artistic genius and of any ability at all which would allow him, now, in the past, or in the future, to be the master of his life and country.

The confluence of modern nationalism and the ensuing modern racism evolved from earlier nineteenth-century national romanticism and developed through theories of de Gobineau and adaptations of the Darwinian revolution. It was echoed in all Western nations, culminating finally in the ideology of Nazi Germany. Because that leading exponent of racism became the enemy of most of Europe and of the United States during World War II, German-championed ideology seemed to have lost some of its popularity. The Hamitic myth ceased to be useful with African nations that have been gaining their independence one by one, and the growing African nationalism drew scholarly attention to Africa's past. Many of the scholars were unencumbered by colonial ties; some of them were themselves African. They began to discover that Africa was not a *tabula rasa*, but that it had a past, a history which could be reconstructed; that it was a continent which knew empire builders at a time when large areas of Europe stagnated in the Dark Ages; that it knew art and commerce.

Some writers started to throw doubts on the Hamitic hypothesis by discovering indigenous Negro achievements of the past, while others attempted to explode it. Still the myth endures, is occasionally subverted by new terminology (such as "Southern Cushites"), and stubbornly refuses to give way and allow an unbiased look at what can be validly ascertained from African culture history. It would be well-nigh impossible to point to an individual and recognize in him a Hamite according to racial, linguistic and cultural characteristics to fit the image that has been presented to us for so long. Such an individual does not exist. The word still exists, endowed with a mythical meaning; it endures through time and history, and, like a chameleon, changes its colour to reflect the changing light. As the word became flesh, it engendered many problems of scholarship.

The anthropological and historical literature dealing with Africa abounds with references to a people called the "Hamites." "Hamite," as used in these writings, designates an African population supposedly distinguished by its race—Caucasian—and its language family, from the Negro inhabitants of the rest of Africa below the Sahara.

There exists a widely held belief in the Western world that everything of value ever found in Africa was brought there by these Hamites, a people inherently superior to the native populations. This belief, often referred to as the Hamitic hypothesis, is a convenient explanation for all the signs of civilization found in Black Africa. It was these Caucasoids, we read, who taught the Negro how to manufacture iron and who were so politically sophisticated that they organized the conquered territories into highly complex states with themselves as the ruling elites. This hypothesis was preceded by another elaborate Hamitic theory. The earlier theory, which gained currency in the sixteenth century, was that the Hamites were black savages, "natural slaves"—and Negroes. This identification of the Hamite with the Negro, a view which persisted throughout the eighteenth century, served as a rationale for slavery, using Biblical interpretations in support of its tenets. The image of the Negro deteriorated in direct proportion to the growth of the importance of slavery, and it became imperative for the white man to exclude the Negro from the brotherhood of races. Napoleon's expedition to Egypt in 1798 became the historical catalyst that provided the Western World with the impetus to turn the Hamite into a Caucasian.

The Hamitic concept had as its function the portrayal of the Negro as an inherently inferior being and to rationalize his exploitation. In the final analysis it was possible because its changing aspects were supported by the prevailing intellectual viewpoints of the times.

Kingship, Archaeology, and Historical Myth

MERRICK POSNANSKY[9]

The Kingdoms of Uganda have for the past hundred years been a focal point of interest to historians and anthropologists. The attention focussed on the Kingdoms, as on other centralized states in Africa, has unfortunately created an imbalance in the evidence available to both historian and archaeologist and led to an overemphasis of the importance of the role of the centralized state in African history. The origin of the Kingdoms has exercised the particular attention of the culture historian. The early visitors and writers from Speke onwards saw the rise of the Kingdoms as undoubtedly due to northern influences, probably Hamitic invaders, though the role of Egypt was always stressed particularly by Johnston who wrote "the influence of Egyptian civilization profoundly affected Negro Africa." Seligman, who concentrated on a combination of language, economy, and physical morphology, enshrined in academic trappings the Hamitic myth, which has lasted until the present day and was restated in a modified form as late as 1963 by Huntingford. The Hamitic myth quite plainly regarded "the civilisations of Africa" as the "civilisations of the Hamites," "the great civilising force of black Africa from a relatively early period." Gorju, as a modification of this myth, linked the origin of many of the Interlacustrine peoples, and particularly the ruling groups, quite firmly with Ethiopia and it is tempting to see in the views of some of the early missionaries the origin of the oral tradition which derives early kings or peoples from Ethiopia.

More recently, Father Crazzolara in his three volumes on the Lwoo has

[9]Posnansky, Merrick, "Kingship, Archaeology, and Historical Myth," Presidential address delivered on 19 January 1966, *Uganda Journal* 30, no. 1 (Kampala, Uganda: The Uganda Society, 1966), pp. 1–12.

Merrick Posnansky (1931–) was educated at Nottingham and Cambridge Universities after which he became the curator of the Uganda Museum, 1958–1962, and the Assistant Director of the British Institute in East Africa from 1962–64. From 1964–67 he was the Director of the African Studies Program at Makerere University College before becoming the Professor of Archaeology at the University of Ghana from 1967–76 after which he accepted the Professorship in History and Anthropology at the University of California Los Angeles. As well as Director of the African Studies Center at UCLA, he has energetically carried out archaeological research in Togo and Benin.

introduced the idea of the Nilotic Lwoo being the progenitors of Kingship.[10] Ogot has reviewed the substance of the Hamitic myth and the Nilotic origin of the Interlacustrine states and come to the conclusion, partly following the lead given by Evans-Pritchard and Lienhardt (in their studies of the Shilluk), that the Kingdoms were not introduced institutions but were "only consolidated either under . . . (Nilotic) . . . rule or in defence against them." Murdock in his monumental study of the whole of Africa's culture history substitutes Cushites for Hamites and sees in the earthworks of Western Uganda and the Kingship of Buganda comparisons with Sidamo earthworks and Kafa Kingship.[11] The Cushite he sees as both pre-Bantu and pre-Nilote. A further study of Africa as a whole has led Oliver and Fage in their *Short History of Africa* to define the "Sudanic" state as "a superstructure erected over village communities of peasant cultivators rather than as a society which had grown up naturally out of them" with "the ideas of ancient Egypt, percolating through the Meroitic filter" as "the basic element of the 'Sudanic' civilization."

The purpose of this paper is to review this welter of conflicting opinion and to decide which, if any, theory is based on fact and fits the Uganda situation. Central to the whole controversy is whether divine-type Kingship (or Sacral rulership, Sudanic Kingship, or African despotism, which are but variants of the same theme) developed independently at different African centres under the same or varied circumstances or whether there is, as Murdock puts it, a mental blueprint of a despotic political structure, transmitted from generation to generation as part of traditional verbal culture, and always available to be transmitted into reality. If there is such a blueprint, was its origin Ethiopia or Egypt and were its transmitters Hamites, Nilotes, Cushites, or some other un-named people? The question of origin raises the problem of defining the role of the Nile Valley civilisations in African history.

Up to now the bulk of evidence used for theorising on the problem has been linguistic, anthropological (both physical and social), historical (both orally transmitted and written), the comparative analysis of political institutions, and, in the case of Murdock, a comparative study of agricultural economies. On the whole the archaeological evidence has been ignored or looked upon only as of secondary importance in supporting a theory formulated on the basis of other approaches. The excuse of the present writer in trying to pose questions for which we may never have the answers, is to add the findings of archaeology to the arguments previously employed. The Nubian campaign, initiated by the urgency of rescue operations consequent

---

[10]Father J. P. Crazzolara, *The Lwoo.* Part I, Lwoo Migrations, Verona, 1960; Part II, Lwoo Traditions, Verona, 1951; Part III, Clans, Verona, 1954.

[11]George Peter Murdock, *Africa: Its People and their Cultural History* (New York: McGraw-Hill, Inc., 1959).

upon the erection of the Aswan High Dam, has recently thrown new light on the later developments of civilisation in the Nile Valley. Dates are now also being released from excavations initiated by the Uganda Museum as part of the Uganda Iron Age Project which add a fresh interest to arguments concerning the builders of Bigo.

It is to Nubia that we have to look for the earliest contacts between Egypt and Africa to the South. The discovery of negroid burials dating to the tenth millennium BC indicates that Nubia was very much a racial as well as a cultural contact zone. Research in Nubia has demonstrated that rather than the influence of Egypt being unbroken, following its extension of administrative control to the south after 1500 BC the influence of the African hinterland of Nubia was perhaps more pervasive than that of Egypt. The pottery of the Meroitic period (?300 BC—310 AD) resembles more closely that of the Group C pastoral folk (2500 BC) than that of the preceding Napatan Egyptian whilst there is a surprising technological continuity from the Meroitic, through the X Group wares, to the Christian Nubian period of the eighth and ninth centuries AD. Detailed study of physical remains from various cemeteries dating to the period of upheaval, between the decline of Meroë and the period of the establishment of the Christian Kingdoms, also indicates continuity. Previously the assumption of many of those who derive the origin of divine Kingship from Egypt is that Meroë fell to attacking barbaric hordes and that the survivors fled to the west carrying with them the Egyptian ideas of Kingship and that these ultimately resulted in the rise of the Sudanic Kingdoms of West Africa. There is no need though, if influences have to be spread, to link them necessarily with the fall of Meroë since at their peak the successor states of Christian Nubia stretched as far west as Darfur and possibly as far south as the Nuba mountains (12 degrees N).

Fairman has suggested that Ancient Egypt was a conservative society and that "African social customs and religious beliefs were the root and foundation of the Egyptian way of life." Taking the sacred marriage of Horus and Hathor as an example he concluded that several strands are closely synthesised. One, connected with Osiris and earth fertility, probably owed its ultimate origins to southwestern Asian prototypes though the other strands suggest underlying pastoral ceremonies which could indicate a possible "common climate of custom and belief" from which both Egypt and later African societies were to draw. This posing of the possibility of African origins of Egyptian Kingship does not eliminate the problem but heightens it. It is often assumed that there was one stereotyped version of Egyptian divine monarchy, it is important however to realise that the institution of monarchy was constantly in process of adaptation to changing circumstances and practically every feature of divine-type monarchy from a large number of examples can be paralleled in 3000 years of Egyptian development. Westcott has shown the weakness of direct derivations from Ancient

Egypt in relation to modern West African, Akan, and Yoruba societies and has indicated the effect of the demand for an ancient pedigree in creating such contacts.

Though Nubian continuity and the African basis of ancient Egyptian society can thus be inferred it does not mean that the contacts between the Nile Valley and other parts of Africa should be minimised. The expeditions to Punt, which probably refers to the Horn of Africa, from Middle Kingdom (2600 – 2100 BC) times, and the dispersal of the ideas of agriculture across to west Africa in the same millennium are evidence of the antiquity of such contacts. Occasional trade items from the Nile Valley dating from the first and second millennia AD have been found in West Africa whilst Ethiopian *abuna* were appointed from Alexandria throughout the Medieval period. By the thirteenth century however, it was Kanem and Bornu which were expanding eastwards towards Darfur. But one of the greatest tangible contributions of the Nile Valley civilizations has often been considered to be that of iron-working via Meroë. The archaeological evidence is perhaps here at variance, in that iron is not in abundance, even in Meroitic grave contexts, until the end of the first millennium BC, whereas iron working is found at Nok in Northern Nigeria by the third or fourth century BC and in Rhodesia by the second century AD. The serious possibilities of iron working being brought by Red Sea traders to Ethiopia and thence conveyed to East Africa cannot be overlooked; nor can the possible role of the Indonesians or other Indian Ocean seafarers in conveying iron-working to Rhodesia. North African contacts via the Ghadames-Ghat Sahara route, attested from prehistoric chariot drawings, may have provided the origins of the West African Iron Age since iron was used in and traded from North Africa as early as the middle of the first millennium BC. The absence of the highly distinctive Meroitic pottery in West Africa or anywhere outside a fairly restricted area of the middle Nile provides further reason to believe that the direct contribution of Meroë to sub-Saharan Africa has been overstressed.

The argument in support of the link with Egypt is that there exists a "substratum" which can be recognised after a long passage of time in the "form of scattered survivals among people now differentiated thoroughly in respect of culture. language and race." If there is this substratum it would not show every feature of the progenitor society but would be distinguishable by the recognition in a given society of "preponderant integrating factors." The difficulty of reconstructing such a substratum is that it is composed of varying elements drawn from different quarters at different times, which means that any overriding hypothesis of African history is subject to weakness since elements from quarters other than the "blueprint" cultural source can quickly be shown by critics of the given hypothesis and the links in time from the progenitor to a society demonstrating the "significant survivals" can rarely be demonstrated convincingly.

The survivals in East Africa which have normally been thought of as significant are traits of Kingship, cattle cults, earthworks and building in stone, physical resemblances of present day peoples to past peoples and isolated elements of language which are often shown to refer to cattle or Kingship. The origin of Kingship has depended solely on where the origin of these traits has been placed. Physical resemblances, cattle and Kingship had been the main considerations of Seligman; isolated language traits and Kingship had been the concern of Wright; monuments and Kingship the main interest of Murdock; and Crazzolara has concentrated largely on language. Within Uganda can be found divine-kingship, cattle-cults, earthworks and items of language which are totally foreign to the language groups in which they occur. A survey of the origins of all these features reveals much about the cultural influences affecting the development of Uganda's present day Kingdoms.

The Kingdoms of Buganda, Bunyoro, and Ankole have royal dynasties which vary in length from eighteen to twenty-two generations. They were preceded, according to the oral traditions of western Uganda, by the three generation rule of the Bacwezi. In Buganda, where the Bacwezi legends are weak, the present dynasty was preceded either by several local dynasties, the mythical Kintu, or was an offshoot of the Bunyoro royal house. According to Crazzolara, the Bacwezi were the first Lwoo movement. He based his conclusion on such linguistic evidence as the *mpako* royal names of Bunyoro-Kitara, the term Bacwezi which he believed was derived from the widespread Lwoo *Cwaa* clan of northern Uganda and the southern Sudan, and various names used for objects and customs associated with royalty by the Bacwezi which were subsequently transmitted to the successor state of Bunyoro-Kitara. Oliver interprets the Kingdoms of Bunyoro and Buganda with their Babito dynasties as the result of the Lwoo movements and as the direct consequence of the breakup of the large Bacwezi Kingdom. The Hinda dynasties of southern Uganda, such as Ankole, are interpreted as the result of a defensive consolidatory response to the Lwoo movement and the establishment of the Babito Kingdoms. What is quite obvious is that, in whatever theory is accepted, the Lwoo movements acted as a catalyst to state development and the Babito Kingdoms had certain closer contact with the northern Lwoo than the southern Kingdoms. These links are seen in the legends of Isimbwa marrying the daughter of the "Lango" Labongo, the northern soothsayers foretelling the doom of the Bacwezi, the disappearance of Cwa Nabaka (the second Kabaka of Buganda) and the burial of the first three Bakama of Bunyoro in Acoli country, the use of coronation mounds and the use of a Nilotic word *Kale* in *ekikale* the Bunyoro word for a royal enclosure.

The Lwoo influence was thus important but the degree of importance largely depends on the interpretation that is given to the Bacwezi. To Wrigley the Bacwezi "never existed except in the minds of men" and "their makers," the Bahima, "had little to do with the making of Biggo." He further contends that there was once a "large loose-jointed Bantu Kingdom" which broke up on the impact of the Lwoo. Wrigley offers no chronology for this Kingdom. Oliver on the other hand accepts the Bacwezi as a parent dynasty breaking up on the impact of the Lwoo as described in the traditions with each of the successor kingdoms, particularly Ankole and Bunyoro, claiming direct descent from the parent dynasty. The Bacwezi he sees as the makers of Bigo and the other earthworks and the date as probably the fifteenth century. The present writer, on the basis of the traditions, would date the Bigo culture at 1350–1500 AD and would also accept the correlation of the Bigo culture with the Bacwezi. The excavations at Bigo in 1957 and 1960 have greatly clarified the problem and it is possible to describe a Bigo "culture" with some certainty and suggest that the Bigo culture was the work of people akin to the present day Bahima. The principal features of the culture which allow these suggestions to be made have only slowly become evident. The pottery which characterises the Bigo culture has been described elsewhere in detail but a brief description is perhaps necessary here. The pottery forms at Bigo and several other large cities, such as Mubende and Kibengo, consist of spherical bowls, jars, shallow basins and footed dishes decorated with roulette patterns made by knotted-pass rollers. Less frequently, decoration also includes an haematite slip applied around the rim (internally) or as vertical zones on the exterior. The forms and decoration are distinctive enough for the distribution of the Bigo culture to be led fairly closely to the short grass country of Western Uganda which has a rainfall largely under 35 inches per annum and stretches from south of the Kagera as far north as the Kafu. Large earthworks situated in undulating country are also a feature of the culture. These normally have a central hill and in several cases, like Kibengo and Bigo, are located on a river. Bigo, with its ditch system of over six and a half miles, was clearly not primarily defensive though could be termed defendable and its inclusion of good grazing in the meadows of a Katonga tributary indicates that its makers intended that it should be able to protect large herds of cattle.

Bigo was the largest site. Nearby on the Katonga are the two smaller earthworks of Kagogo and Kasonko and ten miles to the south the former "reservoir" and village site of Ntrnsi. The scale of the earthworks undertaking at Bigo, where the ditches in some places are more than fifteen feet deep and are cut into solid rock, suggests rulers with a firm control over a relatively large manpower, such as would be possessed by a ruler of a centralised state. At the centre of Bigo an enclosure bank, originally more than ten feet high and now partly destroyed, has been interpreted as a royal enclosure (orirembo) of the type that survived in Ankole, Rwanda and Karagwe until the late nineteenth century. This supports the further suggestion that Bigo was the capital of this state whilst the other earthworks could have been centres of subordinate chiefs. At Bigo the sheer size, its location to include meadow lands, the numerous gaps in the outer ditch together with the enclosures of the inner trench system, and the finds of large amounts of cattle bones clearly indicate Bigo was the capital of a pastoral kingdom situated over western Uganda. It would seem from the paucity of finds and the absence of house sites that the inhabitants could only have lived in flimsy huts, such as are still used by pastoral folk and who most probably made more use of wooden vessels and calabashes than of pottery. The occupation was of a short duration as no thick layers of habitation debris such as food remains, hearths and broken pottery, were found.

Radio-carbon dates from three different structural features of the central enclosure area of AD 1370, 1450 and 1505 reinforce the view that the occupation period was short and provide a date for that occupation of around 1350–1500 AD. The date is identical to that for the Bacwezi worked out from the traditional history. The short occupation fits in with the three-generation rule of the Bacwezi who were pastoral rulers. The Hinda Kingdoms to the south have *orirembo* enclosures at the centre of their kraal capitals. We know from the history of Ankole that the *Abagabe* considered themselves the direct heirs of the Bacwezi; and the form the capital sites took, and the continuity of that form from the Bigo prototype, would support their contention. It is amongst the pastoral Bahima, who formed the aristocracy of Ankole, and their neighbours in Karagwe and southern Bunyoro that the Bacwezi tales are strongest. Further support for this association can be seen in the presence at Ntusi of clay hearth kerbs decorated with rouletted patterns which are similar to the undecorated kerbs of even the simplest Hima hut today. Wrigley dismissed the Bahima as the makers of Bigo because of their present pastoral life and "light cultural luggage" but there is every indication that the Lwoo had even less material culture. Nor does question of the possession of iron arise as a decisive factor since iron working in Uganda predates Bigo, and weapons in the form of arrowheads have been found in contexts dating to several hundreds of years before Bigo. The scarcity of iron in the southern Sudan and the use by such people as the Dinka of spearheads of bone, horn and wood would indicate that the Lwoo themselves were probably not characterised by the control of the best supplies of iron as Wrigley suggested.

Bigo was abandoned because of the movement of peoples from the north. The ditch system was neglected and the *orirembo* mutilated to build a large flat-topped mound. The newcomers stayed a shorter time than the original builders but left behind them a clue to their origin in distinctive arrowheads, barbed on opposite faces of both edges of a square tang, which are at present only found amongst the Madi of Northern Uganda. This small fact adds some slight support to Father Crazzolara's recently expressed view that the

Lwoo were really only part of a larger Madi movement. Mounds occur also at Kakumiro, Budo and Fashoda and could perhaps be associated with Nilotic customs of royal accession.

Thus the archaeological evidence suggests that a Bahima Kingdom existed before the Lwoo movement. If this contention is correct it is important to decide from where to derive the Bahima. They have previously been called Hamitic and marked on maps as such but for this description there is no evidence. The Bahima speak the Bantu languages of the people they move among, their traditions and songs handed down from generation to generation are also in Bantu forms. The Bahima established a kingdom in western Uganda (including a large part of what is now western Buganda) because that was the area best suited to a pastoral life. Physically the Bahima are negroes and no tests, of which but a few, unfortunately, have been made, have shown blood groups or other biochemical data which mark them off significantly, in a quantitative sense, from the Bairu. Yet they are different in superficial physical appearance, with their tallness, slimness and more aquiline facial features; a fact which was commented upon by most of the early explorers and writers and summed up by Johnston in such terms as "the Bahima have the figures and proportions of Europeans," or "Gala-like negroids," with the inference that they came from the northeast. One may however think of the strongly marked physical differences between Bairu and Bahima as due to nutritional and social factors rather than necessarily inferring a folk movement from the Horn of Africa. Living predominantly on a high protein diet and with definite physical features socially preferred in marriage, it is probable that both the forces of natural and social selection have operated to produce the physical differences so apparent two generations ago to the first European writers. A similar process has been observed in Rwanda and Kivu by Hiernaux amongst Batutsi and Bahutu, whilst the effect of a high protein diet in inducing extra height is a widely observed phenomenon amongst groups migrating in time or space to situations where a better diet is attainable.

Though there is no evidence of the movement of the Bahima into western Uganda, the Ankole cow which they now herd was certainly an immigrant. It is currently suggested, though without much solid evidence, that the Sanga variety of cow, to which those of western Uganda belong, originated in the Ethiopian highlands area as a cross between the Asiatic *Bos inaicits* (humped zebu) and the longer established humpless long-horned cattle. The arrival of these cattle does not of necessity mean the movement of large numbers of people nor is it certain that their movement from a possible Ethiopian highland source area was direct rather than via the southern Sudan. It is just as possible, as has been inferred by Payne, that the southern Sudan has also to be considered as part of the general region for the emergence of the Sanga. The same variety of cow is found in Rhodesia and its arrival there may be dated on the evidence of Iron Age cattle figurines to the latter part of the first millennium AD.

From the same general source area as the cattle, and as uncertain in date, probably came the idea of the use of the roulette in pottery decoration. This simple motif, though now employed for an infinite variety of designs, still characterises the pottery of the larger part of East Africa. It was first found in Renge pottery of Rwanda, the Bigo pottery of Uganda and the Lanet Wares of Kenya (Class C of Sutton). These three classes post date the earliest proven Iron Age pottery, the dimple-based ware, and presumably date from the early part of the second millennium AD. The pottery is found initially associated with pastoral peoples and could have accompanied the cattle movement.

A further index of contact from the north which has been discussed is the idea of building in stone. The variations in construction techniques from Ethiopia to Kenya, Kenya to Tanzania and Tanzania to Rhodesia demonstrated by the writer from Kenya and by Sassoon from Engaruka represent agricultural societies coping with difficult environments which demand the maximum use of limited agricultural land and rainfall, to which is added in several cases the problem of the clearance of stone from steep hillsides. The cairns of East Africa have also been thought of as a possible connection with Ethiopia and have lent some support to the megalithic Cushite theory of Murdock. This assumption largely depends on the pre "Nilo-Hamitic" populations having a Cushitic language, which is as yet far from proven. It also depends on various cultural and social traits, such as circumcision, being indigenous to a certain zone and passed to neighbouring people like the Bantu Kikuyu and Bagisu and to the Nilo-Hamitic Masai and Nandi and not brought in by them. The view is also based on the assumption that the cairns are found in the predominantly bush country of the rift valley and highland zones of Kenya and Tanzania. Similar cairns are however found in a much wider area and in differing ecological zones, particularly in the region west of the Nile in the Bahr-el-Ghazal, where the Bongo cairns have recently received attention and in the Lake Victoria area of Uganda in Kooki and Mengo districts. The cairns of the southern part of the Sudan, described many years ago by Evans-Pritchard and Seligman, would be just as appropriate parallels to those of western Kenya or Engaruka as those of the Ethiopian areas. Seligman illustrates the squatting circles of the Lotuka-speaking tribes and illustrates a Leria circle which are remarkably similar to the *Poret* or elders' "quiet discussion" circles of certain of the Kalenjin tribes.

If the origins of the material and archaeological aspects of the culture of the Kingdoms of western Uganda cannot be accurately delineated the sociological and political aspects present even greater problems. The Kingdoms were clearly influenced by the northern movements, but it is apparent that some centralised organisation preceded them. The Shilluk succession of Reths on no account amounts to more than fifteen generations and cannot be considered as the prototype for the Uganda Kingdoms. The fact that certain features are held in common by the Shilluk and the Uganda Kingdoms can be interpreted as being due to the effect of certain pressures and cultural influences on both groups. The use of terms like *Ret, Kak* and *Ker* which are in common use over a very wide area, may well be derived originally from the Meroitic, but it is impossible to trace direct lines of derivation. It is probable that as individual sacral rulership systems are studied in detail several complexes with similar traits will be distinguished. One of these complexes may well comprise the southern Sudan, but it has to be remembered that it is probably to this same area that we have to look for developments which later resulted in the expansion of certain of the tribal groups, falling within the old Nilo-Hamitic label, which are characterised by societies without rulers.

Too much can be made of similarities in customs. The many aspects of cultural divergence discernible in the universal approach to culture history; such as pyramids and sun-cults in the Americas, regicide in Polynesia, the ritual significance of fire in non-monarchical states, sexual aspects of fire-making, arrows fired into the air for rain making in Bulgaria and ritual incest in the South Seas which any cursory perusal of Fraser's "Golden Bough" and similar encyclopaedic anthropologies can reveal, should warn against the dangers of isolating even a few traits in tracing the origins of divine Kingship. Many of the traits of Kingship would appear to have a purely functional purpose. The link with rain-making is one of these and it would be difficult to prove that this is Egyptian and not a legitimate reaction of an agricultural society in an area where rain is undependable. The fact that arrows are fired in different directions in both ancient Egypt and Bunyoro has been taken by Oliver as almost conclusive proof of the Egyptian origins of divine Kingship but it is only one picturesque (and possibly symbolic) feature of Kingship and cannot outweigh the fundamental differences. The secrecy surrounding the ruler is a measure of ensuring that the status and person of the ruler is maintained and the mystery surrounding death provides against a struggle for power breaking out immediately on the death of a king. Many absolute features of the Kingship of a state like Buganda were only developing as late as the nineteenth century and it is difficult to distinguish between traits that were original and those that may have been adopted during the subsequent twenty generations. The marriage of the king to his sister, besides being found in the Nile Valley civilisations, also occurs in the tales of origin of many Bantu peoples such as the Akamba and in certain kingship groups as in the Kingdom of Mwenemutapa where it is possible to date its inception.

Ogot has suggested that the important question to answer is not what is

the origin of divine Kingship but "what were the circumstances or factors
. . . which produced the attitude of mind which regards Kingship as divine?"
The circumstances producing Kingship amongst the Shilluk and in Bunyoro
he suggests were the "presence of certain economic, political and military
factors." He follows Oberg in suggesting that the arrival of the Bacwezi, an
organised minority group of Bahima, resulted in the first Kingship. In the
popular traditions of western Uganda the Bacwezi are always spoken of as
being very different to the Bahima because of their fair skins (sometimes
even said to be white) and tallness which could be an indication that they
were in fact an immigrant minority. This is a satisfactory explanation but
one which cannot be proven. If eventually the archaeologists discover a
sequence of demonstrable pastoral sites with a sequence of roulette-deco-
rated pottery in which the Bigo forms suddenly appear and then disappear
it may prove possible to say that the Bacwezi [was] an immigrant minority.
So far this is as impossible as demonstrating where the Bahima came from,
if at all they came from anywhere, or saying from where the political organisation of the Bacwezi should be derived. The large structure (or structures)
discovered by Shinnie in his 1957 Bigo excavations would appear to predate
even the earthworks themselves and indicates from the postholes a large
construction which is a unique feature of the site and one which conceivably
may hold a clue to the origins of centralised government within the area.

In conclusion one can only say that the whole question of the origin of
Kingship is, and will be, purely a matter for speculation. Archaeology has
so far only succeeded in indicating the lack of supporting data for most of
the sweeping theories which derive Kingship from one common source.
Though even indirect links with Egypt or Meroë may have been slight, nevertheless, it is important not to minimize the cultural reservoir effect of the
area of the Nile to the south of Nubia in the present Sudanese provinces of
Upper Nile and Bahr-el-Ghazal, which can be termed for the want of a better
simple description, the "Nile Pool." This is the region from which the Nilotes emerged and where the Shilluk still live. It lies between the Sidame
region of Ethiopia on the east and the Nile-Congo watershed on the west.
From this region cultural contacts have been maintained with West Africa
by way of the "Yam Belt" of Murdock. For East Africa it can be said that
the Nile Pool area, received influences from a large number of sources and
like a reservoir it passed streams of cultural influence to the south as well
as to the east and west. Kingship itself would appear to be as old as the
Bigo culture. The first makers of the centralized state were probably the
Bahima or at least a ruling dynasty of Bacwezi. The advent of the Lwoo
movements in all probability was contemporaneous and may have affected
the development of the Bacwezi state. The Bacwezi state was short-lived
and split into successor states, the northern strongly under Nilotic influence,
the southern carrying on many of the practises initiated by the Bacwezi

though with both groups strongly defending their rights as heirs apparent. Even the southern Kingdoms, from the evidence of Bacwezi names and certain details of the Bacwezi traditions in Ankole, were not entirely uninfluenced by the developments taking place to the north of them. It is likely that the Lwoo movements were not as dramatic as they have been made out to be but may have been preceded by increasing pressures from the Nile Pool area from the twelfth or thirteenth century AD onwards, when the forces of Islam were beginning to push down the Nile valley into the area from Egypt and from West Africa via the Congo-Nile watershed. These pressures may have been evidence by a form of "shunting" action in which the Madi, as suggested by Father Crazzolara, may have been initially important in northern Uganda. These first movements may have been initially important in northern Uganda. These first movements may also have provided the loosely-knit pastoralists, who had themselves derived their cattle and pottery from the north, with the stimulus to centralisation.

It is undeniable that the Nile Pool area was influenced indirectly from Ancient Egypt but it was also influenced from other quarters. It was not the "Sudanic civilization" which finally flourished in Uganda, or even a Meroitic filtration of that civilisation, but something which was rooted as much in the environment and economic possibilities of Western Uganda as in the influences seeping down from Nubia. Uganda in its turn provided a fusion of the older and presumably loosely-knit Kingship of the Bacwezi and the newer Kingship of the Babito which it transmitted south into Tanzania and possibly westwards into Rwanda and east into Busoga. The contemporaneity of the Kingship of Mwenemutapa in Rhodesia [and the lack of material culture links between East Africa and the Rhodesian-Katangan] areas would indicate that Uganda cannot be regarded as a "staging post" for the transmission of the idea of "Sudanic Kingship" further south. There, other factors, such as the well-attested trade from the Indian Ocean seaboard as early as the seventh or eighth centuries AD, served as the catalytic force towards the establishment of some form of political centralisation. In the same way in which the Nile Pool area provided some of the major influences affecting the growth of the states of western Uganda the area of Nubia to the north provided influences contributing the state formation in parts of the Western Sudan. But in West Africa influences were derived from elsewhere, particularly North Africa, and as a result it was the western-most states such as Ghana, the furthest removed from the Nile, which developed farther than the eastern-most. In the face of such anomalies and with the large gaps in the evidence available it is premature to accept any single hypothesis to explain either direct links between Uganda and other cultural areas, such as Ethiopia and Meroë or the role of the Nile Valley civilisations in the diffusion of political ideas and institutions.

The African Origins of Western Civilization
CHEIKH ANTA DIOP[12]

What were the Egyptians?

In contemporary descriptions of the ancient Egyptians, this question is never raised. Eyewitnesses of that period formally affirm that the Egyptians were Blacks. On several occasions Herodotus insists on the Negro character of the Egyptians and even uses this for indirect demonstrations. For example, to prove that the flooding of the Nile cannot be caused by melting snow, he cites, among other reasons he deems valid, the following observation: "It is certain that the natives of the country are black with the heat."

To demonstrate that the Greek oracle is of Egyptian origin, Herodotus advances another argument: "Lastly, by calling the dove black, they [the Dodonaeans] indicated that the woman was Egyptian. . . ." The doves in question symbolize two Egyptian women allegedly kidnapped from Thebes to found the oracles of Dodona and Libya.

To show that the inhabitants of Colchis were of Egyptian origin and had to be considered a part of Sesostris' army who had settled in that region, Herodotus says: "The Egyptians said that they believed the Colchians to be descended from the army of Sesostris. My own conjectures were founded, first, on the fact that they are black-skinned and have woolly hair. . . ."

Finally, concerning the population of India, Herodotus distinguishes between the Padaeans and other Indians, describing them as follows: "They all also have the same tint of skin, which approaches that of the Ethiopians."

Diodorus of Sicily writes:

The Ethiopians say that the Egyptians are one of their colonies

---

[12]Diop, Cheikh Anta, *The African Origins of Western Civilization: Myth or Reality* (New York: Lawrence Hill and Co., 1974). Excerpts taken from pp. 1–9, and 138–139. Cheikh Anta Diop (1923–1986) was born in Senegal and educated in France, where he received a Litt. D. As one of Africa's most recognized historians he is remembered for his efforts to prove that Black people played a much greater role in the formation of civilization than is generally acknowledged. Diop founded the first Carbon 14 dating laboratory in Africa and in 1966 was honored by the World Festival of Negro Arts as the Black intellectual who had exercised the most fruitful influence in the twentieth century. Diop also founded two political parties in Senegal that were later banned.

which was brought into Egypt by Osiris. They even allege that this country was originally under water, but that the Nile, dragging much mud as it flowed from Ethiopia, had finally filled it in and made it a part of the continent. . . . They add that from them, as from their authors and ancestors, the Egyptians get most of their laws. It is from them that the Egyptians have learned to honor kings as gods and bury them with such pomp; sculpture and writing were invented by the Ethiopians. The Ethiopians cite evidence that they are more ancient than the Egyptians, but it is useless to report that here.

If the Egyptians and Ethiopians were not of the same race, Diodorus would have emphasized the impossibility of considering the former as a colony (i.e., a fraction) of the latter and the impossibility of viewing them as forebears of the Egyptians.

In his *Geography,* Strabo mentioned the importance of migrations in history and, believing that this particular migration had proceeded from Egypt to Ethiopia, remarks: "Egyptians settled Ethiopia and Colchis." Once again, it is a Greek, despite his chauvinism, who informs us that the Egyptians, Ethiopians, and Colchians belong to the same race, thereby confirming what Herodotus had said about the Colchians.

The opinion of all the ancient writers on the Egyptian race is more or less summed up by Gaston Maspero (1894–1916): "By the almost unanimous testimony of ancient historians, they belonged to an African race [read: Negro] which first settled in Ethiopia, on the Middle Nile; following the course of the river, they gradually reached the sea. . . . Moreover, the Bible states that Mesraim, son of Ham, brother of Chins (Kush) the Ethiopian, and of Canaan, came from Mesopotamia to settle with his children on the banks of the Nile."

According to the Bible, Egypt was peopled by the offspring of Ham, ancestor of the Blacks:

> The descendants of Ham are Chus, Mesraim, Phut and Canaan. The descendants of Chus are Saba, Hevila, Sabatha, Regma and Sabathacha. . . . Chus was the father of Nemrod; he was the first to be conqueror on the earth. . . . Mesraim became the father of Ludim, Anamim, Laabim, Nephthinhim, Phethrusim, Chasluhim. . . . Canaan became the father of Sid, his first-born, and Heth. . . .

For the peoples of the near East, Mesraim still designates Egypt; Canaan, the entire coast of Palestine and Phoenicia; Sennar, which was probably the site from which Nemrod left for Western Asia, still indicates the kingdom of Nubia.

What is the value of these statements? Coming from eyewitnesses, they could hardly be false. Herodotus may be mistaken when he reports the customs of a people, when he reasons more or less cleverly to explain a phenomenon incomprehensible in his day, but one must grant that he was at least capable of recognizing the skin color of the inhabitants of countries he has visited. Besides, Herodotus was not a credulous historian who recorded everything without checking; he knew how to weigh things. When he relates an opinion that he does not share, he always takes care to note his disagreement. Thus, referring to the mores of the Scythians and Neurians, he writes apropos the latter:

> It seems that these people are conjurers; for both the Scythians and the Greeks who dwell in Scythia say that every Neurian once a year becomes a wolf for a few days, at the end of which time he is restored to his proper shape. Not that I believe this, but they constantly affirm it to be true, and are even ready to back up their assertion with an oath.

He always distinguishes carefully between what he has seen and what he has been told. After his visit to the Labyrinth, he writes:

> There are two different sorts of chambers throughout—half under ground, half above ground, the latter built upon the former; the whole number of these chambers is three thousand, fifteen hundred of each kind. The upper chambers I myself passed through and saw, and what I say concerning them is from my own observation; of the underground chambers I can only speak from report, for the keepers of the building could not be got to show them, since they contained, as they said, the sepulchers of the kings who built the Labyrinth, and also those of the sacred crocodiles. Thus it is from hearsay only that I can speak of the lower chambers. The upper chambers, however, I saw with my own eyes and found them to excel all other human productions.

Was Herodotus a historian deprived of logic, unable to penetrate complex phenomena? On the contrary, his explanation of the inundations of the Nile reveals a rational mind seeking scientific reasons for natural phenomena:

> Perhaps, after censuring all the opinions that have been put forward on this obscure subject, one ought to propose some theory of one's own. I will therefore proceed to explain what I think to be the reason of the Nile's swelling in the summertime. During the winter, the sun is driven out of his usual course by the storms, and removes to the upper parts of Libya. This is the whole secret

in the fewest possible words; for it stands to reason that the country to which the Sun-god approaches the nearest, and which he passes most directly over, will be scantest of water, and that here streams which feed the rivers will shrink the most. To explain, however, more at length, the case is this. The sun, in his passage across the upper parts of Libya, affects them in the following way. As the air in these regions is constantly clear, and the country warm through the absence of cold winds, the sun in his passage across them acts upon them exactly as he is wont to act elsewhere in summer, when his path is in the middle of heaven—that is, he attracts the water. After attracting it, he again repels it into the upper regions, where the winds lay hold of it, scatter it, and reduce it into a vapor, whence it naturally enough comes to pass that the winds which blow from this quarter—the south and southwest—are of all winds the most rainy. And my own opinion is that the sun does not get rid of all the water which he draws year by year from the Nile, but retains some about him.

These three examples reveal that Herodotus was not a passive reporter of incredible tales and rubbish, "a liar." On the contrary, he was quite scrupulous, objective, scientific for his time. Why should one seek to discredit such a historian, to make him seem naive? Why "refabricate" history despite his explicit evidence?

Undoubtedly the basic reason for this is that Herodotus, after relating his eyewitness account informing us that the Egyptians were Blacks, then demonstrated, with rare honesty (for a Greek), that Greece borrowed from Egypt all the elements of her civilization, even the cult of the gods, and that Egypt was the cradle of civilization. Moreover, archaeological discoveries continually justify Herodotus against his detractors. Thus, Christiane Desroches-Noblecourt writes about recent excavations in Tanis: "Herodotus had seen the outer buildings of these sepulchers and had described them. [This was the Labyrinth discussed above.] Pierre Montet has just proved once again that 'The Father of History did not lie.'"[13] It could be objected that, in the fifth century BC when Herodotus visited Egypt, its civilization was already more than 10,000 years old and that the race which had created it was not necessarily the Negro race that Herodotus found there. But the whole history of Egypt, as we shall see, shows that the mixture of the early population with white nomadic elements, conquerors or merchants, became increasingly important as the end of Egyptian history approached. According to Cornelius de Pauw, in the low epoch Egypt was almost saturated with foreign white colonies: Arabs in Coptos, Libyans on the future site of Alexandria, Jews around the city of Hercules (Avaris?), Babylonians (or

---

[13]Tanis, the Biblical Zoan, at the mouth of the eastern branch of the Nile Delta.

Persians) below Memphis, "fugitive Trojans" in the area of the great stone quarries east of the Nile, Carians and Ionians over by the Pelusiac branch. Psammetichus (end of seventh century) capped this peaceful invasion by entrusting the defense of Egypt to Greek mercenaries. "An enormous mistake of Pharaoh Psammetichus was to commit the defense of Egypt to foreign troops and to introduce various colonies made up of the dregs of the nations." Under the last Saite dynasty, the Greeks were officially established at Naucratis, the only port where foreigners were authorized to engage in trading.

After the conquest of Egypt by Alexander, under the Ptolemies, crossbreeding between white Greeks and black Egyptians flourished, thanks to a policy of assimilation:

> Nowhere was Dionysus more favored, nowhere was he worshiped more adoringly and more elaborately than by the Ptolemies, who recognized his cult as an especially effective means of promoting the assimilation of the conquering Greeks and their fusion with the native Egyptians.

These facts prove that if the Egyptian people had originally been white, it might well have remained so. If Herodotus found it still black after so much crossbreeding, it must have been basic black at the start.

Insofar as biblical evidence is concerned, a few details are in order. To determine the worth of biblical evidence, we must examine the genesis of the Jewish people. What, then, was the Jewish people? How was it born? How did it create the Bible, in which descendants of Ham, ancestors of Negroes and Egyptians would thus be accursed; what might be the historical reason for that curse? Those who would become the Jews entered Egypt numbering seventy rough, fearful shepherds, chased from Palestine by famine and attracted by that earthly paradise, the Nile Valley.

Although the Egyptians had a peculiar horror of nomad life and shepherds, these newcomers were first warmly welcomed, thanks to Joseph. According to the Bible, they settled in the land of Goshen and became shepherds of the Pharaoh's flocks. After the death of Joseph and the Pharaoh "Protector," and facing the proliferation of the Jews, the Egyptians grew hostile, in circumstances still ill-defined. The condition of the Jews became more and more difficult. If we are to believe the Bible, they were employed on construction work, serving as laborers in building the city of Ramses. The Egyptians took steps to limit the number of births and eliminate male babies, lest the ethnic minority develop into a national danger which, in time of war, might increase enemy ranks.

So began the initial persecutions by which the Jewish people was to remain marked throughout its history. Henceforth the Jewish minority, withdrawn within itself, would become Messianic by suffering and humiliation. Such a moral terrain of wretchedness and hope favored the birth and development of religious sentiment. The circumstances were the more favorable because this race of shepherds, without industry or social organization (the only social cell was the patriarchal family), armed with nothing but sticks, could envisage no positive reaction to the technical superiority of the Egyptian people.

It was to meet this crisis that Moses appeared, the first of the Jewish prophets, who, after minutely working out the history of the Jewish people from its origins, presented it in retrospect under a religious perspective. Thus he caused Abraham to say many things that the latter could not possibly have foreseen: for example, the 400 years in Egypt. Moses lived at the time of Tell el Amarna,[14] when Amenophis IV (Akhnaton, circa 1400) was trying to revive the early monotheism which had by then been discredited by sacerdotal ostentation and the corruptness of the priests. Akhnaton seems to have attempted to bolster political centralism in his recently conquered immense empire through religious centralism; the empire needed a universal religion.

Moses was probably influenced by this reform. From that time on, he championed monotheism among the Jews. Monotheism, with all its abstraction, already existed in Egypt, which had borrowed it from the Meroitic Sudan, the Ethiopia of the Ancients:

> Although the Supreme Deity, viewed in the purest of monotheistic visions as the "only generator in the sky and on earth who was not engendered . . . the only living god in truth . . ." Amon, whose name signifies mystery, adoration, one day finds himself rejected, overtaken by Ra, the Sun, or converted into Osiris or Horins.

Given the insecure atmosphere in which the Jewish people found itself in Egypt, a God promising sure tomorrows was an irreplaceable moral support. After some reticence at the outset, this people which apparently had not known monotheism previously—contrary to the opinion of those who would credit it as the inventor [of monotheism]—would nonetheless carry it to a rather remarkable degree of development. Aided by faith, Moses led the Hebrew people out of Egypt. However, the Israelites quickly tired of this religion (the Golden Calf of Aaron at the foot of Mount Sinai) and only gradually returned to monotheism.

Having entered Egypt as seventy shepherds grouped in twelve patriarchal

---

[14]Tell el Amarano, a city built 190 miles above Cairo in 1396 BC, as the new capital of Akhnoton's empire.

families, nomads without industry or culture, the Jewish people left there 400 years later, 500,000 strong, after acquiring from it all the elements of its future tradition, including monotheism.

If the Egyptians persecuted the Israelites as the Bible says, and if the Egyptians were Negroes, sons of Ham, as the same Bible says, we can no longer ignore the historical causes of the curse upon Ham—despite the legend of Noah's drunkenness. The curse entered Jewish literature considerably later than the period of persecution. Accordingly, Moses, in the Book of Genesis, attributed the following words to the Eternal God, addressed to Abraham in a dream: "Know for certain that your posterity will be strangers in a land not their own; they shall be subjected to slavery and shall be oppressed four hundred years."

Here we have reached the historical background of the curse upon Ham. It is not by chance that this curse on the father of Mesraim, Phut, Kush, and Canaan, fell only on Canaan, who dwelt in a land that the Jews have coveted throughout their history.

Whence came this name Ham (Cham, Kam)? Where could Moses have found it? Right in Egypt where Moses was born, grew up, and lived until the Exodus. In fact, we know that the Egyptians called their country *Kermit,* which means "black" in their language. The interpretation according to which *Kermit* designates the black soil of Egypt, rather than the black man and, by extension, the black race of the country of the Blacks, stems from a gratuitous distortion by minds aware of what an exact interpretation of this word would imply. Hence, it is natural to find *Kam* in Hebrew, meaning heat, black, burned.

That being so, all apparent contradictions disappear and the logic of facts appears in all its nudity. The inhabitants of Egypt, symbolized by their black color, Kemit or Ham of the Bible, would be accursed in the literature of the people they had oppressed. We can see that this biblical curse on Ham's offspring had an origin quite different from that generally given it today without the slightest historical foundation. What we cannot understand however, is how it has been possible to make a white race of *Kermit:* Hamite, black, ebony, etc. (even in Egyptian). Obviously, according to the needs of the cause, Ham is cursed, blackened, and made into the ancestor of the Negroes. This is what happens whenever one refers to contemporary social relations.

On the other hand, he is whitened whenever one seeks the origin of civilization, because there he is inhabiting the first civilized country in the world. So, the idea of Eastern and Western Hamites is conceived—nothing more than a convenient invention to deprive Blacks of the moral advantage of Egyptian civilization and of other African civilizations, as we shall see.

It is impossible to link the notion of Hamite, as we labor to understand it in official textbooks, with the slightest historical, geographical, linguistic, or ethnic reality. No specialist is able to pinpoint the birthplace of the Hamites (scientifically speaking), the language they spoke, the migratory route they followed, the countries they settled, or the form of civilization they may have left. On the contrary, all the experts agree that this term has no serious content, and yet not one of them fails to use it as a kind of master-key to explain the slightest evidence of civilization in Black Africa.

Arguments for a Negro Origin

The concept of Kingship is one of the most impressive indications of the similarity in thinking between Egypt and the rest of Black Africa. Leaving aside such general principles as the sacrosanct nature of Kingship and stressing one typical trait because of its strangeness, we shall single out the ritual killing of the monarch. In Egypt, the king was not supposed to reign unless he was in good health. Originally, when his strength declined, he was really put to death. But royalty soon resorted to various expedients. The king was understandably eager to preserve the prerogatives of his position, while undergoing the least possible inconvenience. So he was able to transform the fatal judgement into a symbolic one: from then on, when he grew old, he was merely put to death ritualistically. After the symbolic test, known as the "Sed Festival," the monarch was supposedly rejuvenated in the opinion of his people and was once again deemed fit to assume his functions. Henceforth, the "Sed Festival" was the ceremony of the king's rejuvenation: ritualistic death and revivification of the ruler became synonymous and took place during the same ceremony. (Cf. Charles Seligman's *Egypt and Negro Africa: A Study in Divine Kingship* [London: Routledge, 1934].)

The monarch, the revered being par excellence, was also supposed to be the man with the greatest life force or energy. When the level of his life force fell below a certain minimum, it could only be a risk to his people if he continued to rule. This vitalistic conception is the foundation of all traditional African kingdoms, I mean, of all kingdoms not usurped.

Sometimes it operated differently, for example, in Senegal, the king could not rule if he had received wounds in battle; he had to be replaced until cured. It was during such a replacement that a paternal brother, who was the son of a woman of the people, seized the throne. As Lat-Soukabe, he initiated the Guedj dynasty, circa 1697.

The practice of replacing the king whenever his vital strength declines obviously stems from the same vitalistic tenets throughout the Black world. According to those beliefs, the fertility of the soil, the abundant harvests, the health of people and cattle, the normal flow of events and of all the phenomena of life, are intimately linked to the potential of the ruler's vital force.

In other regions of Black Africa, the events occur exactly as in Egypt with regard to the actual killing of the monarch. Certain peoples even set a time limit, after which he is assumed to be incapable of ruling and is then really put to death. Among the Mbum of Central Africa, this time limit is ten years and the ceremony takes place before the millet season. The following peoples still practice the ritualistic death of the king: the Yoruba, Dagomba, Shamba, Igara, Songhay, the Hausa of Gobir, Katsena, and Daura, and the Shilluk. This practice also existed in ancient Meroë, i.e. Nubia, Uganda-Rwanda.

A Review of Diop
RAYMOND MAUNY[15]

. . . . One would have thought after reading his doctoral thesis that Diop would have "put water in his wine" and that the advice of his professors . . . would have taken root. This is not the case, as I realized when listening to the lecture given by C. A. Diop on April 19, 1960 at Dakar. . . .

Now, what may be permissible to a student or a young secondary school teacher is not permissible to the *Doctor es lettres* who can, by virtue of his title, begin teaching in a university. And so, despite the understanding that I feel toward the author, whom I know, I feel it's my duty, whatever pain it may cause both of us, to say openly what others do not, out of politeness or for other reasons.

According to Diop, the Pharaonic Egyptians, the Phoenicians, the Carthaginians, the Elam, and the ancient Arabians were all Negroes. Negroes were at the origin of civilization:

> [T]hey were the first to invent mathematics, astronomy, the calendar, science, the arts, religion, agriculture, social organization, medicine, writing, technology, architecture. . . . In saying all this one simply asserts that which is, in all modesty, strictly true and which no one, at this time, can refute by arguments worthy of the name. . . . Moses was Egyptian and therefore Negro.

Thus, according to Diop, Judaism, Christianity, and Islam are basically Negro.

I am all the more confident about rejecting the author's interpretations because I have no intention of attributing to Indo-Europeans what I attribute to races more or less *brown* (I am aware of the author's objection on page twenty to the use of the word brown instead of black, an objection I do not accept) and to the yellow people between the Nile and the Pacific: Egyptians,

---

[15]This review appeared in *Bulletin de l'Institut Français d'Afrique Noire* XXII, Series B (1960), pp. 544–51. Translated by Nell Painter and Dr. Robert Collins. This review is actually directed at Diop's original work *Nations negres et culture*, first published in 1955 by Presence Africaine, Paris. *Nations negres et culture* was translated and published in English in 1974 as *The African Origin of Western Civilization.*

Raymond Mauny has been a prolific writer and commentator on the African past while professor of African history at Dakar.

Syrians, Mesopotamians, Hindus, and Chinese. I recognize without any prejudice that "my ancestors the Gauls"[16] were, before the arrival of the Romans, barbarians, when, at the same time, brown and yellow people already had a civilization for several millennia and when great monuments had already been built in Nubia, a Negro land.

On what does C. A. Diop base his opinion? The whole of modern Egyptology, according to him, has been a vast European racist plot to destroy the evidence that the people of the Pharaohs belonged to the Negro world. This veritable "falsification of history"—it is even the title of one of his chapters—has led to the willful disappearance of thousands of mummies so as to preserve only those with long hair.

It is well known that a number of "archaeologists" working before 1900 and before the legislation concerning ruins in Egypt did neglect to preserve skeletons in order to have only those on the side of "artistic and epigraphic treasure. . . ."

According to C. A. Diop the examination of bone remains and of mummies of pre-Roman Egyptians demonstrates that they were Negroes:

> I assert that the skulls found for the most ancient periods and the mummies of the dynastic period are in no way distinct in anthropological characteristics from the two Negro races existing on earth: the Dravidian with straight hair and the Negro with kinky hair,"

add further on . . .

> When we scientifically clean the skin of mummies, the epidermis appears pigmented in the same way as that of all other African Negroes. . . . I add that today *infallible scientific techniques* exist (ultraviolet rays, for example) to determine the melanin content of a pigmentation. Now the difference between a white person and a black, from this point of view, comes from the fact that the white person's organism does not secrete enzymes. It is the same for that of the ancient Egyptians. That is why, from prehistory to the Ptolemaic period, the Egyptian mummy stayed black. In other words, during all of the known history of Egypt, the skin of all the Egyptians of all social classes (from Pharaoh to peasant) has stayed that of the authentic Negro, as well as their osteology. See: the canon of Lepsius.

We need answers to these statements which only anthropologists and

---

[16]"Nos ancestres les Gaulois" ("Our ancestors the Gauls") is an allusion to the opening sentence in an elementary school textbook widely used in French West Africa. The phrase has since become synonymous with the assimilationist colonial policy of France. *(Editor)*

Egyptologists can give us. *That there were Negroes among the Egyptians and that a prolonged mixing has left profound Negroid imprints among the people of the country has not been denied by anyone for a long time. But this is far from making the whole or even the majority of the Egyptians of the Pharaonic period Negroes.*

I am not an anthropologist no more than an author for that matter, but I suggest to the reader one of the best works concerning the question of the ancient Egyptians: C. S. Coon, *The Races of Europe,* (New York: The Macmillan Co., 1939, pp. 91–98 and 458–62). The racial composition of ancient Egypt is analyzed (pre-Neolithic Mediterraneans, whites; Tasians, whites; Fayum-Merimdians, whites; Badarians, seemingly from the Abyssinian plateau, brown with Negroid features; Nagada, related but less Negroid; Mediterraneans of lower Egypt, whites; and from 3,000 BC up to the Ptolemaic period, the history of Egypt shows "the gradual replacement of the Upper Egyptian type by that of lower Egypt." The later invaders (Hyksos, people of the sea, Semites, Assyrians, Persians, Greeks) all belonged to white races, with the exception of the Ethiopians of the twenty-fifth dynasty who were of Nubian origin.

According to Coon, the conventional impressions show a svelte body, with narrow hips and small hands and feet. The head and face "are those of smoothly contoured fine Mediterranean form"; numerous types of the upper classes represented by the portraits "looked strikingly like modern Europeans." The type of certain Pharaohs, like Ramses III, seems on the contrary to be related to the Abyssinian type.

The pigmentation of the Egyptians "was usually a *brunet white;* in the conventional figures the men are represented as red, the women often as lighter, and even white" and the daughter of Cheops, the builder of the great pyramid, as "a definite blonde." Southward, as one approaches Aswan, the population was evidently darker (brown-red, brown).

In their paintings and sculptures the Egyptians represented foreigners with their racial characteristics: "Besides the Libyans, who have Nordic features as well as coloring, Asiatics, with prominent noses and curly hair, sea peoples from Mediterranean, with lighter skins and more pronounced facial relief than the Egyptians, are also shown, as well as Negroes" and farther "The Mediterranean pigmentation of the Egyptians has probably not greatly changed during the last 5000 years."

Such is the opinion of an anthropologist. I leave each individual to draw his own conclusions. But this does not prevent me from thinking that it would be difficult to support the position that a people composed principally of Mediterranean groups could be Negro, especially after all the precise arguments given by Coon, who, it may be noticed in passing, recognized a Negroid contribution.

According to C. A. Diop the ancient authors definitely affirmed that the

Egyptians were Negroes. Herodotus, the "father of history," who wrote about 450 BC, is very correctly included, for he visited Egypt. But are C. A. Diop's examples the proof that he thought they were?

Herodotus does not mean to speak of Egypt when he says "the heat makes the people black," but rather of the inhabitants of the countries of the South, that of the Ethiopians, from where the Nile comes.

"And when he adds that the pigeon was black, he means us to understand that the woman was Egyptian." Did not the Greeks (the Hebrews had the same reaction) have a tendency, as is well known, to regard the Egyptians as "blacks" only because they were darker than the Greeks? Do we not use the same expression in France (from which the family names Morel, Moreau, Lenoir, Negre, etc.) to designate people with a darker than average complexion? A Nordic is clearly conscious of having a lighter complexion than the ordinary Spaniard or southern Italian. He will speak of dark skin, brown skin, even of black skin, just as one, for that matter, speaks of bathers tanning on the beach in summer. Yet neither the one nor the other is any more Negroid for it.

Is the example of the Colchidians any better? The author cites a passage from Herodotus: "The Egyptians think these people are the descendants of part of the troops of Sesostris. I would suppose the same for two reasons: the first is that they are *black* and that they have kinky hair." But why does Mr. Diop not add the rest of Herodotus' passage . . . "To tell the truth this proves nothing because other peoples are in the same situation." And the adjective *melanochroes* which Herodotus uses does not necessarily mean "black." Legrand, in 1948, translated it as "having a brown skin." Also on this subject I refer the reader to F. M. Snowden's, *The Negro in Ancient Greece.*

In the following example concerning the southern Indians, I see nowhere any mention of the fact that the Egyptians were black. It is a question only of the Ethiopians.

The passage of Diodorus of Sicily concerning Ethiopia's civilization being older than that of Egypt, according to the Ethiopians, is interesting from more than one point of view, because it reports for the first time in history, to my knowledge, the interpretation that the Egyptians were descended from the Ethiopians, and thus raises *the question of the part that the Negro had in the formation of ancient Egypt.* In addition I consider this text more important than those of Herodotus, of Genesis, and of Strabo, for the problem before us. But I insist on immediately saying that archeology has convincingly shown that it was Egypt that was the civilizing element in Ethiopia, and not the reverse. I do not think that anyone can prove that the architectural triumphs of Nubia, to cite only one example, are earlier than those of Upper and Lower Egypt of the period of the pyramids. This does not mean that the Ethiopians did not have a part in the constitution of Egyptian civilization. I am even convinced of the contrary. It is up to the ethnologists, sociologists, and others to determine the precise magnitude of that contribution.

In the following example from Strabo: "Egyptians established themselves in Ethiopia and Colchida." I do not see anything which would prove that the Egyptians were black; they colonized these two countries and that is all.

The same comment may be applied to the passage from Genesis (9:18 to 10:20) where the Egyptians (Mistaim) are, in effect, regarded as descendants of Cham. Cham was only a legendary person, however, just as Noah, Sem, and Japhet, and the Bible's division only indicates the diverse races known at the time by the editors of Genesis: Indo-Europeans (Japhet), Semites (i.e. Hebrews, Arabs, some Mesopotamians, etc.), and Chamites (i.e., the ensemble of people who to their knowledge were darker than Semites: Kush, Ethiopians, Punt, Canaan).

Genesis, which is not a treatise of anthropology, by any means, but a collection of Hebrew, Mesopotamian, and Egyptian legends concerned, among other things, with the origins of the human races as the Hebrews of the second millennium BC might see it, and nowhere does Genesis speak of the *color* of the descendants of Cham or Canaan: the Israelites were only conscious of being lighter than they, that is all.

Thus not a great deal is left after an examination of the ancient texts cited by the author which might lead us to believe that the ancient Egyptians were Negroes. Archaeology leads us to just the opposite conclusion, supported, of course, by the text of Herodotus. It was only from the time when "Egyptian fugitives" were settled in Ethiopia that "the Ethiopians, adopting manners of the Egyptians, became more civilized."

To be sure, there is no lack of hypotheses regarding the origins of the Egyptians; and C. A. Diop is not an innovator in this matter. Here is a passage where G. Hanotaux *(Histoire de la nation egyptienne)* speaks of it:

> What were the earliest people (of the Nile Valley)? Celtes, replies Poinsinet de Sivry—Negroes, said Voley—Chinese, was the opinion of Winckelmann—Indo-Polynesians, pretended Moreau de Jonnes—Africans from Ethiopia or Libya, declared Petrie, supported by the naturalists, Hott, Morton, Perrier, Hamy—Asiatics coming from Babylonia with an advanced civilization, affirm the archaeologists and orientalists, Brugsch, Ebers, Hommel, de Rouge, de Morgan. There is without doubt reason for this variety of opinions: It is that there was such a mixture of diverse races in Egypt.

Egypt is thus a melting pot of races and civilizations, at the crossroads of three continents. This is the real contribution of this country. To want to monopolize the whole to the profit of only one of the composite elements is to contradict the truth. And it is up to us, historians of Black Africa, to unravel what was the part of the *Negro* and of the *Brown* people (the "Africans of Ethiopia and Libya" of Petrie), a fact already widely admitted, as we have seen, in the makeup of ancient Egypt.

As for the rest of Black Africa, the results of archaeology, as we know, are very meager at present. How can C. A. Diop explain that the Egyptians, who he pretends were Negroes, and the Nubians, spiritual sons of Egypt, were the only ones before the first millennium BC to be civilized in all of Africa? For one cannot understand why the inhabitants of the Nile valley would have been *the avant-garde* of humanity when the other Negroes stayed at a "primitive" state just like the Europeans who were their contemporaries. And if West African Negroes descended from the Egyptians, why did they become "decivilized" *en route* between about 500 BC, the date of their departure from Egypt according to C. A. Diop, and 900 AD, the period from which we have texts describing them as rather "backwards"? Which way did they go? How is it that no ancient author speaks of this migration, although, according to the author, it was made during the historical period? And how is it that they have left no trace of their passage along the way?

Let us be very clear that it is *mounds* in the interior region of the Niger Delta and not *pyramids,* as the author thinks, not that one wants to "disparage African achievements," but because a pyramid is a volume with a well-defined form and mounds have a round or oval plan and are roughly hemispheric in form. The first are found particularly in Egypt, Nubia, and in Central America, the second in Black Africa and Europe.

As for thinking that the signs carved on the Baobabs of Diourbel are hieroglyphics, the author is now at home and knows the question well enough, I suppose, to judge for himself whether it is really writing (the old people of the area would give him the information in this case) or simply graffiti carved in the soft bark, which seems more likely.

Another problem rightly preoccupies Mr. Diop: the skin color of the Egyptians as it is represented in tomb paintings and on other documents. According to him . . . "the color called dark red of the Egyptians is none other than the natural color of the Negro," and he gives a text of Champollion-le-Jeune as evidence. Now Champollion-le-Jeune clearly distinguishes between Egyptians (dark red), Negroes "Nahasi," Semites "Namou" skin color tending toward yellow, Medes and Assyrians with a swarthy complexion, Indo-Europeans "Tamhou," with white skin.

Two works with numerous illustrations in color, which I have before me . . . to my mind support the opinions of Champollion-le-Jeune, and many others, concerning the great variety of races represented [in Egypt]. Nevertheless, one thing is clear: when the artist wanted to depict Negroes, he distinctly gave them a black or gray color. And the dark red people are not, with few exceptions, Negroes, but tawny people, brown people. It is, of course, true that the color black is found throughout the paintings, *but to represent the hair and not the skin.* The Egyptians were absolutely conscious of the difference in skin color between themselves, the Negroes, and Asiatics.

We have seen above that an anthropologist, C. S. Coon, called the usual color of the Pharaonic Egyptians "brunet white." This color resembles that of the average modern Egyptian of the Delta, those of the south being darker (reddish brown to a medium brown hue).

I am happy to find myself in accord with C. A. Diop when he speaks of the Ife civilization in Nigeria. It was a brilliant civilization, incontestably Negro, which, with its brass heads in naturalistic style, attained the summits of, not only African, but world art.

I am not competent, on the contrary, to judge the linguistic portion of this work, in particular the relationships between ancient Egyptian and modern Wolof; and I leave this problem to linguists. But I must admit my skepticism when I see a toponym in Songhai country, Tondidarou [Tundi-Daro], a site which I know well, with its megaliths (of which the obvious etymology is Songhai: *tondi daru* = big stone) explained by the Serer *tundi daro* = the hills of the union.

Nor do I think that the Lebu of Cape Verde have any relation whatsoever with the people, of the same name inhabiting the western approaches of the Nile Delta before our era. And to say that several Pharaohs of the first dynasties were of the Serer race "because their name included *Sen*" seems, to my mind, at the least very questionable. Such play on words is possible among all the languages of the world. Would Sun-Yat-*Sen*, Ib*sen*, Eisenhower, and Amund*sen* all be Serer as well?

Logic does not seem to lead to a closer possible relationship between ancient Egyptian and other African languages than to Indo-European languages. *But it is evident that comparisons should be made by competent and specialized linguists.*[17] It will be impossible to speak knowingly about all this until dictionaries and grammars of African languages are published. In order to form an opinion on a similar work of D. P. de Pedrals, *Archeologie de l'Afrique noire,* (Paris: Payot, 1950), a work which unfortunately seems to have had a good deal of influence on the author, I suggest the reader consult the reports in *Man,* September 1951, pp. 122–23, and the *Bulletin de l'Institut Français d'Afrique Noire,* 1951, pp. 1331–33.[18]

---

[17]The student would do well to consult the work of Joseph H. Greenberg, *The Languages of Africa* (Bloomington, IN: University of Indiana Press, 1963), particularly pp. 42–65. *(Editor)*

[18]Unfortunately, the work of D. P. de Pedrals, *L'Archeologie de l'Afrique Noire,* (Paris: Payot, 1950), from which C. A. Diop derives so much of his information, has been described by one authority as "would-be scientific discussions of names and words that add not one jot to our knowledge of African archaeology." (G. W. B. Huntingford in his review of *L'Archeologie de l'Afrique Noire,* appearing in *Man* (London: Royal Anthropological Institute of Great Britain

Despite these questionable hypotheses given as accepted and irrefutable truths, and the failure to include information from recent works concerning West Africa, the book of Mr. Diop is a landmark. It is the first general historical work written by a French-speaking black African, and, besides being an important source of documentation, it includes some excellent parts and it has the great merit of not following the traditional interpretations and of forcing the Egyptologists and others to take a stand and define their positions more precisely. Nevertheless, written before 1955 in Paris, it is inescapably a belligerent book, completely impregnated with the spirit of those years of struggle during which Africans, in particular students exiled in Paris amid the colonizing people and, in addition, frustrated by their national history, prepared the way for independence by exalting Negritude, sometimes even, and this is normal, at the price of taking liberty, perhaps unconsciously, with impartial and scientific truths: only that which could agree with his thesis was included. All this is "quite fair," and to me the attitudes formed during the general struggle of all the different African peoples are to be found therein.

Today, in 1960, times have changed. This is the year of independence for a number of countries in Black Africa, Mali among others. The African historian, without abandoning in the least his political opinions formed during the years of struggle against colonialism, owes it to himself, to science, and to his country to place himself, if he has not already done so, on the level of *strict objectivity,* which does not exclude interpretation or the use of hypotheses to be proven, but without which it is impossible to speak of history, of research, of scientific knowledge of history. *Otherwise the whole of the new school of African history risks being discredited and the sum of errors and exaggerations would be disastrous for the Africans themselves.* For now, and with reason, the African history taught to black children is being reformed so that children no longer learn just the history of the colonizers, but of their own people. it is no longer a question of convincing Parisian audiences or African students in Paris; the former were almost in general incompetent to judge and the latter were obviously already decided by anticolonial reaction, before the rapid acquisition of independence, to applaud this veritable Negro Gobinism. *It is now a question of the author's submitting his ideas to the examination of specialists, who are the only ones qualified to say what is worth retaining.* Or else the author himself must go back to the hard task of historical research to verify a number of his hypotheses.

When modern Egyptologists accept C. A. Diop's thesis that ancient

---

and Ireland, LI 1951), p. 123. Other leading archaeologists agree, seeming to make this work a very questionable source for evidence on Egyptian origins and migrations of the African. *(Editor)*

Egypt was "Negro," then and only then must school manuals be reformed. Would the cultural unity of Africa, from the Egyptians to the Bushman, include the Moroccans, the Tauregs, the Teda, the Pygmies, the Zulu, the Somalis, and the Abyssinians? Why not? On the condition that the ethnologists and sociologists tell us it is so.

A linguistic connection between ancient Egyptian and Wolof? Specialists of African languages could, one day, tell us if this hypothesis is valid. But again, they must be experts and their works confirmed by other specialists.

As for West African prehistory and history to the end of the middle ages, I hope that the author will permit me to think that I may give a relatively authoritative opinion in this matter.

There is, in effect, one urgent problem: *the part of the Negro* in the development of the universal civilization during the course of past centuries. In the meantime, however, what must come immediately is the development of the Negroes' active and original contribution to the elaboration of modern humanity. That the Negro had a part is incontestable, undeniable, but, up to now, the question has only just been touched by specialists. Just like all the other races, the Negro has contributed his stone in the construction [of the edifice of human history], but it is now a question of making this addition more precise, and no longer dismissing the problem by saying that Egypt was Negro and thus solving the problem before it can be properly stated and studied.

This study will no doubt necessitate long years of work before it can lead to any real conclusions: careful scrutiny and commentaries on texts, examination of Egyptian and other collections, innumerable detailed studies will all advance us, step by step, towards the truth. This task should be begun as early as possible, and principally in the three West African universities, Ibadan, Accra, and Dakar, and in Negro universities in America. I am ready to collaborate in this task.

The great merit of C. A. Diop will be to have contributed, after Dr. K. O. Dike, Fr. M. Snowden, J. C. de Graft-Johnson, and others, to the opening of this record to which no African, no Africanist and I would even say that no one should be indifferent at the hour when Africa vigorously affirms her personality.

Black Athena
MARTIN BERNAL[19]

Proposed Historical Outline

Black Athena is focused on Greek cultural borrowings from Egypt and the Levant in the 2nd millennium BC or, to be more precise, in the thousand years from 2100 to 1100 BC. Some of these may be earlier and a few later exchanges will also be considered. The reasons for choosing this particular time-span are first that this seems to have been the period in which Greek culture was formed, and secondly that I have found it impossible to discover indications of any earlier borrowings either from the Near East or from legendary, cultic or etymological Greek evidence.

The scheme I propose is that while there seems to have been more or less continuous Near Eastern influence on the Aegean over this millennium, its intensity varied considerably at different periods. The first "peak" of which we have any trace was the 21st century. It was then that Egypt recovered from the breakdown of the First Intermediate Period, and the so-called Middle Kingdom was established by the new 11th Dynasty. This not only reunited Egypt but attacked the Levant and is known from archaeological evidence to have had wide-ranging contacts further afield, certainly including Crete and possibly the Mainland. The succession of Upper Egyptian black pharaohs sharing the name Menthotpe had as their divine patron the hawk and bull god Mntw or Mont. It is during the same century that the Cretan palaces were established and one finds the beginnings there of the bull-cult which appears on the walls of the palaces and was central to Greek mythology about King Minos and Crete. It would therefore seem plausible to suppose that the Cretan developments directly or indirectly reflected the rise of the Egyptian Middle Kingdom. . . .

[19]Bernal, Martin, *Black Athena: The Afroasiatic Roots of Classical Civilization* (London: Free Association Books, 1987). Excerpts taken from volume 1, pp. 17–18, 440–442.

Martin Bernal was born in London 1937. He attended King's College Cambridge as an undergraduate, graduate student and research fellow. He also studied at Peking University, Berkeley and Harvard. In 1973 he was appointed to the faculty at Cornell University where he remains today as a Professor Emeritus. After 20 years he changed his field from the history of China in the 19th and 20th centuries to the origins of Ancient Greece. In the series of books with the general title *Black Athena* he argues that we should take Ancient Greek historians seriously when they maintained that Egyptians and Phoenicians played central roles in the formation of their culture. Conversely we should take into account the political and ideological pressures on 19th and 20th century scholars who wished to deny the ancient interpretation. The books have stimulated widespread discussion and controversy.

Conclusion

. . . . The main body of the book began with a description of the ways in which Classical, Hellenistic and later pagan Greeks from the 5th century BC to the 5th century AD saw their distant past. I attempted to trace their own vision of their ancestors' having been civilized by Egyptian and Phoenician colonization and the later influence of Greek study in Egypt. I tried to show the ambivalent relationship between Christianity and the Jewish biblical tradition on the one hand and Egyptian religion and philosophy on the other: despite all the centuries of potential and actual rivalry, there was no doubt on either side that up to the 18th century, Egypt was seen as the fount of all "Gentile" philosophy and learning, including that of the Greeks; and that the Greeks had managed to preserve only some part of these. The sense of loss that this created, and the quest to recover the lost wisdom, were major motives in the development of science in the 17th century.

I went on to show how at the beginning of the 18th century the threat of Egyptian philosophy to Christianity became acute. The Freemasons, who made much use of the image of Egyptian wisdom, were at the centre of the Enlightenment in its attack on Christian order. And it was in opposition to this 18th-century notion of' "reason" on the part of the Egyptophils that the Greek ideal of sentiment and artistic perfection was developed. Further, the development of Europocentrism and racism, with the colonial expansion over the same period, led to the fallacy that only people who lived in temperate climates—that is, Europeans—could really think. Thus the Ancient Egyptians, who—though their colour was uncertain—lived in Africa, lost their position as philosophers. They also suffered through the establishment of the new "progressive" paradigm because they had lived so far in the past.

In this way, by the turn of the 18th century the Greeks were not only considered to have been more sensitive and artistic than the Egyptians but they were now seen as the better philosophers, and indeed as the founders of philosophy. I suggested that as the Greeks were now viewed as such paragons of wisdom and sensitivity, intelligent counterrevolutionary intellectuals saw the study of them as a way of reintegrating people alienated by modern life; and even of re-establishing social harmony in the face of the French Revolution. Classics as we know it today was created between 1815 and 1830—an intensely conservative period. The same period also saw the Greek War of Independence, which united all Europeans against the traditional Islamic enemies from Asia and Africa.

This War—and the philhellenic movement, which supported the struggle for independence—completed the already powerful image of Greece as the epitome of Europe. The Ancient Greeks were now seen as perfect, and as having transcended the laws of history and language. Thus it was now thought profane to study any aspect of their culture as one would the culture of other peoples. Moreover, with the rise of a passionate and systematic racism in the early 19th century, the ancient notion that Greece was a mixed culture that had been civilized by Africans and Semites became not only abominable but unscientific. Just as one had to discount the "credulous" Greeks' stories about sirens and centaurs, so one had to reject legends of their having been colonized by inferior races. Paradoxically, the more the 19th century admired the Greeks, the less it respected their writing of their own history.

I see this destruction of the Ancient Model as entirely the result of social forces such as these, and the requirements put upon the Ancient Greeks by 19th-century Northern Europeans. My belief is that no internalist force—or advance in the knowledge of Ancient Greece—can explain the change. Having said this, I accept that the establishment of the Aryan Model was greatly helped by the working out of the Indo-European language family, which—though inspired by Romanticism— was an internalist achievement; and by the undoubted fact that Greek is fundamentally an Indo-European language. But here, too, the same social and intellectual forces that had brought down the Ancient Model in the 1820s were even more intense in the 1840s and 50s, and they clearly played a role in the increasingly "northern" picture of Ancient Greece that developed in the late 19th century. At the same time, the sense that only 19th-century men knew how to think "scientifically" gave the—mainly German—scholars the confidence both to dismiss ancient descriptions of early Greek history and to invent new ones of their own without any regard to the Ancients.

With the intensification of racism in the 19th century there was increasing dislike of the Egyptians, who were no longer seen as the cultural ancestors of Greece but as fundamentally alien. A whole new discipline of Egyptology could thus grow up, to study this exotic culture and at the same time maintain and reinforce Egypt's distance from the "real" civilizations of Greece and Rome.

The status of Egypt fell with the rise of racism in the 1820s; that of the Phoenicians declined with the rise of racial anti-Semitism in the 1880s and collapsed with its peak between 1917 and 1939. Thus, by the Second World War, it had been firmly established that Greece had not significantly borrowed culturally or linguistically from Egypt and Phoenicia and that the legends of colonization were charming absurdities, as were the stories of the Greek wise men having studied in Egypt. Indeed, these beliefs survived the years between 1945 and 1960, even though their ideological underpinnings of racism and anti-Semitism were generally being discredited in the academic community.

Since the late 1960s, however, the Extreme Aryan Model has been under heavy attack, largely by Jews and Semitists. The important role of Canaanites and Phoenicians in the formation of Ancient Greece is now being increasingly acknowledged. However, the traditional attribution of much of Greek civilization to Egypt is still denied; and in Greek language studies—the last bunker of Romanticism and the Extreme Aryan Model—any talk of significant Afroasiatic influence on Greek is ruled absurd.

The main point I have been trying to make throughout this book is that the Ancient Model was destroyed and replaced by the Aryan Model not because of any internal deficiencies, nor because the Aryan Model explained anything better or more plausibly; what it did do, however, was make the history of Greece and its relations to Egypt and the Levant conform to the world-view of the 19th century and, specifically, to its systematic racism. Since then the concepts of "race" and categorical European superiority which formed the core of this *Weltanschauung* have been discredited both morally and heuristically, and it would be fair to say that the Aryan Model was conceived in what we should now call sin and error. . . .

Black Athena Revisited
GUY ROGERS[20]

The editors of this volume present here some preliminary answers to [the] questions [raised in Bernal's work]. These preliminary answers are based upon summaries of the articles edited for this volume (although there obviously are some differences among the contributors about details). In setting out these preliminary answers, we hope to provide scholars and the general public with a handy reference to the state of expert judgment on some difficult scholarly questions.

We recognize that Bernal (and other scholars) may well disagree with our answers to these questions. We welcome his response. At the end of this conclusion, we make some suggestions about how the debate about the roots of classical civilization might be framed most productively in the future. We look forward to the next round in the debate.

Who were the ancient Egyptians? Although the population of ancient Egypt had ties to the north and to the south, and was also intermediate between populations to the east and west, the population of ancient Egypt was distinct and basically Egyptian from the Neolithic period right up to historic times.

Were the ancient Egyptians "black"? Many of the scholars who contributed to this volume found this question to be disturbing, at least as it was formulated in *Black Athena*. Several contributors specifically have been concerned that ancient evidence and archaeological remains have been identified with concepts of race and racial issues which belong to the modern world. Such issues appear to have been absent in the conceptual world of ancient Egyptians and Greeks. Indeed, in the ancient Mediterranean world in general, color terms did not carry the stigma of inferiority similar to that associated with color terms in postclassical societies, which have sub-

---

[20]Lefkowitz, Mary R., and Guy MacLean Rogers, ed., *Black Athena Revisited* (Chapel Hill, N.C.: The University of North Carolina Press, 1996). Excerpts taken from pp. 448–451, *Quo Vadis?* by Guy MacLean Rogers.

Guy MacLean Rogers (b. 1954) holds a Ph.D. in Classics from Princeton University. He has received numerous grants and fellowships, including ones from the National Endowment for the Humanities, the American Philosophical Society, and All Souls College, Oxford. His first book, *The Sacred Identity of Ephesos: Foundation Myths of a Roman City*, won the Routledge Ancient History Prize. Chairman of the Department of History of Wellesley College from 1997–2001, he grew up and still lives in Litchfield County, Connecticut.

jected darker skinned peoples to terrible forms of discrimination on the basis of the color of their skin.

But since Bernal himself has raised this question, both in *Black Athena* and in subsequent public comments, scholars have felt obliged to set the record straight for the sake of their peers as well as the general public.

We believe that the attempt to assign the people of the Nile valley to "Caucasoid" or "Negroid" categories is an arbitrary act and wholly devoid of historical or biological significance. It would be inaccurate to describe the ancient Egyptians as either black or white; the population of ancient Egypt was one of mixed pigmentation. Essentially, the Egyptians were the Egyptians. To describe them otherwise promotes a misconception about the ancient Egyptians, with racist undertones, that reveals much more about those who wish to make such attempts than about the ancient Egyptians themselves.

Was Egypt African? Although Egypt lies geographically on the continent of Africa, in anthropological terms the categorical labeling of the civilization of ancient Egypt as "fundamentally African" is misleadingly simplistic. In fact the archaeological evidence of African kingdoms south of Egypt suggests distinctly different cultures that were often in conflict with ancient Egypt. *Black Athena* hardly treats these relations—and still less so the widespread evidence in other parts of the continent for the independent evolution of civilizations. In tracing the alleged Afro-Asiatic roots of classical civilization, Bernal has almost nothing to say about the entire continent of Africa and its many and diverse ancient civilizations. In short, *Black Athena* is not about ancient Africa at all.

Did the ancient Egyptians or Hyksos colonize Greece? In *Black Athena* Bernal claims that Greece was colonized from Egypt not once, but twice: first during the third millennium B.C.E., when Egyptian colonists arrived in Greece, bringing advanced building skills, their cults and religion; and second, during the eighteenth/seventeenth centuries B.C.E., when the Hyksos, having been driven out of Egypt, invaded the Argolid and ruled there.

Unambiguous archaeological evidence in support of an Egyptian colonization of Greece is absent from the Aegean area, despite decades of field research. Nor do the historical records of Egypt or any other Near Eastern culture support the idea of a Hyksos invasion and colonization of the Argolid.

Did the ancient Egyptians and/or the Phoenicians massively influence the early Greeks in the areas of language, religion, science, and/or philosophy? No expert in the field doubts that there was a Greek cultural debt to the ancient Near East. The real questions are: How large was the debt? Was it massive, as Bernal claims? Was it limited to the Egyptians and the Phoenicians?

The consensus of the contributors to this volume is that the debt cannot be described as massive; nor was the debt limited to Egypt and Phoenicia.

Certainly the evidence shows that the Eighteenth Dynasty and the Aegean world were in close contact at certain levels; but such contacts are not equivalent to "suzerainty" and do not imply the substantial cultural impact upon the Aegean that is required by Bernal's claims.

All of the contributors agree that the early Greeks got their alphabet from the Phoenicians; but little else. Indeed, in terms of language, the evidence that Bernal has presented thus far for the influence of Egyptian or Phoenician on ancient Greek has failed to meet any of the standard tests which are required for the proof of extensive influence, including a large percentage of undisputed vocabulary borrowings, phonetic similarity, and parallelisms in grammar. Overall, the fact remains that Egyptian and Canaanite scripts were never used widely in historical Greece.

Similarly, in the area of religion, Egyptian and Canaanite deities were never worshiped on Greek soil in their indigenous forms. Nor does the abundant archaeological evidence support claims of deep and pervasive influence in the area of cult.

The case for Egyptian influence on Greek mathematical astronomy, mathematics, and medicine is only somewhat stronger. In these areas the Egyptians definitely influenced the Greeks; but Greek achievements, especially in the fields of mathematics and medicine, became quite distinct and original.

Several contributors, while convinced of the influence of the Mediterranean cultures of the ancient Near East on early Greek civilization, especially through the medium of trade, nevertheless could not agree that Egypt or Phoenicia was the principal axis of that influence. Instead they point to relations that were probably more critical to long-term developments in Greece, including (especially) relations with the northern Levant, Anatolia, and, ultimately, Babylonia, which was much more influential culturally than Egypt generally in the Near East. Furthermore, there were more geographical routes available by which that Babylonian influence could travel.

Finally, several contributors have drawn attention to a different model of interaction between the ancient Near East and early Greece. Instead of Bernal's model of colonization and/or massive influence moving from Egypt and Phoenicia to Greece, Near Eastern specialists suggest a model of regular, widespread, and mutually profitable contacts between many different Near Eastern cultures and the early Greeks over a much greater time span. Several scholars emphasized that there is, in fact, increasing evidence of Minoan and early Greek influence on the culture not only of Egypt, but of Palestine as well. The cultural road to early Greece apparently was not a one-way street; rather there were many two-lane highways of cultural exchange, connecting many different Near Eastern cultures not only with the early Greeks but also with each other.

Did the Greeks believe that they were descended from the Egyptians and the Phoenicians? There were rival traditions propounded about the origins of the Greeks, at different times and for different reasons. We might call such rival traditions competitive subjective ethnicities. The Cadmus and Danaus myths, for instance, upon which Bernal places such weight, were created or revised (in the forms which we now have them) by Athenian poets and historians who wished to emphasize the autochthony of Athens by contrast with the alleged foreign origins of rival city states. Greek myths of ethnic origins, in other words, do not bear unmediated, literal truths about the origins of the Greeks.

Did eighteenth- and nineteenth-century scholars obscure the Afro-Asiatic roots of classical civilization for reasons of racism and anti-Semitism? Some eighteenth- and nineteenth-century scholars who wrote about the question of Greece's cultural debt to Egypt or Phoenicia did so from a point of view that today would be considered racist or anti-Semitic. Some of those scholars denied or underemphasized that debt for the sake of maintaining the uniqueness and originality of European culture in their own day.

But not all or even the majority of eighteenth- and nineteenth-century classical scholars who downplayed Greece's debt to Egypt or Phoenicia were racists or anti-Semites. Rather, the majority of those scholars downplayed that debt because they saw little evidence for the kind of massive influence that Bernal has argued for. Nor has he been able to produce new evidence or a new interpretation of old evidence which might convince the majority of scholars today that the majority of eighteenth- and nineteenth-century scholars were essentially wrong.

Furthermore, as the essays collected in this volume have shown, Professor Bernal's attempt to portray figures such as Herder and Grote as racists or romantics is not supported by a careful, contextualized study of all of the evidence. Too often in *Black Athena* he has selected only a few sentences from the works of earlier scholars and has decontextualized those sentences in order to build up a picture of undifferentiated racism and anti-Semitism—but only on the part of those previous scholars who have questioned the depth of Greece's debt to Egypt or Phoenicia.

The scholarly record is, in fact, far more complex and contradictory than Bernal allows. The picture of attitudes toward blacks in Britain and America, for instance, is far more complicated than he makes it out to be. There certainly were many prominent and outspoken intellectual antiracists in Britain and America, a fact readers would never discover from reading *Black Athena*.

More to the point, many scholars in the eighteenth and nineteenth centuries questioned the depth of Greece's debt to Egypt and Phoenicia, not for reasons of racism and anti-Semitism, as Bernal would insist, but because evidence leading to that conclusion was lacking; or, more importantly, because the discovery of new evidence led in the opposite direction. In particular, the discovery of the Indo-European language group, of which Greek was proved to be a member, encouraged nineteenth-century scholars especially to think of Greek civilization as being fundamentally different from the civilizations of Egypt and Phoenicia.

In sum, Bernal's presentation of European classical historiography of the eighteenth and nineteenth centuries as pervaded by racism and anti-Semitism that prevented scholars from accurately assessing the Afro-Asiatic roots of classical civilization, is oversimplified and unconvincing.

Suggestions for Further Reading

Adams, W. Y., *Nubia: Corridor to Africa* (Princeton: Princeton University Press, 1977).

Diop, Cheikh Anta, *The Cultural Unity of Black Africa* (Chicago: The Third World Pres, 1978).

———, *Cheikh Anta Diop: An African Scientist: An Axiomatic Overview of His Teachings and Thoughts,* edited and compiled by E. Curtis Alexander (New York: ECA Associates, 1984.

Drake, St. Clair, *Black Folks Here and There: An Essay in History and Anthropology,* 2 volumes (Los Angeles: Center for Afro-American Studies, 1990).

Smith, Grafton Elliot, Sir, *The Ancient Egyptians and the Origin of Civilization* (London: Harper, 1923).

Gardiner, Alan Henderson, Sir, *Egypt of the Pharaohs* (Oxford: Clarendon Press, 1961).

Goody, Jack, "The Myth of a State," *Journal of Modern African Studies* 6, no. 4 (December 1968), 461–74.

Huntingford, G. W. B., "The Peopling of the Interior of East Africa by its Modern Inhabitants," in Oliver, Roland, and Mathew, Gervase, eds., *History of East Africa,* vol. 1 (Oxford: Clarendon Press, 1963), 58–93.

Lucas, Jonathan, *The Religion of the Yorubas, Being an Account of the Religious Beliefs and Practices of the Yoruba Peoples of South Nigeria, Especially in Relation to the Religion of Ancient Egypt* (Lagos: C.M.S. Bookshop, 1948).

———, *Religions of West Africa and Ancient Egypt* (Apapa: Nigerian National Press, 1970.)

———, Meyerowitz, Eva, *The Akan of Ghana: Their Ancient Beliefs* (London: Faber and Faber, 1958).

Mokhtar, G., ed., *Ancient Civilizations of Africa,* volume 2 of UNESCO's *General History of Africa* (London: Heinemann, 1981).

Tarharka, *Black Manhood: The Building of Civilization by the Black Men of the Nile* (Washington, D.C.: University Press, 1979).

Trigger, Bruce, "The Myth of Meroe and the African Iron Age," *African Historical Studies* 2, no. 1 (1969), 23–50.

———, "The Rise of Civilization in Egypt," in Clark, J. Desmond, ed., *The Cambridge History of Africa,* vol. 1 (Cambridge University Press, 1982), 478–547.

Van Sertima, Ivan, ed., *Egypt Revisited* (New Brunswick: Transaction, 1989).

Welsby, Derek A., *The Kingdom of Kush* (Princeton: Markus Wiener Publishers, 1998).

Wescott, R. W., "Ancient Egypt and Modern Africa," *Journal of African History* 2, no. 2 (1961), 311–21.

PROBLEM II
BANTU ORIGINS AND MIGRATIONS

The term "Bantu" was first defined by Dr. Wilhelm Bleek in his book published in 1862 entitled *A Comparative Grammar of South African Languages*. Bleek observed that nearly every language spoken on the southern third of the African continent used prefixes that could be attributed to a set of what he called "Proto-Prefixes," presupposing a generic relationship and implying an aboriginal source. Many scholars of Africa have since studied the Bantu languages, and all have come to the general conclusion that these languages definitely form an organic unity suggestive of just such common origin. This hypothesis, however, has created in the past a number of linguistic, geographical, historical and even national problems in identifying the relationship of the Bantu languages, which presently occupy such a vast area of the African continent. Today the problem has been fundamentally resolved in the work of many scholars in many disciplines, but primarily through the linguistic work of Prof. Joseph H. Greenberg. The disputes that have divided scholars of virtually every nationality over the past generation have now been largely laid to rest as a consensus has been formed as to the relationship of the overwhelming millions of Bantu speaking peoples of the continent of Africa. Moreover there is increasing agreement as to the homeland of the Bantu speaking people, and what is more important, their relationship with the speakers of West African languages forming a larger speaking group known as Niger-Kordofanian.

The present problem, however, is concerned principally with those Africans who speak a Bantu language, their origins and their diffusion throughout much of the African continent. Although there is widespread consensus that indeed the Bantu-speaking Africans originated in the area of the Cameroon Nigerian borderlands known as the Benue region, there is still controversy as to what factors were introduced or developed within their society to enable them to increase their numbers and to migrate over such an expansive geographical area as the whole of central and southern Africa. Although there is general understanding that their migrations began to take place about 500 BC there is still dispute as to the direction and the rate at which they populated the African continent.

For many years the fashionable theories of Sir Harry Johnston (1858–1927), that implacable imperialist, were widely accepted as properly identifying the cradleland of the Bantu. Johnston identified the parent Bantu speech as the tongue of "West African" features spoken originally in the heart of Africa "somewhere between the basins of the Upper Nile, the Bahr al Ghazal, the Mubangi, and the Upper Benue in the Shari Basin." He traced the first movement of these archaic people eastward to the Nile Valley north of Lake Albert. There they settled and developed into what Johnston called "the proto-Bantu." Then from this homeland on the Upper Nile and the great lakes the proto-Bantu began their migrations that swept them into the other parts of Africa. Although Johnston wrote most of his work at the end of the Victorian period, he recognized the relationship between the Bantu languages of central and southern Africa with those of West Africa, an important contribution that was not fully realized until the work of Prof. Greenberg. Recognizing the similarities between many of the West African languages and the Bantu, Johnston termed these tongues "semi-Bantu" and explained their development in three ways. First, some of these languages had descended from the archaic Bantu ancestors whose origins were in the Shari Basin. Second, others had descended from the early southward migration of the proto-Bantu before their main migration began. Third, some were formed by the fusion of the language of the Cross River and the Benue Basin areas with the Bantu who finally broke through the great Congo rain forest and migrated into the more salubrious climates to the south. Modern scholarship has modified much of what Johnston saw at the end of the nineteenth century, but outside of being a preeminent British proconsul in imperial Africa, he recognized the fundamental importance of the relationship between Bantu and West African languages, and even if he did not define the migration of Bantu with precision he was not far from wrong.

The very early work of Sir Harry Johnston, which is more historical than linguistic, was challenged by Malcolm Guthrie whose long association with central Africa and methodology ultimately placed the origin of the Bantu people south of the tropical rain forest of Zaire and their growth and dispersion from the southern savannah into eastern Africa and, of course, ultimately to the Cape of Good Hope. Although there is wide agreement that the Bantu did prosper and disperse from the southern savannah this is certainly not the source of their origins nor of their relationships linguistically

with the West-African languages so fundamental to the Greenberg hypothesis. Despite the fact that his work on the prehistory of Bantu languages is
no longer tenable, it still forms an important part of the history and evolution
of the languages of the African continent. Of greater importance, perhaps
because of its acceptance by the scholarly community, is the work of Joseph
H. Greenberg and particularly his methodology that has resolved the relationship of not only the Bantu languages but those with West Africa. Not
only does Prof. Greenberg incontrovertibly demonstrate that Prof. Guthrie's
empirical evidence is in error but that the efforts have been completely
vindicated by the work of Prof. Colin Flight who has described both historically and linguistically the validation of Prof. Greenberg's work.

The influence of this long, technical, and historical debate has perhaps
found its resolution by a new generation of historians of Africa in the work
of Thomas Spear, who, although dealing only with Kenya's past, succinctly
shows the impact of the resolution of the Bantu problem.

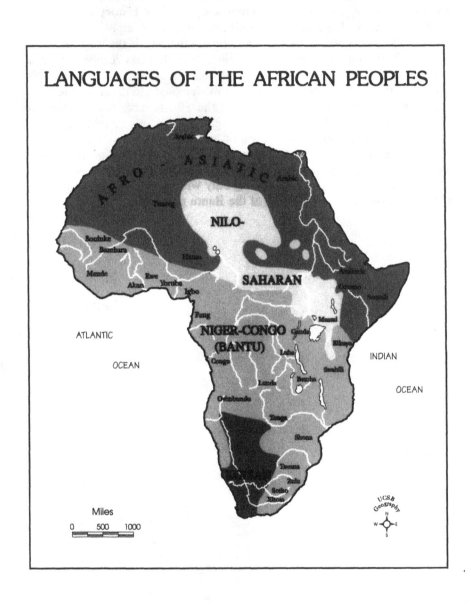

LANGUAGES OF THE AFRICAN PEOPLES

AFRO - ASIATIC

Arabic

Arabic

Tuareg

NILO-

Soninke
Bambara

Hausa

Mande

Ewe
Akan Yoruba

Igbo

Amharic

Oromo

Somali

SAHARAN

Fang

Maasai

NIGER-CONGO
(BANTU)

Ganda

Kikuyu

ATLANTIC

Congo

Luba

Swahili

OCEAN

Lunda

Bemba

INDIAN

OCEAN

Ovimbundo

Tonga

Shona

Tswana
Zulu
Sotho
Xhosa

Miles

0   500   1000

UCSB
Geography

N
W   E
S

58

Bantu Languages
SIR HARRY JOHNSTON[1]

The Bantu languages . . . do not strike one as foreign in their origin to Negro Africa, less so, in fact, than the Fulani. Probably the parent speech was a prefix-using tongue of "West African" features spoken originally in the very heart of Africa, somewhere between the basins of the Upper Nile, the Bahr al Ghazal, the Mubangi, and the Upper Benue, one of a chain of similar prefix and concord languages stretching from westernmost Africa to Kordofan. The first invasive move of the archaic Bantu seems to have been eastward, toward the Mountain Nile and the Great Lakes. The proto-Bantu folk were certainly once—many centuries ago—settled in the Nile valley north of the Albert Nyanza. One can trace their place-names still, in countries long since colonized by Nilotics or Sudanese. In this direction (the southwestern part of the Anglo-Egyptian Sudan) they must have remained till at least as late as three or four hundred years before Christ—late enough to have been in full possession of goats and oxen and to have received the domestic fowl from Egypt or Abyssinia. Then they embarked on their great career of conquering and colonizing the southern third of Africa.

The most archaic Bantu languages at the present day are those of Bunyoro, Bukonjo, Ruanda, Buganda, the islands of the Victoria Nyanza, and the region of the northwest slopes of Mount Elgon (Masaba). It is reasonable to suppose that after the Bantu language-type came into existence, perhaps between the Shari basin and the Bahr al Ghazal (its nearest relations are found in the Niger and Cross river basins), its first great concentration lay in the region of the Great Lakes, in Equatorial Africa. Here it was shut off for a while from westward extension by the dense wall of Congoland forest. Southward, down the shores of Tanganyika and thence southwest and west across the mountains and plateaus of southern Congoland to the Atlantic; eastward and southeastward to the Indian Ocean and the Zangian coasts; southward across the Zambezi and Mashonaland to temperate South Africa swept the Bantu invaders, armed, it may be, with novel iron weapons and led by a Hamiticized aristocracy. They progressed, no doubt, as rapidly as the Zulu or Basuto hordes overran Central Africa under the white man's

[1]Johnston, Sir Harry H., *A Comparative Study of the Bantu and Semi-Bantu Languages* (Oxford: Clarendon Press, 1919). Excerpts taken from pages 22–39.

Sir Harry Hamilton Johnston was a famous explorer, administrator, and author of Africa.

observation in the nineteenth century. Here our forefathers or contemporaries have been able to testify to the spread of the Zulu clans and the Zulu tongue from the thirty-fifth to the third degree of South latitude in about fifty years.

The original Bantu invaders found no empty Africa before them. We may be certain from abundant evidence that Central and South Africa have been inhabited by man for many thousands of years, and probably by some black-skinned forest Negro, Sudanese Negro, or Congo Pygmy—for an indeterminately long period, as far south as the Zambezi river. But South Africa proper, between the high plateaus of northern Becuanaland and the seacoast of Cape Colony and Natal may possibly have been the domain exclusively of the Bushman and of the Hottentot hybrid down to the first Bantu invasions from across the Zambezi in (at a guess) about 700 AD. South Africa then or earlier may have been partially depopulated from some cause—some epidemic of germ disease. Anciently—thirty, fifty thousand years ago, farther back still, perhaps—there existed in southernmost Africa a remarkable cave dwelling type, the "Strandlooper," whose skull bore less of a resemblance to the Bushman or the Negro than to some round-headed, semi-Caucasian stock of the Mediterranean. This Strandlooper either coexisted alongside the Bushman or preceded and was followed by this specialized desert Negro. In time the Strandloopers died out, leaving perhaps some traces of their presence in varied Bushman strains, and bequeathing to the Bushmen their wonderful gift of drawing and engraving, so reminiscent of the cave and rock pictures of the Solutrian and Megdalenian Cave men of Europe or the Paleolithic and Neolithic nomads of Algeria and the Sahara. We may imagine, however, some two thousand years ago, a South Africa beyond the Zambezi and Kunene rivers given up for a time to the dwarfish, steatopygous, yellow-skinned, click-using Bushman.

The next disturbing element may have been the Hottentot; a hybrid between Negro and Negroid and some more northern Bushman race, which seems to have migrated from Equatorial East Africa southwestwards to the Central Zambezi and thence to the Atlantic coast near Walfish Bay, and on again southwards till the Hottentots entered (what is now) Cape Colony and displaced the Bushman. Later, it may be, there came other invaders from the northeast, by sea, rather than by land, the mysterious gold-mining, stone-building monolith- and phallus-worshipping people who originated the Zimbabwe walls, temples, and emblems. These are amongst the unsolved mysteries of Africa; but the most striking of these stone cities, together with this whole impulse and procedure of gold mining, most certainly were foreign to the Bantu arts and pursuits. The Bantu have seldom any word for gold. The tribes oldest in legendary history in South and East Africa use for gold an Arab word meaning "moneys." Zimbabwe and its like originally, perhaps, and certainly later, early in the Christian Era, became associated with the exploring and trading voyages of the south Arabians; and among the early writers of Islamic times there were to be gathered traditions that when the Arabs first visited the southeast coasts of Africa they found them peopled with "Wakwak" savages, who from the brief allusions may strike one as more like Bushmen than Bantu. The arrival of the Bantu hordes (the ancestors of the Karana, Bechuana, Zulu-Kafir, Masangane, and Ronga peoples), may have been the cause of the abandonment of the stone fortresses and mining depots by the sea-people whose forerunners designed or built them. After a time, however, the Arabs got into friendly relations with the Bantu colonizers, who in a much clumsier fashion imitated their mining and their stonebuilding. The Arabs, indeed, by their trade, their influence, and their slavemarkets seem to have molded the conquests of some early Bantu warrior-chief into that empire of the Mwenemutapa—Lord of the mine—which the Portuguese found still a potent state when they reached Southeast Africa at the commencement of the sixteenth century.

The Bantu were quite possibly settled on the more northern coast of the Indian Ocean—the land of Zanj—at the beginning of the Christian Era. The early Arab traders from Mokha, Aden, Mokalla, and Maskat cultivated friendly relations with them. A hybrid type sprang up, the Swahili, or men of the "Suahil" (coast-land). With the aid of the Arab daus (sailing vessels) many of these Swahili from the land of Zanj or Zang (the Persian or Arab name for Black man's country, and the origin of "Zanzibar") colonized the Komoro islands and even reached Madagascar, supplying the Malagasy dialects with numerous Swahili words.

In the Congo basin the Bantu invaders often appeared as solitary huntsmen, boldly attacking the big wild beasts with their iron spears. Bantu culture throughout the Congo basin is closely associated with the iron spear—Songo, Kongo, Lionga. They probably found the Congo forests peopled already with forest Negroes speaking tone languages of West African type or with a still more primitive people, the Congo Pygmies. There would even seem to be portions of the innermost Congo basin which the tall Bantu have not yet penetrated and where there are only Pygmies. On the Northern Congo there still remain patches of non-Bantu territory inhabited by Negroes speaking languages of an as yet unclassified type, vaguely styled "Sudanic." Somewhat similar to these are the Forest Lendu to the west of the Albert Nyanza.

The first great Bantu migrations undoubtedly emanated from the vicinity of the Victoria Nyanza and north Tanganyika, and were directed round and not through the Congo forests. But in course of time, the Bantu communities founded in the region of the Albertine Nile and the Nyanzas, or farther still to the northwest between the sources of the Wele and the Aruwimi, broke through the wall of forest, and sent streams of migrants across the northern parts of Congoland to the Gaboon and the Cameroons; reaching as their final effort the island of Fernando Po, which was not very anciently severed from a Cameroons promontory by some volcanic rift. Such an east-to-west propulsion might, in contact with the Nigerian peoples of the Cross river and Benue basins, have created by fusion the semi-Bantu languages; and no doubt one or two groups of such arose in this way and not very anciently. But it is more probable, taking all known facts into account, that a large section of the semi-Bantu speech forms is either descended from sisters of the Bantu parent tongue (born in that central region north of the Benue, east of the Niger, and west of the Shari river), or has been originated by early, very early, southwestward migrations of the proto-Bantu before the great eastward move into the Nile basin and before the exact shaping of Bantu features had taken place.

One is led irresistibly to deduce from the linguistic, ethnological, and anthropological evidence before us that at some such critical period in their career the Negro speakers of the early Bantu languages were brought under the influence of a semi-Caucasian race from the north or northeast. Perhaps it was a gradual drifting into Central Africa of Egyptian or Gala adventurers coming up or across the basin of the Mountain Nile; an infiltration of a superior type of man rather than a forceful invasion. Descendants of such ancient civilizers of Central Africa are undoubtedly to be seen at the present day in the Bahima, Ruhinda, Batutsi aristocracies of the Nyanza regions, the Mangbettu and Azande "royal" families of the Nile-Congo water-parting, the Basi-busongo of central Congo-land, the Luba chieftains, and the many handsome-featured pale-skinned castes and ruling clans in so many of the Bantu peoples. Such good-looking "Negroid" types may be encountered among the Zulus, the Bechuana, the Herero, the Alunda, Baluba, Many-uema, and the northern Congo riverain tribes, the Fang peoples, and the Duala of the Cameroons. Livingstone, Burton, Stanley, as well as later travelers, were all struck with the Egyptian-like features of the aristocratic families in the big Bantu states and kingdoms or among the warlike tribes of Central Africa. Similar aristocracies were noted by the pioneer missionaries and traders in southernmost Africa.

The Bantu-speaking peoples of Africa, it might be here stated, do not constitute a race apart from other Negroes or offer any homogeneity of physical type. But on the whole they represent so much the average Negro type that "Bantu" is still in favor as a physical definition among craniologists. In reality, they are just fifty millions of Negroes whose speech belongs to one of the many language families of "Negro" type; only in this case the language family, instead of being confined in its range to a hundred villages or two hundred square miles, is spread over the southern third of Africa say over 3,500,000 square miles—from the Cameroons, the Northern Congo, the Nyanzas, and the Mombasa coast to Cape Colony and Natal. Bantu languages are spoken by Congo Pygmies and forest Negroes of marked prognathism and stunted stature, by fuzzyhaired brown-skinned Fernandians still in the stone-and-wood age of culture, by tall-statured, handsome pale-skinned Negroids with Egyptian profiles—the Bahima and Batutsi, by great, burly, coarse-featured, downright, "West Coast" Negroes like the Wanyamwezi, the Baganda, the Ovambu, and the folk of the Angola coastlands; by tribes with the yellow skins, broad, wrinkled faces of the slit-eyed Bushmen, by the very black-skinned, large-eyed, comely Atonga of Nyasa, the semi-Arah Swahin or Karaiia, the stately Zulu, the mean-looking Batwa of Bangweulu, the Assyrian-like Baluba and Busongu, the simiesque Banandi of the Ituri forest or Babongu of the Gaboon, and the all-round, moderately ugly, black Negroes of average stature and average Negro characteristics throughout the rest of South and Central Africa.

Yet about the Bantu speech and the culture which accompanies it (ordinarily) there is a suggestion, strengthened by the association of these languages with metal-working (iron more especially), with agriculture, cultivated plants, and cattle-keeping, that adds to the impression derived from their legends, their religious beliefs, games, and weapons. It is that the Bantu language family was finally molded by some non-Negro incomers of possibly Hamitic affinities, akin at any rate in physique and culture, if not in language, to the dynastic Egyptians, the Galas, and perhaps most of all to those "Ethiopians" of mixed Egyptian and Negro-Nubian stock that down to one thousand years ago inhabited the Nile basin south of Wadi Halfa and north of Kordofan. Such a race may even have been akin to the Tibu farther west, the Tibu of Fezzan, the Eastern Sahara, and the Libyan desert. We know that some of the weapons of the Central Congo are to be traced northwards to Tibu weapons and implements of ancient date.

In spite of the suggestion of Egyptian influence in the domestic animals and plants of Bantu Africa (as also of the Western Sudan) and of the Egyptian profiles among the Bahima, I cannot but think this "Egyptian" influence over the Bantu was wrought indirectly through Gala, Ethiopian, and perhaps Tibu, through more or less Hamitic peoples influenced by Egyptian civilization of an early type. If much direct Egyptian influence had found its way to Central Africa from the Lower Nile it must surely have imported into Darkest Africa that deep attachment to stone—for building and for worship—which emanated from the Mediterranean and southwest Asiatic peoples. But no skill in stone quarrying, stone carving or stone building ever reached the Bantu, or for the matter of that, the Fula, the Mandingo, or the Hausa. Of all such arts the Bantu culture and languages are ignorant.

The Baganda and Banyoro legends of the incoming strangers of remote antiquity, the wandering demi-gods ("Bacwezi"—ghosts, spirits) who came with long-horned cattle, trained dogs, iron weapons, religious theories, and the elements of civilization generally, make no mention of building in stone or of building at all. The very similar Ful shepherd aristocrats of Western

Africa likewise had the "Bantu" culture, the herdsmen's craft, a simple agri-culture with the hoe, an acquaintance with iron and copper (though copper plays a very secondary role in Ful and Bantu thought, legend, and speech); but no notion of stone building. With the exception of the Bube or Fernan-dian indigenes, no Bantu people has been found living in an age of stone implements, though there are abundant evidences to show that nearly all Negro Africa (except perhaps the innermost forests of the Congo basin) went through ages of using flaked, chipped, bored, and polished stone weap-ons and tools. The Bushmen and Hottentots had remained in this stage, without knowledge of metals, using stone and also horn, bone, stick, thorn, and shell. Most of the forest Negroes apparently adopted—or reverted to—wood before they were introduced to the use of copper. An industry in smelting and hammering copper, in exporting copper in the ingot or in manu-factured form seems to have arisen a long while—many centuries—ago in Katanga, where the copper deposits are singularly rich; and this trade in copper to have spread from south Congoland to north and west Congoland; and southward as far as Nyasaland: Was it pre-Bantu? We have no means of telling; but there are many indications showing that the invasion of the Bantu was facilitated by the use of iron weapons, and that the working of iron ore and the fabrication of iron weapons and tools in Central and South Africa dates only from the Bantu conquest of the southern third of the continent.

The spread of the more aristocratic "Negroid" Bantu is also associated with the ancient Egyptian or Gala long-horned ox *(Bos taurus aegyptiacus)*. This breed possibly had a west Asiatic origin, and it is evidently nearly related to the Indian humped ox. No trace of any wild progenitor has yet been found in its ancient habitat, Egypt and Ethiopia. It was obviously the first type of domesticated cattle in Africa. Later there entered East Africa the Indian Zebu breed, which may have also replaced the *aegyptiacus* type in southern Arabia. The Zebu, or humped type, crossed Africa from the east coast to western Congoland, the western Sudan, and western Zambezia, and traveled down the southeast coast of Africa to Zululand. The Hamites, I should say, had already introduced the long-horned *aegyptiacus* cattle to the regions south of the Vic-toria Nyanza. And here they were brought by that mysterious race, the Hotten-tot hybrid, to central South Africa and down the southwest coast to Cape colony. At some unknown period afterwards the Bantu peoples round the Ny-anzas received these long-horned cattle from the north and conveyed them in their southward migrations as far as Damaraland. Probably in all but the ele-vated regions of Central Africa these straight-backed, long-horned cattle died out from germ diseases, which is why so many Bantu tribes at the opening up of Africa by the modern white man were without cattle or had adopted the humped cattle of Indian origin. Cattle, both of the *aegyptiacus* and *indicus* breeds, seem to have been introduced from Bantu Africa into Madagascar by

Arab intermediaries and slavedealers; which is why a Bantu word for "ox" is the chief term employed in Malagasy.

One of the difficulties attending the acceptance of the theory that the "Bantuizing" of one-third of Africa has been a long process in unwritten history and cannot be compressed within a period of about two thousand years is the splitting up of the mother tongue into more than two hundred twenty distinct languages, and the improbability of these languages with their marked idiosyncracies having sprung into existence in so short a period as is assigned by writers like myself. By searching Portuguese records in regard to the Kongo or Karana tongues we do not find a great difference between the speech of the sixteenth and seventeenth centuries and the speech of today; the numerals of the Bakwiri or Barundo at Ambas Bay (Cameroons) written down by some French or Dutch trader at the close of the seventeenth century are almost identical with the modern form.

But with the evolution of languages, as of species, Nature—I believe—proceeds *per saltun,* alternately with slow progression. A great jumble of events, and lo!—new languages spring suddenly into existence. Those that suit the altered circumstances remain and continue their course for centuries with slow modifications. Not more marvelous would have been the rapid differentiation and specialization of the leading Bantu languages in Central and South Africa, between—let us say—the year One of the Christian Era and the twelfth century, than was the coming into existence of the Romance languages, engendered by the impact of the Goth, German, and Slav on the vulgar Latin of the decline and fall of Rome. No Romance language existed in the sixth century AD. But, by the close of the twelfth century, Italian, Sicilian, Provencal, French, Castilian, Portuguese, and Rumanian were distinct, mutually unintelligible tongues; analytic where the parent Latin was synthetic, possessing an individual character which has not greatly altered in the slow subsequent changes. Dante's Italian of the thirteenth century would be perfectly intelligible in the streets of Florence today and is not very different from the dialect spoken in Central Italy from the tenth century onwards. Yet in the sixth century no such language existed. We might almost say, judging from the Oaths of Strasbourg and other scanty evidence, that the French language was born and Saxon of 1000 AD was created between the sixth and the tenth centuries. English which would have been almost unintelligible to an orthodox Anglo-Saxon of 1000 AD was created between about 1100 and 1350 AD.

I am disposed to agree with Lepsius in the belief that the Bantu language-type, like the parent speech of the Aryans, has taken a very long time to shape out of some Negro speech in the heart of Africa; I am only arguing that the commencement of the sudden and rapid invasion of central and southern Africa by the Bantu cannot be referred back much earlier than the second century BC; and that the differentiation of the more than two hundred distinct forms of Bantu speech occurred subsequently and rapidly. Six thousand years ago the Aryan *Schwärmerei* was probably just beginning, somewhere in eastern Europe. And there were then—I suggest—but the slightest dialectal differences in tribal speech amongst the Aryan Russians to indicate that one group of clans would become the progenitors of the Aryan-speaking Asiatics—would in Asia generate the Tokhari, the Pisacha, the Sanskrit, Prakrit, and Zend languages; another tribe Aryanize the Lithuanians; yet another section (as they marched northwestward, westward, southwestward, or southward) become ancestors of the Slavs, or the Goths and Germans, the Kelts and Keltiberians, the Itali, the Dakians, Thrakians, and Greeks.

But if close resemblance in structure and syntax, if similarity of numerals and pronouns, and the possession in common of a great number of rootwords of nouns and verbs, adjectives and prepositions are to be given full value as evidence of near relationship and of a recent origin from a common source, then we must regard the expansion and differentiation of the Bantu languages as a much more recent and rapid process than that which brought about the Aryanizing of all Europe and much of Southwest Asia.

The map of Bantu Africa will show the main directions taken in presumed history by the different streams of Bantu migration; and an examination of the groups of Bantu languages will, after detaching true and widespread Bantu roots from their vocabularies, leave a residue which must represent the assimilated fragments of prior languages spoken by the peoples whom the Bantu armies conquered and fused with; just as in the Keltic tongues, the Armenian, Albanian, and the modern Romance dialects there are words retained from languages of utterly different affinities which were in occupation of the land when the Aryan or Aryanized invaders came with their overpowering influence. Some very slight influence of Gala (a Hamitic "white man" speech) can be traced through the East African Bantu, about four hundred miles south of the present Gala range in East Equatorial Africa. The Sudanic tongues, the Nilotic and Masai, even the Nubian and Kordofan languages have sent words from the north—chiefly of domestic animals, wild beasts, and trade goods—circulating through northern and western Congoland, through the Nyanza Bantu, the speech of Kikuyu, Kiliminjaro, Usambara, and the coast-belt of Equatorial East Africa. The unclassified, somewhat monosyllabic tongues of the Niger delta and the Cross river have influenced the worn-down Bantu languages of the West Cameroons. The influence on Bantu of Arabic, Portuguese, English, French, and Dutch is so palpable and (excepting that of Arabic and Persian) so comparatively modern that it hardly comes within the range of philological studies. It needs no explaining. Considering how long the Arabs and the Gala Hamites have been in influential contact with the Bantu of East and Southeast Africa, and how powerfully the Aryanized Persians of the tenth, eleventh, and twelfth centuries AD influenced the Zangian coasts and islands, it is surprising how comparatively few Arabic and Persian words have crept into

Bantu speech. Swahili is by far the most Arabized of the Bantu tongues; yet except in refinements of vocabulary often ignored by the common people, it remains essentially and very typically a Bantu language. The fact that the ancient and medieval Bantu invaders of eastern Zambezia and Southeast Africa knew and cared nothing for gold till some incoming foreign people from across the seas taught them the value of that metal is shown by the absence of any true Bantu root word for "gold." The word by which "gold" is rendered in the Zambezian and Southeast Africa Bantu languages is—if not a variant of the Portuguese "ouro" or the English "gold"—derived from Arabic, and usually a corruption of *dirham (ndarama, ndalamu)*.

Subtracting the foreign, the pre-existing elements from the modern Bantu tongues, we are left in nearly every group with a surprisingly large proportion of words traceable back to a common inheritance from Old-Bantu, from the pristine Bantu of North Equatorial Africa. Most of the defections from this rule are due to that human love of metaphor and trope, that dislike in timid or refined minds to calling a spade a spade, a devil a devil, a urinal a urinal. Totemism, superstition, would start a practice of referring to dreaded snakes not as "nyoka," "the snake," but as "the long animal," "the hisser," the "coiler." The Bantu tongues have as many paraphrases for alluding shamefacedly to the genital organs or the functions of generation and defecation as the most modest speech of Europe and America. The variations of Bantu vocabularies, especially in the south, have been mainly caused by Hlwnipa. This word, a verb in Zulu meaning "to have shame, to be ashamed," covers the practice of not calling some common object, some beast, bird, fish, utensil, or geographical feature by its proper name if that name happens to be the cognomen of a near relative, a husband, father, brother, mother, great friend, or respected chief. The custom refers more to women's utterance than men's; unhappy Woman throughout the long history of the ascent of the human species having always been regarded as unlucky, as an Eve doing the wrong thing and bringing down ill luck by offending the vague Powers of Nature and Fate. Consequently, in parts of Bantu Africa, if a woman marries a man named "Lion," though she may continue to call her husband shyly and whisperingly by his name, she will henceforth call the real lion, the "roarer," the "slayer of beasts," the "big cat." Farther north, if the totem animal of the clan, or the most striking local example of divine or demoniac power is a crocodile, it might not do to be heard calling "crocodile" (on the principle of letting sleeping dogs lie). So the crocodile—to the confusion of the inquiring philologist—is not called Ngrt'ena or Ngandu, by one of its widespread Bantu names, but "the long one," "the sly one," "the snapper-up," or some other roundabout nickname. Evidently, however, as with family slang in our own land, a fashion in misnomers seldom starts from the vagaries of a few fantastics; otherwise the Bantu languages would not have remained after some two thousand years of dispersal so astonishingly true to type.

Some Developments in the Prehistory of the Bantu Languages
MALCOLM GUTHRIE[2]

In a field like Africa it is reasonable to hope for some assistance from linguistic data for the general study of prehistory. In fact there is a real temptation to use material of this kind in such a way that the results cannot be verified, or, to put it more baldly, to make guesses that are no better than their guesses. Clearly the serious investigation of the prehistory of Africa demands something more than speculative hypotheses, and for this reason it is essential that any conclusions drawn from linguistic information shall be based on a firm basis of codified data.

There are areas in Africa where it still proves to be impracticable to find linguistic data that are coherent enough for prehistorical purposes. In the case of the Bantu languages, however, the situation is different, and this has been recognized for a hundred years since Bleek first put forward in 1862 a theory of common origin based on the material that was available to him. The relationship between the members of the Bantu family has never subsequently been called into question, and further investigations have merely served to make it even clearer. As more and more of the Bantu languages have been studied by means of increasingly accurate techniques, the volume of data available for comparative purposes has become very great indeed. Nevertheless, the techniques of comparative study used in the treatment of the material provided in this way have remained almost unchanged since the last century, when Meinhof first propounded his reconstruction of Ur-Bantu. The main characteristic of this type of study is that it introduces speculative hypotheses into the handling of the data, so that few of its conclusions can really be substantiated. The persistent use of this approach to Bantu prehistory has led to a crop of unverifiable theories which have gained gen-

[2]Guthrie, Malcolm, "Some Developments in the Prehistory of the Bantu Languages," *Journal of African History* III, no. 2 (Cambridge: Cambridge University Press, 1962), pp. 273–282.

Malcolm Guthrie was a missionary in the Belgian Congo and later head of the Department of Africa Studies and Chair of Bantu Languages at the School of Oriental and African Studies, University of London, from 1950 until his death in 1972.

eral acceptance, the latest of these being the Niger-Congo group introduced into Greenberg's classification of African languages, which in turn has been accepted by Murdock as having a factual value.

In order to meet the fundamental condition that hypotheses should be built only on facts that are demonstrably true, I began some fifteen years ago to adopt a quite different method of comparative study. The aim of the investigation was to produce results in prehistory that would be based on verifiable observations. To do this involved a great deal of sifting and codifying of the evidence before even a beginning could be made in the direction of discovering the probable origins of the Bantu family. A detailed statement about the technical details of the method I developed has been presented elsewhere, and all that is necessary here is a bare outline of the procedure adopted.

Collecting and Arranging the Data

The raw material for any comparative study of languages is the existence of groups of cognates from language to language, characterized by what are known as sound-shifts. The difficulty is that the recognition of cognates may call for a degree of precision and skill that can be commanded only by a specialist. Frequently there are instances of a specious relationship that can easily mislead the inexperienced investigator, who may equally find it difficult to believe that some true cognates are related at all. Thus for example Kikuyu *rut* (teach) is very similar in shape to Sotho *rut* (teach), but this can be shown to be a purely fortuitous resemblance, whereas Hai (Chaga) *ifwoo* (bone) and Mbundu *ekepa* (bone) really are cognates in spite of their dissimilarity. Although the working out of the rules governing the relationships between cognates is sometimes a complicated operation, it does prove to be possible to formulate rules that can strictly be applied in the construction of numbers of sets of cognates. In this way a coherent corpus of organized data is obtained that can provide an adequate foundation on which theories about prehistory can be built. In practice over 2300 such sets of cognates have been constructed with items from some 200 of the Bantu languages.

Once a corpus of this kind has been formed, it is possible to infer that all the items in a given set are due to some item in some ancestor language, which is then termed a "root," while the items contained in any set of cognates are known as "reflexes" of the root to which they are attributed. In other words there are as many roots involved as there are sets of cognates, but it would be a quite unjustified assumption at this stage to speak of all these 2300 roots as though they belonged to the same ancestor language. Indeed, certain features of these roots make it highly unlikely that they could all be attributed to one language, as for example the fact that there are seven roots meaning "yesterday," five meaning "egg," and four meaning "six." It is clearly improbable that any language would have such a wealth of words for meanings of this kind. One of the first things to be attempted is to produce some classification of the roots into various types, and this does not prove to be very difficult. If it is possible to discover all or most of the reflexes of a given root, the area covered by the languages in which the reflexes are found can be considered the geographical spread of the root itself. Although there are many languages where the available evidence is inadequate, those which have been examined cover a sufficiently large proportion of most parts of the Bantu field to provide a reasonably clear picture of the spread of each of the 2300 roots. As is inevitable, the patterns of geographical spread are of many different kinds, and a certain amount of experimenting was necessary to discover how to assort these patterns so as to produce the greatest possible simplification of their variety. One type of root, however, presented no difficulty in this respect, since its reflexes cover the whole or the greater part of the Bantu area. The total collection of these roots, which are known as "general," forms a very important body of information, which we may term the "general group" of Bantu roots.

The other patterns of geographical spread which are less than general can be assorted into two main groups according as they are confined mainly or exclusively to (a) the western part, or (b) the eastern part of the Bantu area. These two distinct subdivisions of the Bantu field are termed "regions," and the two groups of roots just referred to are known as "western" and "eastern" respectively. The miscellaneous group of roots that cannot be classified as either general, western or eastern contains less than fourteen percent of the total. In order to increase the usefulness of the information contained in the eighty-six per cent of classified roots, it proved necessary to choose a certain number of "test languages," and to make a note of every reflex of the roots found in them. In all, twenty-eight test languages were selected, and the noting of all the reflexes they each contained increased the total collection of cognates to about 22,000. It is, then, this body of codified data which provides the basis for the investigation of Bantu prehistory.

Even when the roots with their reflexes have been classified, a considerable amount of work has to be done to bring out facts that have a bearing on the probable origins of the family. For one thing some analysis of the actual structure of the different roots is necessary, and in particular the way these structural features are distributed in the three main groups of roots. In addition, a number of statistical operations are possible, ranging from the simple adding up of the totals of reflexes from each of the test languages to computations based on special formulae to obtain a measure of the relationship between any two languages. There is also a need to codify the features that distinguish some pairs of roots which have everything else in common. Thus for example there are a number of cases where two roots with the same meaning differ in that one of them has "U" where the other has "O," as for example between *NUN* (get fat) and *NON* (get fat). The geographical spread of each of such pairs then has to be determined, as well as any correlation between the difference in the vowel of the root and the difference in the spread of the reflexes.

From such an investigation it is possible to obtain a reasonably clear picture of the whole situation as reflected in the body of data contained in the sets of cognates, and this is set out briefly in the next section.

The Overall Comparative Bantu Picture

At this point it is not proposed to introduce any hypotheses about Bantu origins, but simply to outline the state of affairs that will require some explanation in terms of prehistory in the concluding section of this paper. Some facts will be given first of all about the meanings expressed by the general roots, and then about the relative totals of reflexes found in the test languages. A certain amount of statistical information obtained from computations will also be presented but in a very general form. Finally it will be possible to set out a few typical facts only about the way pairs of apparently related roots differ in their geographical spread.

In all there is a list of over 500 general Bantu roots which show a relatively uniform spread of meanings. Thus the list contains some thirty names of animals, birds, and insects, which include most of those found throughout the Bantu area, such as "dog," "goat," "cattle," "pig," "elephant," "hippopotamus," "buffalo," "ant-eater," "squirrel," "puff-adder," "guinea-fowl," "hawk," "pigeon," "tick," "spider," "bee," "mosquito." There are a number of omissions from the list, and the more interesting of these are the following. There are several roots for both "domestic fowl" and "hyena," and while the total spread of all the reflexes covers most of the field, no individual root has a wide geographical spread. The case of the roots meaning "crocodile," "lion," and "bat" is somewhat similar except that here there is a sharp division between the western and eastern regions. The reflexes of the roots for "scorpion" and "parrot" are confined to the western region, and those for "frog" and "louse" to the eastern, no satisfactory set of cognates having been made from the other region in these cases; while no set whatever has so far been constructed from words for a few animals and insects, as for example for "jigger."

The list of general roots also contains about thirty names of parts of the body, but these call for no special comment. Among the remainder of the general roots there are terms for various kinds of cultural activity, and a few of these may be noted, such as words for "pot," "to mould pottery;" "basket," "to plait;" "to fish with line," "fishhook;" "trap," "to set trap," "birdlime;" "iron ore," "iron," "to forge metal," "to blow bellows," "hammer," "knife;" "cloth," "to sew;" "canoe," "paddle," "to paddle;" "journey," "to carry on the head," "headpad." The actual geographical spread of the general roots with these meanings varies slightly, but in a brief outline of this kind cannot be described in detail, and one or two examples only must suffice. The root meaning "to paddle" has no known reflexes in the central part of the eastern region, while that meaning "paddle" has none in the southern part of the same region. The root meaning "to forge iron" covers the whole area except certain parts on or near the coast in the centre of the eastern region, where two quite distinct sets of cognates occur, one being reflexes of a peculiar root, and the other apparently related to a root meaning "to pound."

In respect to trees and items of food the number of general roots is limited, containing mainly those meaning "fig-tree," "palm-tree," "banana," "bean," "honey," and "mushroom." The roots for words referring to other foods have mainly a regional distribution. Thus there are distinct western and eastern roots for "sugar cane" and "salt," while there are western sets of cognates only for "palm-nut," "palm-oil," "kola nut," "yam," "maize," and "pepper," but eastern sets only for "pumpkin," "ground nut," and "millet."

There are many other categories of meaning represented among the general roots, among which the presence of the following may be noted, "chief," "polygamy," "war," "bow," "courtyard," "fireplace," "platform," "bedstead," "pestle," "ladle," "year," "cold wind."

A simple procedure by which the total number of reflexes of the general roots in each test language is reckoned up provides a series of figures that can be plotted on a map as percentages of the total number of general roots. The state of affairs revealed by the map includes a belt of high figures, termed the nucleus, stretching right across the Bantu area on both sides of the boundary between the regions. Thus there are on the western side Kongo 44, Lwena 46, Luba-Kasai 47, Luba-Katanga 50, and on the eastern Bemba 54, I'la 43, Rundi 44, Swahili 44. From the nucleus the figures decrease both to the north and to the south, but the diminution, which is fairly uniform to the south in the west, and on both sides in the east, is more abrupt to the north in the west. Thus from Kongo 44 and Lwena 46 in the west, going southwards there are Mbundu (Umbundu) 38 and Herero 33; and in the east southwards from Bemba 54, Swahili 44, and I'la 43, there are Nyanja and Yao both 35, Zezuru (Shona) 37, Venda 30, Sotho 28, Zulu 29, and Xhosa 26, and northwards from Bemba 54, Rundi 44, and Swahili 44 there are Sukuma 41, Ganda, Nyoro, and Nyankore—all 37, Kikuyu 32 and Kamba 30. To the north of Kongo 44 and Luba-Kasai 47 on the other hand are Bali (Teke) 28, Tetela 26, Bobangi 24, Bulu 20, and Duala 14.

A similar operation performed on the two groups of regional roots gives a very similar pattern of distribution in that the highest figures for all are obtained for languages in the nucleus. The principal difference in these figures from those obtained for the general roots is that apart from Kongo, which has the high value of 53, there is an even diminution in both regions from around 38 in the centre (in the western region Bali 38, Bobangi 38 and in the eastern Bemba 38, Swahili 39) to about 20 or just under at the extremities (N.W.: Duala 17; S.W.: Herero 17; N.E.: Kamba 21; S.E.: Xhosa 16).

A more complicated statistical procedure exists on the basis of which a taxonomic classification can be produced by taking into account the joint occurrences of reflexes of individual roots in each pair of languages. This is feasible only with the aid of an electronic computer, but its results show a nuclear area that is similar to that revealed in the distribution of the percentages of the general roots.

One further aspect of the statistical characteristics of the roots and their reflexes has been investigated by means of a special formula designed to express numerically the degree of relationship between any two pairs of test languages. This has been applied to the reflexes of the total range of roots as well as to the general and the two regional groups taken separately. By this means many very detailed indications have been obtained that supplement the taxonomic picture just referred to. To attempt to present even part of this here is scarcely practicable, but the following diagrammatic representation expresses in a very concise form the situation revealed by the computations. The siting of the names in the diagram roughly corresponds to

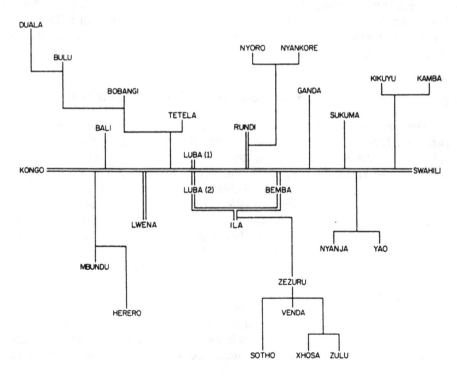

the relative geographical location of the languages, the linking lines being based on the information shown up in the whole range of statistical operations, including the taxonomic classification just referred to. The double connecting line links the languages of the nucleus, while the single lines give an approximate indication of the order of relationship of the remaining languages.

This diagram inevitably grossly oversimplifies the picture presented by the statistical analysis that has been carried out, but it must suffice as an illustration of the situation revealed in a large number of such diagrams that have had to be constructed. From the investigation of sets of cognates that have to be attributed to roots which differ in one respect only, a great deal of information has been obtained. The following typical example must suffice to show the kind of facts that are involved. There are a number of pairs of roots where one begins with "ob" and the other with "op," such as *obega* (shoulder), *opeca* (shoulder), but in no case is either root in the general group, nor are there any clear cases where the reflexes of the one root are in one region and those of the other are in the other. On the other hand, in pairs where one root as "og" and the other "ok," as for example *o-gonib* (scrape), *o-hofilbo* (scrape), there are two or three where the root with "ok" is general, and at least one where the one with "ok" is eastern and the other western. It is therefore clear that any distinction between "ok" and "oc" has a different status from one between "op" and "ob." A number of differences of this kind have been established and these provide a means of classifying some of the roots.

Provisional Hypotheses about Bantu Prehistory

The very brief outline given in the previous section of the picture built up from features present in the corpus of Bantu roots and their sets of reflexes has disclosed a situation that calls for some hypotheses to account for it. These hypotheses fall roughly into two types according to what object is in view. This may be (a) the probable nature of the ancestry of the Bantu family or (b) the more difficult question of the provenance of any hypothetical ancestor or ancestors. As the first of these involve mainly inferences and the second much more speculation it is convenient to consider them separately.

THE FAMILY ANCESTRY

Not only can a large number of direct inferences be made which do not involve recourse to speculation, but in practice a relatively detailed network of such inferences has been constructed. As is inevitable in any procedure of this kind, however, it can never be asserted that no other hypothesis fits the facts. The only claim made therefore for the suggestions in this subsection is that no more satisfactory explanation of the situation has yet been found. In a paper of this kind it is possible to give no more than the barest outline of such tentative conclusions as have been drawn, but the following are the more important of them.

(a) As there is a well-defined group of general Bantu roots, it may be inferred that these occurred in a single ancestor language to be called "proto-Bantu." Assuming then that such an ancestor existed, the fact that every Bantu language contains reflexes of the general roots must mean that all the Bantu languages are descended from the one original stock.

(b) Since proto-Bantu was presumably a language of the same general type as the present-day languages, it probably had at least 2000 unrelated items in its vocabulary. The fact therefore that there are no more than just over 500 general roots means that a large amount of the proto-Bantu material has disappeared. It is conceivable that some of the lost proto-Bantu roots are preserved in the regional groups of the sets of cognates, but since they could not be identified even if present, inferences about the original stock can be drawn only from those sets of cognates that are indisputably general.

(c) The pattern of geographical distribution of the reflexes of the general roots seems to indicate that proto-Bantu was spoken some at the centre of the nucleus, i.e. in the bush country to the south of the equatorial forest midway between the two coasts.

(d) The meanings expressed by the general roots suggest that the speakers of proto-Bantu were presumably a people with a developed culture that included a knowledge of such things as iron-working and river craft.

(e) The occurrence of two well-defined groups of regional roots with exactly the same sound-shifts can only mean that dialectal variants developed within proto-Bantu. The statistical features displayed by these regional groups seem to show that the western dialect separated from the original stock well before the eastern dialect came into being.

(f) As the figures obtained to express the degree of relationship between the test languages display well defined patterns of distribution, it is probable that there was a certain amount of cross-contamination between the original stock and its dialects while the ancestor languages were still in the nucleus area. The information revealed in a study of roots that differ in one feature only confirms this inference and even throws some light on the details of the contaminations.

(g) The fact that the figures for the distribution of the reflexes of roots in each of the three groups show a progressive diminution from the nucleus presumably means that the ancestors of the present-day languages dispersed northwards and southwards from the nucleus. As the sharp drop in the percentages in the reflexes of the general roots to the north in the west coincides with the boundary of the equatorial forest area, it is probably due to a greater rate of decay under forest conditions. The fact that there is no comparable drop in the figures for the reflexes of the western roots could be due to the development of a large number of fresh items in some intermediate ancestor of the northwestern languages.

(h) Since there is regularity in the sound-shifts in the reflexes of all the roots, it is probable that the development of the present-day languages from proto-Bantu and its dialects proceeded uniformly without noticeable contamination. This means that it could in theory be possible to construct a genealogical table with the proto-language and its dialects at the source, and the diagram of relationships in the diagram may well provide a framework for this.

THE ORIGIN OF PROTO-BANTU

The general outline of the probable ancestry of the Bantu languages just presented is clearly incompatible with either of the two previous theories of Bantu origins. Johnston located the ancestor language in the Lake Victoria region, while more recently Greenberg has speculated that the point of origin was near the Cameroons-Nigeria border. Since the Greenberg theory has gained a wide currency, it is worth noting that it apparently ignores such things as terrain and vegetation, but treats Africa as though people could have migrated equally easily in any direction. Any coherent hypothesis however must take account of the possibilities of movement as well as of the linguistic data.

There is a certain amount of evidence found scattered here and there throughout West Africa that may shed some light on the probable origin of proto-Bantu. The significant fact is that features reminiscent of Bantu languages occur irregularly in a number of apparently unrelated West African languages. If we assume that these are vestiges of some earlier language, fragments of which were absorbed into various languages at some time in the prehistorical period in West Africa, then such a language, which we will term "pre-Bantu" might also have been the source of proto-Bantu. If that were so, then we have to imagine the speakers of pre-Bantu moving in two directions, some to the proto-Bantu area, and others to West Africa. One hypothesis which could fit this requirement is to suppose that pre-Bantu was spoken somewhere in the Lake Chad region by people who had some skill in the use of canoes, and that one group of these used the waterways of the Congo basin to traverse the otherwise impenetrable forest.

An elaboration of this basic speculation could envisage that the original proto-Bantu speakers had no knowledge of ironworking, but that this arrived subsequently by the same route, being brought by descendants either of their own ancestors who had remained in the Chad area, or of collaterals. This would mean that when the skill of ironworking reached them, the proto-Bantu speakers may well have become fairly numerous, since there could have been a considerable lapse of time between the coming of the first group and the subsequent arrival of "the smiths." The acquisition of iron tools and weapons could then have been a major factor in the ultimate dispersion of the speakers of the proto-Bantu dialects.

The westward movement of still other groups of speakers of pre-Bantu, which could account for the fragmentary occurrence of Bantu features in West African languages, may have taken place at any time. It is however conceivable that it was provoked by the same events, whatever they were, which impelled the smiths to make their journey southward.

As is inevitable in a hypothesis involving so much speculation, pre-Bantu has a much smaller degree of certainty than proto-Bantu, the picture of which is constructed largely from direct inferences.

The Languages of Africa
JOSEPH GREENBERG[3]

North of the Bantu languages, whose very obvious unity was early noted, stretches a region of vast linguistic diversity roughly coincident with the geographical area of the Sudan. In the first of two general studies devoted to the languages of the Sudan, Westermann sought to show that the languages of this area (presumably most or all of them, since no exact listing was given) formed a single family he called the Sudanic. His citations were almost all from eight languages, five in the western Sudan (Twi, Ga, Ewe, Yoruba, and Efik) and three from the eastern area (Dinka, Nuba, and Kunama). It is noticeable in Westermann's material that, whereas the five western languages occur in all of the lexical comparisons, the eastern languages are cited far less frequently and the majority of these examples are unconvincing. From this it is clear that the five western languages form part of some real unity while the eastern languages, if related at all, display a connection of a more remote nature. The weakness of the case for a language family embracing the entire Sudan has frequently been noted, and Westermann in a later study explicitly admitted this, remarking that the term Sudanic languages "bezeichnet Sprachen eines gemeinsamen Typus, deren genetische Einheit nur teilweise nachweisbar ist."

In his second study, Westermann, ignoring the central and eastern areas, showed that almost all the languages of the western Sudan (i.e., the area west of Lake Chad) formed a real unity within which he distinguished a number of genetic subfamilies. This stock he called West Sudanic. He also pointed out that the Bantu languages show important lexical resemblances to the West Sudanic languages and that the Bantu noun-class prefixes find close analogues in the class affixes (prefixes, suffixes, and sometimes both) of many West Sudanic languages. This further point was elaborated in a subsequent publication.

The proofs presented by Westermann for the interconnection of the bulk of the languages of the western Sudan (hereafter referred to as the West Sudanic nucleus) is adequate, and the references have already been given to Westermann's material to which those may refer who wish to convince

---

[3]Greenberg, Joseph, "Languages of Africa," *International Journal of American Linguistics* XXIX, no. 1 (Chicago: Chicago University Press, 1963), pp. 6–38.
Joseph Greenberg is an Emeritus Professor of Linguistics at Stanford University.

themselves firsthand. . . . The evidence presented by Westermann, in the studies already cited, is sufficient to show genetic relationship and on one occasion he stated this conclusion explicitly. In other publications, however, where tables of classification are presented, he always lists Bantu separately doubtless because of the size and importance of the Bantu group and because of the long-continued tradition of assigning it a separate status. In fact, the evidence for the inclusion of Bantu is actually better than for many languages of West Sudanic whose affiliation has never been questioned. Bantu does not even form a single genetic subfamily within the entire complex, but belongs within one of Westermann's already established subfamilies, the one he calls Benue-Cross or semi-Bantu, precisely because of its close resemblance to Bantu. There is no more justification for the term semi-Bantu than, let us say, a term semi-English to describe German, Dutch, Swedish, Danish, Norwegian and Icelandic. I have renamed this subfamily of which Bantu is a member Benue-Congo as more appropriate in view of its much greater geographical extension resulting from the inclusion of Bantu.

Westermann's treatment stops with the Benue-Cross (semi-Bantu) languages of Nigeria. Consideration of the languages east of this area shows that many of them show clear evidence of affiliation with the West Sudanic nucleus. To the entire family consisting of the West Sudanic nucleus inclusive of Bantu, plus this eastward extension, I have preferred to adopt a new name of a noncommittal geographic nature, Niger-Congo, from the two great rivers in whose basins these languages predominate.

The eastward extension of the Niger-Congo family forms an additional genetic subgrouping beyond those distinguished within the West Sudanic nucleus. It includes such well-known languages as Mbum, Gbaya, Zande, Sango and Banda. . . .

In an earlier section of this chapter, the position to be assigned to the Bantu languages within the vast Niger-Congo family was indicated without the presentation of detailed proofs or the refutation of arguments that might be presented in favor of the traditional view.

As has already been seen, the great mass of languages in the western Sudan were demonstrated by Westermann to be genetically related and to this group he applied the name West Sudanic. In the first part of this chapter I attempted to show that many languages farther east in the Sudan, though by no means all of them, belonged to this "West Sudanic" family; for this entire stock I proposed the designation Niger-Congo.

Westermann, who, it is worth remarking, is an eminently cautious investigator, pointed out many resemblances in fundamental vocabulary between the proto-West Sudanic forms he had reconstructed and the proto-Bantu forms postulated by Meinhof. This material, which might be vastly extended, showed regular correspondences such as the following: proto-Bantu v = proto-Sudanic b, proto-Bantu y = proto-Sudanic g; in the vowel system proto-Bantu i, e, a, o, ū, ~u corresponded respectively with the proto-Sudanic i, e, a, ua, u, u. Occasionally the proto-Bantu "u" corresponds to proto-West Sudanic "i." Moreover the noun classifying affixes of West Sudanic, which appear as prefixes in some languages, suffixes in others, and as both prefixes and suffixes in still others, showed close resemblances to the well-known prefixes of Bantu—both in form and meaning, thus:

PWS	PB	Meaning
u	γu	Singular, personal class and animate non-personal class
ba	va	plural, personal class
i	γi	plural, animate non-personal class
li	li	singular of paired objects
a	γa	plural of paired objects
ma	ma	liquids and other mass nouns
bu	vu	abstract
ki	ki	plants, objects
ku	ku	infinitive, locative
ka	ka	diminutive singular
ti	tu	plural of diminutives.

I list here the English equivalents of a selection of morphemes for which cognate forms may be found in Bantu and West Sudanic. A full listing, with forms from the relevant languages is not attempted for reasons of space: head, ear, mouth, tongue, jaw, arm, hand, leg, knee, breast, belly, back, tail, skin, bone, saliva, excrements, mother, father, sun, stone, wind, water, blood, fat, charcoal, animal, leopard, fowl, egg, dog, bird, goat, fly, crab, tree, two, three, four, inside, not, I, he, we, you, they, be, go, send, speak, eat, drink, sleep, die, laugh, call, steal, break, defecate, sit, bad, soft, large, black.

In order not to duplicate material already available, the reader is referred to the above-mentioned study of Westermann. Likewise a number of proto-Bantu forms are incidentally cited in the Adamawa-Eastern comparative word list earlier in this chapter. Some idea of the extent of these resemblances may be gathered from the following. They are more numerous than for many of the languages already accepted as West Sudanic and the case is somewhat better than for the affiliation of English to Indo-European. Thus, of fifty nouns, taken at random from Johnston's study of Bantu, twenty-one were referable without trouble to proto-West Sudanic. Of these same fifty nouns in English only seventeen could be traced to proto-Indo-

European. Of these some fifty nouns in Dyula, a typical Mande dialect which had always been reckoned as West Sudanic, only eleven could be shown to be derived from proto-West Sudanic.

If we may, on the basis of this evidence, admit that the Bantu and West Sudanic (i.e. Niger-Congo) languages are related, the question arises regarding how this relationship is to be conceived. One alternative is to regard Bantu as coordinate genetically with West Sudanic (i.e. Niger-Congo) as a whole. In view of the size of the Bantu group and the independent position accorded to it in every previous classification of African languages, this was my assumption during the earlier phases of the investigation. However, another possibility soon forced itself on my notice, namely, that the Bantu languages are simply a subgroup of an already established genetic subfamily of West Sudanic.

For this to be true, there must exist a subfamily of West Sudanic which shares common linguistic innovations not found elsewhere among West Sudanic languages. There is such a group of languages, those called Benue-Cross by Westermann and semi-Bantu by other writers. An example of an innovation of the type referred is the word for "child." The proto-West Sudanic form is *vi* and it is found virtually everywhere outside of the Benue-Cross group. These languages, along with Bantu, show a form *ana* which is evidently an innovation dating a period of common historical development in which both semi-Bantu and Bantu languages shared. Many other such innovations could be cited. Their sum total is so great that, as will be seen later, several Bantu languages, about which only very limited information existed, have been classified as Bantu while other observers have on occasion classified the same language as Bantu or semi-Bantu. Of the fifty Bantu nouns discussed above, forty-three are found commonly in semi-Bantu languages, while for the same fifty in English, only thirty-nine are traceable to primitive Germanic.

The position of the semi-Bantu Languages has always been a paradoxical one. They have been considered, with every right, as a subdivision of West Sudanic yet they show a resemblance to Bantu which is so close as to earn them the name semi-Bantu. If Bantu and West Sudanic are really distinct, such a group of languages should not exist! But we have seen, that apart from any consideration of the semi-Bantu group, there is sufficient evidence that Bantu is in some manner related to West Sudanic. The denial of the relationship between the Bantu and semi-Bantu languages, which is almost comparable to denying the genetic relationship of English and German, is the reductio ad absurdum of the conventional assumption of the independent status of Bantu.

The only alternative explanation, and one must suppose that this has been more or less tacitly accepted up to now, is that the semi-Bantu languages owe their special resemblance to the Bantu languages through borrowing, and that the resemblance between West Sudanic and Bantu is likewise the result of borrowing from Bantu. This explanation seems to be precluded for the following reasons:

1. The nature of the phonetic correspondences. For the bulk of the semi-Bantu languages we have nothing beyond word lists. In the case of Efik, however, one of the languages of the Cross River group, we have a dictionary with tone markings by R. F. G. Adams and a number of Efik forms cited in Ida Ward's excellent tonal study. A comparison of Efik with related proto-Bantu forms shows a high degree of correspondence in tones, about as great as that exhibited by most contemporary Bantu languages to the reconstructed proto-Bantu forms.

   We also have Abraham's tonal material for another semi-Bantu language, Tiv. Here again there is, in general, excellent agreement with reconstructed proto-Bantu tonal forms. Most striking of all is the following. In Bantu, the nominal prefixes have low tone. However a number of Bantu languages agree in having high tone except for Meinhof's classes 1 and 9 (the singular of the personal and animal classes) for certain forms in concord with the noun. These include one or all of the following: adjective prefixes, prefixes of numbers, genitive particle including the possessive adjectives and pronouns and verb subject pronouns. Thus, for all classes except 1 and 9 which have low tone, these concord elements have high tone as against low tone for the nominal prefix. This precise irregularity occurs in Tiv where for the "long form" of the pronouns as subject of certain verb form classes 1 and 9 have low tone and the remaining pronouns have high tone. A more intimate point of contact or one less likely to be borrowed is difficult to imagine.

2. The irreversibility of certain changes. In Meinhof's classes 3 and 4, Bantu has the prefixes mu- and mias against semi-Bantu and West Sudanic u- and i. This is certainly a Bantu innovation. In the pronominal referents for these classes Bantu has, however, yu- and yi-. This can be explained in the light of semi-Bantu and other West Sudanic forms as a survival from the period when the noun prefixes did not begin with a nasal. On the other hand, the Bantu forms cannot explain the semi-Bantu and other West Sudanic forms.

   Bantu has a verb *vi-ala* "to give birth." As a derivative from *vi* "child" + *ala*, a verbal formative, it is quite understandable. But *vi* "child" does not exist as a word either in Bantu or the semi-Bantu languages, whereas it is the ordinary word for child practically everywhere else among the West Sudanic languages, and a proto-

West Sudanic form *bi* is generally assumed. The verb formation, on the other hand, is peculiar to Bantu. For the West Sudanic languages to have borrowed this word, would have required an analysis of the form *vi-ala* into its constituent elements and the abstraction of the form *vi-* in the meaning "child." I think we must reject any hypothesis which makes professional linguists out of the ordinary speakers of a language. But if not borrowed, then, unless the resemblance is accidental—a highly unlikely hypothesis—it must be the result of genetic relationship.

3. The nature of the vocabulary involved. It is precisely the most fundamental and common words, and in overwhelming numbers, which are involved. Thus there is correspondence between Bantu and the West Sudanic languages, including the semi-Bantu, in the numerals two, three, and four, with semi-Bantu in the numeral five also, while in the numbers above five there is no resemblance between Bantu and West Sudanic forms. Surely a set of languages which were so strongly influenced by another language that they borrowed the lowest numerals would not create the higher ones out of their own resources. In all examples of borrowed numerals of which I am aware, a language which borrows lower numerals also borrows higher ones.

Again one would expect that an influence which was strong enough to cause the borrowing of terms for parts of the body, pronouns, etc., would necessarily lead to the borrowing of less fundamental terms. But such Kulturworter as the terms for axe, maize, Guinea-corn, mat are not among the terms which show agreement between Bantu and the semi-Bantu languages. All our experience and common sense suggests that these would be the first terms borrowed.

4. Some common Bantu words are found widely in West Sudanic, others are not found at all. The first situation is far more common because of the closeness of the relationship. For example, the Bantu word for "tongue" *deme* shows related forms in a large number of languages as far west as the West Atlantic group. On the other hand, the word for "belly" *bumo* is not found outside of Bantu. On a theory of spread from Bantu we would be unable to account for a gigantic conspiracy of the numerous and diverse West Sudanic languages to borrow from a specific group of Bantu words roots and not from others. On the view that Bantu is simply one among many Niger-Congo groups, roots confined to Bantu are more recent innovations which arose during the period that Bantu was differentiating from the most closely related languages of the Bantoid sub-

group of the Benue-Congo division of Niger-Congo. Indeed if a language such as the reconstructed proto-Bantu were spoken by a small population in the Nigeria-Cameroons area, it would occur to no one to consider Bantu as anything but another language of the semi-Bantu (Westermann's Benue-Cross) group.

5. Supposedly transitional languages are really Bantu. Certain languages of the northwest Bantu border area have generally been considered to be semi-Bantu, although some difference of opinion exists. Such languages, for example, are Bamum, Bali, Banen, and Jarawa. These resemble the Bantu languages more than the more distant semi-Bantu languages, so that Bantu seemed, as it were, to spill over in this direction. The closer resemblance of these languages to Bantu seemed to suggest borrowing from Bantu which was less intense the farther one removed from the Bantu-semi-Bantu borderline. These languages show lexical innovations characteristic of Bantu languages as against the remaining Benue-Congo languages and what is known of their grammars confirms this conclusion. They all seem to show, moreover, specific evidence of membership in the Northwestern subgroup of Bantu of which Duala and Yaunde are the best known. In the present work, absence of mention in the list of Benue-Congo languages of a border language is tacit evidence of my opinion that it is Bantu.

If the evidence presented here is accepted, the reader will naturally inquire after the reasons which have induced all previous writers on this subject to accept the Bantu-Sudanese dichotomy as fundamental in African linguistics. I believe that the explanation is to be found in the history of our knowledge of Africa. The Bantu languages, which cover such a large section of Africa, were the first to come to the attention of scientifically trained observers and their unity was obvious, so that the existence of a Bantu language family was early established. By contrast the Sudanese area presents a chaotic picture and it was only in 1911 with the appearance of Westermann's Sudan-sprachen that the presence of widespread relationships among languages of the Sudan was demonstrated. By this time the separate status of Bantu was so traditional that a fundamental separation of the two groups was assumed. This was reinforced by evolutionary reasoning, in which, starting from a few well-known languages of the West Coast (e.g. Ewe, Twi, which were atypical in having lost their noun affixes), a sequence Sudanic = isolating, Bantu = agglutinative became fundamental for African linguistics. Moreover, the field is so vast that workers in one area had little knowledge of the languages in the other.

Another consideration which has played its part is that the vast area and large numbers of speakers of the Bantu languages seemed to guarantee separate familial status. I have no doubt that if a language resembling proto-Bantu were spoken by a small number of people in the Nigeria-Cameroon border area, it would have been classified with the other languages of the Benue-Cross (i.e., semi-Bantu) group. Considerations of this kind are, of course, irrelevant. At present the speakers of Germanic languages number over 350,000,000, while those of the Tokharian branch number zero, Tokharian being extinct. This does not prevent Indo-Europeanists from considering Germanic and Tokharian as being coordinate branches of Indo-European and providing equally valid evidence for the reconstruction of Proto-Indo-European.

If the view of the position of the Bantu languages presented here is accepted, there are certain historical conclusions of considerable significance which follow. When Sapir demonstrated that the Algonkian languages were related to the Wiyot and Yurok languages of California, it was clear that, if this demonstration was accepted, it constituted a powerful argument for the movement of the Algonkian-speaking peoples from the west to the east. In the present instance we have, not two languages, but the vast Benue-Congo group of languages all of which except Bantu are spoken in Nigeria and the Cameroons. Moreover the location of the other languages of the Bantoid subgroup suggests even more specifically the Central Benue valley as the ultimate area of Bantu origins. The evidence thus becomes strong for the movement of the Bantu-speaking peoples from this area southeastwards. The usual assumption has been a movement directly south from the Great Lake region of East Africa. It will also follow that this is a relatively recent movement, a conclusion which has generally been accepted on the basis of the wide extension of the Bantu languages and the relatively small differentiation among them. The assumption of Bantu movement made here also agrees well with the analyses of Herskovits, Ankermann, and Froebenius, which make the Guinea Coast area and the Congo basin part of the same culture area. Bantu culture would then be a relatively recent southeastward expansion of the Guinea-coast type of culture.

Trees and Traps
COLIN FLIGHT[4]

> For the present series there will emerge a complete genetic reclassification of
> the languages of Africa. These results are so at variance with the commonly
> accepted scheme that a brief methodological foreword seems in order. There
> is nothing recondite about the method which I have employed. . . .

These abruptly articulated sentences form the opening of the first in a
series of articles which, with time, would be seen to have initiated a new
phase in the historical study of African languages. Seven of these articles
appeared, at quarterly intervals, during 1949–1950. They offered not only a
fresh classification for the languages of the African continent; they also
exemplified a fresh approach to the problem of language classification anywhere in the world. Since then, the classification itself has been revised and
extended on several occasions, and the methodology has been made more
explicit in some respects. But of none of these subsequent developments
can it be said that they were not latent in the original publications. Even if
the author had lost interest in the subject soon afterwards—which happily
was not the case—the indications would still have been there for others to
follow up, if and when they chose. In that sense, the achievement was complete by 1950. Recognition of the achievement, however, was only slowly
gained. Among Africanists these articles became the focus for a prolonged
and sometimes acrimonious controversy, the echoes of which are with us
even now. In some quarters, the classification was not at all willingly accepted; nor was the methodology which lay behind it. On the contrary,
especially in British circles, they both encountered severe and solidary disapproval. In the course of this controversy as it developed during the 1950s
many questions arose which I am frankly incompetent to discuss; but that
does not deter me from trying to comprehend some of the basic issues. Why
was there so much disagreement on certain points, but not on others? Why
was there so much mutual misunderstanding?

In the present article I seek to acquire some grasp on one strand in the
controversy which, if I am right, is important not only for linguists. In the

---

[4]Colin Flight, "Trees and Traps," *History in Africa* (Atlanta: African Studies Association,
Emory University, 1981), pp. 43–66.
Colin Flight is a professor of history at the University of Birmingham.

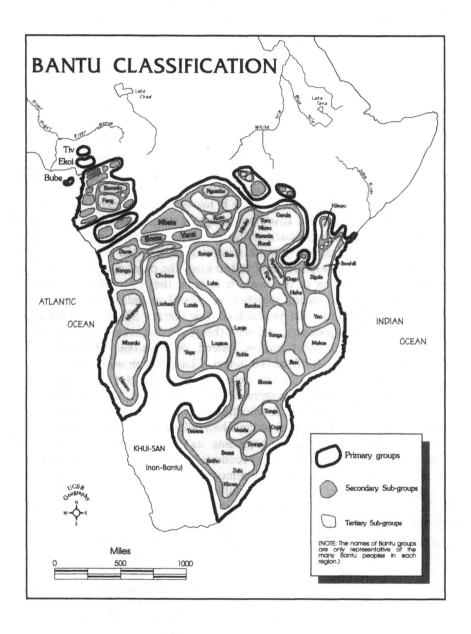

BANTU CLASSIFICATION

Lake Chad

River Niger

River Benue

Lake Tana

Blue Nile

White Nile

Nile

Juba River

Tiv
Ekoi

Bube

Ewondo
Fang

Ngombe

Mbete

Boma

Yansi

Yaka

Kikuyu

Toro
Nkore
Rwanda
Rundi

Ganda

ATLANTIC

OCEAN

Duma

Kongo

Chokwe

Luchazi

Lunda

Songe

Luba

Bembe

Goga

Hehe

Zigula

Swahili

Lenje

Yao

Tonga

Makua

Mbundu

Yeye

Luyana

Subia

Rua

Shona

Tonga

Tswana

Venda

Tonga

Copi

KHUI-SAN

(non-Bantu)

Swazi
Sotho

Tsonga

Zulu

Xhosa

INDIAN

OCEAN

UCSB
Geography

N
W-E
S

Miles

0   500   1000

Primary groups

Secondary Sub-groups

Tertiary Sub-groups

(NOTE: The names of Bantu groups are only representative of the many Bantu peoples in each region.)

87

debate over the possible existence of so-called *Mischsprachen,* or "mixed languages," there is much of interest for those of us who possess no specialized knowledge of linguistics, nor of African languages, but who are still rash enough to hope that we may be able to use linguistic evidence in our attempts to reconstruct the history and prehistory of Africa. For us as well these seven articles held revolutionary implications.

Of much that had been written on the subject by others before him, Greenberg was thoroughly contemptuous, and not inclined to disguise the fact. Previous classifications, defined less by agreement than by an abstention from disagreement, were never fully reliable, and sometimes grossly misleading. The criteria that were supposedly decisive—for including a language in one group, or for excluding it from another—were only partly valid and partly not linguistic at all; they were often even demonstrably incompatible. Some classifications which had been widely accepted, such as that of the German linguist Carl Meinhof, were underpinned by racist assumptions which Greenberg made it his business to expose, in words vibrating with indignation. Elsewhere a lighter touch was enough to topple some baseless speculation: parts of the text are extremely entertaining. Even in the passages of close linguistic analysis, there is the occasional aside which serves not merely to amuse but to mark the point where one stage in the argument leads on to the next. It is from the skill with which these various passages are strung together, with bold modulations of pace and texture, that the articles derive much of their literary effect. A non-linguist can read them with pleasure, and with the sense that these matters are not entirely beyond his comprehension. Indeed, this was one of the points on which Greenberg insisted from the outset. Classification was not a mystery, understood by none except a few devoted specialists. Not uncommonly, in Africa amateurs "with a minimum of formal linguistic training" had succeeded in finding a correct classification for the languages of some region that they knew, while the professionals had failed because they were blinded by preconceptions. At the very beginning, as we have seen, Greenberg emphasized that there was "nothing recondite" in the methods which he had employed: they arose from "the commonsense recognition that certain resemblances between languages can only be explained on the hypothesis of genetic relationship." For Greenberg there is a category of resemblances which cannot conceivably exist except between languages which are of common origin—which are the surviving forms, variously modified, of a single proto-language. It follows from this that genetic classifications have to be discovered, not invented. They are not arbitrary constructions, imposed upon reality; instead they express a pattern of relationships which does objectively exist and which linguists must try to recognize.

Greenberg would claim that a genetic classification can always be found by following a few quite simple rules—rules which decide the admissibility of different types of evidence. These heuristic principles were not explicated fully in the original series of studies. They were discussed at some length, however, in an eighth article published in the same journal four years later, and also in a number of other papers written at roughly the same time. Here I intend only to give some indication of their scope. The most basic rule—which was in fact the last to be made explicit—is that languages have to be classified on linguistic evidence alone. Everything else is irrelevant. As Greenberg remarked, this rule would not have been worth mentioning if it had not been so frequently disregarded. The important rules are three.

First, when languages are compared, the only significant resemblances are those that result from the conjunction of similar forms with similar meanings. In practice, the main effect of this rule is to eliminate "structural" or "typological" similarities of the kind which may exist between languages which are not genetically related—and which conversely may not exist (i.e., may have ceased to exist) between languages which are. Such similarities cannot be relied on as evidence of genetic relationship. For this the only evidence which counts is that which comes from the comparison of individual morphemes—lexical items (words, roughly speaking) and grammatical elements like inflections or affixes. In any language, there are bound to be thousands of these items, each representing an arbitrary association of form and meaning. For purposes of comparison such data could hardly be bettered.

Second, it is only when resemblances can be shown to occur in some number, and with some consistency, that a genetic relationship between the languages in question can safely be assumed. A few accidental resemblances are almost sure to be found, even between a pair of unrelated languages. Consistency matters most: an individual similarity has no significance unless it is part of a pattern. For this reason there is no point in comparing two languages in isolation. Each pair of languages, each pair of items, has to be compared within the context provided by all the other languages, all the other items. This is the principle of "mass comparison," on which I shall shortly have more to say.

Third, not all the resemblances which are genuine result from genetic relationship: some result from borrowing. The genetic relationships must therefore be disentangled from the others, and this can be done—usually without much trouble—if we introduce a rough-and-ready distinction between "fundamental" and "cultural" vocabulary. Under the former heading we would include pronouns, low numerals, words for parts of the body, and so on. Common sense, supported by a great deal of empirical evidence, will tell us that "fundamental" vocabulary is much less affected by borrowing. An exact definition is not needed; nor do we have to assume an absolute immunity. In a doubtful case, however, where the indications seem to be contradictory—if we find, for example, that low numerals suggest one relationship, high numerals another—it is the more "fundamental" resemblances to which, under this rule, we attach the greater weight. A genetic classification cannot be expected to account for every resemblance which is historically significant. Nonetheless, it will cover a large proportion of them; and those which are left can then be explained piecemeal as the product of borrowing between already separate languages.

What exactly does it mean to say that two languages, or groups of languages, are "genetically related," "of common origin"? In the first place it means that we are defining a binary relation on some given set of languages. Suppose that we write this as A *t* B or "A links with B." If we wish, we can treat this as the statement that "A is of common origin with B." If we prefer, we can take it to mean that "A belongs to the same group as B." This latter interpretation appears to have the advantage that we are simply stating a fact, without guessing at what it signifies. We shall soon see, however, that each statement implies the other. "Links with" is an equivalence relation: it is reflexive, symmetric, and (most importantly) transitive. If A links with B, and B with C, then it must also be true that A links with C (and C with A, by symmetry). As Greenberg has said, it is through the insistence on transitivity that his classification can be sharply distinguished from those constructed by British linguists.

In a links-with analysis we are assuming that the languages will lend themselves to a classification which is hierarchical in structure. If this is true, if relationships between languages are hierarchically patterned, the only conceivable explanation lies in the nature of the evolutionary process. Unless we are determined to be perverse, we have to infer that languages evolve by repeatedly splitting apart—always by fission, never by fusion. And if *this* is true, it supplies a theoretical justification for the assumption with which we started. Languages which have evolved in this way must be related hierarchically; languages which are related hierarchically must have evolved in this way. In other words languages belonging to the same group must be of common origin, and vice versa. In Africa, with a few minor and marginal exceptions, there is no direct evidence—no written documents—which will tell us how the languages have really evolved. Thus there is only one question worth asking. Is it true, as a matter of fact, that the languages can be classified hierarchically, without too much distortion, and without recourse to arbitrary decisions—decisions, that is, which might be made differently by a different classifier? Greenberg would insist that it is, if we follow the rules. For what my opinion is worth, I am perfectly satisfied that he is right. The arguments which can be deployed in support of this proposition are very strong—about as strong as they could be, given the circumstances. Greenberg has shown, for example, that his method, applied to the existing European languages, is capable of producing very quickly the partition which, "by universal consent and much other evidence," is accepted as correct.

Written documents give corroboration, but they would not be indispensable. Even in the absence of such evidence, an internal check can generally be made by demonstrating that grammatical resemblances agree with the pattern of relationships displayed in fundamental vocabulary. On Greenberg's assessment of the available data, contradictions did not appear in Africa, any more than they did in Europe or the Near East. To this, the only possible exception came from a language called Mbugu, spoken by a small population in the Usambara region of Tanzania. In grammar there are pronounced similarities between Mbugu and the Bantu languages which surround it; in fundamental vocabulary there are not. Though he conceded that this was a difficult case, Greenberg proposed to classify Mbugu as a Cushitic language, much modified grammatically as a result of heavy borrowing from Bantu. Most linguists appear to agree with that diagnosis.

We thus appear to be justified in concluding that a hierarchical scheme, despite its simplicity, is appropriate for the classification of languages. If it fits, then simplicity is a virtue, not a vice. Again, a genetic classification of the hierarchical type must also be unique: there can only be one such classification which is objectively correct. In the short term any classification which is actually proposed may well be incomplete—either in the sense that it fails to include all the existing languages or else in the more important sense that some of the details are left unspecified. To that extent there is scope for disagreement between one linguist and another, but only of a superficial and temporary kind. In the long term, any two linguists, if they agree on which are the languages to be classified, and if they agree on the rules, must also agree on the final classification.

Greenberg's classification, even in its most recent recension, is very far from complete. The most that has ever been claimed for it is a partial, one-sided correctness: it is not wrong (except perhaps in a few points of detail, to be blamed on human error or on a shortage of information), but it is not completely right. In his very first article, Greenberg insisted that the groupings he would propose were all "in the class of the obvious," and that he had been deliberately "conservative." Many questions to do with the definition of subgroups and supergroups were left without an answer—but with the implicit promise that, by following the rules, an answer could be found.

From a different point of view—for historians and prehistorians—the significance of Greenberg's classification is no less obvious. The historical implications are immediate. A genetic classification of African languages is an outline plan of African history.

It was British Africanists who expressed the most strenuous opposition to Greenberg's classification. . . . In short, the reaction from British Africanists was almost uniformly unconstructive. Their attitude at first was one of amused indifference. Privately they felt they knew, publicly they were committed to the proposition, that classification was a task of the utmost difficulty. Anyone who thought that it was easy did not deserve to be taken seriously. Even by making it *look* easy, however, Greenberg was threatening their authority. It is clear that he aroused deep feelings of resentment—feelings which were betrayed by a remarkable propensity on the part of British linguists for misunderstanding and misrepresenting what Greenberg had to say. On the whole, they preferred to ignore him for as long as possible.

The real disagreement arose, I think, from the collision between two rival strategies, two discordant conceptions of the classifier's task. Greenberg's strategy has already been briefly described; more briefly still, it consisted of feeding the data through a succession of sieves, until a fraction (sometimes a very small fraction) was left, which would lend itself to classification on strictly hierarchical lines. It could thus be said, with some justification, that this strategy does not exhaust the data. But such an observation will carry no critical charge unless it is thought that there exists an alternative strategy, capable of transcending this limitation. Is it possible to classify languages "in full"? British linguists believed or hoped that it was. From what they did more than from what they said, from specific statements rather than from programmatic utterances, we can see that their classifications differed from Greenberg's in the manner of their construction and in the criteria by which they were meant to be judged.

For most British linguists, most of the time, classification was not a matter of any great urgency or interest; but there were some circumstances in which it demanded their attention. . . . As each small group of languages was described in turn, the question of its classification was raised—and then answered with a statement like the following:

> Mbo languages show vocabulary affinities with Ewondo, Bulu, N.
> Mbene, and Duala; phonetically their relationship tends toward
> Bamileke; grammatically they seem to be linked especially to
> Ewondo, Bulu, and N. Mbene.

American linguists could see no sense in a statement of this kind. For their British counterparts, this was not only a perfectly sensible thing to say: it was just the sort of answer that they expected. By treating this statement as typical, and by analysing its form, I think we can reach the root of the disagreement.

The first point is obvious: we are dealing with three statements, not with one. This was what baffled American linguists—the juxtaposition of two or more statements, ostensibly contradictory.

If we persevere, however, the contradiction dissolves. Each substatement is identical in form. It does not simply assert that A is related to B. The full meaning is conveyed in the two qualifying phrases which must always be present, explicitly or by implication. In the first place, the statement asserts it to be true that, given A, the language to which it is *most closely* related is B. I shall express this by writing "A links to B," or A~B. The links-to relation has peculiar properties which, in ways that I shall shortly try to explain, determine the characteristics of the resulting classification. As a preliminary indication, we may note that it is neither symmetric nor transitive. In the second place, the statement is always made with regard to some specified aspect of the data: A~B is claimed to be true lexically, phonetically, grammatically, or in some other restricted sense. Among British linguists it was not taken for granted that the pattern of relationships would be the same for every aspect. On the contrary, the presumption was that lexical relationships, for example, would *not* in general be congruent with any of the rest.

Ideally the groups distinguished by links-to analysis could themselves be subjected to similar treatment. That is, the analysis may need to be repeated over and over again, the groups defined in one pass through the data being treated as units in the next. In practice, though they recognized the possibility, British linguists saw little chance of success in this direction. The attempt, they felt sure, would soon grind to a halt. During the first pass, the links-to relation could probably be defined for most of the "basic units": except in areas where the data were very thin, "groups" could thus be identified with a fair degree of confidence. During the second pass, however, the relation would have to be left undefined in so many instances that "larger units" could seldom be distinguished satisfactorily. It would generally not be possible, given a group, to specify any second group as the one to which it was most closely related—either because there was no second group at all which seemed to fit the bill, or because there were two or more such groups which looked about equally eligible.

What *did* develop from this pessimistic prognosis was an ostensible justification for the belief in "mixed languages." We are now in a position to see, I suggest, that this arose out of the assumption that classificatory difficulties of the kind encountered were, in origin, at least partly objective. In other words, it came to be supposed that they were not entirely due to deficiencies in the data, or in the techniques of analysis employed, but that also there was—or might well be—a point beyond which linguistic relationships became intrinsically indeterminate. By an easy transition, it was further assumed that such indeterminacy would have to be explained historically, as the outcome of some process or processes of linguistic hybridization, whereby two or more languages might merge into one. These assumptions, thoughtlessly made, would not have confused the issue so thoroughly if they had not also succeeded in distracting attention from what, in my view, is the most significant charactertistic of any classification constructed by links-to analysis—the fact that its validity can only be synchronic.

The history of African languages is just as historical, as rational, as irreversible, as open-ended as that of languages in any other part of the world. We risk forgetting what a preposterous notion it seemed, even among Africanists, even twenty years ago, that Africa had a history. Remembering that, however, we can understand why Greenberg's work was at first so controversial—so badly received in some circles, so well received in others.

Bantu Migrations
THOMAS SPEAR[5]

The great majority of peoples of eastern, central and southern Africa today speak one of the more than four hundred different Bantu languages. The Bantu languages are not only numerous and widespread, they are also closely related to one another, indicating their rapid spread over this vast area within the last two or three thousand years. By looking at the classification of the Bantu languages, it is possible to see how this occurred.

The greatest differentiation among the Bantu languages occurs in the northwestern corner of their distribution—in southeastern Nigeria, Cameroon, Gabon, and Zaire—where seven of the eight primary subgroups of Bantu are found, according to the most detailed classification of the languages to date made by Bernd Heine. The Bantu languages are also part of a larger family of languages, known as Benue-Congo, most of which are centered around the Benue-Cross rivers area of southeastern Nigeria. It is thus clear that the earliest Bantu speakers lived in this area where their closest relatives are, and that they spread throughout the forest zone of equatorial Africa where the initial differentiation of Bantu into its eight constituent subgroups occurred. Eventually the speakers of one of these subgroups emerged from the southern fringes of the forest zone onto the savanna along the lower Congo River and slowly expanded south down the west coast into present-day Angola and Namibia and east towards the Great Lakes. This too must have been a slow process, because seven of the eight subgroups of savanna Bantu developed along the forest fringe. On reaching the area of the Great Lakes, however, the spread of Bantu speakers must have quickened as all the Bantu languages from eastern to southern Africa are closely related languages belonging to a single eastern highlands subgroup of savanna Bantu, as we can see on the map. While it is not possible to say precisely when these various movements occurred, the differentiation among the Bantu languages indicates that the initial spread of Bantu speakers through the equatorial forest must have occurred during the second millennium BC, while that of the savanna Bantu took place from early in the

[5]Spear, Thomas, *Kenya's Past* (Essex: Longman, 1981). Excerpts taken from pages 29–33. Thomas Spear is Professor of African History at the University of Wisconsin.

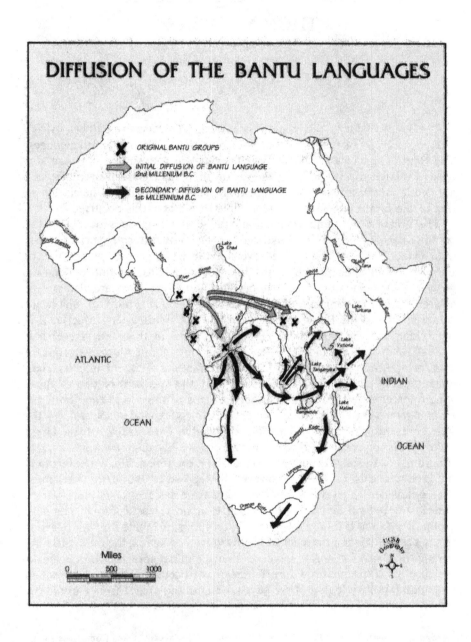

DIFFUSION OF THE BANTU LANGUAGES

X   ORIGINAL BANTU GROUPS

INITIAL DIFFUSION OF BANTU LANGUAGE
2nd MILLENIUM B.C.

SECONDARY DIFFUSION OF BANTU LANGUAGE
1st MILLENNIUM B.C.

ATLANTIC

OCEAN

INDIAN

OCEAN

Lake
Chad

Lake
Turkana

Lake
Victoria

Lake
Tanganyika

Lake
Bangweulu

Lake
Malawi

River Gambia

River Benue

Congo River

Zambezi River

Limpopo

Orange River

Miles

0   500   1000

UCSB
Geography

first millennium BC, and of the eastern highlands Bantu during the later first millennium BC and early first millennium AD.

By comparing the common words, or cognates, widely spread in the present Bantu languages, linguists have also been able to reconstruct substantial portions of proto-Bantu as it may have been spoken prior to the expansion of the Bantu-speaking peoples. From this reconstructed vocabulary it is obvious that the earliest Bantu speakers in the Congo basin were fishermen and root crop cultivators, for they had words for fishing with a hook and line, fishhooks, fishtraps, dugout canoes, paddles, yams, oil palms, and goats, but they did not have words for grains or bananas, cattle herding, iron working, or pottery, making it improbable that they practised any of these activities. Iron working is a good example. The present Bantu languages have at least fifty roots for the word "iron," some borrowed from other languages and some derived from their own words, such as "white" or "stone." It is thus obvious that Bantu speakers acquired the skills of iron working after significant differentiation had already occurred among the various Bantu languages. With no common root to draw on, all had to devise their own words for the new process. Bantu speakers must thus have been present in the savanna before the beginnings of iron working in this area in the last centuries BC.

Nor are there words in proto-Bantu relating to grain cultivation or herding cattle. Forest-dwelling Bantu speakers were root cultivators. Since grains were unsuited to a forest ecology and tsetse prevented herding cattle, Bantu speakers could only have adopted those practices after they had emerged on to the savanna. Sorghum, millet, and cattle had already been domesticated in eastern Africa at this time, and the Bantu speakers of the area generally borrowed Southern Cushitic terminology for irrigation, fertilization, sorghum, eleusine, and livestock. It would thus seem that eastern highlands Bantu speakers adopted iron working and mixed agriculture within East Africa from earlier peoples speaking Southern Cushitic languages.

The first Bantu speakers must thus have expanded into the equatorial forest as fishermen and root cultivators early in the second millennium BC. After nearly a millennium, during which they spread along the rivers throughout the equatorial forest zone and their language became differentiated into eight different languages or subgroups of closely related languages, some emerged on to the savanna south of the Congo Basin. Over the next millennium, the last one BC, these Bantu speakers spread throughout the savanna zone, adopting mixed agriculture and, later, iron working. We cannot be sure precisely where or when these innovations took place, but grain cultivation and herding had already been long established in East Africa and the earliest iron-working sites in sub-Saharan Africa are those associated with Urewe-ware pottery in the Lake Victoria region dating from the fifth century BC. It thus seems likely that Bantus speakers first adopted mixed agriculture and iron working in western East Africa and then introduced those industries into eastern Kenya and subsequently into the rest of eastern and southern Africa during the first millennium AD.

Previously historians have assumed that Bantu speakers were responsible for the spread of mixed agriculture and iron working throughout sub-Saharan Africa. If West African Bantu-speaking Negroes practised agriculture and iron working, so the reasoning went, their population would have grown, forcing them to expand, and they would have been able to clear and cultivate the savanna easily and quickly, enabling them to spread rapidly. As we have seen, however, the earliest examples of mixed agriculture and of iron working were both in eastern Africa, and Bantu speakers did not adopt these until the later stages of their expansion from West Africa. The diffusion of these industries and of Bantu-speaking peoples was thus far from even. This can be seen further in the physical types of present Bantu speakers. Coming as they did initially from West Africa, Bantu speakers are usually assumed to be Negroid, like other West Africans, but today they vary quite considerably, reflecting the influence on them of the peoples among whom they settled. These included the Pygmies of the Congo forest, who themselves speak Bantu languages today, the tall, thin Africans of the East African savanna and the Sudan, and the Khoikhoi and San of southwestern Africa. Negroes thus did not displace earlier peoples, but assimilated many and converted others to Bantu speech. Such assimilation not only explains the differences among the Bantu-speaking peoples today, it also helps account for their spectacular population increase and expansion. Just as the Ngoni assimilated thousands of people as they moved north from South Africa in the early nineteenth century, the present Bantu-speaking populations of eastern Africa are probably largely the descendants of the earlier inhabitants of the area who have adopted Bantu speech. In summary, then, the so-called "Bantu migration" should not be seen as a single migration of cultivating, iron-using, Bantu-speaking Negroes sweeping across Africa from west to east displacing all in their wake, but as a series of interrelated diffusions and syntheses as small groups of Bantu speakers interacted with preexisting peoples and new technical developments to produce a range of distinct cultural syntheses across the southern half of Africa. The variety of these syntheses is pronounced in eastern Kenya where the earliest Bantu speakers encountered Southern Cushitic, "Khoisan," and probably Sudanic speakers and still mix with Eastern Cushitic and Eastern Nilotic speakers today along the northern borders of Bantu speech. This complex and fascinating area can thus tell us more about the history and development of the Bantu languages.

Suggestions for Further Reading

Bellwood, Peter, and Colin Renfrew, eds., *Examining the Farming/Language Dispersal Hypothesis* (Cambridge, U.K.: McDonald Institute for Archaeological Research, 2002).

Ehret, Christopher, *The African Classical Age: Eastern and Southern Africa in World History, 1000 B.C. to A.D. 400* (Charlottesville: University of Virginia Press, 2001).

Flight, Colin, "Malcolm Guthrie and the Reconstruction of Bantu Prehistory," *History in Africa* 7 (Atlanta, Ga.: The African Studies Association, Emory University, 1980).

————, "Trees and Traps," *History in Africa* 8 (Atlanta, Ga.: The African Studies Association, Emory University, 1981).

————, "The Bantu Expansion in the S.O.A.S. Network," *History in Africa* (Atlanta, Ga.: The African Studies Association, Emory University, 1988).

Greenberg, J.H., "Linguistic Evidence Regarding Bantu Origins," *The Journal of African History* 13 (Cambridge: Cambridge University Press, 1973).

Guthrie, Malcolm, review of Greenberg's *The Languages of Africa* in *The Journal of African History* 5, no. 1 (Cambridge: Cambridge University Press, 1964).

Hiernaux, J., "Bantu Expansion: The Evidence from Physical Anthropology Confronted with Linguistic and Archaeological Evidence," *The Journal of African History* 9, no. 4 (Cambridge: Cambridge University Press, 1968).

Oliver, Roland, "The Problem of the Bantu Expansion," *The Journal of African History* 7, no. 3 (Cambridge: Cambridge University Press, 1966).

Posnansky, M., "Bantu Genesis: Archaeological Reflections," *The Journal of African History* 9, no. 1 (Cambridge: Cambridge University Press, 1968).

Vansina, Jan, "Bantu in the Crystal Ball," *History in Africa* 6 and 7 (Atlanta, Ga.: The African Studies Association, Emory University, 1979, 1980).

————, *Paths in the Rainforest: Toward a History of Political Tradition in Equatorial Africa* (Madison, Wis.: University of Wisconsin Press, 1990).

Problem III
AFRICAN TRADE AND STATES

While the phenomena of state formation is by no means unique to Africa, the student of Africa's history should appreciate the specific geographical and cultural conditions that gave rise to states in pre-colonial Africa. Development of long-distance trade networks played an important role in the formation of many African states. But numerous states arose in response to insular, local trading networks, or in reaction to internal dynamics of culture, lineage, and religion. In *The Zulu Aftermath,* Professor Omer-Cooper demonstrates how the powerful Zulu state developed apart from the influence of external trade. In Zululand the pressures of population growth, manipulated by the technical and political innovation of Shaka, produced a centralized political organization. The depth and devotion of the Zulu to the ideal of the nation created by Shaka was whimsically observed by the British Prime Minister Benjamin Disraeli in 1879: "A very remarkable people, the Zulus. They defeat our generals [Lord Chelmsford], they convert our bishops [John William Colenso], they have settled the fate of a great European dynasty [Prince Louis Napoleon, the son of Napoleon III and the Prince Imperial of France, killed by the Zulu on 31 May, 1879]." In fact this powerful state nearly brought down Disraeli's government at Westminster. The great Zulu state arose not from economic integration with the outside world, but from the ethnic pride and political organization which they retain to this day.

Long before the dramatic rise of Shaka and the Zulu nation itinerant Lwo-speaking peoples had imposed their supremacy upon stateless Bantu communities in what is now the Republic of Uganda. C. C. Wrigley shows how the Lwo utilized unique techniques of political organization to establish their rule over the acephalous peoples in the Interlacustrine region. The

101

appearance of the Lwo produced a political revolution among the Bantu population. This resulted in the centralized control of the land, and a concomitant revolution in agricultural production. Jan Vansina has observed a similar process at work in Central Africa. There, like the Lwo of the Upper Nile, the Balopwe invaders, brought techniques of political organization to the Luba-Lunda peoples. Applying these methods, they forged disparate, localized, and fragmented polities into a centralized state.

Thus many stateless societies developed into organized states with no outside influences. But many other states owed their existence almost entirely to the catalytic effect of external trade. Thomas Reefe expands on Vansina's example to show how the advent of trade with other African regions increased the wealth and power of the state. This allowed the Luba-Lunda to strengthen their trading networks. This symbiotic relationship, with trade and political organization spurring one another's growth, enabled the Luba-Lunda to bring extensive new regions and peoples under their control.

D. N. Beach found that internal and long-distance trade played a similar role in the rise of the Zimbabwian empire. In Southern Africa the Gumanye peoples built Zimbabwe by dominating the gold and ivory trade with the East African coast. The Gumanye state emerged after a dramatic population increase gave them the power to exact tribute from passing traders. As their wealth grew they eventually required sophisticated political institutions to systematize the profits from the trade. Soon a stratified society and a centralized and hierarchical state developed to meet their needs.

The economic dynamics of state-building is nowhere better illustrated than in the prosperous city states of the Niger Delta. G. I. Jones demonstrates how in the eastern Niger Delta the growing trade with Europe disrupted the traditional lineages of the stateless societies. The demands of administering the trade, and the new opportunities provided by the accumulation of wealth, created a "new equilibrium." As in many other societies, ancient or modern, greed soon subverted traditional respect for authority based on family, lineage, and seniority. New centralized institutions founded upon the wealth and control of trade replaced traditional ones. New leaders pooled their economic gains into political power. The states they established outlived their founders, many surviving through and after the colonial era.

States form in response to a wide array of stimuli. Local environmental and demographic dilemmas, ambitions for power and control, and the novel social demands brought by long-distance trade can contribute to the genesis of new states. In Africa, as elsewhere, these motivations span the spectrum of man's desire for power which cannot be measured solely in cowrie shells.

The Zulu Aftermath
J. D. OMER-COOPER[1]

The whole process of expansion which brought the Bantu from their original home to occupy the vast area of their present habitat can only be explained on the assumption of continuous population growth. Our uncertainties about the time span involved and the currents and crosscurrents within the overall movement prevent an accurate assessment of the rate of this growth or of how it may have varied from time to time and place to place. When the Bantu began to settle in South Africa, however, there can be little doubt that their rate of natural increase was very high. Once they had emerged from malaria and tsetse country into the healthy South African climate the mortality rate must have declined sharply. Many of the most deadly diseases which now affect the population were unknown before contact with Europeans (smallpox, measles, tuberculosis, syphilis). So long as there was abundant land for settlement there could be little to prevent the population increasing very steeply. The process of constant subdivision which characterized the history of Southern Bantu tribes in the pre-Mfecane period implies rapid population growth and gives us some idea of its order of magnitude.

The eastern coastal strip of South Africa was particularly favourable to Bantu settlement, with relatively high rainfall, fertile soil, good grass and excellent crops of millet, maize or pumpkins. As early as the seventeenth century we have evidence of a substantial population in Zululand and Natal. . . . As this population continued to grow, grazing land became scarce.

In the coastal areas inhabited by the Nguni group the position was different, for their habitat was a narrow corridor between the escarpment and the sea. Expansion within this corridor could only take place on a very narrow front and by the eighteenth century this had advanced as far as the Fish River. Further growth of population at the northern end of the corridor would inevitably produce a bottleneck. It is true that the Drakensberg was not an absolute barrier to human movement and some expansion of Nguni peoples onto the plateau did take place across it (Transvaal Ndebele onto the Transvaal highveld and Phuthi into Basutoland, for example). But the

---

[1]Omer-Cooper, J. D., *The Zulu Aftermath* (Essex: Longman, 1967). Excerpts taken from pages 24–37, 170–175.

J. D. Omer-Cooper is a professor at the University of Otago, New Zealand.

natural inertia of all human groups would predispose tribes living in the coastal area to fight for their lands before making the arduous trek across the mountains to a less hospitable environment, inhabited by tribes whose languages they did not understand.

Thus by the end of the eighteenth century Zululand and Natal were becoming overcrowded in terms of current methods of land use and warfare became more frequent and severe. The general conditions which favoured small-scale political organization and encouraged fissile multiplication had been reversed. Lack of space and the demands of more serious warfare dictated larger units and a process of aggregation began. Initially three large blocs emerged—the Ndwandwe, under Zwide; the Ngwane of Sobhuza; and the Mthethwa, under Dingiswayo.

The growth of larger political units was closely bound up with a revolution in military organization. Before this time the northern tribes of the Nguni group were organized along the same lines as their cousins living further down the coastal corridor. They practised circumcision rites and they organized their fighting strength on a territorial basis. Some of them continued to do so and after the Mfecane had driven many of these tribes from their homes, the refugees still clung to the ancestral pattern. In some Northern Nguni tribes, however, a double change took place. The circumcision ceremonies with subsequent period of ritual seclusion which deprived the tribe of part of its fighting strength for considerable periods and left the initiates very vulnerable in case of war, were abandoned in response to conditions of more frequent fighting. At the same time tribal armies were reorganized on an age-grade basis. It is probable that contact between Nguni and Sotho groups in northern Zululand played an important part in this change, for with the Sotho closer settlement pattern went larger initiation schools and permanent age-groupings with a military role. Though the Sotho military system was still very closely bound up with the circumcision ceremonies and provided only a very rudimentary form of military organization, it may well have suggested the idea of employing age-mate groupings as the basis of the military system. This would explain why the process of change began north of the Tugela River rather than in neighbouring Natal where population pressure was presumably just as great.

In the new system adopted by some Northern Nguni tribes young men of like age, who would normally have been initiated, were assembled together by the chief and constituted as a regiment with a name of its own. These regiments were not associated with particular princes but were assigned to one or other of the royal households (known as "heads") which formed their rallying points. This provided a more efficient fighting force and increased tribal coherence by bringing men from different territorial segments together and uniting them in a common regimental loyalty. It also facilitated the assimilation of new groups. Under the earlier Nguni system a newly incorporated group would furnish a separate contingent in the tribal army, thus preserving its sense of identity and capacity for independent military action. Aggregations based on this system were naturally unstable. Under the age-regiment system, however, young men of newly incorporated groups were divided up according to their ages, fought alongside their age-mates from other sections of the tribe and were associated with one or other of the "heads." A means of welding originally different tribes into a permanent and stable unit had been created but the effects of the system were limited by the fact that the regiments only assembled occasionally.

The introduction of age-regiments is often attributed to Dingiswayo. . . . [I]n his youth Shaka took service in Dingiswayo's regiments and soon gained a reputation for reckless bravery. . . . But Shaka's ambition was not satisfied by the position of trusted subordinate to the great chief. . . . Shaka thus became a chief in his own right with a following he could train in accordance with the new military ideas which had been maturing in his mind during his service in Dingiswayo's army. . . . Tribe after tribe was defeated and either incorporated or driven away as homeless refugees. In a long series of campaigns the entire area between the plateau and the sea, northward from the Tugela River to within a few days' journey from Delagoa Bay, was brought under his control. South of the Tugela, Natal was devastated, and the Pondo between Umzimkulu and Umzimvubu Rivers were severely chastised. Fynn, on his arrival in Natal in May 1824, met several of Shaka's regiments returning from a prolonged campaign which had taken them right through Natal to attack Faku the Pondo chief. Bryant maintains that Shaka had undertaken four previous campaigns in Natal: in 1817, 1818, 1819, 1820. As his conquests continued Shaka constructed a new type of state. Its primary purpose was to maintain and expand an efficient fighting force completely loyal to its leader. The normal method of incorporating new elements in an expanding tribe was employed without any important change as far as the civil administration was concerned. Conquered tribes were simply grafted onto the territorial hierarchy, their chiefs becoming territorial sub-chiefs. Shaka not infrequently removed the existing chiefs of tribes he had con-quered and appointed his own nominees in their place. Even when he did not do so he made clear that they ruled at his good pleasure. In Shaka's system, however, the territorial chiefs lacked the power and importance which they had in the traditional system. Though they might continue to adjudicate over cases which arose in the territory under their control, their authority was restricted to the older men and women who still lived in traditional fashion. All young men were drafted into the army and it was in the army that all power resided. Without an effective backing the sub-chiefs could exercise no great influence on policy and were entirely at the mercy of Shaka's whims and fancies. In the central area of the Zulu kingdom a series of military settlements was established at Gibixhegu, Bulawayo,

Nobamba, Isikiebhe, Mbelebele, and Dukuza. These were a development of the system of "heads," modified to meet the requirements of a permanent standing army. Each of them was circular in construction and contained a royal section opposite the entrance. On either side were the huts of soldiers around a central cattle enclosure. Gibixhegu was more than three miles in circumference and contained about one thousand four hundred huts. Each settlement was under the command of a military *induna,* generally a commoner, appointed personally by Shaka. Each settlement also contained a section of the royal women under a senior woman of the royal family who exercised considerable authority in association with the commanding officer. Shaka, however, never officially married and the large numbers of royal women were officially his wards. At these settlements young boys gathered from every section of the kingdom. They were employed at first to help guard the cattle and act as shield bearers, then when they reached manhood they would be enrolled in age-regiments. The regiments were kept on permanent service until they were officially dissolved by the king. During this period they were forbidden to wear the insignia of manhood or to marry. In Shaka's time the period of active service was very prolonged as a consequence of almost continuous warfare, and women of thirty and forty were without husbands. Each regiment was commanded by an officer appointed by the king with junior officers under him in charge of squadrons. They were distinguished from one another by shields of different colours and other such as headgear. The shields and other items of military apparel were supplied by the king. Each regiment had charge of a section of the herds. So far as possible the herd attached to a particular regiment would be made up of cattle of the same colour as their shields. These cattle served to provide the soldiers with meat and milk, and, in addition, millet beer was provided from the royal bounty. . . . This military system not only provided Shaka with the most efficient fighting machine in Bantu Africa but also a means of rapidly assimilating conquered tribes. The young men, split up amongst the regiments, soon came to feel a strong sense of *esprit de corps* and the nature of the system was such as to strengthen and emphasize the loyalty of the soldiers to their ruler in every possible way. From him they received their arms and regalia; their immediate leaders owed their position to his will. Through him lay the only hope of advancement, and from him they would ultimately receive their wives. Even their food was largely provided from royal resources, and, as they ate, the warriors would shout his praises and thank him for his generosity. The regiments had a direct interest in the wars of their ruler, for they were allowed large quantities of meat which tended to outstrip the natural reproduction of the royal herds. Only by repeated victories in the king's service could their standard of living be maintained.

The concentration of power in the army and its extreme dependence on the king, raised Shaka's authority far above that of the traditional Bantu chief. The sub-chiefs had lost the power to act as effective checks on the central authority. Shaka did not need to consult the traditional tribal council. He ruled to a great extent as an absolute despot, deciding cases while taking his morning bath and ordering men to death with a nod of the head. Ultimately, however, his position depended on the loyalty of his troops and their commanders. The military *indunas* now held the position traditionally occupied by the territorial chiefs. Their position was weaker as they were creations of the king and had no hereditary authority of their own, but Shaka was very sensitive of the need to maintain their loyalty. The military *indunas* were thus treated as counsellors and were assembled to discuss all important questions. Shaka also took care to ensure that they did not meet behind his back and unauthorized conferences between military leaders were punished by death. In addition he tried to get at least apparent public support for his policies. When he wished to embark on a course that was likely to prove unpopular he would put the proposal in the mouth of one of his *indunas* and pretend to accept it reluctantly under pressure of public opinion.

The reorganization of society on military lines was accompanied by a new ethos. The informality, hospitality and naïve curiosity which meant that the visitor to a Bantu village was immediately surrounded by a mob of men, women and children, staring, asking questions and openly begging for gifts, was replaced by a more reserved attitude. A pride almost amounting to arrogance and an indifference to human life were accompanied by a sense of discipline, order and cleanliness which at once attracted the attention of European travellers. At the same time political loyalty was enhanced to a high degree, and came to be regarded as an absolute value.

The essential features of this revolution in its centre of origin were the adaptation of the initiation ceremonies to military purposes and creation of a permanent standing army organized in age-regiments. This was a reaction to conditions of frequent and severe warfare and probably stimulated by contact with the rudimentary age-regiment system of the Sotho peoples. It implied much greater internal unity within tribes, as the age-regiments made up of youths from all parts of the tribal territory took the place of the territorial chieftaincies as the immediate foci of political loyalty. It also went with a greater concentration of power in the hands of the ruler. As the balance of power which had given meaning to the traditional system of consultation disappeared, true despotism began to emerge. This in turn was associated with an administrative change of vital importance. There was a transition from a bureaucracy of "royals" to a situation in which effective administrative authority passed into the hands of the class of commoner *indunas* personally chosen by the ruler and dependent on him.

This change involves a principle which can be seen in any human society developing in the direction of greater political centralization and more active government. It can be paralleled in the transition from feudal to bureaucratic administration which marks the emergence of the modern European state. It can also be seen in the history of many African kingdoms. In Bornu a change of this general type took place between the break-away of the Bulala and the reign of Mai Idris Alooma and was one of the main reasons for the relative stability of the kingdom. In the Oyo empire the same principle is seen in the Alafin's administrative hierarchy of slaves and eunuchs. In Buganda the power of the Kabaka depended on the fact that the highest officials were commoners, personally appointed by him and transferable at will from post to post, district to district. In Ethiopia the accounts of Alvarez show that the strength of government at the height of its powers depended on the same principle. Only in the Mfecane, however, can we see this transition in the administrative organization of an African people in its entirety.

As the rising pressure in Zululand forced various groups out of the area they took the basic pattern developed there to far-distant parts of the continent, modifying it in various ways in the light of circumstances. The Swazi who left the storm centre before the revolution reached its climax never developed the full Zulu-type military system but adopted a form of organization half way between it and the traditional system of the Sotho tribes. They also did not develop the highly centralized system of government which was typical of the Zulu. The traditional checks and balances were retained in, for example, the relationship between the king and the Queen Mother and under Sotho influence they even evolved in the direction of increased democracy. The Ngoni combined the age-regiment system with the development of greatly expanded quasi-lineage groupings. This led to an ambivalence in their societies. The military system operated in the direction of centralization and the increased power and prestige of kings, but the growth of lineages encouraged decentralization and fragmentation.

One of the most striking features of the Mfecane is indeed the very general success which attended the numerous and different attempts at forming political units out of originally separate peoples. It suggests that the task of instilling a sense of political unity into peoples of different language and culture in a limited time, the task which faces every political leader in the newly independent African countries, is not so difficult as pessimists tend to maintain.

State Formation in Uganda
C. C. WRIGLEY[2]

Leadership and organization account even more clearly for the successful penetration of the Alur country by initially small numbers of Lwo-speakers, who, as Southall showed, were obeyed by the indigenous Sudanic peoples because they expected to be obeyed. But this only pushes the problem one stage further back. From where did the founders of the Alur chiefdom acquire the habit of authority? Moral ascendancy of this kind belongs only to those who, like the British officials of Southall's parable, were brought up as members of a ruling group; and the only likely explanation in this case is that the first Alur came from the upper ranks of the already established government of Bunyoro.

Since the means of Lwo expansion were political in nature it is reasonable to surmise that the motive force behind it was political as well. This, too, is an unorthodox suggestion, for insofar as any explanation of the Lwo diaspora has previously been offered it has usually been in terms of population pressures, perhaps generated by adverse climatic change. Yet one of the clearest characteristics of the economy of precolonial Africa is that land was very rarely a scarce factor. It was mainly for this reason, as Goody has pointed out, that feudalism of the European seigneurial kind did not occur: the economic base of that system, control of a scarce resource, was lacking, since disease and occasional famine kept the population well below the normal carrying capacity of the land. It is true that minor fluctuations in east Africa's rainfall during the last millennium can be detected, and for this reason among others local imbalances probably did occur and may sometimes have been a cause of movement. The migrations so caused, however, would in the nature of things be gradual and unspectacular, and the society under stress would almost certainly remain a geographical continuum. By contrast, the Lwo diaspora was a movement of explosive force, as can be seen from the wide scattering of the fragments, the continuing close resemblance between the dialects and the absence of clear secondary linguistic groupings that would result from the stage-by-stage outward spread of land-

---

[2]Wrigley, C. C., "The Problem of the Lwo," *History in Africa* (Atlanta, Georgia: African Studies Association, Emory University, 1981), pp. 234–241.

C. C. Wrigley was a British administrator in Nigeria and has taught history at the University of Sussex.

hungry farmers. Moreover, it has been convincingly shown that the political instrument of that kind of expansion is not chiefship but the segmentary lineage system, of the kind operated so successfully by the Nuer, the Tiv, and some of the Ibo. That model might well apply to the growth of the Luo communities after their establishment in Kenya, but not to the adventure that brought them there in the first place.

For abrupt and long-range movements of the Lwo kind the quest for food cannot be an adequate explanation. We naturally turn, therefore, to that other great motive force of human action, the quest for power. What is sought for here is the right to dominate, to be attended and praised, to be exempted from labor (at any rate in its more disagreeable forms), to have first claim on meat and beer, and to have many wives and thus a better than average chance of genetic survival. The incentive to acquire power was obviously very strong, but the means of acquiring and maintaining it were very few, especially in eastern Africa. Since land was not scarce it could not be effectively controlled by any single person or class. The techniques of production did not lend themselves to capitalist organization, nor the techniques of warfare to military dominion, for every man had a spear or a bow and no man had any more lethal weapon. Suppose, however, that a center of power has nevertheless been established. In a polygynous society a ruling lineage will increase its numbers much more rapidly than the rest of the population, in fact at their expense. Thus there will never be enough room at the top for those who believe themselves to be there by virtue of their royal blood. And here we have a potent stimulus to migration and to the spread of the institutions of government. Most members of the ruling house can gratify the expectation of power only by moving out and finding subjects outside the orbit of their successful kinsmen. In practice, moreover, it is hard to distinguish the quest for power from its obverse, the desire for independence, the urge to escape from domination and be one's own master—an urge which can be satisfied only by secession in the literal sense of the term. In either case, once a focus of power and exploitation has emerged anywhere, it is likely to repeat itself throughout neighboring lands and in so doing generate major currents of population movement and cultural mixture. Not only, it is suggested, did monarchical institutions rarely come into being otherwise than by diffusion, but having once come into being they were extremely likely to be diffused.

This assertion will no doubt meet with strong resistance, since the present intellectual climate, not only in African studies, is radically hostile to diffusionist explanations. Certainly few would want to restore the old picture of special "state-forming peoples" roaming around Africa and conferring the blessings of government on the anarchic natives. But it would be equally misguided to assume that African governments were everywhere an endogenous response to local circumstances and needs. It is true that an institution loosely related to government, namely sacred or ritual kingship, can now be seen to have existed in the Interlacustrine region since the beginning of the Iron Age, and was, I believe, present in some other parts of Africa much earlier than that. But ritual Kingship is not government, even in germ. The sacred king is a mascot, a victim of his people's symbolic needs. He wields no executive authority and the radius of his influence is necessarily short; ritual works only for as many people as can observe it, and in the absence of electronics that means that they must be numbered in hundreds rather than in tens of thousands. So Kingship of that kind is no more than a peg on which government can be hung when the conditions of its development become present; and those conditions, it has been argued, were very rare.

Now it is evident that in a great part of east, central, and southern Africa profound social and cultural changes took place between the eleventh and the thirteenth century. This inception of the "Later Iron Age" originally marked for archeologists by the generally sudden cessation of the long-lived and distinctive Early Iron Age ceramic tradition, is now associated with an obvious growth of population, a greatly increased role for cattle, a simultaneous extension of cereal agriculture, and the emergence of much larger scale and more clearly stratified societies. There seems to be a linguistic correlate, in that a particular form of Bantu speech came to exert very widespread influence, overlying the older forms and making the present languages of the "Savanna Bantu" group more alike than they would be if they had descended separately from the speech of the first Iron Age settlers. This makes it unlikely that the changes began with a "Pastoral Revolution" carried out by intruders from the north, as Oliver proposes, and more likely that the epicenter of the disturbance lay within the Bantu world. Phillipson in fact locates it in the region of the Congo-Zambezi watershed, and this is plausible both on linguistic grounds (it was here that Malcolm Guthrie, perceptively but wrongly, located the original Bantu nucleus) and on economic grounds. For the area of course contains the continent's richest deposits of copper, which in part were easily accessible, and that rare, attractive, and semimagical substance would have provided its owners with the opportunity to accumulate wealth and power. The "pastoral revolution" should probably be seen, not as the cause of state-building, but as its consequence, cattle being the only means by which copper-trading princes could invest their profits and display their power.

We postulate that the repercussions of events in the Shaba area were felt far and wide, not least in the Interlacustrine region, where copper was not mined before 1950 yet had long been the universal emblem of royalty. Stimuli from the south led to the creation of the political system whose most obvious monument is the Bigo earthwork, and the northward continuation of this process was the Lwo diaspora.

Although the Lwo spread into northern Uganda and the lands beyond as a politically dominant minority, their coming was the signal for the full peopling of the land. It is now clear that at the end of the Early Iron Age the transition from hunting and gathering to herding and tilling was far from complete in "Bantu" Africa. Farming settlements were thinly spread and limited in the main to areas of unusual fertility. The establishment of cereal farming in the vast tracts of average steppe and woodland savanna, with their undistinguished soils and their erratic rainfall, was no easy undertaking and was unlikely to succeed without a measure of group discipline, cooperative effort, and, perhaps most important, communal storage of reserve supplies. In the first instance these things would probably require political authority of a kind that was forthcoming only after the upheaval of the Later Iron Age. Northern Uganda is as thin-soiled and uncertainly watered as most parts of the Bantu territory, and, although the indigenous Sudanic and Eastern Nilotic peoples had crops and livestock, it was the coming of the Lwo chiefs that provided the conditions for a really effective agricultural economy. This point is acknowledged by the people themselves in their own idiom; many Acholi and Alur traditions state that the founder of the chiefdom brought the rain-stones with him from Zoka, although in ethnographic fact that magical technique was the ancient property of the Sudanic peoples.

Two clarifications should be entered here. The social organization required for the conquest of the savanna wilderness was still on a modest scale, the optimal size of the political unit being some two thousand people or less. Secondly, leadership was needed only for the initial establishment of the new economy. Once agricultural endeavors and disciplines had become routine, exemplary and coercive authority was redundant and in some Lwo communities, especially those in Kenya, it tended toward disappearance. It could be claimed, indeed, that the Lwo peoples, operating on the furthest frontier of the Later Iron Age, got the best of both worlds, generating enough political power to achieve remarkable economic and demographic successes but not succumbing to the servilities and the militarism that were the price of development in the larger Lacustrine Bantu states; cruel punishments and large-scale ritual murders were alien to the Lwo until the late nineteenth century, as were the social neuroses that found expression in the spirit-possession cults of their southern neighbors.

First, let us suppose that the assumption made in this essay is correct, namely that a language recognizable as Lwo was spoken on the banks of the Victoria Nile, and only in that region, before the end of the first millennium, and that the Later Iron Age innovations, by the mechanisms suggested, detonated an explosive northward movement early in the second. At that time, it can be supposed, Lwo-speakers kept to their familiar riverain environment, and the impetus carried some of them as far down the Nile as the Shilluk country. Much later, new tensions developed as the result of the rise of the Nyoro state, which probably took place in the sixteenth or seventeenth century and may itself have been an indirect consequence of the opening of oceanic trade. By this time agrarian organization was well established and the political stimulus thus provided the opportunity for a wider-ranging and more intensive movement of colonization that gave rise to the Alur, Acholi, Dhola, and Luo communities, and probably also to the Paari and the Anywak.

This hypothesis would be proven if it could be shown that the Shilluk use words and names of Bantu origin. It must be admitted however, that such things are much harder to find in Shilluk than they are in the central and southern dialects of Lwo. Nevertheless, there are certain items which seem to me to have high probability. In some Soga states and formerly in Buganda the royal title was Mulondo (witness the name of the Ganda throne: *Namulondo,* "Mulondo's mother"). The base of this is the verb *kutonda,* which in Ganda means both "to find" and "to choose," the reference being to the common idea that the ritual king has to be "discovered" by the kingmakers. The verb belongs to common Bantu, though its original meaning was slightly different: to search for or track down. And it recurs in Shilluk, where the process of electing a new king was described by the verb *rony* and the king was said to be *aronyi Juok,* "chosen of god." The chiefly title *Moronyo* used by the Pajook, the northernmost Acholi group, seems to supply both a geographical and a linguistic link, since it combines the Shilluk shape of the stem with the Bantu nominal prefix. Then there is Nyikang's brother Dimo, thought of by the Shilluk as ruling a country to the west. The myth which they tell about a man who followed a cow into the land of Dimo clearly echoes the Nyoro myth of king Isaza, who likewise followed a cow into the land of ghosts, *oku-zimis.* Since the Lacustrine Bantu stem *-zig* is a development from an earlier form *dimu,* it seems likely that Dimo, the Shilluk king of the land of the setting sun, derived his name from the universal Bantu word for "spirit."

However, a compromise hypothesis is also possible, according to which the initial southward movement of Western Nilotic speech from its ultimate homeland in the Juba-Malakal region took place later than has been proposed in this essay, but earlier than in the orthodox construction. That is to say, the first separation occurred approximately at the time indicated by the Blount-Curley data, no ancestors of the Shilluk ever lived in Uganda, and the ancestors of the central and southern Lwo arrived there about the twelfth or thirteenth century, dispersing again in the seventeenth. On this view the Lacustrine Bantu political culture which emerged about that time would result from the convergence of movements from both north and south and the incoming Lwo could be credited with the introduction of the cord-rouletted pottery which is characteristic of that period and is believed to have northern antecedents.

Finally it has to be acknowledged that enquiries of this sort carry a certain inherent risk. If this essay were read in Uganda it could conceivably be taken to have some bearing on current politics, since categories such as "Acholi," "Nyoro," "Bantu," and "Nilotic" are terms of political discourse. If this were to happen it would be a very unfortunate misapplication, for my own view is that the use of ancient history as ammunition in ethnic factionalism is inutterably childish. The methodology of what might be called the Makerere school of traditional history seems to me open to criticism, but there can be nothing but applause for its most important message, namely that the people of Uganda are the result of long and complicated interactions and there is no permanent connection whatever between linguistic affiliation and political or cultural capacity.

Kingdoms of the Savanna
JAN VANSINA[3]

The peoples of the savanna south of the equatorial forest show a considerable degree of cultural homogeneity, and this fact has been recognized in most culture-area classifications. Most scholars feel that the Lozi, Ovimbundu, and Bolia are marginal and they are often classified separately. Within the remainder of this huge area, the cultures are still different enough to be brought together in subgroups.

It has been demonstrated by Greenberg that the Bantu originated in the area between the Cross River and the middle Benue, and this may well account for the origin of a great part of the present populations in the area. There may have been a Negroid population in the area long before the arrival of the Bantu, but if so they must have been few in number since no trace of any language other than Bantu has been found in the area, indicating that they must have taken over the language of the newcomers. It is likely that the bulk of the present population was of Bantu ancestry. By 800 AD at the latest, agriculturists probably lived everywhere in the area. Evidence from the Ovimbundu country and from Katanga shows that by this time iron was known in both regions, and from the presence of channeled ware in Kasai and in Lou land it is likely that it was known at an even earlier date.

By 800 AD at the latest, then, the peoples of the area, probably the direct ancestors of those who founded the kingdoms we will describe, had the technological means to operate societies and cultures of the type existing in 1900 since no great changes in the basic patterns of economic production occurred in the meantime.

The question can be asked: What were the origins of the kingdoms in Central Africa: would there be but one original center where a state structure was elaborated and then diffused or would there be many? In actual fact, at least three possible centers of origin for state structures, which were widely separated geographically, can be traced to 1400 AD or before. One lay around the lakes of Katanga where the Luba and the Songye place the

---

[3]Vansina, Jan, *Kingdoms of the Savanna* (Madison: University of Wisconsin Press, 1966). Excerpts taken from pages 19–24, 34–36, 70–71, 81–83, 97, and 245–248.

Jan Vansina has traveled and taught extensively in Africa. *Kingdoms of the Savanna* won the Herskovitz prize as the best book on African history in 1967, and his latest publication is *Paths in the Rainforest*, 1990. He is the J. D. MacArthur and Vilus Professor of History and Anthropology at the University of Wisconsin, Madison.

origins of their states, which seems to be in agreement with the known archaeological facts or which at least is not in contradiction with them. Another center lay in the depths of the tropical forest from where the Bolia came. The third one lay north of the lower reaches of the Congo River—the later Kongo, Loango and Tyo (Teke) kingdoms. It is unlikely that there will ultimately prove to have been but a single center of origin for all the Central African kingdoms. A hypothesis involving multiple invention, stimulated by contact diffusions and internal evolutions, seems to be the most appropriate one. It also becomes clear that, short of a miracle, no data will be found which would document in detail the beginnings and the spread of the state systems in the area, for these beginnings may well go back to the beginning of the iron age or even beyond.

The Birth of the Luba-Lunda Empire

Deep in the savanna of Central Africa—in the region west of the upper Lualaba and north of the Katanga lakes, a profound change in political structures took place during the sixteenth century. Invaders—the Balopwe—occupied the area and founded a major kingdom, the Luba empire. From there they went further west at a somewhat later date and established a kingdom in Lunda land. Groups of emigrants would leave this latter area for more than a century after 1600 and carry their political organization with them to the west, the south, and the east, so that by 1750 Luba/Lunda culture was spread from the Kwango River in the west to Lake Tanganyika in the east. This chapter describes the origins of the Luba kingdom and its further internal history and the origins and history of the Lunda empire, and the story of Lunda expansion in Angola, in northeastern Rhodesia, and in the area between the Kwango and Kasai. The history of the area is somewhat arbitrarily limited to 1700, before the expansions into the lands of the watershed between the Congo and Zambesi and into the lands later known as Kazembe.

The Birth of the Luba Kingdom

Around 1500 the area between Lake Tanganyika and the upper Kasai was organized into a multitude of smaller chiefdoms. In the western part these were ruled by the Bungo, the ancestors of the Lunda. In the central part, between the Busbimai River and the Katanga lakes, lived the ancestors of the Luba Katanga; here there were two bigger kingdoms, that of the Kaniok and the Bena Kalundwe. East of the Bushimai the chiefdoms were very small and the people who lived in them were called the Kalanga. Between the lakes and Tanganyika lived the ancestors of the Hemba and perhaps even then some Bemba-speaking groups. The degree of political organization which obtained there is unknown, but by 1500 a great immigrant named Kongolo appeared in the Kalanga lands and was to become the founder of what has been called the first Luba empire.

There is no unified tradition with regard to the origins or the coming of Kongolo and the versions that have been collected indicate only how badly we are in need of a general study of Luba oral traditions. The traditions which are extant tell that he was originally either from the northeast—from the area where the town of Kongolo stands now; or from the northwest—from the Bena Kalundwe of Mutombo Mukulu. In one version he was even said to be born near his later capital. Whatever his origin, he arrived in the country, subdued isolated villages and tiny chiefdoms en route, and built his capital at Mwibele near Lake Boya.

There was no regular standing army (although in the nineteenth century a small regiment was constantly raiding the Sala Mpasu), but there were *kawata* or traveling chiefs who would constantly travel with a militarized retinue to collect tribute or carry out orders in distant parts of the empire. They were not used in the Lunda homeland. In addition to the *kawata,* there was only a small police corps at the capital. The military strength of the Lunda was therefore quite small, which makes their expansion over such a large part of Africa all the more remarkable. Tribute was paid once a year, in the dry season, by the cilool who were farther away whereas those who were nearer to the capital had to pay tax several times a year. Payments would be made in the form of specialized products for which an area was famous or in food. The capital, which comprised from eight to ten thousand inhabitants in 1875, relied entirely on tribute in food for its sustenance. And, as Professor Biebuyck notes, tribute paying seems to have been the outstanding characteristic of the Lunda empire. The outer provinces could do as they pleased as long as tribute was paid.

The whole political structure rested on the twin mechanisms of political succession and perpetual kinship. A successor inherited personal status of the deceased, including his name and kinship relationships. Thus, ancient kinship relations were reenacted every generation and new links were created only after all the old "positions" in the system had been filled. In practice, these mechanisms proved to be extremely useful; they divorced the political structure from the real descent structure since they were not bound to any principle of descent in particular. For example, the northern Lunda are bilateral, but matrilineal with regard to succession for the mwaantaangaand; elsewhere in the empire matrilineality would prevail or it might be, as in Kazembe or with the Yaka, that the people would be matrilineal but the chiefs patrilineal. All this did not matter, however, for the principles of positional succession and perpetual kinship could be applied everywhere. Therefore the mechanisms could be used without necessitating any change in the existing social structures, which explains why so many Central African cultures could take over the system with little or no cultural resistance even when, as with the Lwena, there were already segmentary lineages with political functions.

Other basic aspects which enabled the system to be adapted anywhere were its "indirect rule" features. Local chieftains could be assimilated to mwaantaangaand and the newcomers would be cilool. They would settle and found a Lunda colony [iyanga] which would become a neutral place from the point of view of the non-Lunda residents in an area, a place where one could go for arbitration, a place to which one was ultimately subjected without the use of force. When the Luba and the Lunda political systems are compared, it can be understood why the Luba kingdom did not expand far beyond its homeland while the Lunda did so successfully. The Luba did not practice positional succession or perpetual kinship. They did not exploit the division which existed between "owner of the land" and "political chief" and they never did assimilate foreign chiefs into their own system even though they would put Luba villages near tributary chiefs to supervise payments. From the point of view of the tributary chief, the Lunda system was better since he became an honored and respected "owner of the land," while in the Luba system he was but a defeated chief who was usually overtaxed.

The crucial event in the earlier history of Central Africa has been not the creation of a Luba kingdom by Kongolo and Kalala Ilunga but the introduction of Luba principles of government into Lunda land under Cibinda Ilunga and their transformation by the Lunda. The new political patterns which evolved around 1600 in the Lunda capital, could be taken over by any culture. Its diffusion was to condition until 1850 the history and the general cultural evolution of a huge area. Even now its effects on the peoples of Central Africa are still discernible. But curiously enough, by 1700, when this expansion had already touched so many peoples in the savanna, the organization of the Lunda homeland had just been completed and the last districts between Lulua and Lubudi had not yet been organized. The paradox between the expansion in the areas and the slow growth of the nucleus shows that it was not the military might of the Lunda which was responsible for the upheavals: it was the superiority and the adaptability of their pattern of government and the adventurous spirit of the conquistadors who spread it wide and far. And this diffusion was facilitated by the simple fact that this was an open savanna where no natural boundaries could stem the flow.

All the major kingdoms in Central Africa shared three structural features which led to similar developments, or "consequences," in their history. Everywhere, even among the Ovimbundy to some degree, not only was the ruler at the apex of the political structure but he was its prime mover. Therefore, the varying personalities of kings have left a deep imprint on the history of their realms. States undergo "expansions," "ages of splendor," and "pe-

riods of decadence" in rapid succession and in no logical order of development because of the happenstance of the changing personalities of their
rulers.

Another common feature of the major kingdoms was a system of territorial rule whereby the outer provinces were considered as tributaries, often
enjoying an internal autonomy and even sometimes being ruled by the very
houses of chiefs who had been their rulers before their incorporation into
the kingdom. This was least true of the kingdom of Kongo—but even there
the province of Mbata was a case in point. And in all the states that were
not on the coast, this autonomy was a prominent feature. The practice of
"indirect rule" and the concomitant ubiquitous fading away of the power and
authority of the central government in the outlying provinces explains why
a balance of power never existed between the major states, and why there
never was a struggle for hegemony over large parts of the savanna. For
instance, the power of the Luba and the Lunda over their peripheral provinces was too weak to lead to a conflict between them; there are many cases
similar to that of the province of Kayembe Multulu, which lay between Luba
and Lunda and which paid tribute now to the Lunda, now to the Luba, and
was left in peace by both. The Luba, Lunda, Kazembe of the Luapula,
Bemba, and Lozi never fought each other for long and never participated in
a system of alliances, of building up a balance of power over the whole
interior. The same is true of the coastal states, with the partial exception of
the colony of Angola, which was striving for hegemony; but even here the
fringes of Portuguese-controlled land were ruled by "vassal" chiefs who
essentially were in charge of tributaries.

A second consequence of autonomy was that the existing system of territorial control often reduced itself to sheer exploitation: outer provinces paid
protection money against possible raids from the center, and the center tried
to obtain maximal tribute from these regions but felt no obligation to protect
them against enemies from the exterior. The populations of these provinces
resented this and could not be expected to remain loyal followers of the
kingdom. When they saw an opportunity to free themselves from the exactions of the center, they took it. A good example of this is provided by the
developments in the Luapula kingdom, where the chiefdoms of what is now
southern Katanga defected to Msiri.

The regularities outlined are evident and the link with structural features
of the political system are obvious. It is the task of anthropologists to work
them out in greater detail.

The history of Central Africa is the story of a number of kingdoms that
underwent a regular and fairly predictable development. It is possible that,
despite the succession problem, the development of the African states would
have gone on had there been no influence from outside. But as it actually
happened, the political structures could not cope with the new stresses fos-

tered by the slave trade and tended to collapse during an interregnum, when their power was weakest. The interaction between the growing slave trade and the normal evolution of the political systems explains most of the history of the kingdoms in Central Africa from 1500 to 1900.

The Luba-Lunda Empire
THOMAS REEFE[4]

A system of trade running no less than 1,000 kilometers on a south-north axis linked the people living on the copperbelt in southern Shaba Region with the groups living on the fringe of the rainforest in the Kasai Region of Zaire. This system of extended regional trade in goods was essential to savanna subsistence economies, as well as being a means of distribution of African-produced specialty and luxury products. A trade route spanned hundreds of kilometers, and trade journeys lasted weeks or even months. Exchanges involved the use of currency and the development of emporia. The Shaba-Kasai trade network reached its full territorial extension in the eighteenth century, when it was integrated into a larger system of African long-distance trade encompassing a zone bounded by the Kasai River in the west, the Zambezi River in the south, and the lakes of the Great Rift Valley in the east. This trading zone was one of the largest to develop in central Africa without being directly affected by the international economy in slaves and ivory.

No specialized trading groups emerged to challenge the right of political leaders to expropriate the surplus of savanna production. Rather, villagers organized themselves for a single trip into ad hoc groups under a designated leader, and after having solicited the protection of spirits, they travelled to near or distant regions to trade. These groups, which ranged in size from about five to twenty individuals, consisted of adult males accompanied by their clients and by women who carried and prepared their food. Once at their destination, people might manufacture at least some of the products they needed, like salt, and remit a portion to local earth-priests in return for the right of exploitation. However, the smelting of ore and even lake fishing required technology that visitors often did not possess or specialized materials they could not bring with them, in which case they had to trade with local producers for all the goods they sought.

Small-scale state formation preceded the maturation of extended regional trade on the savanna by several centuries, but the emergence of territorially

---

[4]Reefe, Thomas, *Rainbow and the Kings* (Berkeley: University of California Press, 1981). Excerpts from pages 3–5, 93–97, 101, 192, and 200–203.

Thomas Reefe is an associate professor of African History at the University of North Carolina at Chapel Hill.

extensive states is related, in part, to the growth of trade. The decades on either side of 1700 mark the period of the full extension of Shaba-Kasai trade and the beginning of the Luba dynastic history. It is no coincidence that the Luba Empire and several other states, including the kingdoms of Mutombo Mukulu and Samba, Kanyok chiefdoms, and Songye chiefly towns, lay across the path of this trade.

State expansion brought more and more villages into a common polity that tended to minimize conflict and facilitate travel and trade. Extended regional trade raised the standard of living by more effective distribution of resources essential to the subsistence economy than was possible through village to village trade. The advent of the bambudye society in the Luba Empire, with its emphasis upon cooperation and mutual support when members travelled, could only have had a salutary effect on trading voyages. Luba kings exploited this trade by demanding as tribute a portion of the goods in the hands of subordinate client-chiefs and villagers. Courts acted as magnets to attract prestige and royal goods; the larger the Empire became and the more the influence of its rulers grew, the larger became the quantity of goods collected by the royal court. Womersley has explained the role of Luba royal courts in the redistribution of such prestige goods as beads: "Baskets of unfinished beads were brought in tribute over a period of several generations to the King of the Baluba and gradually spread over the country."

Luba royal males who were victorious in dynastic-succession disputes gained direct access to the iron, salt, and other resources of the Luba heartland. The development of the heartland as an emporium in Shaba-Kasai trade was by the eighteenth century of major importance to the political regime. Luba kings participated directly in the benefits of trade, because their courts were only a few dozen kilometers, at most, from the salt and iron districts of the heartland. A large volume of trade meant that a large quantity of all sorts of imported goods that were produced in areas not controlled by the Luba royal dynasty came to the villagers of the heartland. Portions of these goods were passed along to Luba kings as tribute and gifts. Conversely, the creation of a single state in the heartland during an earlier epoch and the maintenance of political order could only have served to encourage the development of the area as an emporium. Nowhere is the role of trade more vividly demonstrated than in the development of Luba relations with the Songye and the kingdom of Samba, at the northern and southern poles, respectively, of Luba influence by the eighteenth century Luha-Songye Trade.

The proto-Luba state was one of the many small-scale lineage-based states whose rulers participated in a relatively homogeneous politico-religious culture. The origins of this culture go back to the beginning centuries of this millennium, and it is likely that the earliest experiments in collective action occurred among the fishing and agricultural populations of the Upemba depression. The survival of the depression's relatively dense population in an environment of lakes, marshes, and streams required cooperation and political rule beyond the village level. No such imperatives existed among the scattered hamlets and villages of the nearby savanna, but once institutions and techniques of overrule had been developed in the Upemba depression their attraction to leaders and men of ambition on the savanna must have been irresistible.

Rich deposits of salt and iron ore are located in adjacent districts approximately sixty to eighty kilometers northwest of the Upemba depression; it is no coincidence that the small-scale state that was to become the Luba Empire was located here. The Luba genesis myth contains a rich overlay of symbolic associations that tied the ruler of the Empire to the ancestral spirits venerated in this territorial center. Eventually, Luba sacral kings came to have direct and easy access to the specialized products of this heartland, and scarcity of essential goods was manipulated to guarantee the loyalty of client villages and states. The Shaba-Kasai network of extended regional trade developed from about the fifteenth century to the beginning of the eighteenth century. During the same epoch a shift occurred in the scale of political action, as some states began receiving tribute from their neighbors. Expanding trade did not cause this state growth; rather, trade and politics interacted, feeding upon one another. Extended regional trade led to improved communication between peoples and polities. The growth of states facilitated the flow of commodities essential to subsistence society while encouraging the flow of prestige and local goods essential to political life. The Luba heartland became a major emporium on Shaba-Kasai trade routes and the general lines of the Empire's early expansion coincide with the axis of trade that ran from the Songye in the north to the kingdom of Samba in the south.

The ruling lineage of the emergent Luba state acquired clients by lineage powerbrokering, conquest, and resource manipulation. Then the mechanisms and institutions of more permanent allegiance which had been created in its heartland were exported to the periphery. Special relationships were established between the Luba royal dynasty and the diviners and spirit mediums venerating the ancestral spirits from whom client kings derived their sacral authority. Oral traditions were formulated that legitimized ties between local ruling lineages and the royal dynasty by claiming a putative ancestry from primary and secondary characters of the Luba genesis myth. Political insignia were bestowed upon client kings, who then participated in the aura of a superior Luba sacral Kingship. Local rule and overrule were thus merged.

The proto-Luba state emerged in an area producing salt and iron goods essential to the life of savanna subsistence agriculturalists. Although the presence of extensive deposits of salt and metal ores does not make state formation and growth inevitable, there have been interesting correlations between the availability of natural resources and centralized political action. Several of the Mbundu states upcountry from the port of Luanda in Angola emerged around salt pans and iron deposits in the sixteenth century, at a time when a surplus of salt and iron was converted into assets for the growth of political authority. A similar process seems to have gone on in the emergence of the proto-Kanyok kingdom. The path of the eastward expansion of the Lunda in the early eighteenth century and the related growth of the kingdom of Kazembe at that time were determined, in part, by the availability of salt and copper between the upper Zaire and Luapula rivers. The penetration of long-distance trade routes carrying non-African commodities from the Atlantic and Indian oceans and directed by commercial specialists has long been recognized as having served as a catalyst for the expansion of states in central Africa. The Zimbabwe culture and the Mwenemutapa Empire traded gold with the port of Sofala on the Mozambique coast for goods coming across the Indian Ocean in the fourteenth and fifteenth centuries, and political growth is associated with the successful exploitation of this trade. The Lunda Empire expanded into eastern Angola in response to the opportunities of long-distance trade from the port of Luanda in the late eighteenth century and the early nineteenth century. The kingdom of Kasanje in central Angola was located astride trade routes into the interior, and its rulers exploited their position as commercial middlemen. However, other systems of exchange have figured prominently in central African history from a period well before the penetration of long-distance trade. Extended regional trade systems developed, and pedestrians and paddlers covered hundreds of kilometers to acquire African subsistence and prestige goods. The Kongo and Loango kingdoms are the earliest and best-documented examples of dynastic states intimately involved in extended African regional trade before the first agents of international maritime trade, the Portuguese, established their Atlantic coastal bases in the sixteenth century.

During the middle centuries of this millennium, Shaba-Kasai extended regional trade came to link the populations along the southern fringe of the rainforest with the villagers of the copperbelt, and dynastic states larger than a handful of village clusters emerged in this area during the same span of centuries. However, we cannot say that the emergence of Shaba-Kasai trade led directly to state expansion on the open savanna, because the relationship between trade and politics was symbiotic. A leader had to accumulate clients in order to increase his political power and prestige. The savanna population was dispersed, and growth of political power on the grasslands meant, inevitably, the development of territorially extensive states. As these states grew in size they promoted a degree of peace and order that encouraged people to seek subsistence and prestige goods from their near and distant neighbors.

The greater the quantity of goods moved across the savanna and exchanged between villagers, the larger the quantity and the more varied was the tribute that flowed into royal courts; the more goods available at court, the greater was the possibility of holding old clients and attracting new ones through the redistributive tribute-network. Extended regional trade led to a high degree of economic specialization. Standardized trade goods, like copper crosses and salt cones, served as currency, and centers of rich natural resources became emporia for barter and purchase. No class of specialized traders emerged, however, and tribute mechanisms exploited whatever surpluses there were. Tribute collection did not have to be transformed into the direct taxation of trade in the Luba Empire, because the royal court was located near or in the trading emporium created by the salt and iron districts of the heartland. The sheer proximity of resources and the longevity of control in the heartland/emporium meant that tribute and gift exchanges yielded the surpluses of locally produced and imported goods necessary to keep court personnel loyal, with enough left over for redistribution to outlying clients. Later, during the radically expansive phases of Luba history in the eighteenth and nineteenth centuries, Luba kings often acted as tribute mongers, directing their attention and their agents to districts noted for the production of important resources.

The overall low population density of the central African savanna contrasts with the occasional pockets of relatively high population density scattered across the landscape. The Upemba depression has been, in this millennium, a densely populated region. The ecological imperatives for collective action are clear in the depression and are matched by its archeological record showing craft specialization, social stratification, and the existence of political insignia in grave goods. The Luba heartland and the Upemba depression are separated by a distance of only sixty to eighty kilometers. Their populations participated in a common political culture in earlier centuries, and they are linked by the issue of population density.

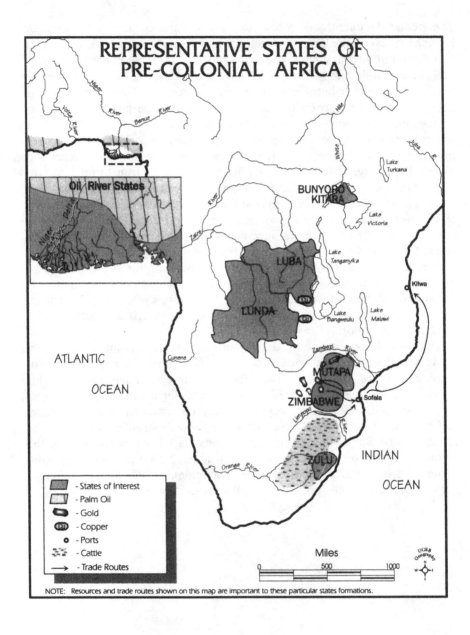

REPRESENTATIVE STATES OF PRE-COLONIAL AFRICA

Oil River States

BUNYORO KITARA

LUBA

LUNDA

MUTAPA

ZIMBABWE

ZULU

ATLANTIC OCEAN

INDIAN OCEAN

Kilwa

Sofala

Lake Turkana

Lake Victoria

Lake Tanganyika

Lake Bangweulu

Lake Malawi

Niger River

Volta River

Benue River

Nile

White

Juba R.

Zaïre River

Cunene

Zambezi River

Limpopo

Orange River

- States of Interest
- Palm Oil
- Gold
- Copper
- Ports
- Cattle
- Trade Routes

Miles

0   500   1000

UCSB Geography

NOTE: Resources and trade routes shown on this map are important to these particular states formations.

126

The Rise of the Zimbabwe State

D. N. BEACH[5]

This rather lengthy section on the economy is here for a good reason. Much of the rest of this book is devoted to political and ethnic history, with most of the attention being paid, perforce, to the doings of rulers and their dynasties. Yet, even though the evidence available has little to do with the economy, at first sight, the economy had a great deal to do with the evidence. Since each of the states, dynasties, and groups to be described was operating in the same environment and in an economy which, by and large, seems to have changed remarkably little, a clear understanding of what was happening in the Plateau in the economic sphere is of fundamental importance.

A feature of the history of the Shona since they occupied the Plateau has been the formation of states. This term requires definition. Whereas the Shona were normally divided, throughout their history, into territories under rulers of which many were in turn subdivided into wards under subrulers and househeads, each made up of a number of villages under village heads these territories varied greatly in size and their rulers varied equally in their wealth and power. It is therefore difficult to draw dividing lines on the scale between a large and powerful territory such as Teve, a medium-sized unit such as Bocha and a small area held by a minor ruler. But it is easy to distinguish between all of these on the one hand and four major Shona political units, on the other hand: Zimbabwe, which flourished in the south of the Plateau before about 1500; Torwa which existed around Khami in the southwest from the late fifteenth to the late seventeenth centuries; its successor, the Changamire state, which lasted until the 1840s; and the northern state of Mutapa which survived in one form or another from at least the fifteenth to the late nineteenth century.

For reasons that will be made clear, we have little more than archaeological evidence for the existence of the first two, but we can look forward briefly to the last two to show why all four can be termed "states." The basic difference between the Mutapa and Changamire territories and all their

[5]Beach, D. N., *The Shona of Zimbabwe* (New York: Homes and Meier Publishers, 1980). Excerpts taken from pages 35–43.

D. N. Beach teaches at the University of Zimbabwe, at Harare.

Shona neighbors was that they were able to raise large armies and exact tribute or intervene in the politics of other territories over long distances and for long periods. No matter how large and powerful some Shona-ruled territories such as Barwe or Minyika became, they were not able to do this. In the cases of both the Mutapa and the Changamire it is possible to distinguish between a large and fairly compact area under the close control of the rulers of one dynasty—whether they exercised that control through members of that dynasty or not—and a much larger region of fluctuating size which from time to time paid tribute to the overlord but which might at other times be independent or even at war with him. The frequency with which tribute was paid would have a lot to do with the distance involved. These, then, would form the "states" proper and their tributaries. There is very sketchy documentary evidence on the Torwa state and virtually none on Zimbabwe, but the sheer economic strength and social complexity revealed by the large-scale public works of these two makes it probable that they too conformed to this definition of the external attributes of statehood, and it is also probable that the distinction between "state" and "tributary area" applied to them. Because they succeeded Zimbabwe, the rise of the Mutapa, Torwa, and Changamire states is not difficult to explain in the context of Shona history, because they were able to draw upon economic, political, and social techniques that had, to some extent, been pioneered by the state of Zimbabwe. But the way in which Zimbabwe started the whole process is not so easy to understand. Two facts are clear from the archaeology of the Plateau as a whole: there had been increasing trade between the Plateau and the East African coast from about the ninth century, yet none of the Shona cultures known to us from archaeology or documents show any traces of political or social traits borrowed from the Muslims of the coast that could explain the rise of the Zimbabwe state. On the other hand, the rise of the state was obviously linked directly to the development of the economy. Therefore, it seems reasonable to interpret the rise of Zimbabwe in terms of general characteristics of Shona society that were allied to this economic development, on the assumption that Shona society as observed by the Portuguese in the sixteenth century and interpreted with the help of more recent evidence would not have been very different in its essentials from Shona society of a few centuries earlier. Even within this framework, however, the Zimbabwe state offers some problems since the connection between the developing economy and the formation of a state was not quite as straightforward as it might appear.

Essentially, the chief problem is as follows: the Zimbabwe state, as will be shown below, developed locally in the environment of the southern Plateau, which however was not an important gold-producing area. Therefore, for the rulers of Zimbabwe to have accumulated enough power either to control the gold trade or to control gold production elsewhere, they must already have developed their wealth by other means; and in the Shona economy the only other means was that of cattle herding. The history of the rise of Zimbabwe, therefore, appears to involve a group which, basing its strength initially on its herds, managed to dominate enough of the gold trade to found a state structure. This, in turn, involved a rather complex and sensitive system of trade routes on the Plateau itself which joined up the goldfields with the sea routes. The goldfields of the Plateau fell into two main blocks. One, the biggest, started in the southwest, crossed the west of the central part of the Plateau in the region of the sodic-soil zone described earlier, and curved round the northern edge in the general area of the Mazoe valley. The other was a much smaller field that straddled the eastern highlands about halfway down their length. The evidence for the dating of the Shona mines is fragmentary and likely to remain so, because the mines were reopened in the twentieth century: but whereas it is clear from the Portuguese documents, that all of the goldfields of the north and east had at least been opened by about 1500, it seems likely that mining first started in the southwest. This is because there is no definite link between gold mining and either the last of the northern Early Iron Age groups, the Maxton phase, or the early phases of the Harare and Musengezi cultures that replaced it; furthermore the relative poverty of the earlier Musengezi people would suggest that they were not carrying on a great deal of trade. On the other hand, while these Musengezi people were living a relatively isolated existence at this stage, between about 1210 and 1290, much more impressive developments were taking place in the southwest. The only available radiocarbon dates for Shona mines both come from this region, and range from about 1210 to 1300, and although this is limited evidence it does suggest that mining started in the southwest much earlier than in the north, especially if account is taken of the considerable growth in prosperity of the Leopard's Kopje culture of about that time.

The Leopard's Kopje culture, it will be recalled, was the first of the Shona groups to settle on the Plateau, from the tenth century onwards. At first, their settlements had been hardly more prosperous, except for their herds of cattle, than those of the Early Iron Age people who preceded them, but by the thirteenth century real changes in society were taking place that strongly suggest an overall increase in wealth. The settlements were occupied longer, they were much bigger, rough stonework was used to terrace hilltop living sites, more elaborate huts were made for the rulers, and there was evidence of much more trade with the coast, in the shape of beads. The conclusion to be drawn from all this is that the Leopard's Kopje people had developed both herding and gold mining to a point where there was an actual surplus of wealth, in both livestock and imported goods such as cloth and beads. It would seem that all the ingredients for state formation were present, yet the irony is, that the Leopard's Kopje people did not reap the greatest benefit from their efforts and did not form a state, as far as the archaeological evidence can show this. They did have at least two centres in the Limpopo valley drylands in the south—possibly not as dry then as they are now—at Mapela and Mapungubwe; but although the latter site has attracted attention on account of its prominent position on a hill and the gold burials found there, its importance can be exaggerated. It is true that a great deal of labour went into the carrying of earth to the top of the hill, and that some elaborate huts were built there, but in the last resort there were only three people buried with gold ornaments and objects, and suggestions that Mapungubwe was a religious centre are based on a misunderstanding of the equivalent evidence for Zimbabwe. Given its position well to the south of the Leopard's Kopje gold mining area, away from trade routes to the coast, it is remarkable that Mapungubwe developed as far as it did. The overall conclusion to be drawn from the evidence on the Leopard's Kopje culture, when it is considered that its people seem to have possessed the greatest resources in terms of cattle and gold on the Plateau in the first few centuries of the Shona settlement and to have exerted the greatest effort in terms of production, is that the culture represented a case of arrested development. This, of course, was true for all the Shona peoples of the Plateau, in that there was a lack of balance between the real value of what the Shona exported and what they imported, but in the case of the Leopard's Kopje people this was taken a step farther, in that the people who derived the most benefit from their efforts belonged to a different culture within the Shona complex: the rulers of the Zimbabwe state.

To understand how this was possible, it is necessary to look at the way in which the Leopard's Kopje people were able to export their gold. In the first place, given the good communications that probably existed on the Plateau since the Stone Age as the result of hunters and traders passing on news, it is probable that the Leopard's Kopje people had a clear idea of the location of the various Muslim trading ports along the coast, from the mouth of the Sabi northwards to the mouths of the Zambezi. It is also likely that, once regular trade was established, news of the varying terms of trade at the ports would travel rapidly along the trade routes. Consequently, if the evidence for the period from the sixteenth century to the nineteenth is any guide, Leopard's Kopje miners would have had a choice between taking their own gold to trade it at the coast or trading it locally with a trader from the coast, probably a Muslim Shona, at a lower price. Since the small quantities of gold that were traded at any one time were not too bulky, and even the weights of cloth and beads that went the other way may not have been too heavy, the main problem of either the Leopard's Kopje trader or his coastal counterpart would probably have been to find enough men to guard his goods against robbery rather than to carry them. Certainly robberies were common enough. It would follow from this that trade routes need not necessarily have followed rivers, although where such rivers as the Sabi, Buzi, or Zambezi were navigable by canoes for short or long stretches they would be used. (This explains such trading sites as Ingoinbe Ilede or the islands of Chiluane and Bunene south of Sofala.) Nevertheless, long overland trails could be and were used, such as the route from the Mutapa state round the north end of the eastern highlands and down to Sofala. Certainly, the eastern highlands were not an impassable barrier, and such gaps in the ranges as that which occurred in the territory of Manyika would offer an easy route. Overall, however, the most logical route for gold exports from the Leopard's Kopje people's area was due east or slightly northeast, across the southern edge of the Plateau and either down to the navigable lower Sabi or over the eastern highlands to the port of Sofala. In terms of distance, the routes to the north that led to the Zambezi were not so much longer, especially since such a lot of the travelling was by water, and later in the era of Zimbabwe these routes were to become important; but for the early period of the Leopard's Kopje culture's development the eastern routes seem to have been crucial. And here we return to the rise of the Zimbabwe state.

The Zimbabwe state arose out of the Gumanye culture, the second of the two Shona cultures to have settled the southern half of the Plateau. The Gumanye culture was, as has been pointed out, much like the other three early Shona cultures; but within this similarity it was distinct from them, mainly in its pottery tradition. Its villages were found across the southern part of the Plateau from the middle Mtilikwe to the Lundi, and although its people had many cattle, judging from the animal remains and the figurines that were common in their villages, they were anything but wealthy in terms of imported goods and, therefore, by implication, in terms of goods that could be exported. Nevertheless, one of the dynasties of the Gumanye people appears to have managed to build up enough power to dominate the trade between the southwestern goldfields of the Leopard's Kopje people and the coast, and this led to the foundation of a state at Zimbabwe. Zimbabwe (the term seems to be derived from the Shona term dzimba dze-mabwe, houses of stone, and was widely used from the sixteenth century to mean Shona capitals of any type) arose in a complex of rocky hills and valleys on the southern edge of the Plateau just to the west of the Mtilikwe river. It is not known precisely why this particular site was chosen, for generally similar environmental conditions could be found over a much wider area. There is no evidence as will be explained later in this chapter, that a religious shrine existed there before the state arose. On the other hand, there are suggestions that whereas the nearest reef mines were not rich enough to warrant working, there were some alluvial goldfields in the river valleys nearby, not nearly as rich as the southwestern mines but sufficient to aid the foundation of the state. But perhaps the simplest answer is that those who started the whole process did not foresee the complexity of the society that they were founding and therefore had no special reason for choosing the site.

The site itself included a whale-backed hill, crowned with great boulders and with a steep, smooth rock face on its southern side, overlooking several broad valleys and lower granite hills nearby. A Gumanye village was established on the top of the western end of the hill in the late eleventh century and its cattle enclosures and millet fields would have been spread out in the valleys around, to form a site territory which, because of the nearby hills, would probably have had a most irregular shape on the map. At some time after about 1100, this society began to develop into a state. The evidence for this comes from a sequence of building and changes in the local pottery tradition allied to an increase in imported goods, all of which made up the most spectacular aspect of the Zimbabwe state. The exact dating of all this is uncertain, but the process was far advanced, although not complete by any means, by about 1300. Indeed, dates from an outlying Zimbabwe on the coast to the southeast suggest that this level of advancement may have been reached by about 1200.

In outline, what happened was that the Gumanye people, or to be more accurate, a ruling dynasty of the Gumanye people, began to grow more wealthy after about 1100. They began to make superior huts with walls made of thick daga rather than poles and daga, and then they started to make use of the natural tendency of much of the local granite to break off in even sheets, as described earlier, in order to build walls. These walls were used to enclose or screen the huts of the rulers from the gaze of the ordinary people, and the social stratification that this implies was echoed in the pottery styles, in that a special class of pottery was developed for the rulers to keep liquids in—almost certainly beer—while they were served with ordinary foods that were prepared elsewhere on the site. This development was first apparent on the hill and a number of spots up and down the valley at Zimbabwe, where stone walls in an early style that were used to enclose the rulers' huts have been dated to about 1300, 1310, and 1360.

How was this development possible? The most obvious answer is that the rulers at Zimbabwe were beginning to tap the wealth that was travelling between the southwestern goldfields and the coast. Shona rulers in the sixteenth century are known to have tried to control the trade that passed through their lands, and they were evidently following the example set by Zimbabwe much earlier. It may well be wondered how the Zimbabwe rulers did this, for, although Zimbabwe lay on the general trade route, it was not in such a position that those who wanted to avoid paying tax could not spare themselves the annoyance by making a detour to the north or south. The simplest answer is that the rulers of Zimbabwe already possessed enough men to compel the traders not to do this. In short, the Zimbabwe state rose by exerting military strength to benefit from the exertions of others, specifically, the Leopard's Kopje people. It has been suggested that the architecture of Zimbabwe does not have a military function, and that therefore the state could not have had a military foundation. This misses the point that the whole effort made would have been offensive, not defensive, and that at least two of the Shona states known from documents to have raised large armies, the Mutapa and Changamire, did not have military architecture either: defensive walls are made by the weaker party in most cases. More to the point, once the Zimbabwe state had established a presence over an area wide enough to dominate the trade routes, major military efforts would not be necessary as long as the taxes levied were not so high as to encourage people to avoid them. As for the foundation of this body of armed men, few of whom would have been anything like full-time warriors, the rise of the cattle herds of the Gumanye culture, and the implications this would have had in a society where cattle were used to acquire wives and thus eventually relatives and supporters, supplies the simplest answer.

From these beginnings, the Zimbabwe state developed in three main ways: the life style of the rulers became ever more elaborate, the condition of the people at the capital became more urbanized, and the culture as a whole began to spread over the rest of the Plateau. The first and second features are known to us only through archaeology, but the third can be linked to a certain extent to documentary and traditional evidence. Of the first two, only the first is at all well covered in most works on Zimbabwe, but it can be argued that the second is of more real significance, in that it involved the lives of more people.

Between about 1300 and about 1450, the Zimbabwe state became very prosperous, as it succeeded in increasing its grip on the gold trade and, probably, building up its cattle herds even further. This wealth was reflected in the life style of the rulers. It became possible to finance skilled builders, descended from the first wall builders, who improved the stone building technique, while at the same time the new wealth made it possible to divert labour from the agricultural cycle into the cutting, dressing, carrying, and laying of stone for the walls on a much grander scale. Additions were made to the walls on the hill, new stone enclosures were built around more ruling-class huts in the valley, and major changes were made to one of the existing wall-and-hut complexes there: an existing screening wall was partly rebuilt and an opening was cut in it to permit access to a solid stone tower of a curved, conical shape. Around the whole complex a continuous wall was built, pierced by entrances under wooden lintels; although it varied considerably in height, thickness, plan, and construction it still represented the best and most impressive construction in the state.

These walls, then, were the outer signs of the wealth of the rulers who lived in the huts behind them, screened even more than before from the gaze of the ordinary people. There were other signs of their wealth. There were relatively few huts within the buildings, so that the rulers had far more living space than the ordinary people. Their pottery was different, and was supplemented by a limited amount of imported ceramics, and an astonishing variety of imported goods. . . . Judging from the conditions of the sixteenth century, the cloth that was imported would have included the finest silks and embroidered materials. A proportion of the gold that was brought in was not exported but was worked by local goldsmiths into ornaments, and there were even some iron gongs of the kind used by the rulers north of the Zambezi that had been imported. In short, the rulers of Zimbabwe lived in considerable luxury, and this situation seems to have lasted up to the end of the state, probably in the last half of the fifteenth century.

Trading States of the Oil Rivers

G. I. JONES[6]

In my own case, and in attempting to classify and differentiate between political systems in Eastern Nigeria, I find it convenient to regard the two main divisions of *African Political System* as polar or extreme types rather than as exclusive categories. At the one pole political authority is centralized and derives from the central government as "personified" by the king, the head of the state. At the other there is no central government, authority remains with the members of the territorial segments which are held together by ties of common interest, traditions, descent, common ritual institutions, and similar bonds. The Zulu or Tswana systems could be said to represent the one type, the Dinka or Nuer the other, and most other African systems could be graded between these two extremes. In Nigeria the kingdoms of Benin and of Idah would fall closer to the A pole, the political system of the Tiv close to the B pole, while most of the societies of Eastern Nigeria would occupy a more central position. All Ibo, Ibibio, or Ijo societies that have been studied can be said to possess the requirements of a primitive state, in that they have some centralized administrative and judicial institutions and cleavages of wealth and status corresponding to the distribution of power and authority. They are also segmentary in Fortes's sense, in that power is ultimately resident in the segments not in the central government, which consists essentially of a federation of politically equivalent segments. In the case of Ibibio and Ijo these federations can be called villages and in that of Ibo, village groups.

It is hoped as a result of this present study to show that the political system of the Eastern Delta states developed out of the kind of segmentary political system characteristic of other communities in the Eastern Region. The hypothesis is put forward that in systems of this Eastern Delta type one is concerned with a cycle of development through which a political system, which is essentially segmentary in character, passes in moving towards a

---

[6]Jones, G. I., *Trading States of the Oil Rivers* (Oxford: Oxford University Press, 1963). Excerpts taken from pages 5, 6, 59–66, 178–181, 204, and 205.

G. I. Jones was a district officer in Southern Nigeria, and later a lecturer in anthropology at Cambridge University.

new equilibrium when it has been upset by external factors. These factors in the Eastern Delta states were, firstly, the control of the overseas trade with western Europe and, secondly, the acquisition of very considerable state revenue which was provided by European trading vessels in the form of trading dues (comey). The cycle begins with an exceptionally able and wealthy political leader who replaces a federal system of equivalent political units with a monocratic system of his own. But the political group which he has created itself divides into segments and in due course these new segments either develop into the units of a new federal system similar to the one they have replaced, or become involved in a conflict which is resolved either by political fission or by the emergence of another successful leader who develops another similar monocratic system. Such an achievement involves leadership of a high order operating under very favourable conditions, as was found in the Eastern Delta during the eighteenth and early nineteenth century. But this pattern of an exceptional leader being able to establish himself as the supreme ruler of his community was not confined to these Delta states. It was occurring throughout the region, being least in evidence in the areas most actively involved in territorial expansion, and most common in the more populous areas, where there were greater opportunities for specialization and for the acquisition of wealth through trading and other professional occupations. The British colonial government, as it brought the region under its control, gratefully recognized such self-made rulers wherever it found them and sought to create them for communities where they were lacking. These were the "warrant chiefs" who became their principal instruments of local government. But, at least during the recent past, such self-made chiefs were never able to alter the structure of their tribe or village group and the office in almost every case died with its creator. In earlier stages of their development, however, such restructuring may well have taken place, to judge from the traditions of a number of these communities. But for clear examples of the processes involved in such restructuring we must refer to the Oil River states whose oral traditions can be supported by historical records.

In other Ijo communities, as in those of the hinterland, age and descent were the cardinal determinants of a man's status. Only a man who was of advanced age could aspire to the headship of the house or lineage and then only if he were a lineal descendant of its founder. Social mobility existed but it was a slow process, a matter of several generations before the descendants of slaves and of strangers became accepted as full members of the lineage or house. In the principal Oil River states, on the other hand, social mobility became so rapid that it was possible for a bought slave to become the founder of his own canoe house[7] and for some of these to become first

---

[7]A canoe house is a single or group of armed trading boats that form the basic political unit on the Niger Delta.

the chief of a group of houses, and eventually the most powerful chief in the state, for example, the two Braid brothers and George Amakiri in Kalabari, and Jaja Anna Pepple in Bonny. Indeed, the majority of the *opuwari* houses were founded by slaves of this type.

Although in ritual matters descent still counted and priests of ritual cults still had to be lineal descendants of the patrilineage that "owned" the cult, it ceased to be a prerequisite for social advancement in political and economic spheres and was replaced very largely by other qualities, particularly those of administrative and business ability. With this exaggerated emphasis on wealth and economic leadership went a rather different status evaluation which, as it was never properly appreciated by nineteenth century Europeans and has been partly forgotten or misrepresented in contemporary local tradition, will have to be examined in some detail.

People in these states were classed or ranked by a number of different and frequently conflicting criteria which can be seen as belonging to two very different systems—a traditional one based primarily on descent and a newer one based mainly on wealth. The traditional system probably indicated where power resided in the past, the new one very clearly showed where it lay in the Eastern Delta in the nineteenth century. . . . The traditional system distinguished two main categories, namely, slave and freeborn with a superior class of freeborn, royalty. The last categorized king and the princes, that is, freeborn persons who were direct lineal descendants of the founder of the dynasty. . . . The essential difference from the traditional system was that every one of these positions could be acquired and could also be lost. It was also very much a competitive system. A king, if he lacked the resources associated with kingship, could find himself deposed. A nigger[8] of the lowest category if he possessed the requisite capacity could rise to the rank of chief of a main house, and, in the case of Jaja Anna Pepple, to the rank of king.

Under the earlier political systems the office of head of the community is said to have been one for which the chief of any of its houses (wards) was eligible. Under the nineteenth century system this office was vested in a particular lineage and passed from founder to sons (provided they were able enough) and then to sons' sons. This office originally carried with it little additional authority except in ritual matters, the community head ranking as little more than the senior of a number of ward heads and performing the function of presiding over village council meetings and similar public gatherings. With the advent of European trading vessels the office which was now dignified by the European title of king developed into one of considerable power. The king represented the community in its external relations with other powers and he was the person to whom the Europeans looked to

---

[8]Dr. Jones earlier explains that this was the term used for slaves in the trading houses of the Niger Delta and is not meant in the pejorative sense as in the United States.

arrange the conditions under which they traded and to whom they paid trading dues or comey, which, in the early nineteenth century, amounted to a very considerable revenue. An able king could use his position to obtain favourable trading concessions from these Europeans, and so add to the wealth of his canoe house, and he could manipulate the distribution of comey in ways that would secure the maximum of political support from the heads of other houses. Although there was a royal lineage there was no royal house. The son who succeeded to the Kingship was already the chief of his own canoe house. While his father was alive, this canoe house was a subordinate house in the group which looked to the king's house as its main house. When the father died this group broke up and the new king's house expanded and became the main house of a new group of houses, which were derived from this house and not from his predecessor's.

Local traditions do not distinguish between the formal conciliar organization of these governments and their administrative and executive machinery. During the nineteenth century the distribution of power between the different parts of the system changed very radically so that by the end of the century most of it lay with chiefs of the dominant canoe house groups. This situation was then consolidated by the British consular government, which constituted a council consisting of the chiefs of main canoe houses as the local administrative and judicial authority. My informants were very much aware of this change but they tended to oversimplify it by saying that in the colonial period it was the chiefs who ruled, while in the period before it was the secret society, *Ekine*. It seems clear, however, that in internal matters each canoe house, and each canoe house group governed itself.

It was also possible throughout the region for an exceptionally able political leader to acquire sufficient power to become the recognized and de facto political head or chief of a ward or a village and less frequently of a whole community. This was frequent enough among the Northern Ibo for the position to become institutionalized under the title of *eze*, a term usually translated as king. Such a self-made chief might very well succeed to the traditional headship of a ward or village or of a community if he could satisfy the hereditary and other qualifications required for these offices. What they were unable to do in the hinterland was to establish this position of king and the political authority they had been able to associate with it, so that it became an office which passed to their descendants. In the Eastern Delta states things were different, thanks to the wealth brought by the overseas slave trade and to the organizational demands of this trade. In these states the qualifications required for succession to headship of a ward were not restrictive or exclusive. Any member was eligible provided he could trace his descent to the founder of the ward. It was therefore easy for an able and politically ambitious man if he were also a good business man, to accumulate sufficient wealth and with it a sufficient following to secure his election to the headship of his ward. It was also to the advantage of the ward in its competition with other wards to have at its head an able and powerful leader, and to support him in his efforts to secure election to the headship of the community. The political authority of a ward chief in these Oil River states thus tended to be greater than that of the corresponding ward or village heads of most hinterland communities.

At the same time the needs of the European traders produced an even more striking development in the power and authority of the head of the community. They expected to find, and to a very considerable extent they either found or developed in each of the Oil River states with which they traded, a supreme administrative head who had the authority to negotiate with them the conditions under which they conducted their trade, and the power to see that these conditions were adhered to by the members of this community. This person they called the king and to enable him to carry out these duties effectively they provided him with revenue in the form of comey (trading dues). It is clear that the heads of the other wards saw to it that they had a share in these duties and rewards, but it is also clear that the king was in a stronger position than they were in controlling their distribution. He was also able to use his position as the head of the community to obtain other "spoils of office" from the European supercargoes in the form of additional and superior gifts and trading advances and concessions. The office of king thus developed into one of considerable political authority. It involved the control of very considerable wealth by West African standards, and it enabled a man who was already wealthy and powerful when he attained the position of king to enhance his wealth and power still further. As the trade with Europeans increased so did the power and authority which could be exercised by the holder of this office, and the more valuable a prize did it become for the chiefs of competing wards.

Once a ward and its chief had obtained the Kingship however, the office tended to remain with it and with that chief's descendants. But this did not mean that there was a "royal ward" the chieftaincy of which went with the Kingship. During the time its chief was king a ward expanded and segmented into a number of sub-wards founded by the king's sons; on the king's death the princely chief of one of these succeeded to the throne while the other segments became separate and independent wards. When this second king died he was succeeded as king either by one of his brothers who was the chief of one of these independent wards, or, should his reign have been a long and a successful one, by one of his sons who was the chief of one of the sub-wards into which his, the second king's, ward had expanded. . . . Alternatively, if the expansion of a king's ward resulted in undue competition and conflict between would-be chiefs of its sub-wards, political fission replaced lineage segmentation. The cohesion of the ward was lost and the field was open for the chief of another ward to claim the Kingship. This is what seems to have happened in Kalabari when the Korome Ward or group of wards, which had been dominant in the time of King Owerri Daba, split and the Kingship passed to the Kamalu dynasty of the Endeme ward.

What were the sources of this superior power? Neither the African nor the European traditions tell us much about it. It is obvious, however, that one of the principal sources of this power was the control of the wealth which the king received as money from the European trading vessels. We do not know exactly how he disposed of this revenue but we can assume that a strong king would be able to exercise a greater control over its distribution than a weak one and that in the hands of an able king it would constitute a very powerful political weapon. There were also, particularly in the eighteenth and early nineteenth century, the standardized "gifts" made to the king by vessels on their arrival and departure, and there were later in the nineteenth century similar gifts made by agents of assumption and resumption of office. In addition to this there were other trading concessions which the king could expect to receive from supercargoes desirous of obtaining and retaining his "goodwill."

We can conclude from this that one of the main sources of a king's political authority derived from his control of wealth, this wealth being used to build up a power structure, directly through the enlargement of the king's own house group, indirectly by securing the goodwill and support of the heads of other groups. The wealth he was able to use for this purpose came from three sources, the state revenue (comey), the spoils of his office ("dashes" and trading concessions) and house funds, namely, the trading profits made by him as head of his house and the work bars, customs bars, and other contributions made by house members.

It is not only inaccurate but misleading to attempt to describe the political systems and the social structure of these Oil River states as they existed before the establishment of British Colonial rule in the form of a static model, whether based on a synchronic study of one phase of their development or on a general characterization that would perforce ignore and misrepresent the structural changes that occurred. It is equally unsatisfactory to regard them as systems in a state of oscillation between political systems of the group A and group B type. They appear to conform more closely to systems which pass through successive stages of accretion, segmentation, and fission. Whether power is concentrated in the hands of an "absolute monarch" or one who rules by maintaining a "balance of power"; whether power is in the hands of a leader of a particular ward who controls a puppet king or the Kingship is open to the head of any ward that may be temporarily dominant depends on which stage has been reached when the system is examined.

The political systems of communities in the Eastern Region of Nigeria can be said to belong to the same general type, one in which power is distributed between the primary segments of the community, that is the villages in the case of the Ibo, the village sections, wards, or canoe house groups in the case of the Ibibio and the Oil River states. In some of these systems, for example in those of the Northern Ibo, these segments are so structured that a balance of power is maintained between them and these can be distinguished as stable systems in which this balance of power remains relatively unaffected by the temporary political activities of political leaders. Others, notably those of the people we have been concerned with in this study, can be distinguished as unstable systems, in which the distribution of power in the system was upset by the intrusion of external factors. These factors made it possible for one of these segments and its leader to become unduly powerful so that the former structure of the segment or, in extreme cases, of the whole community was destroyed.

We can in the case of these states, identify the principal disturbing factors as the sudden access of wealth provided by the overseas slave trade, the recognition by the European traders of their village heads as kings and the association of this office of king with the control and distribution of very large trading dues.

We can also attribute the greater degree of instability which characterized the Eastern Delta states after this period to the increased wealth brought by the eighteenth century slave trade and to the increased warfare that accompanied it, which resulted in the replacement of the ward by the canoe house whose chieftaincy was open to the ablest members in the house without regard to their origin.

Suggestions for Further Reading

Bovill, E.W., *The Golden Trade of the Moors* (London: Oxford University Press, 1958).

Brenner, Louis, *The Shehus of Kukawa: A History of the al-Kanemi Dynasty of Bornu* (Oxford: The Clarendon Press, 1973).

Fage, J. D., "Some Thoughts on State Formation in the Western Sudan Before the Seventeenth Century," *Boston University Papers in African History* (Boston: Boston University Press, 1964).

Goody, Jack, "Feudalism in Africa," *The Journal of African History* 4, no. 1 (Cambridge: Cambridge University Press, 1963).

Maquet, Jacques, "A Research Definition of African Feudality," *The Journal of African History* 2, no. 2 (Cambridge University Press, 1962).

Marcus, Harold G. *A History of Ethiopia* (Berkeley: University of California Press, 1994).

Miller, Joseph, *Kings and Kinsmen: Early Mbundu States in Angola* (Oxford: Clarendon Press, 1976).

Reyna, S.P., *Wars Without End: The Political Economy of a Precolonial African State* (Hanover, N.H.: University Press of New England, 1990).

Spaulding, Jay, *The Heroic Age in Sennar* (East Lansing: Michigan State University Press, 1985).

Thornton, John K. *The Kingdom of Kongo: Civil War and Transition, 1641–1718* (Madison, Wis.: University of Wisconsin Press, 1983).

Trimingham, J.S., *A History of Islam in West Africa* (London: Oxford University Press, 1962).

Vansina, Jan, *The Children of Woot: A History of the Kuba Peoples* (Madison, Wis.: University of Wisconsin Press, 1978).

Wilks, Ivor, *Asante in the Nineteenth Century: The Structure and Evolution of a Political Order* (London: Cambridge University Press, 1975).

PROBLEM IV
ISLAM IN AFRICA

Islam came to the Sudan during the fourteenth century from the Maghrib, across the trade routes of the Sahara. There on the vast grassland plains of the Sahil it was carried southward by Muslim merchants and teachers who integrated themselves into the African community, accommodating Islam to the customs and traditions of the western Sudan.

The religious example of these Muslim traders or *dyula* came to be emulated by the traders of the Western Sudan. These new converts soon found themselves wielding influence within the state of Ghana, and later played a role in the development of the states of Mali and Songhay. Islam eventually became the religion of the ruling and trading classes, and by the eighteenth century was making inroads in converting people who resided outside of urban centers.

When the Islamic world experienced a religious renaissance in the eighteenth and nineteenth centuries the growing Muslim community in West Africa underwent a religious revival that profoundly changed its Islamic character. The tolerant and accommodating ways of the past were replaced by an uncompromising and militant determination to adhere to the one true faith as defined in the Quran. As a result of these reform movements, begun by the Islamic religious brotherhoods and spearheaded by Islamic ethnic groups on the Saharan fringe, Islam came to the nonbelievers in the south.

The jihad became the motor for the spread of Islamic influence throughout the western Sudan. These wars began in the early eighteenth century and continued into the colonial era. Perhaps the most successful, and most significant jihad was that of the Fulani cleric Shehu Usman Dan Fodio in Hausaland (located in modern Nigeria) in 1804. By the time it ended six years later the Shehu had created the powerful Caliphate at Sokoto and confirmed the rule of Islamic law and government. Historians have studied the Shehu's jihad in an effort to answer broader questions regarding the spread of Islam in Africa. How did the jihad expand Islam? What were the motives of its leaders and followers? What did these movements accomplish? The answers to these questions cast light on the appeal of Islam, and the impact it had on the peoples of Africa.

Mervyn Hiskett's introduction to *The Sword of Truth* places the jihad of Usman Dan Fodio in its historical context, establishing the social, ethnic, religious, and geographical setting in which the movement arose. Hiskett attributes the success of the Shehu's jihad to the potency of his religious message, and the favorable ideological climate in which it was received. The eighteenth century found the passive attitude of the Muslim literati gradually changing. Slowly from within this group individuals emerged for whom life within a pagan community became increasingly intolerable. These clerical leaders began asserting their claim to act as arbiters of personal and social morality, a claim they based on their exclusive ability to interpret the Quran. Their dissatisfaction with life in the Hausa kingdoms as it contrasted with their Islamic ideal paved the way for the reformist movement of Shehu Usman dan Fodio. Hiskett locates the Shehu's movement within the broader framework of Islam's inexorable spread throughout the western Sudan. At this time the powerful appeal of Islamic culture enabled it to penetrate into remote areas previously removed from the Islamic political or religious community.

In "The Jihad of Shehu Dan Fodio: Some Problems," M. G. Smith examines the historiography of the Shehu's jihad and the Sokoto Caliphate. Smith finds that the divergent views of historians (such as Hiskett) with others' conclusions regarding the jihad to be "so opposed that instinctively one suspects the truth—that is, the historical reality of the jihad—to lie somewhere in between." Historians have failed to appreciate the jihad's tremendous complexity. While the Shehu's spiritual fervor was unquestionably sincere, such leadership can only succeed in an environment receptive to rebellion. In any event, the Shehu's cause became overshadowed by the myriad motives of his followers. Smith believes that opposition between Muslims and non-Muslims became confused from the earliest moments of the jihad by other factors such as ethnicity, kinship, secular and political resentments and loyalties, calculations of advantage, and communal solidarities and antagonisms. These latent hostilities and cleavages between Muslim and heathen, pastoralist and farmer, immigrant and indigenous people, Fulani and Hausa, all found expression in the jihad. These considerations often obscured the Shehu's sincere religious principles. Smith concludes that the very nature of the Islamic concept of jihad dictated the form the Shehu's jihad had to take if it were to succeed. His jihad was ambiguous because the concept is intrinsically ambiguous. Therefore, the Shehu's jihad was typical of all the jihads of this period because the pursuit of political advantage is a general feature of all jihads undertaken against "heathen" rulers.

M. O. Junaid argues conversely that historians who concentrate on the social and ethnic elements of the conflict ignore the reality of the jihad: that it was inspired and followed predominantly because of sincere religious convictions. He examines the Shehu's writings for evidence of the religious rather than the social basis of his movement. Junaid states that these texts' religious character, and the Shehu's subsequent establishment of an Islamic state ruled by the Sharia in Sokoto, evince the true motivations of the jihadists. Historians concentrating on social considerations misunderstand the religious nature of the social questions: the Hausa's social and political practices were as contrary to Islamic religious standards as were their pagan rites. Junaid maintains that the jihad cannot be attributed to a dichotomy between the supporters and opponents of Dan Fodio, based entirely on ethnic or tribal lines. He concludes that the nineteenth century jihad movement in Hausaland was launched mainly to revive Islam and to establish an ideal Muslim state fashioned after the historic state of Islam in the seventh century.

Peter Waterman, in "The Jihad in Hausaland as an Episode in African History," states that analyses that emphasize one determinant factor cannot satisfactorily explain the jihad, and studies like Junaid's that isolate the religious element in particular have been surpassed by more historically sophisticated approaches. Waterman's article attempts to explain the jihad within the process of historical developments, from which he believes historians have removed them. He examines the views of historians who have concentrated on either the social, economic, ethnic, or ideological elements of the jihad, and finds each approach inadequate. Studies that focus on the social dynamics of the jihad have been either too broadly or narrowly framed, while ethnically oriented research has shown that the ethnic element was a marginal rather than a central cause of the conflict. But neither does he accept the explanation of historians, such as Smith, who vaguely assert that several "latent hostilities" combined to spark the movement. Waterman believes that historians must first understand the economic structure prevailing in Hausaland before and after the jihad before they can determine the movement's causes and effects. Once this is identified (he calls this structure the "African mode of production") the relevant social, ideological, and ethnic dimensions of the jihad become explicable. The jihad occurred when the existing raiding economy came into conflict with the expanding economy based on long distance trade with Europe. He concludes "the jihad can probably be interpreted as a crisis within society based on the tributary mode of production that led to changes in the ethnic relationships, advances in political organisation, and development in the economy through increased trading and raiding, and through increased exploitation of servile labour agriculture. Changes, advances and developments, then, not a social revolution." Al Haj Umar, one of the most formidable of the leaders of militant Islam in nineteenth century Africa, would not have agreed.

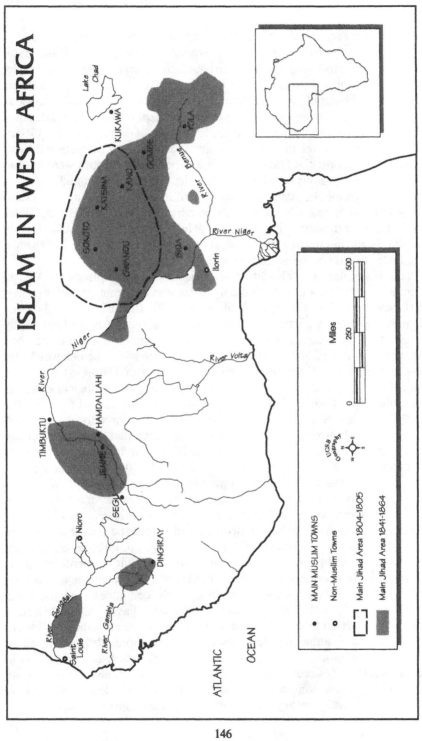

ISLAM IN WEST AFRICA

Lake Chad

KUKAWA

KOLA

GOMBE

KATSINA · KANO

SOKOTO

GWANDU

River Benue

BIDA

River Niger

Ilorin

Niger

River Volta

River

HAMDALLAHI

TIMBUKTU

JENNE

SEGU

Nioro

DINGIRAY

River Senegal

River Gambia

Saint Louis

ATLANTIC

OCEAN

UCSB GEOGRAPHY

MAIN MUSLIM TOWNS

Non-Muslim Towns

Main Jihad Area 1804-1805

Main Jihad Area 1841-1864

Miles

0   250   500

The Sword of Truth
MERVYN HISKETT[1]

At the turn of the eighteenth to the nineteenth century a revolutionary movement arose in Hausaland (now part of northern Nigeria) that was to have a profound influence on the subsequent history of the area. At its center was a man who bore the Hausa name Shehu Usuman dan Fodio—the Shaikh 'Uthman, son of Fodio. The movement he led, and the successful jihad, or holy war, he fought to reform Islam in Hausaland, brought about important changes in this part of Africa. This book is about the history of his movement and the effects it had on the subsequent development of Hausa society.

The Early History of Hausaland

The Hausas are not a tribal group. They are a community of people of various ethnic origins who speak a common language—Hausa. They emerged as a result of migration from the north into the western Sudan, probably in the tenth century AD, although the sources, of which the most important is the Kano Chronicle, may be chronologically unreliable. These immigrants mixed with the indigenous inhabitants, who were pagan hunter-gatherers, and after the lapse of several generations established mastery over them. The hunter-gatherers at the time the immigrants arrived lived in dispersed hamlets, were organized on a clan basis, and were not subject to any central authority. But the immigrants built walled towns and set up city-states that controlled the surrounding countryside and thus territorial boundaries were acquired.

By the first half of the fifteenth century Hausaland was partially under the control of Bornu—allegedly an Islamic state since AD 1085—to the extent that, during the reign of Dauda (1421–1438), a Bornu prince arrived in Kano City at the head of a large army. He appears to have been a "Resident" representing the Bornu interest, and the Kano Chronicle suggests that tribute in slaves may have been paid to Bornu at this time. But by the end of

---

[1]Hiskett, Mervyn, *The Sword of Truth: the Life and Times of Shehu Usuman dan Fodio* (New York: Oxford University Press, 1973), pp. 3–11.

Mervyn Hiskett is the author of several books on Nigeria and Islam. His most recent book is *The Development of Islam in West Africa*.

the fifteenth century whatever power Bornu had over Hausaland had declined. The enduring legacy of this period was the introduction of some Islamic words into the Hausa language, and Bornuese titles into Habe government; also perhaps, some fragments of Islamic law.

By the sixteenth century a homogeneous people was in being, with a common language, and it is probably early in this century that they acquired the label Hausa. According to their legends of origin, seven true Hausa states had by then emerged—Kano, Daura, Rano, Katsina, Zazzau, Gobir, and Garutt Gabas. They were associated through kinship ties and trade links, with seven others, known somewhat disdainfully as "the bastard seven," who were not Hausa by blood but who followed a way of life similar to that of the Hausas. These were: Kebbi, Zamfara, Nupe, Gwari, Yauri, Yoruba, and Kwararafa.

In the sixteenth century the Saharan empire of Songhai extended its conquests into Hausaland. Kano, Katsina, and Zaria became formally subject to it and paid tribute. But the power of Songhai lapsed and by the seventeenth century a warlike people from the Benue area, called the Kwararafa, had conquered part of Hausaland, including Kano. They in turn receded, and by the eighteenth century a number of virtually independent kingdoms had emerged, each under the discrete and arbitrary rule of a Hausa or Habe chief. Some of these were nominally Muslims; but most did little more than extend patronage to Muslim scholars and traders in and around their courts. By the middle of the eighteenth century the extent of the Habe kingdoms was . . . broadly from the river Niger eastward to the river Jamaari; and from a point just south of the Saharan town of Agades southward down to the river Benue.

While these shifts of power and ethnic developments were taking place, yet another group of people were establishing themselves in Hausaland: the Fulani, a nomadic people whose early records show them to have lived in the medieval Saharan kingdom of Mali. As early as c. 1450 certain Fulani clans migrated from Mali into Hausaland. In the reign of Yakubu of Kano (1452–1463) a party of Fulani visited that city. Most of them seem to have continued on to Bornu but some stayed and settled in Hausaland. Gradually their numbers increased, until by the end of the eighteenth century there was a considerable Fulani population in the area, consisting both, of nomadic cattle-raising clans and the sedentary clan of the clerical Toronkawa. As will be seen, their presence proved to be of profound importance.

The Establishment of Islam in Hausaland

The religion of Islam may have penetrated into Hausaland as early as the fourteenth century AD, for there is some evidence of Islamic names in the king-lists of that time. But it was not until the end of the fifteenth century that an Islamic presence was firmly and unmistakably established. Traditionally, Islam's law and constitution are said to have been brought by a North African cleric, Muhammad al-Maghili (d. 1504). In fact, it is likely that this was the result of a more complex pattern of events made up of influences from Islamic Bornu, and the impact of North African, and later Egyptian, Islamic culture, brought in across the Sahara desert by the penetration of the medieval desert trade routes down into sub-Saharan Africa.

But although Islam was established by 1500, it was certainly not generally accepted. What seems to have happened is that individual Muslims from the peripheral areas of North Africa and Egypt—traders seeking the gold and slaves of the Sudan, and scholars after the lucrative patronage of the courts—came into the Habe kingdoms and settled. They formed the nuclei of small Islamic communities that gradually began to affect the surrounding animist culture of the native people. The first stage was the nominal acceptance of Islam by some of the chiefs and courtiers. But this amounted to, little more than the adoption of Islamic names in addition to indigenous titles, and participation in certain Islamic rites—for instance, the annual sacrifices—and perhaps attendance at Friday mosque. This much identification with Islam was regarded as prestigious by the chiefs' still-pagan subjects. But they were certainly not prepared to see their traditional cults wholly abandoned; and the chiefs were probably unable to accept Islam wholeheartedly even had they wished to do so. The result was that the two cultures existed side by side, and sometimes merged to produce "mixed" Islam—some Islamic practices carried on with animist customs and rites.

As for the representatives of Islam, they began to widen their circles and make converts among the indigenous people. In this way coteries of native scholars grew up in certain urban centers of Hausaland—particularly Kano and Katsina. These scholars were, of course, literates in an otherwise preliterate society; and this gave them the status and power of an elite. They functioned in such roles as court astrologers, religious teachers, scribes, Islamic rainmakers, military advisers, and physicians. Their literacy was seen as evidence of superior magic, and the local rulers valued their presence at court for the prestige it brought. The scholars seem to have acquiesced quite readily in this comfortable situation. Only occasionally did one of them have enough courage to protest the mixing of Islam with paganism. While the careers of such activists were sometimes spectacular, their tangible achievements were few; although occasionally, as in the case of al-Maghili, their writings did become important sources of ideas for future generations. But usually they were content to follow a life of scholarship and to study the books brought in across the Sahara from North Africa and Egypt. Then they themselves began to write. Soon they produced a corpus of local Islamic literature written in classical Arabic—the liturgical and legal language of the Islamic religion—from which it is clear that by the first half of the seventeenth century the small Islamic communities were fully at home in the intellectual world of Islam, and therefore not so far removed from the ideas and attitudes of late medieval and Renaissance European Christendom. But, of course, in Hausaland, as in Europe at an equivalent stage of intellectual development, such scholarship was the preserve of a tiny minority and its impact on the lives of ordinary people was slight. It did, nevertheless, have some significant consequences. The existence of literacy in Arabic and the Hausa-speaking areas meant that the themes of early Islamic history, the tales of the Prophet Muhammad, and much of Middle Eastern folklore as it was recorded in Arabic sources must have begun late in oral form, far beyond the circle of those who were able to read Arabic books. The results of this can be seen in the strong Islamic coloring in Hausa folktales. Also, it is likely that Islamic astrology and various forms of Islamic divination and fortune-telling were also sifted down to a popular level as early as the seventeenth century, when they began to enter the culture of the animist population. The sources are insufficiently informative to prove this conclusively, however.

The Beginnings of the Islamic Reform Movement

The generally passive attitude of the Muslim literati changed, slowly but perceptibly. For there began to emerge from among them individuals, by now deeply influenced by Islamic ideology and conditioned by an Islamic literate culture and scholarly disciplines, for whom the surrounding pagan way of life became increasingly offensive. One of the earliest manifestations of their pious discontent occurred in Kano, during the early seventeenth century, when two native Islamic theologians energetically disputed with each other as to whether or not the customs and behavior of the nomadic Fulani: for instance the games they played in the bush; the ritual flogging by which young men were initiated into full membership of the tribe; and almost certainly the "bundling" that was part of their courtship ceremonies—[all] were compatible with Islam. By the end of the eighteenth century the increasingly urgent tone of Islamic disapproval became apparent in a number of works in which Muslim scholars pointed accusing fingers at local un-Islamic customs and behavior and urged the adoption of Islamic alternatives. The kinds of things they objected to were the idolatrous rites of animism—sacrifices and libations to various objects of worship; failure to observe the Islamic food prohibitions and prohibited degrees of marriage; the survival of inheritance through the female line in defiance of Islamic law prescribing inheritance through the male line. They also frequently expressed puritanical disgust at the bawdy songs of the Hausas and their addiction to dance and traditional music; while the bombastic formal praise-singing of the Habe courts struck these ardent monotheists as both idolatrous (according to the strict teaching of Islam, only God and the Prophet Muhammad are worthy of such unbounded praise) and vainglorious. For instance, a certain Shaikh Jibril b. 'Umar, a scholar noted for his zeal and doctrinal rigor, and an early teacher of the Shehu Usuman dan Fodio, complained that many of his contemporaries confessed Islam "with an ample mouth" but at the same time hypocritically continued to practise pagan customs and rites. Particularly offensive to him was what he called "nakedness with women" by which he meant failure to adopt the lengthy Muslim robe and the veils as well, of course, as the un-Islamic practice of the mingling of the sexes in public, at celebrations, dances, and the like. Another of his accusations was that people who claimed to be Muslims made their own rules concerning private and public behavior instead of referring to the learned scholars for an authoritative ruling. Here, of course, he was asserting the ancient and persistent claim of the clerics in Islam to be the sole arbiters of personal and social morality, on the grounds that they alone could interpret divine revelation correctly.

This mounting dissatisfaction with life as it was in the Habe kingdoms, as contrasted with the Islamic ideal, ushered in the movement of the Fulani reformer, Shehu Usuman dan Fodio, and his associates, a group of scholars who were among the most able and articulate of the dissenting intellectuals.

The Shehu, who was a descendant of the early Fulani settlers in Hausaland in the fifteenth century, spent his youth in the devout pursuit of Islamic religious education, and his early manhood in preaching teaching, and authorship. His frustration and that of his companions and pupils at their continued failure to achieve their ends by argument eventually persuaded them to use force. The result was the Fulani jihad, or holy war, which in the end gave them control of most of Hausaland. The story of his life is largely that of the events that led up to this holy war, the war itself, and the immediate sequel to it, all of which it will be the task of subsequent chapters to record. But first, it is necessary to continue the introductory account of the history of the area down to more recent times. For it is against the subsequent history of the Hausas that the true significance of the Shehu's life is to be judged.

The Fulani Caliphate of Sokoto

The jihad or holy war, which erupted in Hausaland during the early years of the nineteenth century, under the Shehu's leadership, was an event of great importance. It swept away the majority of the Habe states leaving only a few rump kingdoms, such as Maradi and Daura Zango. In the place of the Habe chiefs the Shehu appointed his own flag bearers—that is, his senior lieutenants—as emirs (Arabic, amir = army commander) over the conquered kingdoms. Muhammad Bello, the Shehu's second son and successor as caliph, or Islamic ruler, later founded the city of Sokoto on the site of what was previously a small hamlet. The new walled city became the administrative capital from which the Fulani empire was governed.

The Fulani now claimed authority over nearly all Hausaland and extended their political influence westward, across the river Niger into Gurma, and southward to the river Benue, which marked the farthest point of their initial expansion. They did not subdue Bornu; although they fought several campaigns in an attempt to do so. But they did eventually spread to the southeast, to what is now Adamawa. They protected their empire by a screen of *ribats* or border fortresses, behind which they strove to create a society modeled according to an ideal Islamic pattern, as they interpreted this from Islamic history and literature. Yet they were not entirely secure behind their ramparts. In the west their power over the lands across the river Niger fell away because their arm was not long enough to reach that far; while the people of Kebbi remained in constant revolt, in the end winning virtual independence of Sokoto. From the north they were constantly harassed by the Habe, who had been driven out but not destroyed, and who remained vigorously bent on revenge. This situation had its effect upon the outlook and ethos of the Fulani, as well as upon their military dispositions. They became a closed, exclusive society whose members saw their survival not only in terms of maintaining their frontiers, but also the strict orthodoxy of their religion and the hierarchical structure of their feudal organizations. Their hold, both physical and ideological, was firm enough over the towns within their empire, many of which grew up around the ribats. In the more distant bush areas, however, it remained tenuous and large groups of animists continued to live in virtual independence. Yet so powerful was the appeal of Islamic culture that its influences penetrated even to these remote areas, and a process of Islamic acculturalization, as distinct from direct conversion and political allegiance to the Islamic state, became steadily more pervasive.

The first Fulani rulers were forceful men with considerable administrative ability. And during the period of their rule the nature of their government, and of society in general, was more in conformity with the Shari'a or Islamic legal and social code, than it had been under the Habe. In later generations, however, it became increasingly difficult to contain the dynastic and tribal rivalries that the jihad had pushed into the background; but which now began to emerge again to weaken the solidarity and strength of the empire. Nevertheless, the caliph's moral authority proved sufficient to surmount these difficulties, and the core of the empire remained intact. It was the situation that developed in the newly conquered territories of the south that, in the end, proved the most dangerous.

Unlike the western, northern, and eastern borders, the southern border of the Sokoto empire had always remained open. For the threat from the fragmented pagan tribes that inhabited the wooded country of the river

Benue was negligible and the area offered scope for the more restless scions of the Sokoto dynasty to carve out new kingdoms and enrich themselves by slave-raiding. One who took ample advantage of such opportunities was Umaru Nagwamatse, a restless, turbulent son of Abubakar Atiku, the second caliph of Sokoto. In 1859 he established himself in the hitherto unconquered pagan enclave to the southeast of Sokoto and set up the emirate of Kontagora. He and his successors ruled as robber barons nominally in allegiance to Sokoto, but in fact too powerful to be disciplined by the central authority. Together with their Nupe allies they ravaged Gwariland and southern Zaria by constant, indiscriminate slave-raiding against Muslim and pagan alike, and Sokoto was unable to restrain them. It was their excesses that proved disastrous for the caliph, and not any action for which he himself was directly responsible.

The Jihad of Shehu Dan Fodio
M. G. SMITH[2]

Among universalistic religions, Islam is distinguished by its emphasis on war as a means of spreading the Faith. Where likely to succeed, such war is a duty for the Faithful, and it was largely due to the zealous prosecution of this profitable duty by its adherents that Islam spread as far and fast as it did. During the eighteenth and nineteenth centuries the western Sudan experienced a succession of these jihads. Beginning in 1725 at Futa Toro, this wave of militant Islam was halted only by the French occupation. The leaders of all these recent West African jihads were Torodbe clerics from Futa Toro, who are usually classed as Fulani. Perhaps the most successful of these Torodbe jihads was that which Shehu Usumanu dan Fodio (also called Shaikh 'Uthman ibn-Fodiye) launched against the Hausa chiefs of Gobir, Katsina, Zaria, Daura, their allies and congeners, in 1804. In six years of hard fighting the Shehu's followers overran these ancient states and passed beyond to carve out new chiefdoms in areas where no states had previously existed. Thereafter the northwestern segment of what is now Nigeria has remained under the control of the Shehu's successors and their lieutenants. This dar al-Islam has been ruled mainly by Fulani Muslims. By 1840 it extended from Adamawa in the North Cameroons to Illo on the Niger, from Adar in the North to Ilorin on the borders of Yorubaland.

Assessments of this jihad have always varied. According to J. S. Trimingham, dan Fodio "from 1786 preached the jihad in such a way that it became a racial as well as a religious war; [it] . . . differs from the other jihads on account of the number of nomads who joined in." For S. J. Hogben:

> Religion was often made the pretext for the acquisition of worldly power . . . that had as its confessed object the purification of the Muslim religion, and it was directed against the corrupt rulers of Hausaland, who had been supposedly oppressing or ignoring the rights of their Muslim subjects. In reality, it was originally a national fight of the Fulani, both Muslim and pagan, against the forces of Yunfa, the king of Gobir, who had decreed

---

[2]Smith, M. G., "The Jihad of Shehu Dan Fodio: Some Problems," in *Islam in Tropical Africa*, I. W. Lewis, ed. (London, published by the Oxford University Press for the International African Institute, 1966), pp. 408–19.

M. G. Smith is the Crosby Professor of Human Environment at Yale University.

their extermination. Only after the victory, when the pagan Fulani
who had borne more than their full share in order to achieve it,
had retired to their flocks and herds, did the malams who had
been the leaders, exploit the opportunity under cloak of religion
to oust the native rulers and put themselves into their places,
with Usuman dan Fodio at their head. Henceforth the movement
was no longer confined to a particular race; yet from its very
nature it appealed most strongly to the fanatical and more highly-
strung element in the Fulani clans.

For W. F. Gowers, on the other hand:

> The *jihad* was the raising of the standard of revolt by Othman
> dan Fodio against the tyranny of the non-Moslem rulers of Gobir,
> in defence of his co-religionists whether Hausa or Fulani. It was
> not in any sense a conquest of the Hausa race by the Fulani;
> indeed, the Hausa adherents of Othman were probably as numer-
> ous as his Fulani followers. Even the leaders were not, strictly
> speaking, Fulanis. The Torabbe or Toronkawa (the tribe from
> which Shehu dan Fodio came) owe their origin to a mixture of
> the Jolof . . . element. They are blacker in colour than most Fu-
> lanis . . . they originally spoke the Wa-Kore language and are
> connected with the Suleibawa, who, like the Torabbe are not Fu-
> lani—if there is any such thing as a pure Fulani race.

Trimingham observes that Torodbe or Tokolor and Suleibawa are regarded
as *rimbe,* assimilated free groups, but not as Fulbe proper.

Sir Ahmadu Bello, Sardauna of Sokoto, the late Premier of Northern
Nigeria and a descendant of Shehu dan Fodio, has recently affirmed the
"official" Fulani view.

> The Shehu Usumanu was a Fulani leader . . . a great preacher
> and man of the utmost piety . . . [he] was among a people who
> were nominally Muhammadan; . . . the religion had become very
> corrupt, and many pagan practices had crept in and had taken
> firm hold even in the highest quarters. The Shehu Usuman de-
> clared a Holy War against the polluters of the Faith. In 1804 he
> started by attacking the Chief of Gobir, one of the worst offend-
> ers, in whose territory he was living . . . . Meanwhile, to cleanse
> the religion, the Shehu had organised revolts in all the great Hausa
> states; the Fulani living in them rose and overthrew the Hausa
> king. The Shehu appointed new rulers, either from among the
> victorious generals, or from among other important Fulani.

There are also other popular interpretations, radical and dissident. In one view, the jihad was a political revolution against oppression and misrule; in another it was a cloak for racial conquest and imperialism.

These differing interpretations raise some important problems which can only be treated allusively here. As Trimingham observes, "the history of the *jihad* of 'Uthman dan Fodio and of the Fulani states has yet to be written." Until this is done, and perhaps even afterwards, it may be wiser to suspend judgement between these conflicting views. They are in any case fully intelligible only in context. The late Sardauna saw himself as heir and custodian of a great and vital tradition derived from Shehu Usumanu. In 1959 those young Muslims who stressed the radical view of Shehu's *jihad* also advocated radical reforms in the Emirates of Northern Nigeria which were founded by this jihad. Others, with a dissident view of the *jihad,* preferred the wholesale elimination of the old regime and of the traditional Fulani ruling stratum. As we have seen, assessments of the Shehu's *jihad* made by British administrators who have worked in this area are very similar to these Nigerian views. Such divergent opinions might well reflect differing personal appraisals of the Fulani performance as a ruling stratum, *since* the *jihad* and especially during this century.

Despite such contextualization, these differing viewpoints present important problems. Together, they obstruct and might well deny that an impartial historical account of these events is possible; yet the viewpoints are so opposed that instinctively one suspects the truth—that is, the historical reality of the *jihad*—to lie somewhere in between. What remains problematic is whether such "historical truth" can be discovered at this stage, or would get a fair hearing if it were. Clearly, an individual's view of this *jihad* is closely related to his ideological preference and his personal experience of recent Fulani administration. Traditionalists, Muslim or British, have tended to see the jihad as a genuine attempt to purify and spread Islam in this region. While admitting many subsequent lapses by its supporters and custodians, they argue that its historical effect was overwhelmingly beneficent in various ways; and that fairly moderate reforms, which will preserve and realize the spirit and aims of the *jihad* more effectively, are all that is necessary. Radicals and dissidents, who view the *jihad* as a revolutionary or imperialist war, derive quite different consequences which correspond with their ideology and personal experience. The British parallels to these Nigerian views strongly suggest that political involvement in North Nigerian affairs underlies all these conflicting interpretations. If so, this also seems to reduce the likelihood of an impartial historical account and assessment of the *jihad,* since this presupposes such knowledge and experience of the area that some sense of personal commitment is likely. Indeed, it may be unavoidable, since the *jihad,* whatever its merits or demerits, has had a decisive political impact on the region, and still exercises a predominant influence on current policy.

It is clearly unsound to seek an understanding of the course of this struggle, or the motives of its actors, in events which occurred long after the conflict had ended, but one suspects this retrospective interpretation to be rather common. Since the events of 1804–1810 are fundamental to the present political order, there is scant hope that they will escape such ideological interpretation, or even that their presentation will proceed unaffected by political considerations, future and present as well as past. There is no doubt that the ruling Fulani, particularly in Sokoto Province, have actively nourished and reinterpreted the memory of this *jihad,* and especially the charisma of Shehu dan Fodio, in ways politically serviceable to their rule. The Shehu's books and writings, some of which might well be politically explosive, even today, have long been difficult for commoners and subjects, especially Habe, to come by. In their new independence and Federal political context the Northern rulers might now see fit to distribute them widely. Early British administrators, such as H. G. Harris, F. Edgar, Major Burdon, E. J. Arnett, and Sir H. R. Palmer, had access to various writings of primarily historical interest, such as *Tazyin al-Waraqat,* by 'Abdullahi dan Fodio, the *Tazyin al-Ikhwan,* by Shehu Usumanu, and the *Infaq al-Maysur* by Sultan Mamman Bello. The great majority of free subjects in the Fulani empire were illiterate, and may hardly have known these titles, much less their contents. As late as 1959, Hausa Arabists in Northern Nigeria were surprised to learn of Shehu Usumanu's *Kitab al-farq* and *Bayan wujub al-hijra 'ala al-'ibad.* Yet it is clear from internal evidence that the Shehu intended these books for a wide public. No accurate assessment of Usumanu's jihad can ignore these critical documents. As political testaments, they rank with Lugard's Political Memoranda.

A further problem which these conflicting viewpoints raise concerns the nature of this jihad and of the jihad as a general form of Islamic expansion. Jihads fall into two main classes: revolts by Muslims against their non-Muslim rulers; and attacks by Muslims organized in autonomous political units against non-Muslims. The historically notable jihads are those which succeeded; but providing that over conditions are fulfilled, unsuccessful attacks might well be included.

The character of the Fulani jihad of Northern Nigeria is disputed mainly because it was launched against rulers who claimed to be Muslim, although undoubtedly lax in their observances. As the Sardauna put it, "the Shehu Usumanu declared a Holy War against the polluters of the Faith"; that is, an armed rebellion aimed at enforcing correct observance of Islamic ritual and law. Much of the debate about the legitimacy of this jihad derives from the fact that it was a revolt against chiefs who were formally Muslim.

This problem receives extensive treatment in Shehu Usumanu's *Bayan Wujub al-Hijra,* especially section 1, 4–6, 12, 16, 31, 46–7. Citing a wide range of Muslim authorities, Koranic texts and traditions, the Shehu carefully distinguishes the various contexts in which jihad is obligatory or unlaw-

ful, and the rules which regulate it. He begins by discussing the obligation
of hijra—that is, for Muslims to withdraw from the lands of the heathen.
Except for the physically disabled, this obligation is shown to be unconditional. Shehu argues that:

> Withdrawal from the town of the heathen is an essential duty,
> both in the Koran and the Traditions, and in the consensus of the
> learned. . . . Now the capital cities of the Sudan are included in
> the towns of the heathen; . . . these cities fall into three
> classes. . . . In one class of these towns, paganism predominates
> and Islam is very weak, for instance . . . Mossi, Gurma, Bussa,
> Borgu, Dagomba, Yoruba . . . and Gombe. The rulers of these
> countries are all heathen, and so too . . . their subjects. . . . An-
> other class of towns are those in which Islam is dominant and
> there is little paganism; but the countries of Bornu, Kano, Kat-
> sina, Songhai and Malle, as Ahmed Baba shows, . . . all these
> are heathen states without any doubt, since the chiefs . . . are
> heathens like the first group, although they practise religion of
> Islam, because they are polytheists also. They have obstructed
> the way of Islam, and have put worldly standards before the Faith.
> In the view of all the 'ulama, all this is simply heathen.

With these arguments, Shehu justifies his flight of 21 February 1804 from
Degel in Gobir territory to Gudu near Kwonni just over the boundary, and
also his summons to other Muslims to withdraw from the (heathen) Hausa
states. In the *Infaq al-maysur,* Sultan Mamman Bello, the Shehu's son and
successor, devotes more space to the documentation of heathen practices
among rulers of Hausaland and Bornu, and also reproduces the correspondence between the Shehu and himself, on the one hand, and the Shaikn
Al haji Aminu al Kanemi, who defended Bornu, concerning this charge of
heathenism and the countercharge of an illegitimate "jihad" on the other.
    The charge of Heathenism seems crucial to the legitimacy of this jihad,
since the general weight of Muslim authorities prohibits rebellions against
unjust or tyrannous chiefs, provided they observe Islam. The Shehu writes
that:

> The Prophet said . . . "he who obeys my Representative undoubt-
> edly obeys me also; he who disobeys my Representative undoubt-
> edly disobeys me also" . . . . Subki says "it is unlawful to
> withdraw allegiance from the ruler. All agree on this if the ruler
> is righteous, and even when he is not righteous this is the better
> opinion, that is, unless he becomes a heretic (muntazil)." Ahmadu
> Zaruk says "It is forbidden to withdraw allegiance from a ruler,
> either in speech or in deed, and this consensus extends to praying
> under all rulers and their officials, good and bad alike."

For the classification of heathen, the Shehu relies on Muhammad al-Magh-ili's Epistle to the Askia:

> There are three classes of heathen; first those who are clearly heathen by descent; second, the man who has been a Muslim, and then openly apostatized, returning to heathendom and aban-doning Islam. His apostasy is quite open and he declares it with his own mouth; . . . third, there is the one who claims he is a Muslim while we for our part classify him as a heathen because that which does not occur apart from heathenism occurs with him openly.

It was the substance of Shehu's and Bello's charges that the Hausa rulers of their day fell into this third category; that for this reason the withdrawal of Muslims from their kingdoms was obligatory, since the Prophet said "he who associates with the heathen or lives with them is just like them"; and thus, that a Holy War against them was obligatory as well as legitimate.

Besides the evidence which Shehu and Mamman Bello cite themselves, observations by Landeroin in the Hausa successor-states of Tsibiri (Gobir), Maradi, and Tasawa (Katsina), and the recent account of Abuja, to which the Zaria Hausa retired, tend to support this charge of heathenism, while emphasizing that the Hausa rulers were formally Muslim. Shehu argues also that:

> Holy War becomes obligatory under three conditions. Firstly, on the orders of the (Muslim) ruler. . . . Secondly, if the enemy launch a sudden attack on Muslim territory. . . . Thirdly, to res-cue captured Muslims from the hands of the heathen.

The relevance of these doctrinal points is shown by the following outline of events which precipitated the jihad of 1804. For some year previously an uneasy situation had prevailed in the dominions of Gobir, where Shehu lived and taught, and where there were also many Fulani, some Muslim and seden-tary, others pagan and nomad. Some time around 1802 the Sarkin (Chief of) Gobir proclaimed "that no one should be a Muslim unless his father had been one; and that without permission no man could wear a turban nor any woman a veil." Bello says, "Nothing . . . caused us so much fear as this proclamation. When Shehu saw the number of his assemblies and their de-sire to withdraw from the infidels and to begin the jihad, he began to urge them to prepare weapons for one year; and we set to prepare it." Nafata died shortly after, and was succeeded by Yunfa, who pressed the anti-Mus-lim policy. In December 1803, at the request of his officials, Yunfa sent a force against a group of Arewa tribesmen who had accepted Shehu's teach-

ing and leadership, under their head, 'Abdusallasni. Following Natafa's proclamation and Gobir harassments, these non-Fulani converts had already
withdrawn from Gobir territory to Gimbana, a site in the Kebbi chiefdom
from which they originally came. They were ordered by Yunfa to return to
Gobir, but refused unless the Shehu expressly ordered this. Gimbana was
then overrun by Yunfa's troops during the fast of Ramadan; its surviving
occupants were captured and escorted towards Alkalawa, the capital of
Gobir. 'Abdusallami, the Gimbana leader, escaped with some of his closest
aides to a Fulani settlement near by.

> The Sheikh ordered them (the Fulani) not to deliver him (Abdu-
> sallami) up to his enemy, and the enemy sent to them saying
> "Hand over to us the remnant of the Muslim fugitives." But the
> enemy was afraid to prove them and matters were adjusted for
> them, so they (the pursuers) returned, and as they returned they
> passed by the settlement of the Sheikh (at Degel); and they (the
> Gobirawa) began to mock at the Muslims and say "You are the
> only ones left and you shall see us again soon." And our foolish
> ones opposed them and took from them some of the treasures
> (booty from Gimbana) and let them (the Gimbana captives) go.
> The Gobir people fled. And when news of this reached their chief,
> he sent word to the Sheikh, "Come out, thou and thy sons and
> thy brethren, from the village, for I propose to make an attack
> on the rest." And the Sheikh made him refrain until he had emi-
> grated with his company; and he fled from out of their country
> to a district called Gudu, and he bade the Muslims flee from the
> land of the infidels to the region to which he had removed. So the
> people emigrated to him steadily, until the infidels prevented the
> Muslims from further emigration, and his followers swore alle-
> giance to the Sheikhu, on the Koran and the Law.

The Sarkin Gobir sent a messenger to recall Shehu. Even before the Shehu's
messenger could set out with his reply to Alkalawa:

> When the Sarkin Gobir blocked the roads to those who were
> fleeing to us, our people rose on a Thursday and fell upon the
> Sudanese who were in the district and slew and captured and
> plundered and caught slaves. When God brought us to Friday,
> Shehu rose up and preached to his people. He commanded them
> to release those whom they had captured and to restore what
> they had taken away. Thereupon they released their captives and
> restored the property they had taken. It also happened before the
> journey of our messenger that the chiefs of Gobir were making
> war on us and harrying us. They were expelling our people and
> making captives of them. Shehu protested against this.

While the Shehu's emissary to Yunfa was at Alkalawa, a force of Gobir horsemen attacked. The Shehu's followers defeated them at Matankare. The Shehu was also attacked three times by the chief of Kwonni near Gudu. By then the situation was quite out of hand and war was inevitable. "The prince of Gobir with Tuareg allies came out against us and met us in a place called Tabkin Kwotto, and God routed them." This was in June 1804. To celebrate the victory the Shehu's brother, 'Abdullahi, wrote a poem in which he says:

> Now the different races among us Mohammedans were first
> the Toronkawa (Torodbe): they are our kindred; then our Fulani
> and our Hausas. There were also some of other races who assem-
> bled and aided us in the service of God.

In July 1804 the Shehu withdrew from Gudu to Nagabci and wrote circular letters to the chiefs of Sudan relating the cause and course of his dispute with the chief of Gobir, enjoining their observance of Islam and its Law, and calling on them to assist him against Gobir, or at least to desist from assisting Gobir.

> The Sarkin Gobir also sent messages to his brother chiefs, the
> Sarkin Katsina, the Sarkin Kano, Sarkin Zazzau, Sarkin Daura,
> and Sarkin Adar. He informed them that he had left a small fire
> in his country and it had grown until . . . now it had burnt him.
> He warned them to be careful lest a fire like this burnt them also.
> Thereupon each one of them rose up and attacked all those who
> allied themselves with Shehu; they slew and captured them. They
> (Shehu's supporters) fled and took refuge in certain towns . . .
> till they became very numerous. Then they rose up, and in self-
> defence drove away the forces sent against them.

This is Bello's version of the way the conflict spread; but when the chief of Gobir received help from other Hausa chiefs as well as the Tuareg, the Shehu also organized this general revolt. In this way conflict spread from Gobir throughout and beyond Hausaland. This general spread was perhaps inevitable, but so were the alignments and composition of the opposing groups.

Some Fulani assisted the Hausa chiefs openly; others secretly; others remained neutral, and yet other Fulani groups sought to assist both parties in order to profit, whichever won. But in most areas as well as Katsina "some of their Fulani kindred (the pagan nomads) joined our folk, the followers of the Faith." From Futa Toro, Sidi al-Mukhtar al-Kunti, the Qadiriyya sufi, sent others, Fulani and Torodbe, to swell the Shehu's jihad. Probably most Fulani who engaged in the struggle sided with dan Fodio's party irrespective of faith. For generations the nomads had suffered oppression and contumely from the Hausa rulers, and they had old scores to repay. They were also tempted by the prospects of plunder and politically privileged positions, such as they received in eastern Katsina in return for their support. With only one known exception, the Chief of Zaria, the Hausa rulers uniformly declared against the Shehu and his followers and tried to help one another in certain campaigns, without much effect. In Bornu the Alhaji Shaik Aminu, to whom this state owed its continued independence, like the nomad Fulani and Hausa warriors, took the side of the Kanuri ethnic group nearest his own Kanembu. The opposition between Muslims and non-Muslims was thus confused from the very start of the conflict by other ties and alignments, such as kinship, ethnic identity, secular political resentments and loyalties, calculations of advantage, communal solidarities and antagonisms, etc. Given this coalescence of very diverse interests among their followers, the control exercised by leaders on either side was uncertain and incomplete. As can be seen from the events just related, the initial conflicts developed inevitably, but were not under the direction of Yunfa or Shehu. Party followers took matters into their own hands: The Shehu's chief lieutenants, his brother 'Abdullahia, his son Bello, exercised a tenuous control over their undisciplined warriors. In Kano, Katsina, and Zazzau the Shehu's supporters disputed precedence and "political claims with one another, even before the struggle was over, and often to their adversaries' advantage.

Especially in Western Hausaland, there was a large and widely dispersed Fulani population, the pastoral nomads being pagan, the sedentary Fulani mainly Muslim. Both divisions were for different reasons dissatisfied with their lot under the Hausa chiefs; before the Shehu's jihad there had been a number of clashes between Fulani and Hausa throughout this area from Zaria to Zamfara. The processes of polarization brought to a head by the Shehu's declaration of jihad would probably have generated conflicts, even without this; but when Shehu and Yunfa came to blows these latent hostilities and cleavages between Muslim and heathen, pastoralist and farmer, immigrant and native peopled Fulani and Hausa, all poured themselves into this conflict, with the result that the critical principles for which the Shehu stood were often obscured. Perhaps it was his recognition of the need to clarify this situation, and to regulate conduct according to Islam, that led the Shehu to devote himself to writing political and religious tracts such as the *Kitab al-farq* and the *Bayan wujub al-hijra,* for the guidance and enlightenment of his followers. Moreover, once this conflict had come to a head at Tabkin Kwotto, it could not be localized within a single Hausa state; inevitably it spread to the limits of the social field in which this combination of forces and cleavages was general. For the Muslim leaders, this multiplied the problems of directing and regulating their jihad in accord with the rules of religion and of good policy. But perhaps this need to pursue political advantage while observing the Law and religion is a general feature of all those jihads which originate as revolts against "heathen" rulers. The results are always liable to differing interpretations. Where religious scruples obstruct effective political action, the jihad will normally fail; where political action of a secular, instrumental type disguises its nature under religious banners, its religious claims are easily discredited; but no one who has studied the Shehu's writings or life can doubt his primary religious commitment. His jihad was successful through a skillful combination of religious apolitical factors; yet it is precisely this combination which lends it an ambiguous character. As I have tried to show, the Shehu and his closest supporters, having identified themselves as the focus of opposition to Gobir government, were very largely governed by the circumstances of their situation and had to adjust, within the limits their religion permitted, to its requirement. This pattern is a general characteristic of Islam, enshrined in the doctrine of ijma', by which consensus legitimates necessary changes. As Weber pointed out, Islam is one of the very few major religions which has a practical orientation to the affairs of this world "an essentially political character," as seen in the injunction of jihad. The ambiguous character of Shehu dan Fodio's jihad derives from the ambiguous character of jihad itself.

19th Century Reforms in Hausaland

M. O. JUNAID[3]

One of the most important events in the history of Northern Nigeria was the Fulani Jihad of nineteenth century. This Jihad movement, led by Shehu Uthman dan Fodio has lasting effects on the political, social and religious life of the people of the region. However, recent literature on this reform movement has advanced various conflicting interpretations to analyse and explain its nature and characteristics. To some scholars, the movement was simply a collective reaction of a lower class people against their oppressive overlords in order to establish a state on the basis of Islam where social justice and equity would reign supreme. Another school of thought maintained that it was a movement motivated by tribal sentiments, planned and executed by the Fulani clerics to overthrow the Hausa rulers. As increasing number of scholars have come to the conclusion that the movement was essentially an intellectual movement aimed at achieving religious objectives.

One problem which these conflicting views raised, concerns the nature of the institution of Jihad as a general form of Islamic expansion. In Islam, the Jihad is a religious duty enjoined specifically for the purpose of repelling all forms of evils from the Muslims and extending the frontiers of Islam.

The purpose of this paper therefore is to examine each of these hypotheses critically, assess their validity or otherwise and develop another hypothesis which will indicate that the Jihad was not the outcome of a conscious planning but the consequence of a political challenge to the corporate existence of the Muslim community.

The Social Theory

From all indications, the exponents of the social theory of the Jihad movement appeared to have been highly influenced by the Marxist philosophy. By abstracting social elements in Dan Fodio's teaching and correlating them

[3]Juniad, M. O., "19th Century Reforms in Hausaland: An Appraisal of Conflicting Hypotheses," (Karachi, Pakistan: The Hamdard Foundation, Nazimabad, volume XII, no. 1, pp. 33–38).

M. O. Junaid is a lecturer in History at the University of Lagos.

with the socio-political conditions in Hausaland, they have conceptualised the prevailing forms of oppression, exploitation and injustice. Such an ideology could indeed be justified to some extent if one considers the views and ideas expressed in the works of the Jihad leaders themselves. These included various kinds of corruption: the selling of justice to the highest bidder, bribery and a host of other oppressive measures such as indiscriminate imposition of taxes and levies. The rulers, it was alleged, seized properties without adequate compensation and appropriated animals which strayed into their own herds, while their own animals were allowed to stray and cause damages to cultivated lands without punity. They paid no attention to the welfare of their subjects and shut their doors in the face of the needy. Dan Fodio went further to compare these abuses of government with the condition which should obtain under an ideal Muslim government. The main pre-occupation of such a government, he asserted, would include improvement of the welfare of the poor and the striving to reform the markets. Its ministers would include a *wazir* (minister) who should be steadfast and merciful with the people, a chief of police who will not oppress the subjects.

A careful study of the social conditions in Hausasland would clearly show that some of the allegations highlighted by Dan Fodio were likely to be substantially true. Most glaring was the fact that when he was summoned by the King of Gobir, Bawa, in (1788–1789) to attend the Sallah festival (Eid al-Kabir) Dan Fodio declined to accept the gifts given to him by the King. Rather, he sought for five special requests from the King which were all granted. These included:

1. Freedom of preaching without hindrance
2. Non-restriction of people to respond to his call
3. That people who put on turban should be accorded due respect
4. Unconditional release of all political prisoners
5. That his followers should not be over-burdened with taxes.

It could be seen that Dan Fodio did not limit himself only to the social grievances, for in the same vein and with equal vehemence, he directed his criticism to the ostentation, luxury and self-indulgence of the Hausa rulers. The variety of ideas expressed in *Kitab al-Farq, Tazyin al-Waraqat, Tazyin al-Ikhwan, Bayan Wujub al-Hijra* and others, on social, political moral, religious and educational issues served to remind us of the totality of Dan Fodio's vision and indeed universal Islam. It would therefore be erroneous and misleading to stress the social aspect of Dan Fodio's teaching as though it was exclusive of the rest. The social and political malpractices of the Hausa rulers were criticised for precisely the same reason as their involvement in pagan practices—all are not in conformity with Islamic religious standard. If such practices are to be regulated by Islamic law, it is clear that government per se has to be religiously inclined. This concern for the establishment of an ideal Muslim state seemed to be the unifying factor in Dan Fodio's thinking, one which eventually precipitated the Jihad movement of 1804.

Ethnocentric Theory

Another viewpoint expressed by some scholars was that the Jihad movement was a tribal conflict between the Fulani and the corrupt rulers of Hausaland and that religion was merely used as a guise for the acquisition of political power. A classical example of this assessment was represented in the following extracts from Hogben's book *The Mohammedan Emirates of Northern Nigeria:*

> In reality, it was originally a national fight of the Fulani, both Muslim and Pagan against the forces of Yunfa, the King of Gobir, who had decreed their extermination. Only after the victory, when the pagan Fulani who had borne more than their full share in order to achieve it, had retired to their flocks and herds did the mallams who had been the leaders exploit the opportunity under the cloak of religion to oust native rulers and put themselves into their places with Usman Dan Fodio at their head.

In the same vein, Trimingham asserted that the "Shehu, from 1786, preached the Jihad in such a way that it became a racial as well as a religious war."

At a glance, this hypothesis would appear to be valid since most of the leaders who prosecuted the Jihad and subsequently became emirs in their respective areas of jurisdiction were Fulani. Moreso, the Jihad leaders wrote a lot of poems addressed specifically to Fulani audiences. All these revealed the special role which the Fulani as a tribe were expected to play under the new dispensation. This role would be further strengthened by the assumption of political power and proper consolidation of the oppressed minority.

This theory however obscures rather than aids proper understanding of the Sokoto Jihad movement. At best, it simplified or clearly avoided the complex issues involved. It did not offer any explanation about the basic concern of the Jihad leaders over religious issues which formed the basis of their prolific writing and the bedrock of the administrative machinery which they established with a degree of success. Since the Fulani were not superior in arms or political administration to their opponents, their numerical inferiority alone would have ensured the failure of the Jihad if they had not enjoyed the active support of non-Fulani allies and associates. That the emergent Sokoto Caliphate was ruled largely by the Fulani Jihadists was a direct result of the fact that the Jihad leaders were mainly Fulani.

A general survey of the role of the Fulani in the diffusion of Islamic faith in Hausaland before 1804 would serve to explain their leadership role in the prosecution of the movement. According to historical sources, Islam penetrated into Hausaland through various channels—trade, war and migration. This penetration was less recognised until the fifteenth century when it began to gather much momentum. The Kano Chronicle refers to the reign of Yakubu (1452–1463) as the period when the Fulani came to Hausaland from Melle bringing books on "Divinity and Etymology." This according to Greenberg represents a second turning point in the Islamisation of the Hausa in that "while the Wangarawa came in small numbers and were never reinforced, the arrival of the Fulani was but the spearhead of a great ethnic movement which continued in increasing strength culminating in the Jihad of the nineteenth century." The numerous works of the Jihad leaders particularly *Ihya al-Sunna, Infaqul Maisur* and *Tazyin al-Waraqat* which shed some light on the state of learning and scholarship in Hausaland before the Jihad illustrated the great intellectual gap between the Hausa and Fulani. As Qadis, Qur'anic teachers and clerics, it was the Fulani who preserved the tradition of Sudanese scholarship and occupied key posts within the Muslim hierarchy. This shows that the Fulani had a long-standing history of Islamisation coupled with their superiority in the art of writing and literacy. The evils of the society against which the Jihad leaders protested were very significant not only to the Fulani as a tribe but also to some discontented elements who felt the oppression keenly. In this respect, the Jihad movement was an expression not of Fulani tribal nationalism, but of the sense of common purpose which a group with ties of education, culture and language is likely to generate. This sense of common purpose was also reflected in the composition of Dan Fodio's followership. They consisted of various elements—Fulani, Hausa, Tuareg etc. There was abundant evidence to suggest that many of the Fulani, even refused to join in the encounter including some of the learned men who openly condemned the Jihad. But with the success of the first major encounter at Tabkin Kwotto in June 1804, many more people rallied round Dan Fodio. However, the Jihad leaders themselves were very categorical when they condemned tribalism in all its ramifications. For instance, in *Bayan Wayan Wujub al-Hijra,* Dan Fodio maintained that superiority based on tribal or racial differences was absolutely unacceptable in Islamic doctrine. This was also confirmed in *Tazyin al-Waraqat* where *'Abdullah bin Fudi,* had to compose a poem to criticise tribal discrimination.

Perhaps the most relevant argument to support the claim of tribal chauvinism was the fact that out of the fourteen flagbearers appointed by Dan Fodio, only one was not a Fulani. It should be noted however, that the flagbearers formed the first set of followers who helped Dan Fodio to achieve victory over the Hausa rulers. It was therefore not surprising that they should be rewarded with political and administrative positions. According to the tradition in Hausaland as well as in most parts of Western Sudan during the period, the religion of the ruler was assumed to be the religion of the entire community over which he ruled. If Dan Fodio could appoint a Muslim ruler for a community, it was assumed that Islam would eventually be established and consolidated in the community.

During his campaign for support, Dan Fodio based his appeals on purely religious grounds thus attracting not only the Fulanis, but also some Hausa faithfuls. If his appeals had been based entirely on racial grounds, it was natural that his kinsmen, being in the minority in Hausaland would have lost the wars because the Hausa who were numerically superior would have overpowered them. Thus, it can be seen that a dichotomy between the supporters and opponents of Dan Fodio, based entirely on ethnic or tribal lines could not be sufficient to explain the force at work.

Intellectual Dimensions

The nineteenth century reform movements in Hausaland sparked off a considerable amount of literary activities. Despite their preoccupation with the reformatory campaigns the leaders of the movement namely Shehu Uthman dan Fodio, Abdullahi and Muhammed Bello left a great legacy in writing and had to their credit hundreds of works on a wide range of topics—jurisprudence, religion, ethics, government, history, etc. From the bulk of their writing, it was absolutely clear that the fundamental cultural values of Dan Fodio and his group were deeply rooted in Islam. This explains why much emphasis was placed by them on the question of belief *(imam)* disbelief *(kufr)* and syncretism *(takhlit)*. Under the Hausa rulers, it was extremely difficult to distinguish between the believers and the unbelievers because of the problem of syncretism. Some of the rulers pretended outward respect for Islam and its institutions, but still glorified some manifestations of *kufr*. The intellectual output of the Jihad leaders undoubtedly helped to sharpen the religious awareness needed for the total reform of Hausaland. More significantly, the titles they gave to many works were indicative of the purpose they intended to serve. Bayan expounding, Diya guiding light, Irshad counselling, Najm guiding star, Naisha advice, Nah Talin educating, Tanbih drawing attention to, are all aspects of conveying the message of Islam.

Conclusion

From the foregoing it could be argued that the basis for the nineteenth century Jihad movement in Hausaland was mainly to revive Islam and the establishment of an ideal Muslim state fashioned after the historic state of Islam in Arabia in the seventh century. The arguments advanced to support the claim that the Jihad movement was either a tribalistic venture or an attempt to evolve a middle course between the privileged and the underprivileged could not be absolutely tenable. It is however true that in order to attain these religious objectives, many literary, political and military activities were highly instrumental. The Sokoto Jihadists regarded their emigration to Gudu as a corollary to the Prophet's flight from Makkah to Medina. They maintained that the Prophet left Makkah at the peak of hostility and persecution and eventually succeeded to establish a militant community in Medina which ultimately overthrew the agelong Quraishite aristocracy and established an Islamic state. In a similar vein, Dan Fodio's hijra to Gudu marked a final break with the Hausa aristocracy and the beginning of a military confrontation which culminated in the collapse and overthrow of the Hausa government and the establishment of the Sokoto Caliphate.

The Jihad in Hausaland
PETER WATERMAN[4]

Introduction

It is now fifteen years since H. F. C. Smith called the Islamic revolts of the nineteenth century a "neglected theme" in West African history. This is no longer true. The bibliography attached to this paper can give only a limited picture of the research that has since been done. Not only has there been a great deal of translating and solid empirical studies, but a great deal of debate on the character of these revolts.

In the first stage, the parties were divided as to whether the jihad (Islamic holy war) of Dan Fodio in Hausaland was primarily religious, social, political or ethnical economic in character. Although we find authors even today declaring, for example, that the jihads were "for the most part . . . a war more against impiety than against peoples." This tendency has been largely surpassed by a more sophisticated approach.

This can perhaps be traced to the search of Olderogge for the social roots of the conflict, though he, unfortunately, took social to mean class conflict. However this piece of academic overreaction permitted others to understand "social" more broadly. As one of these has put it:

> A few writers have recently begun to recognise the complexity of the movement, but they have not explained how the various factors converged to produce the jihad. An adequate explanation depends on a proper understanding of the way in which the various elements were interrelated.

This is well put and the writer goes on to produce a portrait of Dan Fodio in striking contrast to the one- or two-dimensional man and movement with which we have been presented in the past. Yet is this new synthesising approach sufficient? In so far as it is the ambition of any social science to give a total view (and of any study within them to be placed within such a

[4]Waterman, Peter, "The Jihad in Hausaland as an Episode in African History—Some Concepts, Theories and Hypotheses" (Leiden, Afrika—Studiecentrum, *Kroniek Van Afrika* (now *African Perspectives*), 1975), no. 2, pp. 141–50.

Peter Waterman is the author of *African Social Studies: A Radical Reader and Communist Theory of the Nigerian Trade Union Movement.*

context) the recent studies of the Islamic revolutions leave much to be desired. The synthesis has taken place at a low level and on a local scale. The questions that remain are not only such as Thomas Hodgkin put when reviewing one of Trimingham's "scissor and paste" studies of Islam in Africa and that demand fairly straightforward empirical research, but those that have not been asked because a conceptual framework is lacking.

A few questions might clarify the point: What kind of society existed in Hausaland before the jihad? What point did it represent in the development of African history? What was its economic base, its political and social structures, and why did their equilibrium break down? Did the jihad bring about change in the social, economic and political structures of Hausaland or merely place members of a new ethnic group in political power? And if it brought structural change, was this of a quantitative or merely qualitative kind—a revolution or a revolt?

What has been so far lacking is a theocratical framework. What need to be applied are the tools of the economic and social anthropologists—an understanding, for example of the sociology of religion. In the following, an attempt will be made to present some theoretical work that might provide us with more adequate tools and to show their relevance to the problem under discussion. The conclusion will suggest a number of hypotheses that certainly require further discussion. But it is hoped that they will put the jihads back into a process of historical development from which they have been somehow abstracted.

Concepts, Models and Problems of the Jihad

THE SOCIO-ECONOMIC FORMATION

The question has been raised above of what kind of society existed in Hausaland at the time of the jihad. The descriptive accounts usually lack the ambition to go beneath the surface. Even Olderogge, who clearly has such an ambition, is ambiguous here, although he is in no two minds about the feudal character of post-jihad society. The implication is that there was an early feudal society which developed into a fully feudal one as result of the jihad. Such a characterisation is seriously undermined by the combined attack made on the concept of an "African feudalism" by Marxists and non-Marxists over the past few years.

Jack Goody has followed up an earlier attack by an economic one aimed specifically at "paleo-Marxists" and at proving the nonexistence of feudal economics in Africa. His thesis is that while trading patterns and military organisation had some similarities to those of feudal Eurasia, productive relations differed in important respects. Using (perhaps unconsciously, in view of his target) the Marxist terminology of productive relations and means of production he argues that the relative abundance of land and consequent low technological level in tropical Africa militated against that individualisation of land and development characteristic of feudalism. Chiefship tended to be over men, not land, and rulers had to attract and restrain men themselves:

> [D]ifferentiation was confined to chiefs themselves rather than the dynasty as such, being a function of roles rather than social strata; and the most noticeable aspect of the difference lay in control over women and slaves (war booty), and guns and horses, rather than goods and land.

The exception proving this rule is provided, for Goody, by Ethiopia, where there existed the plough, landlordism and a clearly defined leisure class. Goody's points on the military, on productive means, economic and political relations are valuable and require following up. But is a concept of "Not-Feudalism" much help in understanding Hausa or any other African society? This kind of operation is not so far from the kind that resulted in calling African societies feudal because they were clearly neither patriarchal nor capitalist.

Work of a more constructive kind has been carried on amongst French Marxists (whether "paleo" or not, Goody may later tell us) for some years. Discussion has centered around Marx's concept of the "Asiatic mode of production." Marx used this term to characterise those societies where the need for great works (for irrigation, etc.) brought about the creation of a powerful and despotic state and ruling class politically dominating the patriarchal village communities, whilst leaving the subsistence economies unchanged and extracting a surplus from them in the form of tribute.

Godelier and Suret-Canale have attempted to universalise this mode, removing from it its "Asiatic" particularities (great works and despotism) and finding it appropriate for that great number of African societies in which a centralised state coexists with village production and "non-individualised" landownership. This led to a discussion of the forms, dynamic and developmental possibilities of this mode. Suret-Canale stresses, like Marx, the durability of the economic base compared with the political superstructure. And he argues that this mode (for which he tentatively suggests the new title "tributary") does not contain within itself the seeds of structural transformation. Increased exploitation only reinforces the traditional social structures because they provide the very framework for the extraction of the surplus. By itself, therefore, this system can only lead to temporary destruction of the dominant class and state, or reversion to the tribo-patriarchal stage. Here we can perhaps see the outlines of an explanatory scheme for the jihad, as

Suret-Canale does indeed go on to characterise it according to his model. Talking of crisis within this mode he says:

> Most often it results in the replacing of one aristocratic structure by another, of a different form but analogous content. The Fulani and Tukolor "Islamic revolutions" of the eighteenth and nineteenth centuries seem clearly of this type. Thus, in Hausaland, the jihad of Usman dan Fodio and his Fulani and Tukolor supporters was supported by a jacquerie of captives and exploited peasants, against the traditional aristocracy: but the final result was the substitution of a new (Fulani and Muslim) aristocracy for the tribal Hausa aristocracy.

However, Godelier and Suret-Canale have both been criticised by Catherine Coquery-Vidrovitch for their attempts to assimilate Africa to the Asiatic mode of production on the sole strength of the common subsistence economy base. Instead of depriving the Asiatic mode of its dynamic (the necessity for great works) and its dominant political characteristic (despotism) she believes it necessary and possible to outline an African mode of production. In this model there exists the economic base of subsistence agriculture, a dominant bureaucracy that draws tribute but does not intervene directly in production, and a dynamic consisting in West Africa not of the necessity for great works but for trade:

> The specificity of the African mode of production thus rests in the combination of a communal patriarchal economy and the exclusive control of a group over long-distance trade. On the nature of this group depends the form of power at a given moment; if the leaders coincide with the subsistence lineage chiefs at the village level, their preeminence is then uncontested. . . . On the other hand, if (because of hereditary caste recruitment or following the commencement of capital accumulation) there appears within a more differentiated political apparatus a privileged class which succeeds in taking over long-distance trade, the regime expresses a more or less coherent synthesis between the tribal patriarchal system and territorial ambitions of a new type.

Coquery-Vidrovitch opposes that juxtaposition of state and stateless society—because of the contradiction noted by Balandier between lineal descent organisation and territorial organisation—or a tribal-patriarchal society with a subsistence economy and a centralised state with its long-distance trade. She considers the analogy drawn here by Suret-Canale to be doubtful, since what is characteristic of African societies is rather the coexistence of contradictory economic elements within both anarchic and centralised societies.

And it is precisely the dialectic between subsistence economy and long-distance trade that provides one of the motors of history in tropical Africa.

In the conditions of abundant land and low productivity, she says, dominant groups could not obtain a significant surplus by exploitation of the village economy, but only domination of long-distance exchange, by procuring (as much as buying) cheap and selling dear. The peaceful trade and military razzias organised to this end can themselves be considered means of production. Thus the surplus was extracted indirectly rather than directly from the village community, the existence of which continued unchanged [the] condition of supplying tribute. It is in this impermeability of the village vis-à-vis the state that can probably be found that village stability and state instability so much remarked upon. For, she says, long-distance trade was the most dynamic but also the least stable element in these societies. As to the possibility of their evolution, this is subject to frequent blockage precisely because the surplus depends upon trade and war, and because genuine production is "sterile." It is this that explains the complete disappearance of certain Sudanese and coastal slaving states with changes in the section, or character, of trade. Coquery-Vidrovitch does not, unfortunately, apply her model to Hausaland (although she does to the great Sudanese empires), but she does invite anthropologists and historians to carry on further research on her hypotheses, a suggestion which at present we can do little more than pass on.

ECONOMIC STRUCTURES

Perhaps, however we can pick up one or two suggestions from this theoretical discussion in examining the economic structures of Hausaland. The experience of eighteenth century Futa Djalon may be relevant here. In his study of the jihad in the Futa Djalon, Walter Rodney pays great attention to the new kinds and directions of trade developing at this time. He suggests that the new coastal European demand for hides, slaves and foodstuffs was to the economic advantage of the underprivileged Fulani and Mandinka and brought them into conflict with the Djalonke, who exploited them economically and dominated them politically. Analysis along the same lines in Hausaland would be fruitful.

More has been written on the tension between the pastoral and agricultural economies because the two are identified—too easily—with the Fulani and Hausa repectively. After mentioning the conflict between pastoralists and agriculturalists in his area, however, Rodney goes on to stress those aspects of interdependence and solidarity which kept the plural Futa Djalon society together for the lengthy period before fission appeared. The same point about symbiosis and competition in West Sudanic society is made by others. However, one must be more cautious here than Murray Last is when he talks of the permanent possibility of a nomad-peasant conflict. That there was no popular Hausa resistance to the jihad should be proof enough that no threat was felt by the peasants to their means of livelihood.

Clearly we also need to know more about the extent to which the ruling class of Hausaland before and after the jihad was dependent upon raiding, looting and slaving for revenue. This kind of examination has been made, once again, for the Futa Djalon by Rodney. He says that:

> The quest for slaves must have been, not the sole, but certainly the most important stimulus to wars which had long lost their religious significance, but were still called jihad. . . . The strategy of the Futa Djalon rulers was to place a virtual ban on domestic slave procuring activities, while at the same time intensifying the pursuit of slaves beyond the confines of Futa Djalon.

He also points out how the slaves could be used either for agriculture or for sale, depending on which was the more profitable. The terrain, the horse, and the long dry season in Hausaland all encouraged a raiding economy of the pattern described by Coquery-Vidrovitch, and the war machine based on the nomadic Fulani must have lent itself to an activity permitted— whereas not actively encouraged—by Islam. Goody stresses the difference between the heavy cavalry of mediaeval Europe and the light cavalry of Africa, the latter being ideal for raiding and the capture of human booty. The very absence of individual landholding and permanent office holding— that permanent insecurity of the Fulani aristocracy mentioned by Olderogge—indicates the existence of other sources of revenue.

ETHNIC RELATIONS

The nomad-peasant element in inter-ethnic relations has already been deemphasised. How then is the so much stressed ethnic conflict to be interpreted? The Hausa kingdoms were based on agricultural communities of peasant production. Yet, if we are to follow Coquery-Vidrovitch, we would need to seek outside the Hausa village communities for other sources of Hausa state and aristocratic income. Some points on raiding have been made already. And M. G. Smith, talking of fifteenth and sixteenth century Hausa land has described its economy as based on slave raiding for tribute, commerce and forced labour. As outsiders the Fulani were part of this "extra communal" source of revenue.

They were of low status and objects of a political discrimination and economic exploitation possibly greater than that of the Hausa *talakawa* (free peasants). But it is now generally accepted that Fulani discontents were joined to those of low status Hausa and other groups, and were thus opposed specifically to the Hausa ruling class rather than the Hausa as an ethnic economic community. The ethnic element seems thus to be marginal rather than central to the conflict in Hausaland. Moreover, it is difficult to read an exploitation of Fulani-Hausa conflict into the writings of Dan Fodio. And, finally, while it is true that the new ruling class was drawn from the Fulani, the mass of the Fulani achieved a status no better than that of the Hausa *talakawa* under the old regime, and the nomads were coerced into settling (only in Macina?)—presumably so that they could be better controlled and taxed.

THE SOCIAL CONFLICT

In moving ethnic contradictions to one side more room is provided for the social conflict. In the past, however, "social" has been understood either too broadly or too narrowly. Thus, M. G. Smith groups all "latent hostilities" between the Muslim and heathen, nomad and farmer, immigrant and native, Fulani and Hausa. On the other hand, Olderogge reduced social conflict to its economic term (exploiters versus exploited) and is then obliged to imply that the aristocratic Torobe, Dan Fodio, was merely exploiting "religious fanaticism" and mass discontent in the interests of himself and his peers. Clearly we need a more precise definition of terms. If it is to have explanatory value, "social" must be defined as conflict between one or more of the following: exploiter and exploited, rulers and ruled, high status and low status groups.

The next requirement is a sociological analysis of the support for the jihad. This was attempted by Olderogge, who declared that the poorest Fulani rose first, that the Hausa poor were united with the Fulani poor in the cities and that only thus can one explain, for example, the easy fall of a strongly fortified Kano that had earlier withstood the combined assault of Songhai and Kebbi. This crude class-conflict thesis does not stand up to much analysis. What is needed is the kind of differentiated analysis made by Waldman. She first divides the malams—seen as a social stratum—into the satisfied dependents of the Hausa courts and the poor and dissatisfied. She then suggests that even amongst the wealthy *Fulanin Gida* (settled Fulani) of the cities there would have been some support for Dan Fodio.

The *Bararoji* (pastoral Fulani) were mostly non-Muslim but all suffered from the disadvantages that Dan Fodio attacked. The same is true of the Hausa peasantry and non-Hausa pagans to whom Dan Fodio preached. She summarises as follows:

> At the end of the eleventh century, Hausaland was filled with people dissatisfied with the Hausa order, and who were thus potential supporters for a movement of protest. As a result of op-

pressive and arbitrary actions, Hausa rulers alienated many more elements than they benefited or satisfied. All the groups . . . shared one important characteristic; to a great extent they depended for their livelihood and security on the goodwill of others more powerful than them: the malams on the Hausa rulers and Hausa patrons; the Gida on the Hausa rulers; the Bararoji on the rulers, landholders and cultivators, the peasants on the government.

After analysis of support, we need analysis of leadership. Here we can only make some points about its changing character. Waldman points out that although the jihad itself was initiated by a community of mostly Fulani malams around Dan Fodio, it was not supported by the Fulani or Muslims in general until after the successful battle of Alwassa in 1805. When this happened, the clerics around Dan Fodio were no longer able to supply leadership (there had been heavy battle losses earlier). The flagbearers who led the uprising in other Hausa states were usually nominees of the Fulanin Gida. Already in the eighteenth century jihad in Futa Djalon there had been conflict between the religious and military elite, eventually won by the latter. In the Sokoto Caliphate, the clan-based military provided a centre of power that Dan Fodio's successors were obliged to reckon with. This was clearly a movement of considerable complexity. It obviously had a broad popular base. Yet it was initiated by the Islamic scholars who can only with difficulty be presented as the idiologists of the Fulani aristocracy (which was in large measure created during the campaigns). The relatively autonomous role of ideology in this crisis must not therefore be ignored.

IDEOLOGICAL

Despite the placing of religious conflict at the forefront of most studies of jihad it is curiously little understood. Yet the jihad would seem to provide an ideal case for the study of religious ideology in social movement. It is true that M. G. Smith has cited Weber's remark on the essentially political character of Islam, but he hardly follows this up himself. Suret-Canale has commented on the role of Islam in the eighteenth century Sudan as an ideology, saying:

> At the same time a religion and a set of rules for social life, born
> in a very similar social setting (development of a trading economy
> and overthrow of the old kinship structures in Arabia of the eighth
> century) Islam responded exactly to the new needs.

Even more suggestive is Waldman. When she talks of the pattern of "coexistence and tension" between Islam and the ruling class traditional to the Western Sudan, one notes the parallel to that coexistence and tension in the economy, in politics and in ethnic relations that have been stressed above and elsewhere. This does not mean, of course, that the ideological conflict mirrored the opposed terms within the other contradictions. But it does serve to show us how delicate was the equilibrium of this society, and it reminds us that a body of theory, and a corps of propagandists-cum-organisers lay ready at hand that could fuse, form and express the tensions existing in other structures of Hausa society.

But here again we need a critical analysis. It is evident from Waldman's remark that religion can play an "equilibrating" as well as a "disequilibrating" role, and that as a progressive force, it can be found on a scale ranging from reformism at one end to revolution on the other.

The malams of the eighteenth century Sudan were heirs to a rich tradition of intellectual and political radicalism. In the eleventh century the Almoravid provided a prototype for Hausaland:

> [A] militant, activist interpretation of Islam, stressing the necessity for bringing about a total transformation of society, in accordance with the prescriptions of the Sharia, by the method of jihad, combined with a practical interest in establishing a new type of state, on a broader geographical and social basis, with this activist Muslim elite as its ruling class.

Further inspiration and examples were provided by the fifteenth century Muslim scholar al-Maghili, whose conception of the model Islamic state follows:

> The pivot of this system was the just Imam, who upheld the Sharia, imposed Zakat and other canonical taxes, protected the frontiers, conducted jihad against polytheists, suppressed brigandage, safeguarded property rights, consulted with pious and learned ulama and appointed them to appropriate offices, made active efforts to reform surviving pre-Islamic custom, and accepted entire responsibility for government policy in all aspects.

Although he was heir to this tradition, Dan Fodio was also heir to the old tradition of compromise. Therefore it is necessary to analyse his career, since he moved ideologically and politically through a number of phases. He was never so radical as his teacher, Shaikh Jibril ibn Umar, who was forced to leave Gobir while Dan Fodio stayed on. Dan Fodio moved from compromise with the old ruling class, to separation from them, the urging of revolution against them, and then apologetics for the new ruling class. In religious terms this was a movement from quietism, to a peak of radicalism during which he took advantage of popular Mahdist (Messianic) beliefs, and then to a renunciation of these. Olderogge emphasises more strongly the conservative character of the post-jihad phase in commenting on Mohammed Bello's reply to a complaint from Bornu. This reply, he says, is of a purely scholastic character, ignoring the substance of the complaint and thereby condoning the malpractices of the Fulani aristocracy.

The clearest indication of the religious limitations of the jihad is the appearance of second and third generation reforming movements in the Sudan with increasingly radical doctrines and structures.

The second generation is that of al-Hajj Umar who introduced the Tijaniya brotherhood into, and was consequently forced out of, one Islamic state of the West Sudan after another in the 1840s. He finally organised a counter-jihad against the Islamic state of Masina set up by a disciple of the Sokoto regime but a few years earlier.

The third generation is represented by the *empire's combatants* of Samory and others, movements led by men whose claim to leadership was based on personal loyalties rather than descent, and who resisted colonialism actively while Sokoto could only mount a rearguard action against it.

Without dissolving Islam, we clearly do need to see how it functioned, and to consider the malams not simply as the embodiment of Islamic doctrine or doctrines, but as a social stratum, the intelligentsia of the Western Sudan.

Some Hypotheses

If it is possible at this stage to rework the history of the jihad in Hausaland, this would first of all require a critical study of the various theories, and models that have been simply listed here. At this point it is only possible to present conclusions in the form of a few hypotheses that might enrich study of this area and period of African history:

1. That an understanding of the crisis that gripped Hausaland (and the Sudan in general) during the eighteenth and nineteenth centuries demands a more detailed and sophisticated study of the local economies and relations between them than has yet been attempted
2. That pre-jihad Hausaland can best be assimilated to the model of African mode of production, as a series of bureaucracies drawing tribute from subsistence village economies, but basically dependent on a surplus drawn from control of long distance trade and military means of production.
3. That only when we have understood the contradictions within economic structure will we be able to fully interpret those in such other structures as the social (exploiters/exploited, rulers/ruled) the ethnic, the political (state organisation) and the ideological.

4. That the jihad can probably be interpreted as a crisis within society based on the tributary mode of production that led to changes in the ethnic relationships, advances in political organisation, and development in the economy through increased trading and raiding, and through increased exploitation of servile labour and agriculture. Changes, advances and development then, not a social revolution (Pace, Rodney and Olderogge)

5. That the change at the ideological level was limited by these factors. The failure to establish the ideals of Islam within the Caliphate (and other Islamic states of the Western Sudan at other times) is evidenced not simply by the common adaptation of the new states to old patterns and practices, but by the common appearance of competing and more radical Islamic movements to express the old un-righted grievances.

Suggestions for Further Reading

Clarke, Peter, *West Africa and Islam: A Study of Religious Development from the Eighth Century to the Twentieth Century* (London: E. Arnold, 1988).

Hiskett, Mervyn, *The Development of Islam in West Africa* (New York: Longmans, 1984).

Hogben, S. J., and Kirk-Greene, A. H. M., *The Emirates of Northern Nigeria* (London: Oxford University Press, 1966).

Hunwick, John O., *Sharia in Songhay: The Replies of al-Maghili to the Questions of Askia al-Hajj Muhammad* (London: Oxford University Press, 1967).

Johnston, H. A. S. *The Fulani Empire of Sokoto* (London: Oxford University Press, 1967).

"Reform in West Africa: The Jihad Movements of the Nineteenth Century," Ajay, Ade J. F., and Crowder, Michael, eds., *History of West Africa*, second edition, volume 2 (London: Longmans, Harlow, 1987).

Last, Murray, *The Sokoto Caliphate* (London: Longmans, Ibadan History Series, 1967).

Levtzion, Nehemia, *Ancient Ghana and Mali* (London: Methuen, 1980).

Levtzion, Nehemia, *Islam in West Africa: Religion, Society, and Politics to 1800* (Brookfield, Vt.: Variorum, 1994).

——— and Fisher, Humphrey J., eds., *Rural and Urban Islam in West Africa* (Boulder, Colo.: L. Rienner Publishers, 1987).

——— and Pouwels, Randall L., eds., *The History of Islam in Africa* (Athens: University of Ohio Press, 2000).

——— and Spaulding, Jay, eds., *Medieval West Africa: Views from Arab Scholars and Merchants* (Princeton: Markus Wiener, 2003).

Lewis, I. M., ed., *Islam in Tropical Africa* (Oxford: Oxford University Press, 1966).

Martin, B. G., *Muslim Brotherhoods in Nineteenth Century Africa* (London: Methuen, 1973).

O'Fahey, R. S., and Spaulding, J. L., *Kingdoms of the Sudan* (London: Methuen, 1974).

Pouwels, Randall L., *Horn and Crescent: Cultural Change and Traditional Islam on the East African Coast, 800–1900* (Cambridge: Cambridge University Press, 1987).

Robinson, David, *The Holy War of Umar Tal: The Western Sudan in the Nineteenth Century* (Oxford: Clarendon Press, 1985).

Rodney, Walter, "Jihad and Social Revolution in Futa Djalon in the Eighteenth Century," *The Journal of the Historical Society of Nigeria* 4, no. 2 (Nigeria: Impact Publishers, Ltd., June 1968).

Smith, H. F. C., "The Islamic Revolution of the Nineteenth Century; A Neglected Theme of West African History," *The Journal of the Historical Society of Nigeria* 2, no. 2 (Nigeria: Impact Publishers, Ltd., 1961).

Trimingham, J. S., *Islam in East Africa* (Oxford: Clarendon Press, 1964).

———, *Islam in West Africa* (Oxford: Clarendon Press, 1959).

———, *The Influence of Islam Upon Africa* (London: Longmans, 1980).

Problem V
WOMEN IN AFRICAN SOCIETIES

Since the pedagogical methodology of this volume revolves around "problems" designed to provide information, arouse controversy, and instill discussion, *Women in African Societies* before the colonial era presents a more perplexing difficulty than that which George Bernard Shaw presented in "Man and Superman" in 1903, a distinction which is self-evident to any female or male of this century. Africa was no exception, for the relationship between the sexes, which delighted Shaw and his audience, is deeply rooted in every culture from the time of Adam and Eve. It is thus somewhat surprising that historians of the African past, whatever their gender, have shown comparatively little interest in the history of the African woman. Perhaps, this is because the traditions, reflected in most societies by the *griots* (praise-singers and poets), were often the stories of men—warriors, kings, and holy men. Perhaps it is due to the dearth of information on the presence of the African woman in her own culture. Perhaps it is a result of the negligence of scholars to acknowledge the unique and significant contributions women have made to the development of the African past. As in any society there are numerous themes in which women, not men, are the principal players, but five emerge to dominate the literature and oral traditions—women as slaves, women as religious leaders, women as traders, women as the political manipulators in state formation, and women whose gender was neutral or equal in the evolution of pre-colonial African societies where one's entry and position in the lineage group determined an individual's status whether male or female.

Female slavery has been one of the least investigated subjects in African history as it was only recently that African slavery in general, in contrast to the trans-Atlantic trade, began to receive the scholarly attention it deserves (see Problem VI). Even more recently has been revealed the fact that a vast majority of the slaves within Africa were actually women. Because women played such significant and varied roles in societies across the continent, African slave traders—both male and female—desired to retain their female slaves while selling their male slaves to European traders. John Thornton addresses these issues and argues that the trans-Atlantic slave trade reduced the male population at a rate three times greater than the female. Yet, the practice of polygyny—the principle method of familial organization in West Africa—survived and maintained its vitality, although the extrication of African men placed ever greater burdens on African women. Slavery in Africa cannot be understood without the realization of the importance of women to agricultural cultivation, whether slave or free, and the institution of marriage in the context of a society cemented by familial clan and lineage ties in which women were principal figures. Such acknowledgements as these have been the focus of recent scholarship in African history, and have removed women from the periphery of historical discussion to place them back in the center—the very position many of them held in their pre-colonial societies.

Claude Meillassoux concurs with Thornton that African women were important as productive cultivators in the fields whose burden had been imposed upon them by the loss of the exportation of men in the trans-Atlantic trade. Left behind, female slaves were less necessary for procreation than productivity and no longer had the protection of the family, clan or lineage. She was alienated to labor for a master who could dispose of her or her progeny for profit. Many female slaves achieved considerable influence through their skills and intellect, but this did not obscure the depersonalization or desocialization which was her fate.

Martin Klein takes issue with Meillassoux's conclusions with examples from the Western Sudan. While Meillassoux argues that female slaves were not only more numerous in Africa but were wanted for their capacity to work, Professor Klein does not agree, at least for slavery in the Western Sudan. Female slaves were valued more than men, not because of their ability to labor, but because they represented a more secure and stable investment on a social level until age or unreproductive capacity rendered her a liability. The difference in demand, Professor Klein would argue, was that one of the most important functions of a female slave was her reproductive capacity which in the last resort was greater than her value as a producer in the fields and her price in the market place.

The absorption with the African slave trade, and the influential role in which it involved the African woman is a distortion of the influence which they performed in roles other than reproduction or productivity. They were extraordinary entrepreneurs who managed commercial empires and were consummate political manipulators often more astute than their male counterparts. George E. Brooks Jr. describes the development of what became known as "signareship" (female commerce) in the Senegal in which an economic nexus evolved between European men and African women determined to acquire profit from European merchandise. Although one might argue that Brooks' example is not a history of pre-colonial Africa, it most certainly was. The activities of these entrepreneurial, dynamic women of the West Coast of Africa took place in the eighteenth century and still continued long after the age of imperialism, colonialism or proconsuls. Moreover, it was the age of the Enlightenment and the "noble savages" of Senegal could send their elected representatives to the Chamber of Deputies in Paris. What is perhaps more important is the role of the "signares" who skillfully manipulated two trading complexes from two cultures for their own ends. They still do.

If women carved out a unique and specific role in African societies as traders, more so did they as spirit mediums in religious sects. In a study of spirit cults in East Africa, Iris Berger reveals that women achieved prominent positions in East African societies through their roles as spirit mediums—intermediaries between the spirit and material world. Since most animist cultures—including those of East Africa—believed that spirits actively intervened in the material world in the realms of health, prosperity, and fertility, those individuals who served as mediums for the spirits were powerful and influential figures. As many of the cults' primary concerns were with women's issues, and many of the spirits possessed female qualities, those women who served as spirit mediums were able to rise above the traditionally stratified societies in which they resided.

Equally intriguing throughout the continent is the importance of women in the formation of states. Perhaps the best example comes from Nakanyuike B. Musisi and state formation in the Interlacustrine State of Buganda. Here polygynous marriage was essential as a crucial social and political element in state formation whereby "elite polygyny" provided the means to stabilize the state which created the conditions for the expansion of Buganda in the sixteenth century. "Elite polygyny" stratified the male population into which the women were also stratified enabling them to participate through subtlety and sexuality in the manipulation of power. The *bakembuga* (wives of the Bagunda elite) became not only the mothers of kings but king-makers as well.

Finally, there is the intriguing theme of Oyeronke Oyewumi who argues that in Yoruba society gender was not the divisive factor that it has appeared to be in other African societies. In a provocative addition to the "problem" of Women in African Societies, she points out that the distinction between male and female is largely a "myth" constructed by Western scholars, conditioned through the perspective of dominant Western feminism which may apply to George Bernard Shaw in 1903, but is inappropriate to pre-colonial Yorubaland. In traditional Yoruba society Oyewumi maintains that it was not gender that determined relationships between the sexes, but the age at which the individual of either gender entered the lineage group which forged the relationship between male and female and established one's own individuality in Yoruba society, irrespective of gender.

Sexual Demography
JOHN THORNTON[1]

In the past few years, the study of the Atlantic slave trade has shifted emphasis from measuring its volume to judging its effects in Africa. . . . Emerging from this new concentration on the African side of the slave trade has been the realization that the slave trade had a significant impact on the role and life of women, and researchers are increasingly pointing out that the study of women, both as slaves and as free people in areas where slaving occurred, is a necessary corollary to the study of the slave trade as a whole.

The fact that the slave trade carried more men than women to the Americas, about two to three men for every woman according to those statistical series that are available, has long been seen as the cause of the inability of the slave population to grow in America. Low birth rates were largely a product of an extremely unbalanced sex ratio on American plantations, which when coupled with bad nutrition, few incentives to reproduce, and high abortion rates meant that slave populations could not keep ahead of their own mortality except by renewed imports from Africa.

My own work on the Angolan population of the late eighteenth century suggested what were the effects of the very differently altered sex composition in Africa. In Angola, women outnumbered men by nearly two to one in the population left behind after the slave trade. However, unlike in the Americas, the skewed sex ratio did not result in a marked decline in population. Because of the established institution of polygyny, the almost undiminished numbers of women were able to counterbalance some of the losses to the slave trade by continued reproduction. In a study presented at the Edinburgh conference, I charted the probable effects of the slave trade on age and sex distribution in a model population with characteristics similar to those of the population of Angola. Then, operating on the assumption that the rest of western Africa had similar population structures, I tried to sug-

---

[1]Thornton, John, "Sexual Demography: The Impact of the Slave Trade on Family Structure," from Robertson, Claire, and Klein, Martin, eds., *Women and Slavery in Africa* (Madison: University of Wisconsin Press, 1983), pp. 39–46.

John Thornton (1949–   ) was educated at the University of Michigan (B.A.) and took his M.A. and Ph.D. in African History at UCLA. He has taught at the University of Zambia and was the Carter G. Woodson Fellow at the University of Virginia. He is currently Associate Professor at Millersville University of Pennsylvania. His latest book is *Africa and Africans in the Making of the Atlantic, 1400–1600* (Cambridge: Cambridge University Press, 1992).

gest what would be the effect on such a model population of withdrawing a number of slaves equal to the number known from studies of the volume of the slave trade. Working independently, Patrick Manning created another model, which, while differing in approach and assumptions, nevertheless arrived at similar conclusions. Both models supported the conclusion that the population, although showing no long-term growth, suffered little long-term net loss. However, in both models the population, while not shrinking, did undergo fairly substantial alteration in structure, such that the group of males of working age was substantially reduced as a result of the specific demands of the slave traders and American purchasers for slaves in that age and sex group. In my own model, in which I tried to establish the minimum population densities necessary to support the known volume of slave exports in the interior behind each of several slave-exporting centers and then compared these densities with probable densities based on modern population size, I found that at the peak period of the slave trade in the late eighteenth century the demand for slaves must have come close to matching the maximum ability of all these regions to supply them. Moreover, in every region, the sex ratio in the age bracket 15–60 would have been only 80 men per 100 women, and in the hardest-hit area, Angola, as low as 40–50 men per 100 women.

The older debate on the slave trade had concentrated in one way or another on quantitative assessments of the population changes in Africa caused by the slave trade. Thus in Fage's many papers on the subject he insisted that the total volume of the trade was insufficient to offset natural growth and Africa was not depopulated. Criticisms of Fage's approach, such as those of J. E. Inikori and L. M. Diop presented at the Edinburgh conference, maintained simply that Fage had underestimated the total number of slaves exported and that depopulation *had* occurred, with its most important negative effect being a less favorable land-to-labor ratio in the remaining population. The approach to the problem suggested by Manning and myself, on the other hand, involves investigation of the quality of the population left behind, and not simply its quantity. This approach supports an argument that the major impact of the trade was not so much the reduction of the total number of people remaining in Africa as fundamental alterations in the ratio of working to dependent populations or of male to female labor. In this reexamination, the position of women is highlighted, since it is they who suffered the most from the trade in Africa.

The alteration in the age and sex ratios affected women in Africa in two ways, both results of the age- and sex-specific nature of the demand for African slaves by the traders. First of all, since they retained their normal fertility, the burden of child care imposed on them was not lessened by the loss in population—all the more so since children younger than age fifteen or so were rarely taken by the slave traders. At the same time their own numbers, and more important the numbers of males who played a vital role in child support if not in child care, were declining. This can be clearly seen if we examine the change in the dependency ratio of a hypothetical population in which the working group aged 15–60 has been depleted by 10 percent (the effect of having a sex ratio of 80 men per 100 women in this age group). Before the onset of the trade, according to the model life table from which my work was constructed, about 60 percent of the population fell into this age bracket, while the other 40 percent were either younger and required child care, or older and were unable to participate in productive labor. Thus there were approximately 67 dependents for each 100 working people. After the distortion introduced by the slave trade, however, 54 percent of the population fell into the category of able-bodied workers, while 46 percent were dependent, giving a dependency ratio of 85 dependents for each 100 working people. Thus the burden of work falling on the productive members of society was greatly increased, forcing more and more of their time to be spent in purely subsistence activities and reducing their ability to produce surplus for commerce or to maintain an efficient division of labor.

Women were hit in another way as well, however, and this was due to the alteration of the sex ratios among the producers just at a time when the work load of all producers was increasing. The model suggests that there must have been 20 percent fewer males to perform work allocated to men during the slave trade era, work which would then have had to go undone, or be done by females, or compensated for by purchased items. For example, in central Africa women did agricultural work, but men did heavy clearing of the fields, chopping down trees and digging up roots. Without this clearing labor, the women would have had to plant less or move their fields less often, both of which would tend to reduce production. Likewise, because hunting, fishing, and the rearing of livestock were activities which many traditional African societies left to men, the loss of males resulted in a less protein-rich diet for the remaining people.

This model is, of course, an average calculation based on rather crude assumptions. The actual adjustment of particular African societies is much more difficult to determine. The model is a global one applied to all regions of western Africa that supplied slaves, and is based on data obtained from a few rather large areas. How the slave raids affected the population in smaller regions within these larger areas is not considered. For example, a society subjected to raids might lose men and women in equal numbers and the raiding society incorporate the women while selling off the men. Alternatively, slave raiding which matched military forces against each other might result in all the slaves procured by the victor being males of saleable age, since armies select for the same age and sex criteria as plantation managers. My model suggested that the societies that procured slaves selected men ahead of women, and left the societies which gave up slaves with unbalanced sex ratios, while Manning's model assumed that the victims of slave raiding lost men and women in equal numbers, and the unbalanced sex ratios affected the societies that did the raiding. In fact, a variety of different methods were used to procure slaves, from large-scale wars to small-scale kidnapping, including judicial enslavement and raids of organized military forces against disorganized villagers. Each of these methods might have resulted in a different mix of ages and sexes for both the aggressors and the losers, and hence a whole distinct constellation of resulting demographic structures.

In Angola, for example, slaves were procured by major wars between military powers, a method which would probably favor the acquisition of males by the group that sold the slaves, and smaller-scale kidnapping and raiding against villagers which would have resulted in the acquisition of both men and women. Moreover, the census data from Angola show unbalanced sex ratios and distorted age structures for both slaves and free people, suggesting that the depletion of males among victims and the incorporation of females by the groups that acquired slaves were going on simultaneously. Equally diverse means of slave procurement were probably being used in other regions as well, which future research may do much to clarify.

Although a focus on the age and sex distribution of affected African populations does not tell us as much about the qualitative social effects of the slave trade as we would like, it suggests some lines of research that could reveal more about those effects. For example, one result of the unbalanced sex ratios would be an alteration in the institution of marriage. Since the institution of polygyny was present in Africa at the time that the slave trade began, the general surplus of women in the marriageable age group would have tended to encourage it and allow it to become much more widespread, driving down the bridewealth that women's families could demand and weakening the stability of the marriages in existence. It might also have favored men building up large households of wives through the purchase of female slaves; these slaves and their children, unprotected by their kin, would have been subject to abuses. This in turn might have had a detrimental effect on the status of marriage even for free women. These effects might vary according to whether the surplus of women was caused by an influx of female slaves, as in a society that was capturing slaves of both sexes but only selling the males to the Atlantic trade; or by a shortage of men, as in a society in which men were being drained off by warfare to the trade, leaving the women behind.

We can examine such qualitative changes in more detail by looking at one region, that of modern Guinea-Bissau (the Upper Guinea coast), for which descriptive data are available. By the early seventeenth century the region had become one of the foci of slave exporting from the western end of West Africa. Witnesses of the time commented on this fact, as for example the memorial submitted by the Jesuit priest Baltasar Barreira in 1606, or the group of Spanish Capuchins who submitted an open letter to the Pope and several other European rulers in 1686. Extensive slave trade activity is confirmed as well by surveys of the ethnic origins of slaves landing in the New World, such as those compiled from notarial records in Peru by Frederick Bowser. A fairly large percentage of the slaves leaving Guinea-Bissau were from the numerous small political units in the area. From the written observations of many visitors to Guinea-Bissau, we can form some idea of the social ramifications of the slave trade there. It was the wealth of written evidence, much of it from residents hostile to the slave trade, that enabled Walter Rodney to write so poignantly and effectively about the distortion of life and justice caused by the slave trade in the region. These hostile witnesses were mostly missionaries to the coast, which possessed a substantial settlement of Portuguese and Afro-Portuguese residents and was in need of clerical ministrations, and, as a non-Moslem zone, was open to attempts to missionize the African population. The Jesuits worked in the country from the start of the seventeenth century, and were joined by the Capuchins in mid-century. Unlike lay residents, whose writing is also quite extensive, the missionaries took pains to describe daily life and customs, and were not indisposed to denounce the slave trade since it interfered with their successful proselytization as well as offending their sense of justice.

This corpus of writing allows us to see some of the ways in which women were affected by the Atlantic slave trade. Writing in 1684 in an enlarged recension of a manuscript he originally composed in 1669, Francisco de Lemos Coelho, a Portuguese resident of the area, made some interesting notes on the Bissagos Islands. Although he does not mention unbalanced sex ratios as such, Lemos Coelho noted that polygyny was so widespread there that "there are blacks there who have twenty or thirty wives, and no one has only one," and moreover, "the children in their villages are [as numerous as] a beehive." Given the heavy slave trade in the area, the disproportionate number of women and children remarked by Lemos Coelho is not surprising. This unbalanced age and sex structure may also account for the very large share of work done by women on the islands, which astonished Lemos Coelho. After describing their complicated work in making cloth for clothes, he goes on to say: "They [the women] are the ones who work the field, and plant the crops, and the houses in which they live, even though small, are clean and bright, and despite all this work they still go down to the sea each day to catch shellfish. . . ." Lemos Coelho was not the only observer to comment on the burden of work falling on the women of the Bissagos Islands. Over half a century earlier, Andre Alvares d'Almada made almost identical observations, noting "they [the women] do more work than men do in other places." The men, it seems, were absorbed largely in war, which in this case meant slave raiding, while the women had to engage in production and perform more than the normal share of work. In the case of the Bissagos Islanders, it seems probable that the real burden fell upon the extra women, those who had arrived as slaves, although Lemos Coelho's report does not distinguish between slaves and free women.

Elsewhere in the area, other witnesses explicitly drew a connection between slavery, an influx of women, and the peculiar status of slave wives. The Spanish Capuchins, who complained of the state of affairs in the region around Bissau in 1686, believed that the plenitude of female slaves encouraged concubinage. Manuel Alvares, a Jesuit who wrote of conditions in the same area in 1616, observed, "All have many wives," again suggesting the generality of concubinage. Alvares also noted the special vulnerability of slave women: "If a noble takes his own slave for a wife, and she gives him some displeasure, he will sell her along with her child, even if the child is small, without any regard for the child being his own." Others who had lived in Guinea noticed the ease with which subordinate family members might be sold for petty violations of custom, although Alvares added that upper-class women were protected from such dire measures. Much of this testimony was used years ago by Rodney to support his thesis that the slave trade had led to substantial legal distortion, and certainly this particular social custom would allow members of the upper classes to hold or sell subordinates at will and according to other needs or the demands of the trade. Thus slaves held in marriage arrangements such as those described by Alvares could be mobilized for sale without costly wars or risk of retribution. Of course, most witnesses agree that warfare was still the major source of slaves, and one cannot help but suspect that the marriage customs were reported more for their shock value (and perhaps from isolated cases) than for the importance of their incidence.

Nevertheless, the slave trade brought many . . . women into coastal society in Guinea, and the Spanish Capuchins even noted that housing was inadequate, forcing male and female slaves to share quarters during peak periods of the trade. Inquisition authorities were aware that large numbers of slave women were affecting the Portuguese residents as well; in 1589, one Nuno Francisco da Costa was denounced to the Inquisition for having many *mulheres* (an ambiguous word in this case, meaning either women or wives) and reputedly saying that he cared more "for the fingernail of [a particular] slave woman than all the masses and confessions." Slavery and surplus women might even have altered the marriage patterns of theoretically monogamous Christians.

These scattered observations on female roles and marriage customs might be taken for no more than passing remarks of writers who were somewhat unsympathetic to African culture, were it not for their close agreement with our expectations based on demographic trends in the area. Just as Rodney's generalizations about the effects of the slave trade on class structure and the institution of slavery have been criticized as being atypical of West Africa, so too might these remarks on women's roles and the status of marriage. The data are not quantifiable, and were obtained from observers who were antagonistic toward the slave trade and hence anxious to highlight its ill effects. But they do fit some predictions based on a knowledge of the demography of the slave trade, and as such must be taken with new seriousness.

Female Slavery
CLAUDE MEILLASSOUX[2]

While the capacity of the free woman for hard work is often cited to explain the female condition in the domestic community and such institutions as bridewealth, it is the feminine capacity to procreate which is usually given as an explanation for the greater value of women than of men on the African slave market. I believe that these propositions should be reversed. On the first point, I have argued elsewhere that in the domestic society a woman's reproductive capacity is what is most expected from her. Her submission as a laborer follows from her submission as a procreator. In slavery, on the other hand, women were valued above all as workers, mostly because female tasks were predominant in production. Consequently the demand for female labor was greater than for male labor.

Female labor is general in Africa. There are few communities where women are exempt from heavy physical tasks. Still, the Western attitude toward female labor is shaped by the Christian image of female fragility. The assignment of heavy tasks or military activity to women is considered incongruous or incompatible with the "nature" of women, though that assumption is peculiar to the dominant classes of the West. This might be why Western ethnology has generally interpreted the preference of African and Asian enslavers for women in terms of specifically "feminine" qualities such as beauty or fertility. But such a hypothesis contradicts the economic rationale of slavery.

Slavery exists where the slave class is reproduced through institutional apparatus: war or market. In such enslaving societies, "assimilation" amounts to a limited emancipation or simply to some degree of intimacy with the master's family. In an actual slave system the taint of slavery—specifically, prejudice against slaves or those of slave descent—usually persists indefinitely. . . . The slave is kinless, that is, deprived of the protection

[2]Meillassoux, Claude, "Female Slavery," in Robertson, Claire, and Klein, Martin, *Women and Slavery in Africa* (Madison: University of Wisconsin Press, 1983), pp. 49–65.

Claude Meillassoux (1925–) was born in Roubaix France and worked in a factory, in advertising, and as an interpreter before receiving his Ph.D. from the University of Paris in 1964. Recognized for his firmly radical political convictions, Meillassoux is regarded as one of the world's foremost African anthropologists. Meillassoux's recent research has been directed at discerning a theory of slavery in Africa and his most recent work is *The Anthropology of Slavery: The Womb of Iron and Gold* (London: Athlone Press, 1991). Meillassoux currently resides in France.

that comes from belonging to kinship groups. The offspring of slaves, being unrelated both to their begetters and to their owners, also find themselves in the situation of being orphans. Even the children of concubines can only be related to their father's lineage since their mother is without kin. Hence, although these children may be free, they are not protected by the possible arbitration that would come from belonging to two lineages. Hence, they are excluded also from common law and citizenship. This inferior *estate* characterizes the slave's entire existence no matter what his or her *condition* is or how that condition changes. The estate of slaves is linked to their origin and remains constant. Their condition is linked to their function in the slave society and varies according to each individual and, also, to time. It is precisely the social weakness of slaves and of their offspring which explains why genetic reproduction might be wanted by the master, while the same social weakness also sets limits to it. This is observable both within the framework of the kinship system (in domestic societies) and within the framework of a dynastic system (in aristocratic class societies).

The Infertility of Female Slaves

Female slaves were more numerous and more expensive than male slaves. The hypothesis that they were preferred because of their potential for reproduction is not supported by objective data. Neither statistics nor any other kind of evidence demonstrates the maintenance or growth of slave populations by the reproduction of slaves among themselves. On the contrary, in slave societies where women were preferred, such as in sub-Saharan Africa and the Maghreb, the importation of slaves was constant, just as it was in the predominantly male slave societies of America and the West Indies. In both cases, slavery was sustained by the continued acquisition of new slaves by purchase or by capture and not by genetic reproduction. Numerous statistical data for American and West Indian slavery confirm this. Figures are less abundant for Africa, but still convincing.

Female slaves had very few children, and contrary to what we would expect if women were preferred to men for their reproductive potential, they didn't even ensure simple reproduction of the slave population. . . . There was less than one child for each slave woman. If we suppose that half of these children were girls, the "gross rate of reproduction" of the slave population falls below 0.5.

It was the economic law of slave reproduction which operated, independent of any assumed intention of the masters: "The Bobangi didn't bear many children. They just bought people." The low level of natality was not due to some peculiar sterility of slave women but to the fact that they aborted or practiced infanticide. Quite probably, the conditions of existence of slave women and the social climate within which they lived did not encourage them to procreate or to keep their children. If the masters wanted children so strongly, would they have welcomed them with aloofness? . . . If we consider this sterility as a form of resistance to the slave condition, how do we explain that the behavior of these women was marked in other ways by complete acceptance of their condition if not of their alienation? The idea of widespread resistance of female slaves by voluntary sterility is backed up by neither evidence nor testimony. On the other hand, the descriptions of the way of life of slave women show well enough why conditions were not favorable for childbearing. The story of Adukwe, for example, as told by Robertson, indicates a life of wandering and instability, a succession of poor living conditions. Her relations with men were precarious, often illegitimate. Her children were not generally recognized or supported by their genitors. She was never taken care of by any of her lovers. She miscarried several times. Only two daughters survived past infancy.

Thus it does not seem that maternity was as desirable for the female slave as for the free woman. Let us not forget that in a society with a lineage ethic, the wellborn woman prides herself on her fertility. It is not likely that such a society could accept high fertility among slave women. . . . "It is not proper that the slave be comparable to the master," goes a Soninke saying. On the other hand, cases reported in this book show that the fertility of female slaves increased when their condition was transformed, when they enjoyed a form of emancipation or more stable "unions" either with men of their own class or with their masters.

Thus, whatever intentions are attributed to the masters, the facts reported in this book show that slave reproduction took place mostly through purchase or capture in accordance with the economic laws of slavery. The slave class was renewed essentially by the introduction of individuals brought in from outside the society. In the merchant societies, the sole agent of reproduction was money: "If you had no money, the people were finished for good."

The resentment which the masters felt at not having children from their slave women was in contradiction with their general attitude towards slave reproduction. It was convenient to believe that the curse according to which wealth led to sterility was actualized through the infecundity of slave women, inherent anyway in their condition. Lamenting about it helped them to believe that it was due to fate and not to their policy of reproducing slaves by acquisition rather than by marriage as prescribed by the Koran.

The low fertility of slave women was observed also in the royal courts. The palace of the King of Dahomey, where a large number of women lived, many of them slaves, was not a fertile place. The offspring of kings, though very numerous for each of them, were few considering the number of women to whom the kings had access. Glele had 129 children, Gbehanzin 77, while they had access to 5,000 to 8,000 *ahosi* (spouses or dependents) most of whom were in principle prohibited from having any other sexual relationship. In this case, we must speak not of fertility, but of the "sterility" of female slaves.

Other examples confirm the low rate of reproduction in African slave societies. In the Bamum kingdom, where two-thirds of the population was servile, "thousands of slaves remained unmarried." Only those who distinguished themselves received wives as a reward. Their families, however, remained small. Now the Barnum sovereigns made constant war to accumulate slaves for their own use more than for sale. Certain sources suggest a policy of encouraging the reproduction of servile labor, but it obviously was without effect.

In the Sokoto caliphate, Hogendorn's data suggest that sixty percent of slave reproduction was by acquisition. Thus, it seems that the primary value of the female slave was not in her reproductive capacity, unless we assume that slavery functioned everywhere on the basis of a misunderstanding.

The Female Slave as Worker

Swema, a very young girl, after being captured was bought and then transported by an intermediary, who had apparently received an order and payment in advance for this type of merchandise. Swema's mother did not want to be separated from her daughter, and thus gave herself as a slave to the trader. Both were taken away by a caravan, but during the trip each carried a load. When the mother, worn out, could go no further, she was left to die: no work, no food. Swema, also worn out by her heavy burden, was nevertheless brought to her destination, where, sick and comatose, she was considered dead by the consignee and buried alive. She was saved by a passerby. In this case the slaver treated these two women as sheer laborers without sparing them for their reproductive capacity. From that point of view, they had no value. "I do not think that Swema's predicament was affected by her being female," writes Alpers in describing this case. It was thus only in their capacity for work, which did not distinguish them from males, that the female captives were in this case appreciated or rejected.

If the labor that a woman could perform was what determined her [importance], that was because the demand for female slaves was related to the sexual allocation of tasks, that is, to the fact that in African societies, women's participation in labor was greater than that of men . . . the greater demand for girls than for boys "had to do with the sexual division of labor."

In most African societies, women perform a greater number of tasks than men and work longer hours. They are involved in most forms of agricultural labor (sometimes sharing tasks with men) and in all domestic tasks. If we admit that the economy of slave societies was based on a sexual allocation of tasks similar to that of the societies from which the slaves came and that the slaves were intended to perform the same kind of labor, then we should expect a higher demand for women than for men.

Nevertheless, this allocation of tasks was strictly conventional. Certain female tasks which did not demand any apprenticeship, as for example the gathering of wood or water, could be performed by male slaves, though it was humiliating for them to do so. Both men and women were equally well prepared for agricultural tasks. It was different with cooking or with the raising of children, and with certain crafts. It is not that men could not perform these tasks, but women were better prepared because they received knowledge which passed from woman to woman. On the whole, women were thus generally preferred to men. If men could sometimes replace women, women more often replaced men, even in the most painful tasks for which there was hardly any apprenticeship. In about 1840, Duncan said of Dahomey that "women were usually preferred as porters, because it was agreed that they could carry heavier loads of merchandise for longer distances than men who were notorious for desertion." Not only were women in this case considered physically superior to men, but they were also assumed to be more docile. Hence there were no reasons why women would not have been in demand for the "manly" tasks.

In fact, the demand for female slaves was so strong that slave hunters often neglected men or massacred them on the battlefield. The price of men on the African market was generally distinctly lower than that of women. But this situation seems to have evolved with the transformations of the slave economy within Africa.

Women in Slavery in the Western Sudan

MARTIN KLEIN[3]

The introduction to this volume stressed two known aspects of female slavery in Africa: female slaves were more numerous than male slaves, and a higher price was paid for them. The preference for women has been explained by their greater ease of assimilation and by their role in reproduction. In his chapter, Claude Meillassoux has taken issue with the reproduction argument and put forward instead the argument that the greater value placed on female slaves was rooted in their capacity for work. This chapter will assess Meillassoux's argument and describe the situation of women in slavery in the western Sudan.

The western Sudan is an area dominated by Mande- and Fulbe-speaking peoples, which includes Senegal, most of Mali, upper Guinea, Upper Volta, and the northern Ivory Coast. It was a fairly homogeneous area, crisscrossed by trade routes, marked by similar social structures, and dominated by Islam. It was also an area where slavery had existed since early medieval times, if not earlier. Two types of slave system recurred across this zone. The first was characterized by a *household mode of production*. Slaves made up a small percentage of the population, lived within the household, worked alongside free members of the household, and participated in a network of face-to-face links. This system provided for the gradual integration of the slave's offspring into the kinship system as junior branches of the dominant lineage. The second system, which clearly evolved from the first, was marked by a high slave population. Slaves lived in separate settlements, and their labor was the source of sustenance for a ruling class that did not engage in physical labor and lived off the surplus produced by the slaves. I refer to this as a *slave mode of production,* not in an effort to impose a preconceived

[3]Klein, Martin, "Women in Slavery in the Western Sudan," in Robertson, Claire, and Klein, Martin, eds., *Women and Slavery in Africa* (Madison: University of Wisconsin Press, 1983), pp. 67–89.

Martin Klein (1934–   ) was born in New York City and received his Ph.D. from the University of Chicago in 1964. From 1965–70 he was a professor of history at the University of California at Berkeley before he moved to the history department at the University of Toronto.

evolutionary scheme, but simply because slave labor was the major source of both sustenance and surplus.

Demography

The estimates made by French administrators in 1894 and 1904 would suggest that about 60 percent of all adult slaves were female at the time of conquest. To be sure, these data are suspect, but I am inclined to think that, if anything, they minimize the number of women. I find it difficult to explain the few districts that report a majority of men. Certainly, women made up a considerable majority of the adults enslaved during any period. As warriors, the men were likely to resist and be killed. In addition, male prisoners were often killed and were more likely to be sold off. Almost two-thirds of those shipped across the Atlantic were male.

The ratio is even more dramatic for Senegambia, which got most of its slaves from the heart of the western Sudan. The ratio of men to women in exports from the Gambia River approached 8:1 or 9:1 during selected periods, and a sample from the Senegal River was over 4:1. These statistics would suggest that vast numbers of women and children were absorbed as slaves within the Sudan even during the period of the Atlantic slave trade. We can best illustrate this by drawing a model. Let us assume that two-thirds of those old enough to interest European slave traders were female, that ninety percent of the men were exported, and that the ratio of males to females among the exports was 2:1. All are reasonable assumptions. If they are correct, then 45 percent of those in prime ages were exported and 55 percent were kept within Africa. Furthermore, those kept within Africa were almost 95 percent female. Even if we alter our assumptions or feed into them the trans-Saharan trade, we end up with two clear conclusions: first, that a high percentage of those enslaved during the period of the Atlantic slave trade were kept within Africa; and second, that this number consisted almost exclusively of women and children. We can infer from this that the major concern of African slave systems during the centuries up to the closing of the Atlantic trade was the integration of women and children, and that this explains the killing of male prisoners.

Herbert Klein has argued above that the predominance of male exports was in the absence of any strong preference for men in the Atlantic trade. European planters in the New World were willing to pay almost as much for a strong woman as for a man. Except for certain skilled tasks, men and women did the same work on American plantations. In the Americas as in Africa, women were disproportionately represented in field labor. Klein makes a similar suggestion to explain the relatively small number of children in the Atlantic trade. They too were desired in Africa, at least in part because they were more easily assimilated than grown men.

Oral sources also indicate a clear preference for women and children. In fact, with the decline of the Atlantic slave trade, the killing of male prisoners seems to have increased. Roberts reports that Umarian armies often killed male prisoners. Ma Ba's forces also did so. So too did Samori's army on occasion, especially when resistance or revolt was involved. The killing of male prisoners probably declined as commodity production increased and the price differential between male and female captives dropped, but it did continue, though the number of men traded undoubtedly increased. Slave caravans continued to show a higher percentage of women. In 1894, under a civilian governor determined to end the slave trade, 604 slaves were freed— 125 men, 231 women, and 248 children. This number includes some run-aways, but mostly slaves freed when their caravans were interrupted. Toward the end of the century, when the trade became illegal, it focused largely on children, with a small number of women. Men virtually ceased to be traded.

Price data confirm the greater value placed on women. Around 1690, Jakhanke slave traders paid twice for women and boys what they paid for men, though the price on the coast was nearly the same. Over a century later, Mungo Park reported a similar 2:1 ratio between female and male prices. This was gradually reduced towards the end of the century, but prices of women remained higher until the very end and wherever reported. Thus, it would seem that women generally cost up to a third more.

In opposition to the notion that female slaves were valued primarily for their childbearing potential, Meillassoux argues that they were sought primarily for their work potential, and in particular because of the wider range of tasks that could be allocated to them. Meillassoux is not alone in this. Roberts argues that among the Maraka both male and female slaves "were valued above all for their role as commodity producers." I concur with this argument. The incorporation of a slave into a community was based on an act of sale. The trade would not have persisted if there were not people willing to pay the price. The use of slave labor would not have expanded as much as it did had there not been enough of a return to finance the purchase of new slaves. I do not think, however, that the wider range of tasks allocated to women adequately explains the price differential.

Meillassoux's argument is reinforced by a second argument, that slaves did not reproduce themselves. Data from his own research at Gumbu are reinforced by data from other areas. His assumption is that if the masters had been concerned with reproduction, they would have more actively en-couraged it. This argument is sound. Statistical evidence on the percentage of children is less clear than it is for women. There are two reasons for this. First, there was not always a clear definition of "child." Second, the slave trade involved large numbers of children, and in its declining years focused almost exclusively on children. Children grow up quickly, but at the time of the 1904 census, there were still many children who had been enslaved. In spite of this, the number of children was below replacement. Some of the data are especially striking. The figures for Djenne are particularly important because they refer largely to *rimaibe,* a fairly stable population of second-generation Fulbe slaves, who were clearly not reproducing themselves. Equally striking was a census in Beledugu, which reported that 37 percent of the free, as opposed to only 23 percent of the slaves, were children.

Meillassoux may go too far in hypothesizing a slave law of reproduction. The slave mode, as he conceives it, involves the reinvestment of surplus extracted from slaves to buy more slaves. Purchase or capture has the advantage that it is cheaper than the cost of raising a slave and it permits a more rapid rate of accumulation. In this situation, slave owners were not likely to encourage reproduction at the expense of productivity; or as I shall argue below, they were likely to pass the costs of reproduction on to the slaves themselves. This situation did not prevail everywhere, but it did prevail within the area that concerns us. Slaves were cheap and easily available. With the decline of foreign markets, slave raiding increased.

Meillassoux's argument looks very persuasive, but there is a flaw. Most slaves "born in the house" were permitted after marriage to farm for themselves. A fixed sum was paid every year for each man, woman, and child. At Gumbu, this obligation was the same for male and female, though the woman's productivity was lower according to Meillassoux's calculations. In other parts of the Sudan, this lower productivity was reflected in a reduced obligation. Generally, the woman paid half what her mate paid. This lower obligation clearly reflected the woman's domestic responsibilities. She had to cook and take care of children. Because of that, she produced less and paid less to the master. If this was true, we are still left with the problem of explaining the higher price. Even if we introduce textile production into our analysis, it is clear that women did not produce more than men.

Stages of Incorporation

To understand the position of female slaves, we must look briefly at the way in which slaves were incorporated into the society. As Curtin has suggested, slaves had no value at the point of capture because they could easily escape. It was therefore important for the slave to be moved to an area where he or she had no links. During this process, the slave had no social identity. He or she was a thing, who could be worked or beaten. The female slave could be exploited sexually. The slave who faltered on the trail and could no longer proceed was either exchanged for a healthier slave or killed. Men, women, and children were treated with equal harshness.

At some point, the slave was purchased and introduced into a new social unit. A new name was given, and the slave underwent some kind of ceremony in which he or she pledged not to escape. Legally, however, the new slave's status remained different from that of those born into slavery. The literature usually makes some kind of distinction between the trade slave, purchased during his lifetime, and the domestic slave "born in the house" (*woloso* or rimaibe). The usual distinction is that the trade slave was more likely to be harshly treated and was subject to sale. The woloso could not be sold and was part of the domestic unit. In time of famine or other natural disasters, there was often no choice but to sell slaves—and sale was also a threat that could be used against a refractory woloso. In many cases, a domestic slave could only be sold if the other domestic slaves approved. Both famine and debt were widespread concurrences, and the sanctions against sale were very limited. The most important of these was the attitude of the other slaves.

While the woloso might be sold, the purchased slave could rapidly integrate. If purchased young, the slave might soon forget his or her earlier life. The slave was watched carefully during the first years, and if escape was tried, the slave was flogged or put in irons. Rebellious slaves often had to sleep in irons. Women were at an advantage here. Escape by them was less feared, though women did run away. Furthermore, the mature female was likely to find herself someone's consort. She could become the concubine of her master or of one of his sons. Her position was always insecure because she could not turn to her own lineage for support, but it also depended to some degree on her own qualities and on the nature of the master's family. A male slave could become a trusted retainer and had a variety of privileged roles available to him. A female slave was more limited in her options, but she could become wife, mother, lover, companion, or friend.

Slave Systems and Modes of Production

There was a significant difference between the household mode of production and the slave mode. In the former, the slave speedily became part of the family unit. The number of slaves in a given household was small. Descriptions of the household mode generally stress that the master did the same work as the slaves. Thus, one account reported that: "With the Malinke there is no visible difference between master and slave, no disdain of one for the other, no rancor, they eat the same food and work side-by-side." Thus, the female slave spent much of her time on domestic labor within the household. If she were taken into the house of her master or one of his male dependents, she could become a favored spouse. If married to a slave, she and her husband had their own hut within the larger complex. Thus she lived with, worked alongside, cooked for, and even nursed free members of the household. One British administrator tells of an old female slave complaining that her master flogged her. He offered to place her in a free slave village, and she was ready to accept until approached by the master's son, whom she had nursed. As Olivier de Sardan makes clear, the milk tie could be a very important one.

Where the slave mode of production prevailed, the masters supervised, but did not work themselves. Paul Guebhard, the administrator cited above, reported that the slaves were ". . . poorly nourished, poorly treated and poorly rewarded . . . they only work as long as their masters are present to watch them, as a result of which the latter are forced to remain close to them, seated under a tree reading the Quran or chatting with friends. . . ." Within such a society, female slaves could be taken into the master's house, but most slave women were married to male slaves. They were worked much harder, often fed less well, and not involved in face-to-face relations with their masters, who formed a distinctly different class.

Slaves were used within these societies because they were the cheapest and often the only readily available source of additional labor. Thus the societies that were accumulating slaves were those societies that could pay for them. A major difference between the household mode of production and the slave mode was that within the household mode, there was limited expropriation of surplus commodity production, whereas under the slave mode, expropriation and accumulation increased dramatically. The flow of slaves is perhaps the best index of where economic growth was taking place within West Africa. The drop in prices that resulted from the end of the Atlantic trade simply facilitated this growth. Slaves went into the desert-side cities, where they produced grain and wove cotton for sale to nomads, who brought salt and cattle south. Slaves went into the coastal areas that produced commodities like peanuts and palm oil for European markets. Slave plantations developed around the Juula cities, such as Kong, Boundoukou, Bouna, Banamba, and Kankan. Each had a belt of land intensively cultivated by slave labor, as the free peasantry were pushed out to more distant and less safe areas. . . . In some regions, like the Futa Jalon, political elites were important in expanding slave production, but in most regions the decisive influences were the commercial elites. The expansion of the slave sector involved primarily diversification from trade into production.

The Price of Female Slaves

During the crucial years of the Atlantic slave trade, it is probable that relatively few adult males were absorbed into African communities as producers. The system, as it evolved, was primarily concerned with absorbing women and children. With the closing of the Atlantic trade, the number of men increased and the price gap decreased. The majority, however, remained female, and the price of women retained higher.

To understand the reason, we have to return to the demography of slavery.

We must remember that we are dealing with patrilineal and polygynous societies. They had a capacity to absorb an indefinite number of women. Extra wives were desirable at all levels of the system. And they were cheap. In the Futa Jalon, the bridewealth for a female slave was a rooster, a mat, and several loads of wood. But we can go further. A surplus of female slaves became essential to the functioning of the system. Let us look at three levels: the masters, the slave warriors, and the agricultural slaves.

For the masters, increase in the number of dependents was not only a source of status, but also the basis of the perpetuation and expansion of the social unit. Ruling lineages, maraboutic households, and merchant families all sought increase through the accumulation of wives and concubines. The virtue of a slave wife was that she had no family. She had no brothers to support her if there was conflict. She could not divorce her spouse. And her children looked to no matrilineal kin for backing. At the same time, she was part of the cement. Rich and powerful lineages tended to be very large, numbering generally in the hundreds, and sometimes more. The existence of a large patrimony became a factor of cohesion, dissuading the restless from splitting. The largest part of that patrimony was an accumulation of slaves. The female slave also relieved the well-born woman of the burden of domestic work.

Slave warriors represent a different case. Throughout the Sudan, they provided the bulk of the various armies, and the source of key administrative personnel. Slave chiefs were generally well remunerated. The slave warriors were not. Few rulers could afford to feed a large force of warriors: the question becomes how these warriors fed themselves. Jean Bazin reports that the Bambara *tonjon* (slave soldiers) cultivated very little. My informants suggested that the Wolof *tyeddo* (slave soldiers) cultivated, but they probably did little work on their fields. Wars were generally conducted during the dry seasons. Warriors were clearly free to work during the rainy season, but they were generally contemptuous of sustained agricultural labor. They often went on raids during the dry season and spent much time drinking. Booty is an inadequate source of sustenance. It is not regular enough. Furthermore, there were restraints on free-lance military activities. Kidnapping was frowned on, and in some societies punishable by the death penalty because it threatened the stability of the society. Raiding within the borders of a kingdom was also frowned on. Warriors probably brought home some food, but it is likely that most of their sustenance came from the labor of their wives. Furthermore, on long military campaigns, wives were brought along to cook, to carry, and to take care of the camp.

The best-documented example is the French Army, which operated much like a Sudanese army. Recruited largely from slaves, poorly funded, and undermanned, the French colonial forces also depended heavily on booty, particularly on the taking of slaves. These slaves were distributed both to auxiliaries and to *tirailleurs*. Furthermore, it was women who were important. Generally, the military men did not talk openly about the practice, since that could have jeopardized their enterprise, but there are numerous letters in the archives:

> I am going to distribute the slaves in order to have fewer mouths to feed. Of course, it will keep a certain number for your men, who will be available to them after your campaign; you can tell them that from me in order to stimulate them a little.

It is probable that these slave wives fed their husband-masters.

Let us move one step further down the social ladder. I have always been skeptical of statements that some slaves became wealthier than their masters. It was possible, but assuming it did occur, it was probably very rare, given the slaves' obligations. I have also been skeptical of frequent statements that male slaves could take more than one wife. They could, but did they? When I interviewed, one of my first questions was whether a slave could take a second wife. The answer came back with virtual unanimity from both freeborn and servile informants: the master was obligated to provide this male slave with one wife, but the slave could and often did take a second.

Patrick Manning suggests that the surplus of women was a late-nineteenth-century development. If his argument is correct, the western Sudan should be divided into two zones for the period before the mid-nineteenth century. In the coastal zone, most of the exports were men, and there was a surplus of female slaves available for distribution. Polygyny was thus widespread. In the interior, a large part of the savanna exported mostly female slaves north. Here, Manning argues, male slaves predominated, and thus did not marry. This changed only after 1870. If Manning is correct, the validity of my assumptions about slave polygyny is limited in both time and place. I am inclined to think that the death rate among men meant that women were always more numerous among the slaves, but differences in ratios undoubtedly influenced the availability of female slaves for distribution as spouses and concubines. Where there was a significant surplus of slave women, spouses could obviously be provided for male slaves. This was important in the last years of the nineteenth century, because increasingly large accumulations of the newly enslaved posed a real threat to the social order.

It is clear that the importance of slave marriage was not simply the desirability of servile offspring. Marriage permitted both male and female slaves to have some form of normal social existence. It made life more satisfying and gave the slave a stake. Marriage, even in the attenuated form known by slaves, played a crucial role in integrating the slave into the dominant society, and children cemented that integration. But that does not explain the second wife. Richard Roberts's research on the Maraka provides an explanation for that. Roberts discovered that slaves were rarely interested in buying their freedom. Instead, slaves often preferred to buy their own slaves. The reason is simple. The male slave did not control his offspring. His offspring belonged to his wife's master (who was usually also his master). Often, though not always, the master claimed the child's services at circumcision or when his or her adult teeth came in, that is, at adolescence. This meant that the slave had no security. If he became old or sick and could no longer feed himself, he could not count on his children. A good master took care of his indigent slaves, but there were few sanctions to guarantee that the master did this. This led to many slaves buying slaves. But let us note that the same argument is valid for wives. A wife paid her own way, and could be relied on in need. Furthermore, the possibility of a second wife motivated the male slave to work and seek his fulfillment within the system and within his subaltern role. It is probable that relatively few ever took a second wife, but the possibility was important. The female slave seems not to have had a parallel option; but then, her ability to spin cotton meant that she was always of some value.

One other aspect of slave demography is worth exploring. As we have seen, a major limitation on slave reproduction was that it was cheaper to buy a slave than to raise one. This would provide a disincentive to natural reproduction only if we assume that the master paid the costs. He did not. The slave child lived with his parents until he was old enough to work full time, at which time he could be claimed by the master. This meant that the costs of reproduction were borne by the slave menage. The master had passed on the costs, though he kept control of the product. The chief barrier to slave reproduction thus lay in the economics of the slave menage, which Meillassoux has explored elsewhere. The slave owned approximately the amount needed to feed an adult for a year. Given the conditions of the hoe agriculture, there were limits to what a slave menage could produce. A strong healthy male could not produce much over a ton of millet, and a woman not much over half of that. This meant that it was difficult for the slave menage to accumulate enough to buy a slave or a second wife, or to save up a reserve. During famines and after natural disasters, many a slave menage was dependent on the master's reserve. If the master was improvident, it was the slave who starved. If the master was hard, the slave couple could easily lose the right to farm for itself. The slave menage thus could not afford many unproductive members. A small child, an aged parent, or even a sick adult threatened the well-being of the family. Though children went to work young, they had to be fed until old enough to go into the fields. In spite of these barriers to reproduction, slaves did have children and they did constitute families. Having passed on the costs, the master profited. Reproductive capacity must have played some small role in the price of female slaves. The slave family had no juridical existence. The slave, after all, had no lineage. Nevertheless, runaway and freed slaves often tried to free parents and children. And when slavery was deprived of judicial recognition after 1903, the transformation of slave menages into autonomous households was one of the first results.

Frederick Cooper has suggested that within any slave system there was a balance between acquiescence and resistance, between coercion and acceptance. It follows from this line of analysis that slaves must be integrated into the system and motivated, either by fear or rewards, to perform their role within it. Slavery was widespread because it was effective in meeting certain needs. Sudanic slave systems lacked the coercive potential of American slave systems, though they could be harsh and certainly were exploitative. The predominance of women among the enslaved meant that there were enough women to provide concubines for the rich and powerful and agricultural labor for the army, with enough left over to provide a domestic life for the ordinary male slave. Furthermore, in the very act of accumulating, either to buy a slave or marry a second wife, the male slave was seeking fulfillment within the system and enforcing it. It is striking that Sudanic states and slave owners trusted their slaves to bear arms.

Women's Work

Many archival sources insist that the female's labor obligation was the same as that of the male. This varied somewhat from society to society, but the norm was about five days a week from sunrise to early afternoon prayer (2:00 P.M.), with the slaves obligations greater and more strictly enforced within the slave mode. On closer observation, there was a division of responsibilities. Most Sudanic societies have a rather precise definition of what is men's work and what is women's. Women generally had child care responsibilities, and they gathered firewood and water and did the cooking. When slaves worked on the household's lands, they had to be fed—and within the slave mode, noble women did not cook. The men did the heavy work of clearing the fields, but certain crops were women's crops. For example, women cultivated indigo and did the dyeing among the Maraka. In general, there was an understanding about who weeded and who harvested each of the crops. Though this may have broken down from time to time, one slave rising was stimulated by an effort to mix male and female work crews.

Women also freely participated in industrial activities such as mining, salt making, and textile production. Whether gold was mined or salt manufactured by slave or free labor seems to have varied from area to area. In textile production, the major industry in most areas of heavy slave concentration, there was a precise distinction between men and women. Men planted and women harvested cotton. The women spun and the men wove. While much of the cloth produced was white, the most valuable cloth was indigo-dyed blue cloth. Women grew the indigo, made the dye, and dyed the cloth. The entrepreneurs of the Maraka dyeing industry were women, and most of the labor was done by their slaves.

Spinning was a particular problem because it took about eight hours of spinning to produce enough thread to keep a weaver busy for one hour. This meant that spinners were more in demand than weavers. Male slaves were thus free to work at other tasks. During the dry season, many worked as porters on caravans. Others packed goods, built houses, or did other kinds of craft work. Nevertheless, with cloth production crucial to household income, it was important for a Maraka or Juula household to have enough spinners to keep the weavers occupied. The use of women in spinning and dyeing thus became an additional factor pushing up the price of female slaves. It meant that even women too old to do sustained field labor had a price.

Masters generally preferred that female slaves marry within the household, and sometimes insisted that they do so. When a woman married a man owned by another master, she was often purchased or exchanged. If not, she remained the property of her master and continued to work for him. Alternatively, she worked with her husband and they paid her master a fixed sum every year. Women probably produced less wealth than men but worked harder because they combined productive labor with their domestic tasks. Women's work in the savanna was considerable. Water had to be brought from the well, firewood collected, and the millet ground—all before anyone could think of cooking. Whether slaves ate at home or were fed as part of a work gang, the preparation of food involved a substantial investment of labor. Women worked a longer day than men, and probably a harder day. During the rainy season, they brought the men their food, kept the compound clean, and worked their own fields. If life was difficult at home, it was harsher on the trail. Caillie has a description of the organization of domestic life on a caravan to Djenne. The women carried loads when the caravan was on the move. When it stopped, the men rested while the women gathered firewood, cooked, and prepared hot water for the men's baths. They also spun cotton in their spare time, which they sold for their own profit in Djenne.

The woman's path to manumission was also different from the man's. Within the household mode of production, the offspring of slaves were often absorbed within several generations, but where the slave mode prevailed, slave status was hereditary and the only distinction was between those taken in their lifetime and those "born in the house." There were several ways a person could be manumitted. A slave could buy his or her freedom, generally for the price of two slaves—but women seldom had access to such wealth. Much of their labor did not produce income. Islam also encouraged manumission. It was considered a pious act. Deathbed manumissions of trusted retainers have been reported in many Sudanic societies. These probably affected older men who had served their masters well for many years. It is probable that the most frequent kind of manumission and the only one affecting women was the manumission of concubines and slave spouses. Under Islamic law, the child of a free man was born free regardless of the mother's status, and the mother was free if she bore her master a child. There were, however, several limitations on this. According to Richard Roberts, Maraka slave owners often did not acknowledge their offspring and thus avoided freeing their concubines. Such a woman could find herself back in the slave village as she aged. Furthermore, even if freed, she remained within her husband's household as a junior wife and with no kin to turn to for support in a conflict situation. Nevertheless, we can assume that this form of manumission was widespread and involved a constant absorption of slave women into the freeborn population.

Sexual Rights

One of the defining characteristics of the male slave's position was the absence of paternal rights. He could neither bequeath to nor control his offspring, who belonged to his wife's master. The master could claim all or part of the child's services. If the slave child were female, the master chose her spouse, or at least had to give his approval in order for her to marry. The same questions are not relevant for women. A woman would not have had these rights even if free. In fact the question often raised by feminists is whether there was a difference between the wife and the slave. There was, but it was primarily that the freeborn wife was a member of a lineage. She had a family. She could call on her family if mistreated, and could return to that family to visit. The slave had no kin. She had nowhere to go if mistreated. She had little choice, because the sanctions that could be brought to bear were severe. She could be flogged or put in irons. If a concubine, she could be sent back to the slave settlement and her place taken by another more eager to please. If she were a first-generation slave, or if unpopular with other slaves, she could be sold. There are many cases of women being traded numerous times and marched long distances. There was, for example, a Malian slave who claimed to have been traded a number of times and to have been moved from her home in the northern Ivory Coast to Gao, to Segou, to Kano and then back to Gao, much of it on foot, much of it with a load on her head.

A more important defining characteristic of the female slave was her lack of control over her body. One freed slave, in response to a trader's claim that she was his wife, explained to an administrator: "You know that any Juula can take for himself any slave in his troop." For the newly captured and the slave in transit, the matter was clear. The Malian slave cited above talked of being placed in a hut by Samori's *sofa* and visited nightly. While being moved, the slave was a thing. She had been taken by force and had no social identity. Her only protection was the obvious interest of the slave trader in keeping his human merchandise alive. Even after being integrated into a household, the female slave had little control over her sex life. Soleillet talks of the master having the "droit de seigneur" over all of his slave women. He could chose those he desired and give the others to whomever he wished to reward. Female slaves could be given to visitors, in which case the slave was responsible for a full range of domestic chores. According to Soleillet, two slave women were given to Mage and Quinton to keep them from chasing the freeborn. Both women were pregnant when the explorers departed, and one was later visited by Soleillet. Meillassoux goes further:

> The master or his dependents can maintain sexual relations with her [the female slave]. The young noble, who is entrusted to a slave to learn to work, has at the same time a sexual apprentice-ship with the daughters or wives of his host, who if he inadvert-ently surprises the young noble with one of his women, has only the right to give him a symbolic blow with his fist.

The point of view of one slave was plaintively put to a Gambian court: "It was against my wish that the prisoner came to me at night. Being a slave I was afraid."

Conclusion

All of these variables affected the difference between the prices paid for female and male slaves. One irony of the situation is that the gap between male and female prices was declining in the late nineteenth century at the very time when the number of males on the market was increasing. Clearly, a crucial variable was that reproduction was more important within the household mode of production, while slaves were purchased within the slave mode primarily for the production of commodities. Hence, within the slave mode of production the differences between male and female decreased. This is exactly what was happening in the late nineteenth century. Commod-ity production using slave labor was expanding, bringing in its train increased work loads, more intensive exploitation, and lower birth rates.

A slave woman differed from a free woman less than a male slave differed from his free counterpart. She had little control over her children, could not accumulate, and was not sure of being taken care of in her old age; but even free women in most societies had relatively few rights and only limited control over their offspring. All but the elite were doomed to a harsh struggle for survival. The major difference was that the free woman was part of a lineage, to which she could turn for protection or support. She was less vulnerable. The female slave was sought, first and foremost, as a worker, and valued for her ability to produce surplus value, but it was other characteristics that made her more valued than the male. Even within the slave mode, she was valued because she was more easily assimilated, she was less likely to escape, and she helped integrate male slaves. The predominance of women helped Sudanic societies strike that balance between coercion and consensus essential to the functioning of any slave system. If less important, the role of reproducer was not insignificant. Those slaves absorbed as concubines were valued for their ability to produce offspring. For the rest, the production of more slaves was a bonus. Having passed the costs of reproduction on to the slave, the master profited from increase. This was clearly not irrelevant to the price of female slaves.

The *Signares:* Entrepreneurial African Women

GEORGE BROOKS[4]

From the fifteenth century on, Europeans traded along the coast of West Africa—the westernmost perimeter of a vast African commercial complex of whose extent even the most astute Europeans were only vaguely aware. The earliest mariners along the coast were the Portuguese, who initially carried on a shipboard commerce. Soon, however, adventurers from Portugal and the Cape Verde Islands began to settle among coastal and riverine societies in order to benefit from increased proximity to the sources of this African commerce. Termed *lancados* because they "threw themselves" among Africans, these men established relationships with the most influential women who would accept them in order to obtain commercial privileges. In pursuit of their objectives, *lancados* adopted many of the customs and practices of the African societies. . . . Descendants of their alliances with African women were called *filhos da terra,* "children of the soil," and, with their dual cultural background (and sometimes their mothers' social rank and prerogatives as well), were in an advantageous position to serve as brokers manipulating African and European trading networks.

That African women in the Senegambia and Upper Guinea Coast regions did enjoy social rank and prerogatives seems clear. . . . What is certain is that African and Eurafrican women who were wealthy traders or possessed property and influence were treated with marked respect by Africans, Eurafricans, and Europeans alike. In the eighteenth and nineteenth centuries, such women were customarily addressed by titles *nhara* (in Portuguese Guinea), *senora* (in the Gambia), or *signare* (in Senegal)—titles derived from the Portuguese *senhora.* They often possessed numerous domestic slaves, trading craft, and houses, as well as quantities of gold and silver jewelry and

---

[4]Brooks, George E. Jr., "The *Signares* of Saint-Louis and Goree: Women Entrepreneurs in Eighteenth Century Senegal," in Hafkin, Nancy, and Bay, Edna, eds., *Women in Africa: Studies in Social and Economic Change* (Stanford: Stanford Press, 1976), pp. 19–44.

George E. Brooks Jr. (1933–) was born in Lynden, Massachusetts and received his Ph.D. from Boston University in 1962. Brooks has published numerous articles and books on a variety of topics in West African history. He is currently a professor of African and World history at the University of Indiana and has been recognized for his efforts to integrate African history into the study of world history.

splendid clothing. Indisputably they knew how to acquire wealth, how to employ it profitably, and how to enjoy it as well.

Although there were many influential trading women in the Senegambia and Upper Guinea Coast regions in the eighteenth and early nineteenth centuries, the largest number was concentrated in Senegal and it was there that the greatest development and elaboration of what may be termed "signareship" occurred.

The island of N'Dar in the Senegal River—on which the French founded the settlement of Saint-Louis in 1659—is only a mile and a half long and an eighth of a mile wide. Goree is an even smaller island—a half mile long and a few hundred yards wide—cradled by the Cape Verde peninsula. A settlement there was established originally by the Portuguese, who were later ousted by the Dutch, who in turn were displaced by the French in 1677. The population of both islands increased steadily during the eighteenth century: Saint-Louis had an estimated population of some 3,000 by 1764, and more than 6,000 by 1785; Goree had some 1,000 inhabitants in 1767, and some 1,800 by 1785. European residents included the employees of successive French trading companies and the officers and troops of the garrisons. Some who sought their fortunes in Senegal were men with outstanding qualities, but many were of mediocre ability and character. Oftentimes the soldiers represented the dregs of European society—men with criminal records, debauched, and diseased—and were more likely to acquire "civilizing" influences from Africans than to impart them.

The role of African women (primarily of the Wolof and Lebou) was a factor of great influence on the special developments that occurred in Senegal. These women had considerable independence of action in their own societies, and were strongly attracted by the economic opportunities that arose with the coming of the Europeans. And European men were no less attracted to them for their beauty and commercial enterprise. Given the circumstances, cohabitation and economic collaboration for mutual advantage were virtually inevitable.

By mid-century, *signares* had attained considerable economic consequence and had contributed to creating a Senegalese life-style so attractive to Europeans that they refused to obey Company directives against cohabitation and commerce with African women. Pruneau de Pommegorge's account [of 1789] distilled from twenty-two years' experience in West Africa ending in 1765 would serve with few modifications until well into the nineteenth century.

> The women on the island [Saint-Louis] are, in general, closely associated with white men, and care for them when they are sick in a manner that could not be bettered. The majority live in considerable affluence, and many African women own thirty to forty

slaves which they hire to the Company. Each year the domestic slaves make the voyage to Galam engaged as sailors; they bring back to their mistresses fifteen, twenty, even up to thirty weight of gold for the sale of two hogsheads of salt which they are permitted to embark duty-free. The women have some of this gold made into jewelry, and the rest is used to purchase clothing, because they adore, as do women everywhere else, fashionable clothing. Their mode of dress, characteristically very elegant, suits them very well. They wear a very artistically arranged white handkerchief on the head, over which they affix a small narrow black ribbon, or a colored one, around their head. A shift *a la française,* ornamented; a bodice of taffeta or muslin; a skirt of the same and similar to the bodice; gold earrings; anklets of gold or silver, for they will wear no others; red morocco slippers on the feet; underneath their bodice a piece of two ells of muslin, the ends of which dangle beneath the left shoulder—thus appareled when they go out in public, they are followed by one or two young girls who serve as their chambermaids, likewise well dressed, but somewhat more lightly and a little less modestly than is our own custom. One becomes accustomed very quickly, however, to viewing these almost nude women without becoming embarrassed. Their customs are different from ours, and when one becomes accustomed to their nudity it ceases to make any more impression than if they were covered up.

The women being thus escorted when they go out, they frequently encounter a *griot* (a type of man who sings someone's praises in return for money); in such instances he does not lose the opportunity to precede them declaiming their praises with all the exaggerations he can think of, and some immodesties which they know, the women being so flattered that in the rapture excited by this adulation they often fling some of their garments to the singer when they have nothing left in their pockets to give him.

Next to finery, the greatest passion of these women is their dances, or *folgars,* which they sometimes hold until daybreak, and during which one drinks a great deal of palm wine, *pitot* (a type of beer), and also wines from France, when they are able to procure them. The usual way to praise those who have excelled in dancing is to fling a cloth or a handkerchief over them, which they return to the person who has thrown it, making a deep bow to thank him.

Some of these women are married in church, others *a la mode du pays,* which in general consists of the consent of both parties and the relatives. It is remarked that the latter marriages are always more successful than the former; the women are more faithful to their husbands than otherwise is the case. The ceremony which follows the latter form of marriage is not in fact as becoming as is the good behavior of the women.

The morning following the consummation of the marriage, the relatives of the bride come at daybreak and carry off the white cloth on which the couple have spent the night. Do they find the proof they search for? They affix the cloth at the end of a long pole, waving like a flag; they parade this all day long in the village, singing and praising the new bride and her chastity; but when the relatives have not in fact found such proof the morning after, they take care to substitute for it as quickly as possible.

Many aspects of Pruneau de Pommegorge's account continue to be relevant in modern-day Senegal. Senegalese women still possess an unrivaled flair for displaying clothing, jewelry, and other finery. *Or de Galam* (gold from Galam) is still the byword for quality and purity. The single white handkerchief headpiece described by Pruneau de Pommegorge soon evolved into the striking cone shaped turban, artfully constructed with as many as nine colored handkerchiefs, that became the hallmark of *signares* in Senegal and the Gambia. *Folgar* is a Portuguese word that passed into West African languages to describe a carefree frolic or general rejoicing. . . . *Griots* belong to a special endogamous social class, or "caste," associated with many societies living on the coast and in the interior of West Africa. They were (and are) professional entertainers, musicians, singers, and dancers, and their role is analogous to that of the bards or troubadours of medieval Europe: they attached to the leading families as praise-singers, keepers of family histories and genealogies, counselors to rulers, and educators of the young. Traditionally, *griots* had the privilege of mocking people or using abusive language with impunity, with the result that they were generally well rewarded to ensure their favor. Female *griots* were often hairdressers, an occupation that gave them a matchless opportunity to learn and pass on gossip. They also had a reputation for lascivious dancing and for otherwise having all immoral influence on young women.

In another section of his account, Pruneau de Pommegorge testifies to the beauty, intelligence, and remarkable adaptability of Wolof women, which made them much sought after as slaves by French colonists in the West Indies. They were reputed to be so adept that within a few months of their arrival in the Antilles they knew how to sew, speak French, and perform other duties as well as European servants, with the consequence that they were especially sought after for service as chambermaids. This Wolof "adaptability" is a theme discussed by numerous observers.

The Reverend John Lindsay, chaplain aboard one of the British vessels that captured Goree in December 1758, and a subsequent visitor to Saint-Louis, also praised Senegalese women:

As to their women, and in particular the ladies (for so I must call many of those in Senegal) they are in a surprising degree handsome, have very fine features, are wonderfully tractable, remarkably polite both in conversation and manners; and in the point of keeping themselves neat and clean (of which we have generally strange ideas, formed to us by the beastly laziness of slaves), they far surpass the Europeans in every respect. They bathe twice a day, . . . and in this particular have a hearty contempt for all white people, who they imagine must be disagreeable, our women especially. Nor can even their men, from this very notion, be brought to look upon the prettiest of our women, but with the coldest indifference, some of whom there are here, officers' ladies, who dress very showy, and who even in England would be thought handsome. You may, perhaps, smile at all this; but I assure you 'tis a truth. Negroes to me are no novelty; but the accounts I received of them, and in particular the appearance of the females on this occasion, were to me a novelty most pleasing. They were not only pretty, but in the dress in which they appeared, were even desirable. Nor can I give you any drapery more nearly resembling theirs, than the loose, light, easy robe, and sandal, in which we see the female Grecian statues attired; most of which were of exceeding white cotton, spun, wove into narrow slips of six or seven inches, and sewn together by themselves. Their hair, for it differs a little from wool, very neat and curiously plaited; and their persons otherways adorned, by earrings, necklaces, and bracelets, of the purest gold.

And indeed I cannot help thinking, that it was to the benefit of the African company in general, and the happiness of those they sent abroad in particular; that, with such promising inhabitants, the French suffered no white women to be sent thither.

There was, however, no easy fraternization, to the dismay of the British seamen, and Reverend Lindsay was at pains to describe the women's high reputation for chastity and respectable behavior.

Also living at Saint-Louis, Goree, and other West African commercial centers were numerous Africans known as *grumetes,* who were associated with European and Eurafrican trading activities. *Grumete* (Crioulo), *gourmet* (French), and *grumetta* (English) all derived from the word for ship's boy or cabin boy in various European languages, and *grumete* was the name given to Africans hired aboard European vessels as pilots and seamen from the fifteenth century on. *Grumetes* were recruited from West African seafaring peoples for a variety of tasks afloat and ashore: they served as boatbuilders, longshoremen, and guards for slave barracoons, but they were chiefly employed as sailors and their maritime skills made them invaluable to European and Eurafrican traders. They generally spoke *Crioulo,* "Black French," or "Black English," wore European-style clothing, and adopted some Christian practices.

Where Pruneau de Pommegorge and Reverend Lindsay dwelled on the positive attributes of Senegalese women, the noted French botanist Michel Adanson subjected them and the leading administrators in Senegal to a searching critique. . . . He was highly critical of a number of corrupt practices associated with *signares* that interfered with the proper administration of the Senegal Company and were grossly unfair to its lower-ranked French employees. . . . The slaves of *signares* hired in the Company's service carried on trade on behalf of their mistresses and those high-ranking Company officials in collusion with them, with the result that the *signares* obtained the choicest merchandise, including commodities not available to the lower-ranked French employees.

Whether as a result of Adanson's indictment of past administrative corruption or not, the French government introduced significant changes in West African commerce in 1763. Goree was placed under royal administration with an appointed governor, and freedom of commerce was proclaimed. However, independent traders soon learned that free trade was little more than a declaration of principle insofar as West Africa was concerned. Collusion between commercial interests associated with the new Senegal Company (the Compagnie de Guyane) and royal officials made the measure a dead letter. The royal governors proved to be readily corruptible and preoccupied with lining their own pockets. *Signares* must have welcomed the advent of the royal administration, inasmuch as the new royal officials posted to Senegal, like the military officers, had little to occupy their time. Seemingly most followed the example of their superiors and associated with *signares* in illicit trading ventures.

The Abbe Demanet, who accompanied the French expedition dispatched to reoccupy Goree in 1763, criticized the lack of initiative of European traders there and at other trading communities displayed while the women associated with them were becoming wealthy in commerce:

> Each and every one had become absorbed in his own diversions and was debilitated by indolence. Simple clerks, ordinary employees with low-level appointments, reached expenses of 10,000 francs a year. One sees today on Goree, at Senegal, and in the Gambia some of their concubines who have fortunes of 100,000 livres, even though prior to this business, so pernicious in different respects they owned nothing whatever.

Like other sources, Demanet is uninformative on the names of the women or the means by which they carried on their commercial affairs. Besides using their domestic slaves, *signares* presumably employed relatives and took advantage of ties with African traders and rulers on the mainland.

The revelations of Adanson and the Abbe Demanet concerning conditions in Senegal are borne out by the research of Dr. Cariou and Mme. Knight-Baylac on the history of Goree. In 1749, ten of the thirteen private properties on the island belonged to Eurafricans, nine of whom were women. In 1767 the richest woman on Goree, Caty Louette, then associated with a Captain Aussenac, owned twenty-five male and forty-three female domestic slaves. A plan of Goree prepared in 1779 by Evrard Duparel shows that of eighteen compounds belonging to the French government, eleven were occupied by *signares*. . . . *Signares* living on Goree were castigated for spending their days in idleness, for dressing in a manner calculated to arouse violent passions, for inciting whites to debauchery, and for sowing disunity and sickness among them. Royal administrators were accused of collaborating with the *signares* in illicit commerce in order to gain the wealth necessary to attract and support them and indulge their taste for luxuries; in the meantime they prevented other Frenchmen from doing the same.

By the mid-1780s, Saint-Louis and Goree had large populations of Eurafricans and free Africans who owned numerous domestic slaves. According to Golberry's estimates cited earlier, Saint-Louis's population of more than 6,000 included some 2,400 Eurafricans and free blacks and about the same number of domestic slaves, besides 600 French soldiers, government officials, and members of the trading community, and about sixty permanent white residents. (There were, in addition, roughly 1,000 trade slaves held in the fort and in the cellars of houses on the island.) The population of Goree was similar, but on a smaller scale: of an estimated total population of 1,840, there were 116 Eurafrican and free black property-holders and their families; 522 free blacks without property; 1,044 domestic slaves; 70 to 80 Europeans, including government administrators, officers, soldiers, and employees of the Senegal Company; and 200 or so trade slaves held for shipment.

It is impossible to estimate the number of *signares* among the Eurafrican and free black population cited above. Whatever their numbers, *signares* clearly were the chief element in creating a way of life on Saint-Louis and Goree that combined features of Wolof and European society, and that was highly attractive and beneficial to European men who came to Senegal. That *signares* directed affairs for their own purposes is likewise evident.

Signares who were successful in commerce and marriage presided over large households and compounds inhabited by numerous domestic slaves. From the 1760s on, many of the houses in Saint-Louis and Goree were constructed of brick and stone by domestic slaves who were trained to be expert masons and carpenters. Such houses were surrounded by walls of the same material or by palisades of reeds. The ground floors of the houses contained kitchens, pantries, storerooms, and cells for securing trade slaves held for sale. The *signare* and her family lived on the upper floor, which had high-ceilinged, airy rooms with large windows opening onto balconies. The windows were kept shuttered against sunlight during the day and were opened to sea breezes in the cool of the late afternoon before sunset. Indicative of both the expansion of commerce and the increasing affluence of the inhabitants of Saint-Louis and Goree in the 1770s and 1780s are the growing number of such dwellings: on Goree, an increase from fewer than six in 1772 to more than fifty by 1789, all constructed on slabs of basalt and lime mortar made from seashells.

An American shipmaster who traded at Saint-Louis in 1815 described the households and compounds and remarked on the many economic activities that went on there.

> The houses are mostly built of stone and brick; they are large and convenient. The lower floor is appropriated to the servants, storerooms, stables or any other purpose. The second floor is divided into a hall, a sitting room, and several small bed apartments. One or more sides are generally furnished with a piazza running the whole length, which affords a pleasant walk. The whole is surrounded by a high brick wall, the solitary gate to which is constantly guarded by one or two slaves who let no one no thing out but with their master's order. These houses and walls are plastered and whitewashed and at a distance have a very elegant appearance. A closer view, however, so connects the idea of a Prison with thick walls, grated windows, and guarded gates as to destroy the lively interest excited in a stranger's mind on viewing them from shipboard. Each house may in fact be considered a fortress where the master on his sofa views and directs from the piazza his numerous slaves below. These all have their huts ranged round the wall within the yard, and it is not uncommon to see carpenters, coopers, blacksmiths, weavers, tailors, etc., all in operation at once at their respective works belonging to the same yard. For every man of any note makes it a point to have one or more families of his slaves brought up to each kind of work either of use or ornament.

Fortunate indeed was the European who could associate with a *signare* possessed of such a household and skilled labor force.

Perspectives on "Signareship"

If the development of signareship in Senegal has yet to be fully explored—especially with regard to the question of the social origins of the women concerned—the main lines of development seem clear. Signareship represented an economic nexus between European men pursuing personal gain (usually illegally) and African and Eurafrican women determined to acquire

European merchandise. It was the women who provided access to African commercial networks, furnished households with skilled domestic slaves, and proved indispensable as interpreters of African languages and cultures: in short, *signares* skillfully manipulated two trading complexes and cultures to further their own ends. Yet signareship represented a social nexus, too, and *signares* helped create a way of life, an *ambiance,* that went far beyond the economic relationship. Once the process was well begun, it was so advantageous and attractive to all involved, at least in Senegal, that it became self-perpetuating. The two societies, Senegalese and French, partially blending, largely coexisting, created a complex cultural relationship that transcends facile explanation or analysis.

Women as Spirit Mediums in East Africa
IRIS BERGER[5]

Throughout Africa women have played a prominent role in religions centered on spirit-possession. Indeed, in the Interlacustrine and Nyamwezi areas of East Africa—southern and western Uganda, Rwanda, Burundi, and northwestern Tanzania—their participation in other spheres of precolonial religious activity was severely limited. Recent anthropological explanations of this phenomenon have focused on the leverage that possession allowed women to exert in specific conflict situations. I. M. Lewis, for example focused his wide-ranging comparative study *Ecstatic Religion* on tensions between men and women and found numerous cases where predominantly female spirit-possession cults functioned as "thinly disguised protest movements" against the male sex. A study of female mediums in the Interlacustrine and Nyamwezi regions, however, suggests that his "sex war" hypotheses defines only one aspect of the problem; for, in addition to supplying an antimale outlet, religious groups also offered large numbers of women initiates an unusual degree of authority in ritual situations and provided smaller numbers with long-term positions of high status.

Religious beliefs, in these two areas centered on legendary heroes known collectively as Cwezi or Imandwa. Legends trace the worship of these deities to an early state in western Uganda whose rulers bore the name Cwezi. According to traditions, after the Cwezi kingdom declined, people began to honor the spirits of their former kings. By the 1800s closely related religious movements known as kubandwa spanned an area stretching southward from the kingdoms of Bunyoro and Buganda in modern Uganda to Buha, Unyamwezi, and Usukuma in northwestern Tanzania.

Most of these religions were democratic in their inclusion of large numbers of people, both men and women, and most provided a central focus for

[5]Berger, Iris, "Rebels or Status-Seekers? Women as Spirit Mediums," in Hafkin, Nancy, and Bay, Edna, eds., *Women in Africa: Studies in Social and Economic Change* (Stanford: Stanford University Press, 1976). Excerpts taken from pages 157–181.

Iris Berger received her Ph.D. in African history from the University of Wisconsin in 1973. She is currently Professor of History and Director of the Institute for Research on Women at the University at Albany, State University of New York. Her most recent book, *Threads of Solidarity: Women in South African Industry, 1900–1980*, was published in 1992.

ceremonial activity in their respective societies. In Buganda and the nearby Sese Islands in Lake Victoria, however, elitist groups relied on small numbers of professional mediums; and in Unyamwezi, the Swezi society formed only one of a large number of esoteric organizations that filled functions ranging from divination to snake charming. Such organizational divergences combined over time with differences in social, economic, and political settings to effect some variations in women's roles from one area to the next.

The peoples of the Interlacustrine and Nyamwezi regions were similar in many ways. All were patrilineal, lived in scattered settlements rather than compact villages, and spoke closely related Bantu languages. Various combinations of agriculture and cattle raising formed the basis of economic life. With the exception of the Kiga in southwestern Uganda, all the people of these two regions had some type of centralized political structure. The forms of political organization varied considerably—from large, relatively unified kingdoms (Buganda, Bunyoro, Nkore, Rwanda, and Burundi) to clusters of small states (Buhaya, Buha, Unyamwezi, Usukama, and Usumbwa). Nonetheless, all showed a relatively high degree of class division, sometimes between a minority of upper class or family and commoners, sometimes between a minority of upper-class pastoralists and a majority of lower-class agriculturalists. In the latter cases stratification possessed an ethnic as well as a political dimension, with the upper and lower classes identified as Tutsi and Hutu, respectively, in Rwanda, Burundi, and Buha, and as Hima [Huma] and Iru, respectively, in Bunyoro, Nkore, and Buhaya. Religious beliefs and practices reinforced the cohesion of both families and larger political units; but except for some of the rituals performed at royal courts for the benefit of the entire kingdom, most religious observances occurred within either the nuclear family or the lineage (both of which were male-dominated).

In the religious systems of these regions we find scattered references that indicate opportunities for women to rise above their general status of inferiority through various roles and activities. In the culturally related areas of Burundi and Buha, for example, both men and women might enter the hereditary profession of "rainmaker," *muvurati*. And in Heru, one of the six states of Buha, there lived a woman rainmaker (Kicharuzi, "the one who cuts water") whose fame as "the chieftainess of rainmakers" covered all of Buha and extended into neighboring Burundi. With ordinary practitioners as her subordinates, she acted on behalf of the chief of Heru in cases of severe drought. But it was the spirit-mediumship that offered women the greatest opportunity for active participation in religious life. Raymond Firth has defined spirit mediumship and distinguished it from spirit possession. "*Spirit possession* is a form of trance in which behaviour actions of a person are interpreted as evidence of a control of his behaviour by a spirit normally external to him. *Spirit mediumship* is normally a form of possession in which the person is conceived as serving as an intermediary between spirits and men. The accent here is on communication; the actions and words of the mediums must be translatable, which differentiates them from mere spirit possession of madness." Such possession is interpreted favorably as a sign that a god has chosen a person to be inhabited by him periodically for the good of the community. Thus, extending Firth's definition, spirit mediumship implies communication between the supernatural world and a particular social group for which the medium is an agent.

These religions . . . centered on a mythologically defined pantheon associated with long-dead or legendary kings or heroes, natural phenomena, and particular occupations. Frequently the female spirits concerned themselves with women's activities, such as childbirth and agriculture. People consulted the gods on regular occasions as a precautionary measure, and on special occasions when difficulties arose that might have resulted from their neglect. It was felt that, if properly conciliated, the gods could ensure the health, prosperity, and fertility of their followers. Novices usually acquired the ability to intercede with the deities through a formal initiation ceremony, although sometimes direct possession rendered this unnecessary. A person's prolonged illness, for example, might be interpreted by a diviner as a particular spirit's signal of its choice of a medium. When a woman was "signaled" in this way, a ritual was conducted that taught her the necessary professional skills; the ritual also marked her rise to a new and higher social status and, sometimes, to membership in a new social group.

The underlying themes of these ceremonies stressed the initiate's passage through a "liminal" or "indeterminate" phase, one that Turner describes as having "few or none of the attributes of the past or coming state." Following this phase comes admission to a new society that is superior to the profane one and separated from it by special regalia, a secret vocabulary, spirit possession, and esoteric knowledge. Within this new order, the adherent passed through the main stages of life—birth, childhood, marriage—suggesting the idea of a new ritual and spiritual life that paralleled ordinary existence, but on a higher plane. The indicators of this enhanced status varied from place to place. It was implicit everywhere in the intimate relationship to a group of spirits generally conceived of as kings or extremely important and powerful people. Explicit signs included food taboos similar to those of the upper classes, a view of non-initiates as minors incapable of full participation in community affairs, and possession of legal immunity or particular rights and privileges. This high status, however, was temporary and situational except in the case of professional mediums and priests attached permanently to temples. Others probably assumed their normal position between ceremonies, as indicated by the application of food taboos only to ritual situations.

Kubandwa operated on several different social and political levels—from small localized kinship groups to royal courts—but all of these levels remained decentralized and independent both of each other and of political officials. The main rites usually took place among kinsmen or neighbors, although ceremonies also occurred at the courts of local chiefs and kings. Colonial rule disrupted activities at this latter level profoundly, however, making them difficult to reconstruct. Dancing, rhythmic music, mediums speaking in an esoteric language and dressing and acting the role of the possessing spirit all lent a theatrical quality to these ceremonies that has led Michel Leiris to describe similar rituals conducted in parts of Ethiopia as "living theater."

Accounts everywhere emphasize the predominance of women in these ceremonies. Speke described a visit to a District Chief of Rumankia in Karagwe, a former Haya Kingdom in northwest Tanzania:

> Many mendicant women, called by some Wichwezi, by others Mbandwa, all wearing the most fantastic dresses of Mbungu (barkcloth) covered with beads, shells, and sticks, danced before us singing a comic song, the chorus of which was long shrill rolling, coo-roo-coo-roo, etc. . . Their true functions were just as obscure as the religion of the negroes generally; some called them devil-drivers, others evil-eye averters. But, whatever, they imposed a tax on the people.

The early Church Missionary Society members in Buganda invariably described women as the mainstay and most enthusiastic supporters of the "Lubare [spirit] superstition"; a Catholic missionary in the early part of the twentieth century writing of the people at the southwestern tip of Lake Victoria, depicted the Swezi as a secret society "to which most Bazinza women belonged"; and May Edel termed the spirit cult among the Kiga of southwestern Uganda the "*emandwa* of the women." Elsewhere, too, observers have agreed on the large numbers of female members, although rarely have they offered exact estimates, and although the balance of the sexes undoubtedly varied from one community and one deity to the next. In the Ankole district of Uganda, for example, *emandwa* initiates were "at least as likely to be female as male," whereas mainly women joined the more recent cult of Nyabingi. In Bushi, an area of eastern Zaire with close cultural relations to neighboring Rwanda, almost all young girls were dedicated to the deity Lynangombe before marriage. And women formed an estimated ninety-five percent of the members of Benakayange, which developed in the early twentieth century in honor of a group of people killed by Belgian soldiers.

The primary concern of these groups [was] with . . . female problems, most commonly sterility, childbirth, and marital difficulties, with an emphasis on the first of these. F. M. Rodegem calls Kiranga worship in Burundi a "regenerative rite aimed at valorizing fertility." The main object of traditional *mbandwa* ceremonies in Bunyoro, according to John Beattie, was to assist women to bear children; consequently, many Nyoro attributed colonial government and missionary attempts to eradicate these practices to a desire to cause their gradual disappearance as a people. Similarly, among the Sumbwa of western Tanzania, the traditional story of the death of Lyangombe, the central spirit, records the hero's last pronouncement: "Whoever comes to my tomb to pray will be heard by me and I will help him in his trouble. . . . I will help women in their confinements and I will give children to barren women. Let everyone pray to me and I will help them." Although Sumbwa husbands sometimes expressed uneasiness at their wives' joining the Swezi, the case of a nervous or barren wife always proved sufficient arguments; to avoid domestic trouble, the men would pay the fees and ask no questions. Finally Bösch, writing on neighboring Unyamwezi, describes the majority of female members as sterile. This stress on fertility would suggest that *kubandwa* appealed to younger married women of childbearing age and, perhaps, allowed women a religious alternative to the worship of their husbands' lineage ancestors.

Lewis argues that such therapeutic pretensions simply masked the real aim of protest against the dominant sex, offering women both protection from male exactions and an effective vehicle for manipulating husbands and other male relatives. He terms such groups peripheral—that is, they play no direct part in upholding the moral codes of the societies in which they appear, and they are often believed to have originated elsewhere. (Their counterparts, "central cults," support society's moral codes and provide an idiom in which men compete for power and authority.) In brief, Lewis sees peripheral cults as a feminist subculture generally restricted to women (though sometimes including lower-class men as well) and protected from male attack through their representation as a therapy for illness. Underlying this interpretation is the view that these movements stem from threatening or oppressive conditions (physical or social) that people can combat and control only by "heroic flights or ecstasy." They thus represent an attempt to master an intolerable environment.

Both in myth and practice, the East African religions shared some of these features. Women among the Soga of eastern Uganda had control over their husbands during possession, and Shi women in polygynous marriages might feign seizure by the spirit of Chihangahanga in order to get rid of a rival. Colle cites a case in which the deity said through the medium, "Yes, I will leave her, but only if the concubine is driven out; if that other woman is not driven away, . . . I will kill someone here." Possession by such a ghost was seen as harmful; it had to be exorcised. Similarly in Burundi, a medium whose husband threatened to beat her might simulate possession. "Kiranga is there, the husband tells himself, and he will prevent himself from harming her." A more recent Rundi sect, Umuganzaruguru . . . attracted women seeking escape from their husbands' domination. The "cure" for a wife's symptoms of trance, illness, and crying included not only initiation but acceptance of the woman's control over household goods and of her refusal to continue carrying loads; henceforth the husband had to provide her with a servant or transport loads himself.

These examples definitely bear out Lewis's suggestion of the power that spirit possession offers women in disputes with men, although gaining advantages may describe the situation more accurately than engaging in "war between the sexes. . . ."

An additional factor may have been the authority and license of the ritual situation itself, which frequently offered women a share in the status and prerogatives of men. In Busoga, for example, where women normally could not sit on stools, all female mediums had their own skin seats and were treated as men during possession; afterward, however, they resumed their ordinary status and with it all the restrictions that customarily applied to members of their sex. During the Rundi ceremonies, women wore men's ceremonial dress (called *imbega*), sat on stools, carried spears, and had the right—ordinarily denied them—to judge in trials. In Buha, a woman dressed as a man and treated as a great chief led the procession that completed the initiation ceremony. She bore the name Ruhang'umugabo (from *umugabo*, "adult male" or "husband"). During the procession, which involved gathering food and begging, people hurried from their houses and greeted her with the words, *"Ganza, mwami nven'ongoma"* ("Greetings to you, great chief"). In the Nyoro ceremonies to remove a yellow, frothy substance associated with thunder and lightning that could drop from the sky, "The women . . . kept strolling up and down, holding and shaking their spears and shields like men at war. . . ." Similarly, one of the female deities was named Rukohe Nyakalika Irikangabu, she "who wields shields like men." The Rwanda ceremony of *kubandwa* abolished sexual differences; all initiates, men and women alike, acquired a virile masculine quality, *umugabo*. Among the Hunde of eastern Zaire, the spirit Mbalala, which possessed women, carried a spear without "becoming a leper" (apparently the normal punishment for such a transgression of sexual boundaries); sometimes the possessed woman danced with a spear and shield "just as if she had become a man."

A small body of material also suggests that the *Kubandwa* functioned as vehicles for expressing hostility against the social order in general or against particular people, especially superiors. Although none of the examples applies specifically to male-female relationships, it seems unlikely that women would have ignored such opportunities. In Rwanda, a list of highly unflattering or obscene names of spirits included Nkunda abatutsi, "I love the Tutsi" (in this context clearly an ironic expression of attitudes toward the upper class); and possessed persons had complete freedom to express any feelings they wished since others accepted these words as those of the spirit. Individuals bore no responsibility for their utterances. "They could speak inconsiderate words, abuse their parents or their superiors, without anyone dreaming of asking for compensation after the ceremony was finished." These instances are particularly interesting in view of the predominance of lower-class agriculturalists, Hutu, among initiates. In Buha, where the social composition of adherents is unknown, possessed people behaved in a similar fashion. "Another only abuses everyone, even the chief of the country if he is present."

The explanation of this ritual rebellion probably lies in the concept of possession as a liminal state in which all ordinary rules of society are suspended—thus permitting such transgressions as criticism of superiors and men dressing as women and women as men. In Buha, for example, "Initiates who dress as their spirit say that they are no longer men, and they allow themselves many insults and even dishonest actions that they could not permit themselves in a normal state." The temporary nature of this state is of paramount importance; and leadership and prestige often accrue to the medium only while she is possessed. In this way women may be allowed possibilities for status, but the predominant ideas about female inferiority or about women's place in the established social order are not threatened. In fact, the theatrical nature of possession ceremonies may well reinforce the feeling that the occasion is out of the ordinary. Additional evidence in support of this interpretation comes from two facts: most female deities are concerned primarily with female activities (especially agriculture and fertility); and most are also conceived of in positions of subservience to men (usually as wives, daughters, sisters, and slaves of male deities). Although some female deities may have transcended such characterization, the Nyoro view of Nyabuzana probably expresses a general attitude. She had no hut dedicated to her, but "stays at the hearth because she is a woman."

Despite anthropological interpretation of such rites as reinforcing the status quo, and despite the temporary nature of possession, mediums were highly respected members of their societies. Furthermore, *Kubandwa* also provided them with access to more stable and institutionalized high-status positions. In the words of Max Gluckman, becoming a diviner is the "only way an outstanding [Zulu] woman can win general social prestige." Robin Horton, writing on Kalabari communities in Nigeria, echoes a similar theme:

> The fully-developed complex of possession roles typically figures a man: not just an ordinary man, but a man of wealth, power, and status. In adopting this complex of roles a woman is enabled, from time to time, really to "be" what she has always yearned to be but never can be in ordinary normal life.

A small number of women . . . were able to attain positions of national prominence. In the Mubende District of Kitara (the former Nyoro kingdom), the medium of Ndahura, the spirit of smallpox, possessed not only her own temple but an extensive domain. . . . The kings of both Bunyoro and Buganda treated the site with great respect, and Nakaima received offerings from both rulers on the occasion of smallpox epidemics or when they had queries that they wished the spirit to answer. Ndahura, through his medium, also played an important role in the accession ceremony of the *mukama,* "king," of Bunyoro; without this god's aid, the king "could not properly 'eat' Unyoro." Furthermore, the spirit's prestige exempted Mubende Hill from both Nyoro and Ganda attack.

Frequently, the main deities had women dedicated to them as wives, these women not being allowed to marry while in the spirit's service. By far the most important of these women was the official wife of Kiranga in Burundi, Mukakiranga. . . . Mukakiranga played a major role part in the great national ceremony of *umuganiro,* a yearly spiritual renewal of the kingdom in which all Rundi participated. Together with the king, she presided over one portion of the ritual; and she filled a crucial role in the remainder of it.

In Nkore, a female diviner, Nyabuzana, possessed land and a palace at Ibanda Hill at Mitoma. She performed ceremonies at each new moon and directed a four-day ritual of spirit worship that became an important part of the royal accession ceremonies. In addition, she functioned as a source of information to the king on the movements of his enemies and bewitched other chiefs to facilitate their defeat. Her prestige allowed her to walk about in her ceremonial dress and claim any cow she wished; no one refused, believing that the *emandwa* themselves had chosen the cattle.

Much larger numbers of women could attain highly regarded positions as local mediums and priestesses. The Toro clan priestess, the *nyakatagara,* could communicate with one or two of the clan's Cwezi spirits. She directed the construction of shrines, advised on their maintenance, offered prayers on periodic visits to homesteads, and invited initiates, singers, *Kubandwa* and musicians to participate in rituals. Generally, she shared the direction of ceremonies with the most important local medium, the *kazini.* Nyoro group mediums, more commonly women than men, held such high status that even the household head, whose authority was unquestioned in all other matters, had to treat them respectfully at all times. Nyoro informants derive their title, *nyakatagara,* from the verb *okutagara,* "to be free to do what one likes, to be privileged." Beattie doubts the accuracy of this etymology, but notes that the implication is plain. Among the Sumbwa, a leader of the female members organized the work of women and arbitrated in quarrels between them. One account from the Tabora District of Unyamwezi describes a woman named Kanunga as the Mtwale Mkubwa, Great Chief of the Swezi of Uyui; another account refers to the *mnangogo* and the *mnango-*

gokazi, the society's chief and chieftainess. Writing on Shinyaga District in Usukuma, a colonial officer noted that "women have equal status with men, and many female members of the Baswezi have been nominated in the past chieftainesses. . . ."

All of these instances of local female leadership occurred in religious movements that were relatively independent of lineage organization. This independence stemmed from the fact that in some areas the new observance eclipsed those registered lineage ghosts, whereas in others they took the form of autonomously organized groups not based on kinship ties. Since lineage cults represented the husband's family, perhaps their eclipse in itself enhanced the possibility of female religious participation. In Bunyoro and Toro the process was gradual, probably occurring over a period of several centuries; in Unyamwezi and Rukiga, on the other hand, it developed specifically as a result of historical changes during the nineteenth century.

In Bunyoro and Toro by the colonial period, the worship of family ghosts, *bazimu,* had been replaced as the basic religion by the generation of Cwezi *mbandwa.* Today, the cult of the *bazimu* in these areas either is not practiced at all or is of negligible importance. This trend correlated also with the breakdown of residential organization based on patrilineal descent groups. The *mbandwa* groups, in this situation, offered leadership possibilities to many women; although loosely associated with patrilineal clans, they had their own heads and stressed solidarity between initiates rather than between kinspeople.

In Unyamwezi, the divorce from lineage organization was even greater, for by the late nineteenth century secret societies (among them the Buswezi) had begun to fulfill many roles of kinship groups in assisting members in time of need. This trend resulted from people's dispersion through their large-scale participation in long-distance trade. With both family and neighborhood organizations extremely fluid, and with geographical mobility high, secret societies were dissociated from any kinship connections and came to form highly delineated, independent corporate groups. With this decline in the importance of kinship ties came the only instance in the area of women's involvement in cults of lineage ghosts; only here could they preside over the rites to honor deceased members of the group.

Nyabingi worship in northern Rwanda and southwestern Uganda offers another instance of autonomously organized religious groups. By the late nineteenth century, this spirit had successfully eclipsed the *bazimu* and the *emandwa,* both fully integrated with patrilineages. Here the historical setting was the attempt of the Rwanda state, and later of Europeans, to conquer politically decentralized areas. The new cults provided a militant form of organized resistance; and in these groups, centered on a female spirit, a number of famous women were able to exercise substantial power. Pertinent here, though, is the problem of institutionalizing female authority; for although women apparently acted as the chief priestesses in an early period, as the position acquired increasing power in the late nineteenth century male priests became more prevalent. Thus, as in Unyamwezi, women seemed to gain some positions only at times when they possessed relatively low value. This raises the question, impossible to answer from available material, of whether women participated more actively in the initial stages of religious movements when possession might have been more spontaneous and less regulated than in later stages. It also suggests the possibility that the imperfect fit between the Interlacustrine and Unyamwezi areas' religious movements and Lewis's definitions arises from the process of historical transformation by which peripheral cults may evolve into central ones. But although the data do point to a trend toward greater integration with older institutions over time, they do not necessarily verify a process of linear progression from one form to the other. Furthermore, it seems that in its possible historical role as peripheral, *kubandwa* has assumed more importance as a continuing vehicle for popular protest among both men and women than as a strictly feminist outlet. Although these groups allowed women a prominence not otherwise available to them and certain vehicles for pressuring men, other aspects of protest they embodied have been as much against a social order oppressive to men and women alike as against the specific subordination of women. The mobilization of Nyabingi followers against Rwandan and then European overlordship illustrates this theme, as does the earlier involvement of *Kubandwa* in resistance movements against the imposition of new state systems. Nonetheless, deciding on the balance between these themes is difficult since the possibility exists that the latter appears dominant because of its association with militant revolts. Such actions become history, whereas the individual and family-level conflict between the sexes goes unrecorded.

In conclusion, then, regardless of religious or social structure, a small number of women everywhere emerged in institutionalized positions of religious leadership. Thus, as in most stratified situations, a few people were allowed to rise above their customary status without challenging the dominant ideology or structure of subordination. In the Ganda pattern of elitist religions, which lacked mass initiation, women's leadership positions were limited to these few. This may have held true in Unyamwezi as well since the *Swezi* was only one of numerous secret societies, in others of which authority and sometimes even active membership were limited to men. Similarly, in the Nyabingi cults only small numbers of women leaders emerged.

Only in the democratic religions of the Nyoro-Ha area did large numbers of women participate actively in ceremonial life. Although their exercise of power and authority was restricted to ritual situations, they could acquire wealth from their positions and apparently commanded respect at all times because of their religious powers. And here, as in the elitist groups, smaller numbers of women achieved institutionalized high positions either as national figures or, more frequently, as local religious leaders. Yet this religious form arose largely in the most highly stratified societies of the region. This may explain the occurrence in a precolonial setting of a religious form usually associated with the late nineteenth and early twentieth centuries; for the oppression of these societies, like that of the colonial period, may have drawn together subordinate peoples into movements that offered at least occasional and temporary prestige as well as an institutionalized outlet for antisocial feelings. In this context, the form and function of women's religious participation corresponded with that of other low-status groups.

Women and State Formation in Buganda
NAKANYIKE MUSISI[6]

A number of historians and anthropologists have studied the institution of marriage in Africa, but few have studied polygyny in detail, and fewer still have sought to analyze fully the nature or function of precolonial polygynous marriages. In recent years, African polygyny has been viewed as associated most closely with agricultural labor. My own research suggests that polygyny in precolonial Buganda must be distinguished from colonial and post-colonial polygynous practices and viewed, most critically, in the context of elite strategies to create and ultimately to control not only economic but political and social components of a state apparatus as well. . . . I use the term "elite polygyny" in this paper to refer to the "grand polygyny" practiced by the political elite and characterized by the extravagance of having more than four wives, as compared with the more common "small polygyny" involving only two or three wives.

I argue that polygyny, like all institutions, has a history that is rooted in Buganda's origin as an organized kingdom. . . . It [this article] attempts to demonstrate how the social structures characteristic of family and marriage life were influenced by the political and economic underpinnings of the state. In highly stratified Buganda, "elite polygyny" became an integral part of the process of class and state formation. Polygyny augmented both ascribed and achieved rank. "Elite polygyny" thus must be understood in relation to the emergence, consolidation, and expansion of the Buganda state with the concomitant development of social inequality.

With the exception of Karen Sacks's work *Sisters and Wives: The Past and Future of Sexual Equality,* the . . . ethnohistorical and ethnographic

[6]Musisi, Nakanyike, "Women, 'Elite Polygyny,' and Buganda State Formation," *Signs: Journal of Women, Culture, and Society* 16, no. 4 (Chicago: University of Chicago Press, 1991), pp. 757–786.

Nakanyike Musisi was born and reared in Buganda, Uganda. She received her B.A Hons degree from Makerere University; M.A. and M. Lit. from the University of Birmingham, England. Her doctoral thesis from the University of Toronto looked at the history of Baganda women from the earliest times to the demise of the kingdom in 1967. Currently she is an Assistant Professor at the University of Toronto in the Department of History and Women's Studies.

data . . . have not previously been subjected to feminist analysis. The tendency has been to narrate the development of Kingship, kinship, and the state in Buganda with little regard for the ways in which ordinary men and women shaped the destiny of the kingdom or how the processes of state formation in turn shaped women's destinies.

Rereading and reinterpreting these sources [of other Buganda historians][7] offers not only a glimpse into the lives of women but also a wholly new, gendered dynamics of state formation. It is in this respect that this study will differ markedly from those of other Buganda historians who have completely marginalized women's contribution to Buganda's institutions, even when women are very noticeable. This study will also be of interest not only to Africanists but to all those interested in studying the processes through which women become disempowered in the name of state formation.

With population growth, the sons of clan leaders left their fathers' settlements, establishing new clan subdivisions known as *amasiga,* or lineages. In the course of time, these divided into sublineages *(emituba),* which traced their ancestry to the original *maka.* The various settlements, lineages, and sublineages made up the clan. The clan heads, who acquired the title of *abataka* (plural), lived in the original settlements, which came to be called *obutaka,* with their communal property. Whoever held the title of *omutaka* (singular) held clan land in trust for clan members. Indeed, the Luganda word for clan, *kika,* which later referred to a large, spatially dispersed, exogamous unit, is a cognate of *maka,* a single small homestead or settlement. Linguistic evidence suggests that *taka* (land), the term from which *obutaka* (clan land) is derived, and *abataka* (clan heads) are also related. Thus, quite early in Buganda state formation, families *(maka)* and the dispersed clans of which they were part came to be intricately associated with land and with the titles for owning and guarding the land, *abataka* and *abutaka.*

As the internal organization and structure of the clan developed, it assumed additional social, political, and economic powers. It became an administrative structure that judged, protected, taxed, and undertook revenge on behalf of its members. In economic terms, common clan ownership of land, cattle, and sheep prevailed, and, by right of descent, lineage members had potential access to a common labor pool. A person's social authority and claims to labor and products were determined not necessarily by gender but by kinship during this period. These processes contributed to increasing politicization of clans.

---

[7]Roscoe, John, *The Baganda* (Cambridge: Cambridge University Press, 1911); Kagwa, Sir Apolo, *Ekitabo Kya Basekabaka be Buganda (The Kings of Buganda),* printed privately, Kampala, 1900; Mukasa, Ham, *Ebifa du Mulembe gwa Kabaka Mutesa, Uganda Journal,* Parts I and II (Kampala: The Uganda Society, 1934); Kiwanuka, M. S. M. Semakula, *A History of Buganda: From the Foundations of the Kingdom to 1900* (New York: Africana Publishing Corporation, 1972).

The development of *obutaka* (clan land) affected social and gender relations within and among the clans, leading to clearly marked patterns in the marriage system and residential rules. Patriarchy and patrilocality were strengthened with the invention of and emphasis upon unilineal descent and proper identification of the corporate members. The assigning of clan names and identification insignia (or totems) and several rituals—especially *okwalula abaana* ("to hatch the children") and *okusika* (succession rituals)—clearly distinguished clan from nonclan members.

The move toward the consolidation of patrilineal social organization must have had tremendous consequences for women as wives. Roscoe's study of the ritual of "hatching the children" reveals the nature of this control over women's reproductive behavior. The "hatching" ceremony was a time for the affirmation of the superiority of members of the clan on their own ground over nonmembers; wives, as nonmembers of their husbands' clans, had to face some anxiety and threats. In fact, during this time, the distinction between "sisters" and "wives," as characterized by Karen Sacks, was clearly demonstrated.

In addition to strengthening practices related to patrilineality, the preference for patrilocal residence established in the first period became of focal importance in the second period, when the rights and privileges of the clanspersons became clearly distinguished from those of wives. At marriage, women retained membership in their natal clan and did not join their husband's clan. On their husbands' clan lands, wives had only rights of usufruct.

The incipient development of politicized clans as fraternal interest groups, based on both patrilocality and patrilineality, made polygyny a means through which a clan could increase its numbers and consequently its social and political strength. It is at this stage that we can start to trace marriage arrangements, laws, and regulations.

Tradition credits Kimera [a King of Bito Luo origin from the Southern Sudan] with introducing the main features of the constitution as they existed up to the nineteenth century. These constitutional features reflect the emergence of much more marked social differentiation among the Baganda. Kimera is said to have ordained special titles for his descendants, *balangira* (princes) and *bambejja* (princesses), so that they could be distinguished from the rest of the population, which he renamed *bakopi* (common people). Moreover, Kimera created a rank of chiefs, named *bakungu,* for the men who helped him in his power fights. After a political struggle, the clan heads submitted to the king. New laws forbade them from meeting the king face to face and from meeting in one place at the same time, thus inhibiting the growth of possible political plots to overthrow him.

In politico-economic terms, the creation of the Buganda state seems to have been achieved in part through the destruction of the politico-economic basis of the clans and the assimilating of conquered people. With the emergence of *saza* chiefs, overseeing county administrative boundaries (the *sazas*), the state ignored the *butaka* clan boundaries. Control of labor and land became concentrated in the hands of a ruling minority, the bureaucratic chiefs *(bakugu)* and the royal family. The clan could no longer function as a political unit with power to collect, redistribute, and control communal resources, including labor and land. A common state culture that transcended differences of clans, language, and customs united people from different corners of the territory into a common people (the Baganda), with a common language (Luganda) and a common culture (kiganda), in one state (Buganda), all in the common service of the king, who became Buganda incarnate.

In this period of the depoliticization of the clans between the reigns of Kimera and Mutesa I (thirteenth century to mid-nineteenth century), women's position and roles became defined in new ways. First, women were denied political leadership roles. Naku, who reigned just before Kimera (and whose reign was probably very short) became the last recorded female ruler of Buganda. Second, land was now the private property of the *kabaka* and his entourage of chiefs, and to obtain it in exchange for labor and tax, peasants had to enter into client relations with a patron, and only men were qualified to do so. Women could obtain land only through a husband or some other male guardian. In this manner, women became clients of the patron's clients. For a woman to be an acceptable client of the patron's client, she, too, had to show signs of being able to fulfill certain obligations; cultivating and childbearing were most valued. Buganda state formation thus reconstructed a division of labor based on class as well as gender, reflecting patriarchal and class relations. The ways in which women participated in political processes and the production and circulation of wealth varied with their position in the class and state hierarchy. Above all, women themselves became important objects of exchange.

The relevance of all these political developments to the institution of marriage and hence polygyny was tremendous. The economic and political system of patron-client relationships upon which Buganda's bureaucracy was built involved the distribution and redistribution of women. Powerful men in the land could loot, raid, demand, and be given large numbers of women by their clients. One of the strategies the king used for effective control over the clans and the conquered or subdued territories was to link himself by marriage to these populations. This encouraged polygyny on a large scale. As in other despotic societies, the king and his bureaucrats monopolized polygyny. Expansionist warfare with plunder increased the potential for wealth differentiation among men and enhanced men's ability to acquire extra wives. Moreover, all the women captured in war were distributed by the generals, who left most of the warriors empty-handed or with "small change" such as goats. As women became signs and objects of prestige and class, polygyny stratified men. The more wives a man had, the higher his status on the political and social ladder. As a consequence, the king and the chiefs found themselves with tremendous numbers of women, whom they housed in high reed fence enclosures *(ebisakatte)*. Women became a commodity to be accumulated and carefully guarded by the wealthy and powerful men.

Needless to say, the lives of the vast majority, the non-aristocratic women, differed greatly from the lives of princesses (the *abambejja*) and of women of peasant origin who married into the elite. Moreover, due to their special position in the state apparatus, the lives of both princesses and elite wives were riddled with contradictions.

Paradoxically, the state ideology that debased most Baganda women through exchange and distribution privileged the princesses in a number of ways. First, while commoner women never held land in their own right, princesses, like princes, hold land in different parts of the country. Princesses also administered small-scale governments in their designated areas. The chiefs supervising the princesses' estates were allowed to hold titles corresponding to those of the *kabaka*'s chiefs.

Second, all Baganda, including chiefs had to show great respect toward the princesses. According to Roscoe, chiefs bowed low when addressing princesses on the road and often kneeled when they visited them in their homes. Princesses were addressed by the male title *sebo* (sir), rather than *nyabo* (madam), and were exempt from the general rules of behavior and speech that governed commoner Baganda women. Like princes, princesses were free to move about at will and to use obscene language *(okuwemula)*. This set them apart from the ordinary women and men, whose use of language was meant to be cautious. Moreover, they were permitted to engage in what can be called "sexual conspicuous consumption," for it was socially legitimate for them to initiate sexual liaisons with any man they fancied at any time they wished. On the other hand, princesses were not allowed to marry. Thus they occupied an ambiguous gender position—elevated in some respects, circumscribed in others—a situation that demands further examination of the actual conditions of their lives and of their significance for and relationship to the state.

Selective freedoms were accorded to the princesses because these freedoms sustained the class interests of the Buganda royal family and male-dominated social order. The property and power of the royal family and its clients, on the one hand, and the legitimacy of the throne, on the other, are important considerations. First, princesses were not allowed to marry until at least the time of Sunna II, Semakokiro's grandson (ca. 1825–1856). Second, they were barred from having children. Roscoe records that a pregnant princess was required to abort or be punished by death; the man responsible would also be killed. Nevertheless, princesses reportedly defied convention by refusing to terminate their pregnancies, secretly passing their children off as other people's. If they were unlucky enough to be discovered, the children would be killed. Given the methods of abortion in Buganda, the exercise of sexual "freedom" must have been quite problematic for the princesses.

Further illustrations of the relationship between Buganda state formation and control over the sexual behavior of princesses are found in Buganda's succession customs. In a narrow sense, the social ideology with respect to the princesses' state-controlled sexuality can be seen as a reflection of their permanent alienation from the throne and as attempts to prevent their offspring from acceding to the Kingship. Succession in Buganda was patrilineal. As far back as the days of Kimera in the fourteenth century, Buganda's state ideology reserved the throne only to those having royal blood from the father's side. However, the king's mother's clan was the controlling factor. The fact that the rules of exogamy applied also to the royal lineage (apart from the *lubuga,* the king's sister and queen) meant that even if the princesses were to marry and have children, the ideology of patrilineal succession would exclude their offspring from political office. In fact, the *lubuga* (queen) who was the king's half-sister as well as his "wife," was barred from having any sexual relationship with the king. If she were to become pregnant by another man, she would be deposed at once, and, if the king so chose, she could be put to death. This state control suggests a functional relationship between the cultural conventions governing the princesses and the interests of the royal family, which the Baganda regarded as fundamental to the social and political order.

The rules governing the reproductive potential of princesses seem to have been relaxed under later kings (possible in the late eighteenth or early nineteenth centuries), although, as Roscoe notes, pregnant princesses would occasionally be detected and would be "burned to death for their fault." In the reigns of Sunna II and Muetsa I (1825–1884), we learn of princesses being married and having children legitimately in their marriages. Under what conditions did these changes occur? A clue is found in Kagwa and Roscoe's narrations, especially in their terminology "later kings." If these later kings were Semakokiro's grandsons, then the answer may lie in the nature of the Kingship after Semakokiro (ca. 1734–1764). Semakokiro's decree ordering the massacre of all contending princes had far-reaching consequences. The most important of these was to weaken the Kingship, which in turn worked to the advantage of the chiefs, particularly the most powerful chief, the *katikiro* (often referred to as the prime minister). Young kings came increasingly under the control of their powerful and masterful chiefs. Zimbe states that Mutesa I "thought of marrying his sisters (and daughters) to his chiefs, thinking that when chiefs would become his brothers-inlaws [sic], then he would win their confidence." Zimbe finally concluded that by giving princesses away to his chiefs, Mutesa I came to terms with his people. Through these political changes, the princesses had surely entered into the circulation system to augment the king's power and security of tenure. To those chiefs with whom he felt most insecure, the king gave several of his daughters and sisters in addition to other, non-royal, women.

With the weakening of the institution of Kingship, princesses' political power and sexual behavior were curbed and made to conform to patriarchal conventions governing commoner women. Paradoxically, the process by which princesses' sexual behavior was regulated also liberated their reproductive potential (their uteruses) from state control.

As the state developed, the *bakembuga* (the elite wives) were recruited from a range of different sources, including: (1) the Baganda servile masses, the clans; (2) slave women from defeated anti/or tributary areas (such as Ankole, Singo, Buddu, Kyagwe, or Busoga); (3) wives inherited from the dead king; (4) married women abducted from their subordinate husbands; (5) *bakembuga* bringing their own relatives; and (6) women given gratuitously by individuals, both men and women.

Clans aspiring to political power willingly supplied the king with young girls to marry. In fact, the strongest clans were obligated to give him wives. For example, *nanzigu* was always recruited from the Buffalo (Mbogo) clan, her special position having developed historically in relation to the Buffalo clan's struggle with the king in the early days of state formation. *Nakimera* was recruited from the Grasshopper (Nsenene) clan. The king's father had to supply him with a senior wife, the *kaddulubale,* and the king's paternal grandmother supplied him with *nasaza,* who was responsible for cutting the king's hair and nails.

Once a year the king sent his representatives to each district to collect young girls to be recruited as handmaids for his wives. He selected as wives a few of the girls who had been specially recommended. Moreover, chiefs throughout Buganda were obligated to hold marriage councils in their areas to select the most beautiful young virgins roughly between the ages of twelve and seventeen to present to the king. The girls' guardians would then be rewarded with wealth. In return, the king gave women to his chiefs in a number of different ways to "keep up their rank" or to satisfy their sexual urges.

Whenever the king wished additional wives, he simply demanded them from his chiefs, and he seldom took only one wife at a time. The exchange of women between the chiefs and the king carried material and political benefits for both sides. On the one hand, chiefs receiving women from the king pledged political and economic support; and on the other hand, clans, families, or even areas giving the king wives expected and received political favors such as permission to collect or be exempted from certain taxes, or such material rewards as cattle.

Finally, the king received wives as a result of raids made on neighboring states, and he could also force his chiefs to give him their own wives. The increase in the number of the king's wives reflected the clans' insecurity and their need to be allied with the king for potential political gains. It also reflected an increase in royal wealth and power, and possibly the insecurity of the king's office. Indeed, the manner in which the elite wives (*bakembuga*) were recruited illustrates this process. Royalty was never concerned about a woman's birth or rank. Peasant girls or women taken in war as captives became wives as easily as the daughters of the wealthiest chiefs.

The organization of the royal household reflected that of the kingdom as a whole. Moreover, the two spheres—the royal household and the state—were linked by an arrangement through which each wife received taxes in the form of goods from a particular chief or subchief. Hierarchy was recognized within the royal household as well. As A. I. Richards writes, "In the true Ganda style they [the *bakembuga*] used the precedence titles of chiefs to indicate the relative status of one wife to another."

The high reed enclosures (*ebisakatte*) inside which the *bakembuga* resided became a symbol of aristocracy. Within both the king's and chiefs' enclosures, wives were organized in sections, each controlled by a titled senior woman, the *mukyala* or *kaddulubale*. It was her duty to organize the household/*ekisakatte*. She gave orders to and disciplined the other wives, and she distributed goods to them. She also supervised ordinary untitled wives (*basebeyi*, or followers), as well as the *bazaana*, the women of peasant or slave descent who performed much of the arduous work within the household. Titled wives who lived within their own enclosures took care of their own affairs.

As the number of king's wives increased, more offices had to be created. For example, one of the new offices was that of the *mubugumya*, recruited from the Otter clan, whose duty it was to warm up the king's bed before he retired with one of his wives each evening. In fact, so many ordinary wives belonged to the king that his mother, the *namasole*, housed several hundred. She controlled them directly and attended to all their needs. The majority of the women, though, were accommodated outside the king's court in a house called *Bumenya*. Those to be invited to the king's royal couch would stay in three houses called *Balimwagula*.

The elite wives, especially those inside the king's reed enclosures, were of central importance to the state because they became the central figures through which clans rallied to bid for mastery of the throne. Since Buganda Kingship lacked "kinship" or a clan totem of its own, the kin ties and role of the *bakembuga* became of crucial importance because they were the axis along which the Kingship rotated to different clans. Given the ideology of matrilineal descent in the royal family, the *bakembuga* carried responsibility for the clans' biological perpetuation and succession to the throne. The princesses' matrilineal affiliations were so important that they rendered their patrilineal connections largely irrelevant.

Yet while still subordinate to their chiefly husbands, women involved in elite polygyny commanded unprecedented respect from both ordinary men and women. For example, although the exact political relationships between the *abakyala* (the ladies, or titled aristocratic wives) and the chiefs is not precisely specified by Kagwa, the majority of Buganda chiefs, including the prime minister himself were under the jurisdiction of the *abakyala*. The senior wife *(kaddulubaale)* had five chiefs under her, including a county chief, Kangawo of Bulemezi, and the chief gate guard. The *kabejja* had eleven chiefs under her, including two county chiefs, Mukwenda of Singo and Sekibobo of Kyagwe. The chief tax collector was also responsible to her. The *nanzingu* had nine chiefs under her, including the prime minister. The *nasaza* had three chiefs under her, including the maternal uncle of the king (the *sabaganzi*) and the county chief Kasuju of Busuju. In total, the forty-two titled wives (the *abakyala*) had some eighty-six chiefs under them. Those chiefs who resided in the compounds of the *abakyala* also had ranking wives called by the same titles. Any one of these women was a potential kingmaker. Another factor contributing to the elevation of the *bakembuga*'s authority may have been the continued use of kinship and marriage alliances as a means of political and economic control.

Because many of the elite wives were frequently in the company of entertaining, or attending to their husbands, they knew state secrets. Thus, *bakembuga* status became a lifelong occupation. Once a woman or girl became an elite wife *(Mukembuga, singular)*, she could not be married again to a non-elite man, as it was thought that she would reveal sensitive information. One elderly *mukembuga*, who was ninety-two years old at the time, told me in 1986 that the *bakembuga* considered themselves prisoners *(abasibe)* of their masters.

The rules and regulations pertaining to polygynous unions among the elite permitted the *bakembuga* to engage in duties designated for men— although not on a large scale, given the Baganda sexual division of labor. For example, unlike common women, the *bakembuga* became involved in military campaigns. Each chief selected certain wives who were to accompany him in war. They guarded the war gods, cooked, sharpened spears or reeds, performed religious rituals, and at times attended to the wounded. During warfare, it was considered safer to let the *bakembuga* perform these roles than ordinary peasant men. While state ideology held that women could not be prosecuted in their own right, *bakembuga* were above this law. As central figures in succession intrigues and as contenders for power on behalf of their sons and clans, they were often at the center of scrutiny and were treated as men in this context.

Although Buganda's internal political structures enabled the elite to practice large-scale polygyny, it was not prohibited among the ordinary peasants. In fact, prior to Arab and European contact in the mid-nineteenth century, peasants in Buganda could contract marriages in seven different ways, all which were potentially polygynous. For example, in a marriage known as *obufumbo obuwumirize,* wives could be acquired as gifts. It was possible for a chief or king to award his faithful followers with gifts of women. A man could also give his sister or daughter to a friend. More often than not, a second wife was given to remedy the failure of a childless first sister or daughter. In this type of marriage, a polygynist was under no obligation to pay bridewealth, although he could give a small gift in appreciation.

Polygyny among the peasants could also occur through a marriage known as *obufumbo obwenvuma,* in which a man pawned his sister or daughter to satisfy a debt or a fine. The wife could eventually be bought back, often by the woman's matrilineal kin. Additional wives could also be obtained through the leviratic inheritance of a deceased brother's wives. Finally, wives could also be acquired by kidnapping *(okuwuya)* or abduction *(endola).*

In order to suggest that polygyny was inevitable among the masses of Baganda, it has often been argued that Buganda's wars of predation brought in large numbers of women as prisoners, while simultaneously exposing male warriors to death. In addition, ritual sacrifices, the slave trade, the massacres of rebellious princes, and the practice of male infanticide in the royal family are cited as causes of significant sex imbalance. Although the missionaries C. T. Wilson and M. I. Felkin put the ratio of women to men at 3.5 to 1, demographer R. R. Kuczynski dismissed this ratio as exaggerated.

I maintain that an accurate understanding of the causes of any sex-ratio imbalance must involve the following corrections. First, the slave trade intensified only after "elite polygyny" was already well established. Second, women were equally vulnerable as potential sacrifices. Third, the massacre of rival princes involved the deaths of many of their wives as well. In addition, male infanticide in the royal family should not have affected the sex ratio, since the princesses were banned from marriage. And fifth, the women captives brought in from war were often absorbed in elite households. It is clear that more study and more sophisticated demographic analysis will be required before we can reach a conclusion about historical sex ratios.

In practice, high bridewealth payments made it difficult for most peasant men to obtain even one wife. A man wishing to marry more than one wife had to work hard for several years to accumulate the necessary bridewealth. Thus, unless acquired through inheritance or abduction, polygyny became possible for most peasants only as they grew older and accumulated more wealth. When a peasant acquired more than one wife, he arranged his household in the same way as the aristocrats. His wives were stratified and were given titles, such as *kaddulubale* for the senior wife, *kabejja,* and *nasaza.*

In most cases wives shared their husband's residence. But peasants seldom managed to have more than two or three wives, and "the majority were fortunate to have one."

Conclusion

The significance of this study lies in its attempt to pull together strands of information from a number of different sources in order to trace the relationship between some aspects of women's lives and the development of state formation. This has been accomplished by concentrating on one aspect of women's lives, polygynous marriage. The study has revealed how political structures shaped and were in turn shaped by marital and gender relations. On the one hand, Buganda state formation created or produced "elite polygyny," while on the other hand, "elite polygyny" became a critical mechanism in the development of Buganda's political expansion and the institutions of exploitation and stratification. In political and economic terms, "elite polygyny" meant an extension and stabilization of political alliances and relations. Yet in a complex way, patron-client relationships interacted with patriarchy to create categories of "special" women and to make polygyny a preferred and then necessary form of marriage among elite men.

"Elite polygyny" involved the whole state. Peasants and conquered peoples supported the existence of the institution among the elite by supplying them with numerous women, labor, food, and other necessary materials. Yet polygyny as a political, economic, and social statement tended to become a prerogative of the elite class, and thus "elite polygyny" became an expression of class contradictions. It stratified the male population into an elite, with an extraordinary number of wives, and peasants, few of whom had more than one wife. And within polygynous households, women too became stratified.

Although the negative impact of the process of state formation on most women should not be underestimated, not all Baganda women were effectively excluded from direct involvement in Buganda's political process; as wives in alliances and exchanges or as gifts, women played an important role at the state level in balancing internal and regional politics. The *bakembuga* became not only the mothers of kings but king-makers as well.

Inventing Gender: Questioning Gender in Precolonial Yorubaland

OYERONKE OYEWUMI[8]

The preponderant search among feminist scholars for the "status of women" which presupposes the existence of "women" as a social category—always understood to be powerless, disadvantaged, controlled and defined by men—is erroneously conceptualized with regard to precolonial Yoruba society. There were no "women" in Yoruba society in its precolonial past, in that seniority (defined by relative age) and not gender was the main principle of social organization.

"Women" is a problematic category because the term "women" is a nomenclature to identify a particular sex suggesting that women contain a biological uniformity that places them historically and socially in opposition to men. "Sex" denotes the biological differences between males and females and "gender" denotes the meanings that societies attach to these differences.

Gender was not systematically constructed in precolonial Yoruba society. Yet, both feminist scholars and anthropologists have analyzed Yoruba society using gender constructs, as if all societies are structured on the relationship between male and female. These concepts, commonly used in scholarly enquiries about sex, are based on a Western experience, although they are deployed as universals. Therefore, in the process of analyzing any society with these concepts, scholars necessarily create gender categories.

In precolonial Yoruba society, females were not defined as antithetical to men. They were not the *other*. The genitalia and biological sex did not constitute the basis of distinction. Ifi Amadiume, in *Male Daughters and Female Husbands,* writes about the Igbos of south western Nigeria, who share some similarities with the Yoruba, and describes what she calls a "flexible gender system" in which biological sex and gender do not always collapse into

[8]Oyreonke Oyewumi was born in Nigeria and is currently a doctoral candidate in the Department of Sociology at the University of California at Berkeley. This selection is from her dissertation, which examines the position of women in Yoruba society and is reprinted with Oyewumi's permission.

identical categories.[9] In Yorubaland, the term for husband is a non-gender-specific term (includes both males and females), denoting the relationship of wives—females who are married into the lineage—to both male and female members of the lineage. Similarly, one of the major religious cults of the Yoruba, the *Sango* cult, is dominated by females, and according to Babayemi, "They [the males] must dress up their hair as women, assume women's postures . . . and like the female members of the cult, are referred to as wives of Sango,"[10] Contrary to Babayemi, the importance of this observation is not that males are presented as "women" but that the category for wife is a gender neutral category.

In feminist scholarship, it is well documented that in the West women are the "other," being defined in antithesis to men—the norm. Thus the concept "woman" conjures up a number of images such as:

1. Those who do *not* have a penis;
2. Those who do *not* have power;
3. Those who do *not* participate in the public arena.

Hence the *notness* or lack in females defines them as women. These are not the same images that are associated with *obirin*, the Yoruba word that is translated as "woman."

Accordingly, the Yoruba language does not conceive male and females in oppositional terms, since it is non-gender-specific in a number of ways. Personal names are not gendered, nor are there any words for "brother" or "sister" as the words *egbon* and *aburo*, used to denote sibling relationships, are actually gender neutral. Additionally, the subject pronoun does not distinguish on the basis of gender. Thus, Amadiume's following observation about Igbo language and culture is equally true of the Yoruba . . . "The Igbo non-distinctive subject pronoun allows a more flexible semantic system, in which it is possible for men and women to share attributes" and "makes it possible for men and women to play some social roles which in other cultures especially those of the western world, carry rigid sex and gender associations."[11]

The seniority principle was the cornerstone of social intercourse within and without the household. Seniority was not just civility; it conferred some measure of control. The Yoruba focus on age differences in contrast to

---

[9]Amadiume, Ifi, *Male Daughters and Female Husbands: Gender and Sex in an African Society* (London: Zed Press, 1987).

[10]Babayemi, S., "The Role of Women in Politics and Religion in Oyo," Paper presented at the institute of African Studies, University of Ibadan on Seminar on Women Studies: The State of the Art now in Nigeria, 1987, p. 9.

[11]Amadiume, op. cit., p. 89.

their disregard for gender distinctions has been noted by scholars. Bascom observed that:

> Yoruba kinship terminology stresses the factor of seniority including relative age as one of its manifestations, which is important between members of a clan . . . sex is of relatively little importance being used to distinguish mother and father.[12]

Jeremy Eades, in *The Yoruba Today,* underlines the importance of age, noting that many Yoruba may not know exactly when they were born but know precisely who is senior or junior to them because being older confers respect and younger members of the compound must take on the "dirtier and more onerous tasks."[13] In a 1960s study of Yoruba boys and girls, Lloyd found that boys and girls would prefer to be senior [of either sex] than to be junior [of either sex].[14]

The population of a Yoruba town lived in what is described as corporate patrilineages in the anthropological literature. These were large compounds in which male members of a lineage resided with their wives and children. These lineages, "are both land holding and title holding units . . . and in some cases practised specialized crafts such as weaving, smithing. . . ." In these compounds, there was no particular allocation of space on a gender basis. Not even cooking which was mostly done by wives was sectioned off as this activity and almost everything else took place on the verandah. The spatial arrangement contrasts with that of the Igbo who had a clear gender division of space in their households.[15]

In principle, polygyny was the dominant marriage form in Yoruba society, not because all adult males actually had more than one wife, but that all wives of the lineage were ranked in a single hierarchy and related to each other as co-wives whether they shared the same husband or not.

All members of a patrilineage (male and female) were ranked by order of birth, but wives of the lineage were ranked by order of marriage because they were not considered members of the lineage. Thus, it appears as if there were two hierarchical organizations within the lineage but actually, this hierarchical organization operated as one: the birth order ranking of the lineage members and the marriage order ranking of wives was collapsed into the seniority principle which is best understood as organization based on a first-come-first-served basis. The priority of claim was established for each newcomer whether they entered the lineage through birth or through mar-

---

[12]Bascom, William, *The Yoruba of South Western Nigeria* (Prospect Heights, Illinois, Waveland Press, 1969), p. 49.
[13]Eades, Jeremy, *The Yoruba Today* (Cambridge: Cambridge Press, 1980), p. 53.
[14]Lloyd, P. C., *Power and Independence* (1965), p. 36.
[15]Amadiume, op. cit., p. 92.

riage. Consequently, members of the lineage (male and female) were ranked according to their relative chronological age, while wives were ranked relative to the time they married into the lineage. A newly married wife was ranked lower than a one day old child who was born before she entered the lineage because the child preceded the particular wife. In a sense, wives entered the lineage as newborns but they grew with time and therefore their ranking improved vis-a-vis other members of the lineage who were born after they entered the lineage as wives. Thus the hierarchy within the patrilineage was not developed along gender lines; though females as wives entered the lineage at a disadvantage, other females as members of the lineage suffered no such disadvantage. Therefore, wives were not secondary within the household simply because they were female; a bride was subordinate because she was "younger" than all the existing members of the lineage.

Both female and male children in Yoruba society can legitimately be referred to by the non-gender-specific term "offspring," as Yoruba terminology does not make gender distinctions in children. Sons and daughters are both collapsed into one category, *omo-ile,* meaning literally "children of the house," and are ranked according to their chronological age. It is the *omo-ile* that are referred to as husbands by wives—regardless of their sex. Amadiume, in her discussion of the Igbo institution of female husbands states that "daughters could become sons and consequently male."[16] In Yoruba society, the female husbands did not acquire male attributes; the point is that the role of the husband was not defined by sex. The asymmetrical relationship between a Yoruba couple is predicated on the idea that the husband is senior to the wife and therefore enjoys the right of priority in the household, since [with] marriage, it is the wife who moves into the new household.

Scholars have inaccurately evaluated male and female roles in Yoruba society by using the concept of a sexual division of labor. The conventional wisdom in the study of the Yoruba is that long distance trade was the province of males. The primary traded goods in Yoruba society were foodstuffs which traders procured from farms and carried on their heads into the town. Yams and palm nuts, the basic foodstuffs, were processed in town into yam flour and palm oil respectively and then sold in the markets. Since trading might have required that an individual be away from home for weeks at a time, long distance trade has been described as incompatible with childrearing, the domain of the female.

However, I would suggest that motherhood was an impetus rather than an obstacle to economic and trading activities. Part of the definition of motherhood in Yoruba society was that mothers must provide for their children materially. Yoruba mothers, like fathers, were breadwinners too. Therefore,

---

[16]Amadiume, op. cit., p. 15.

it is mistaken to present the role of mothers and fathers in dichotomous terms, as it is often suggested by the concept of sexual division of labor.

In fact there is increasing evidence to show that historically females were indeed involved with long distance trade. For example, one European explorer in precolonial Yorubaland noted in his journal that "we passed several people, primarily women, heavily laden with cloth, plantains and a paste from pounded Indian corn.[17]

Anthropologists, in their focus on patrilineage, tend to reduce females simply to the role of wives, which in reality was but one role among many in Yorubaland. The female did not become a part of her husband's family; though resident in his household, she retained full rights and obligations in her natal compound, to the extent that her children could lay claim to property or gain access to land by invoking their mother's rights. Though a female was a wife in her husband's household, she was a husband (a member of the lineage) in the lineage of her birth.

Motherhood is another institution that reveals that Yoruba society was based on a seniority rather than a gender distinction. Motherhood symbolizes for Yoruba females the height of achievement because it combines two things which Yorubas value most—children and seniority. In fact, the essence of Yoruba marriage is children. In the past, just as in the contemporary, bridewealth was paid to the family of the bride to confer a husband's right to the children born in the course of the marriage, not control over the wife's labor. A successful and fully led life in Yoruba society was one in which one spent old age being pampered by one's children and then at death being despatched to the world of the ancestors with the pomp and pageantry of a big funeral celebration. Rites of passage celebrations, like the funeral, were simply called *inawo,* which literally means "the spending of money." The more money spent on the funeral the merrier and the more enhanced the social status of the spenders and in the case of funerals, the status of the deceased. But, the role of children did not end at death, in that the Egungun cult, which is a cult of ancestor veneration was celebrated yearly to solicit the good will and blessings of the ancestors.

A wife's position as junior changed with the birth of her first child. She became a mother. She began to acquire some seniority after having been in the household longer than "newer wives" and "new" children. To children members of the lineage a new mother was not a "wife" but rather a "mother." This is underlined by the fact that members of the lineage stopped calling her by her given name; instead she was named "mother of . . ." (whatever the name of the child was). This change in name reflected the improvement

---

[17]Clapperton, Hugh, *Journal of Second Expedition into the Interior of Africa* (Philadelphia: Carey, Lea and Carey, 1829), p. 30.

in her rights because in the society, one only called one's junior, peer, or those who one did not respect, by name.

Sociologists have written repeatedly about the ideology of motherhood in western cultures in which mothers have the "natural" responsibility of raising children. This belief is said to have been used to keep women out of public life. Fraiberg and Auerbach argue that this ideology led to the emergence of the concepts "good mother" and "bad mother"—a "good mother" being instantly and constantly available to meet the needs of her children.[18] In Yoruba society, the conception of motherhood and the ideology of mothering were much different from the Western conception. It is true that Yoruba mothers may not have had any higher interest than that of the welfare and success of their children, but this did not result in the domestication of mothers; instead, it meant providing for their children in every way possible, including economically. "Breadwinning," which is associated with fatherhood in the West, was part of the definition of motherhood in precolonial Yoruba society. The task of "breadwinning" was shared between mothers and fathers. From the child's vantage point, there was no good or bad mother. In fact, it was considered sacrilegious to even think in these terms because from the Yoruba point of view, "a mother, is a mother, is a mother." What makes a mother did not depend on what she did after the baby was born, but on the fact of having been pregnant for nine months and having gone through labor pains. Yoruba mothers would never let their children forget this biological fact and often used it as a form of social control. Mothers commonly enforced obedience by invoking their experience of labor pains; T. M. Aluko, in his novel *One Man, One Wife* captures very well this aspect of motherhood in Yoruba society when a character named Gbemi is trying to persuade her daughter Toro to marry the man her parents had chosen. She says:

> Toro, you must heed my words. Toro I enjoin you to marry Joshua. By the womb in which I carried you for ten moons, by the great travail I underwent at your birth, by these breasts which suckled you when you were helpless, by this back on which I carried you for nearly three years. In the name of motherhood I command you to marry Joshua.

Fathers did not command this kind of power over their children.

Edholm et al., in "Conceptualizing Women," conclude that:

> [T]he concepts scholars employ to think about *women* (all empha-

---

[18]See Fraiberg, Selma, *Every Child's Birthright: In Defense of Mothering* (New York: Basic Books, 1977); and Auerbach, J., *Working Parents and Child Care Responsibility: The New Role of the Employer,* Ph.D. Dissertation submitted in the Department of Sociology, U.C. Berkeley.

ses mine) are part of a whole ideological apparatus which in the past have discouraged us from analyzing *women's* work and *women's* spheres.[19]

I could not agree more that concepts are part of the ideological apparatus. However, Edholm and other scholars fall into their own ideological trap by deploying the concept "women" as a given rather than part of the "whole ideological apparatus" they articulate. Woman/women is a social construct invoked asocially, and ahistorically in western gender discourses. There was no "women" in precolonial Yorubaland but there were females in diverse, overlapping, and paradoxical roles, such as husband, wife, mother, offspring, and trader.

In conclusion, what the Yoruba case reveals about gender is that it is not a given social category, and as such, as an analytic tool, it cannot be invoked in the same manner, to the same degree, in different situations across time and space. Gender is both a social and historical construct. No doubt gender has its place and time in scholarly analyses, but its place and its time is not precolonial Yoruba society. The time of "gender" was to come during the colonial period. Among the precolonial Yoruba, seniority was the dominant principle of social organization.

---

[19]Edholm, et al., "Conceptualizing Women," *Critique of Anthropology,* Vols. 9–10, 1977, p. 127.

Suggestions for Further Reading

Allman, Jean, Gieger, Susan, and Nakanyike Musisi, eds., *Women in African Colonial Histories* (Bloomington: Indiana University Press, 2002).

Berger, Iris, and White, E. Frances, *Women in Sub-Saharan Africa: Restoring Women to History* (Bloomington: University of Indiana Press, 1999).

Bullwinkle, Davis A., *African Women: A General Bibliography, 1976–1985* (New York: Greenwood Press, 1989).

———, *Women of Eastern and Southern Africa: A Bibliography, 1976–1985* (New York: Greenwood Press, 1989).

———, *Women of Northern, Western, and Central Africa: A Bibliography, 1976–1975* (New York: Greenwood Press, 1989).

Clark, Carolyn M., "Land and Food, Women and Power, in 19th Century Kikuyu," *Africa* 50, no. 4 (1980): 357–370.

Hafkin, Nancy, and Bay, Edna, *Women in Africa: Studies in Social and Economic Change* (Stanford: Stanford University Press, 1976).

Hakem, Ahmed, et al., "The Matriarches of Meroe: A Powerful Line of Queens Who Ruled the Kushitic Empire," *UNESCO Courier* 32, no. 8/9 (August/September, 1979), 58–59.

Hodgson, Dorothy L., and McCurdy, Sheryl A., eds., *"Wicked" Women and the Reconfiguration of Gender in Africa* (Portsmouth, N.H.: Heinemann, 2000).

Jeffries, Rosalind, "The Image of Women in African Cave Art," *Journal of African Civilizations* 6, no. 1 (1984): 98–122.

Kinsman, Margaret, "Beasts of Burden: The Subordination of Southern Tswana Women, ca. 1800–1840," *Journal of Southern African Studies* 10, no. 1 (1983): 39–54.

Loth, Heinrick, *Women in Ancient Africa* (Westport: L. Hill and Co., 1987).

Marks, Shula, and Rathbone, Richard, "The History of the Family in Africa: An Introduction," *Journal of African History* 24, no. 2 (1983): 145–61.

McCakie, T. C., "State and Society, Marriage and Adultery: Some Considerations from the Social History of Pre-Colonial Asante," *Journal of African History* 22, no. 4 (1981): 477–94.

Mikell, Gwendolyn, ed., *African Feminisms: The Politics of Survival in Sub-Saharan Africa* (Philadelphia: University of Pennsylvania Press, 1997).

Musallam, B., *Sex and Society in Islam: Birth Control Before the 19th Century* (Cambridge: Cambridge University Press, 1983).

Oyewùmí, Oyèrónké, *The Invention of Women: Making an African Sense of Western Gender Discourses* (Minneapolis: University of Minnesota Press, 1997).

Robertson, Claire, and Klein, Martin, eds., *Women and Slavery in Africa* (Madison, Wis.: University of Wisconsin Press, 1983).

Ross, Robert, "Oppression, Sexuality, and Slavery at the Cape of Good Hope," *Historical Reflections* 6, no. 2 (1979): 421–33.

Thomas, Lynn M., *Politics of the Womb: Women, Reproduction, and the State in Kenya* (Berkeley: University of California Press, 2003).

Van Sertima, Ivan, ed., *Black Women in Antiquity* (New Brunswick: Transaction Books, 1984).

White, E. Francis, *Creole Women Traders in the 19th Century*, Working Paper #27 (Boston: Boston University, African Studies Center, 1980).

PROBLEM VI

SLAVERY IN AFRICA

Africa, the slave trade, and slavery have been primarily associated for several hundred years with the trans-Atlantic trade in human flesh which has generated impassioned controversy, moral dilemma, civil wars, violence, and voluminous literature. It has only been within the last generation that scholars have begun to examine the trade in slaves and slavery within Africa itself. The late Walter Rodney was one of the first historians to address the issue of slavery within Africa in distinction to the trans-Atlantic commerce in his research on the history of the Upper Guinea Coast. Rodney makes special reference to the dearth of accounts by early European travelers to the institution of indigenous African slavery. He argues that the insatiable European demand for labor produced not only the shipment of Africans to the New World but was responsible for introducing that "peculiar institution" within African societies themselves. When the European powers eventually abolished slavery in the early nineteenth century, they were only dissolving their own invention.

Professor John D. Fage disagrees. There is no argument that the trade in slaves to labor in the Americas was a devious scheme of European cupidity, but according to Fage the institutions of trade and slavery were well established before the arrival of the Europeans on the coast of West Africa. Fage concedes that Rodney's claim may well apply to the Upper Guinea Coast, a small fragment of the expansive coastline of West Africa sprawling through the surf for over a thousand miles to the east, and the source of only a small amount of slaves for the trans-Atlantic trade, but his argument cannot apply to the Lower Guinea Coast which was for over a century the principle source of slaves for the Americas. In the lower Guinea Coast the European demand for slaves merely provided the African potentates and merchants with the opportunity to decide to retain their slaves for personal use or sell them to the Europeans.

Suzanne Miers and Igor Kopytoff in *Slavery in Africa* regard this debate as irrelevant for neither Professors Fage nor Rodney address the issue of defining African slavery. According to Miers and Kopytoff slavery in Africa was a diverse, heterogeneous institution and was not the chattel experience typically associated with the plantations of the Americas. They argue that slavery in Africa was "institutionalized marginality" in which virtually no society had a single definition for "slave." In fact, Miers and Kopytoff believe that the word "slave" is misleading since it embraced so many forms of servitude from the most harsh exploitation in the salt mines of Taghaza to the benign domesticity within the household of the Ottoman Pasha. With delicacy the authors place quotation marks around the word "slavery," preferring to define the slave not by his or her position within the household of the master but rather the position he or she held in the society which defined him or her as a slave.

Other historians have criticized Miers and Kopytoff's rather beneficient definition of who was or who was not a slave. To them a slave was a slave no matter how one defined the terms of servitude. According to this view Miers and Kopytoff have failed to understand the reality of slavery, for in fact slaves had a very limited ability to become acceptable in a free society and consequently remained "marginalized" throughout their lives. As slaves within African societies, they serve as economic assets to sustain otherwise uneconomic enterprises such as the panoply of the courts of the Sudanic kingdoms. Although African slaves, like their American counterparts, did not have their previous cultural consciousness crushed by the experience in the New World, exploitive or benign, the slaves' very ability, indeed determination, to retain and utilize their own cultural identity branded them as permanent outsiders to the African societies that they served. Thus slavery in Africa was not simply a "marginalizing" experience but was as oppressive when required as that which took place on the plantations of the Americas. In fact the American and African institutions of slavery were more similar than different; a slave was a slave, and although opportunities to improve one's position as a slave often were made possible in African societies, the status of one's origin in slavery was never forgotten.

Paul Lovejoy reinvigorates the debate by proposing that the terms of slavery in Africa were transformed over time. If kinship relations were the foundation of many African societies then dependent kinship relations were often times the mortar. But, external elements unrelated in kinship steadily altered those relationships throughout the generations of the African past. The trade in African slaves by Muslims preceded that of the trans-Atlantic trade by many centuries. The Islamic slave trade certainly exploited Blacks for labor, porterage across the Sahara to serve as slaves in Muslim societies, but slaves were not only accepted into commerce and Islamic intellectual life but many through their abilities and loyalties rose to positions of authority in the states of the Islamic world. Women were, of course, purchased as concubines, but their position in the Muslim household and their sexual role rapidly integrated them into the indigenous Islamic familial structure. Slavery, whether African or Islamic, became much more a part of the culture, whatever the religion, than the trans-Atlantic trade, which redirected the flow of goods and resources to the coast and ultimately out of Africa. Under the pressure of the intense market of the trans-Atlantic trade, African servitude was transformed into a much less benign institution.

Igor Kopytoff disagrees. Not only does Lovejoy appear to romanticize the life of a slave in the African past, but appears to make the African an observer rather than a participant in its own historical experience. Moreover, according to Kopytoff, Lovejoy provides a "model," of sorts, that describes events across time and space which have not received the scrutiny of strict historical research.

The understandable obsession by the public, politicians, and scholars with the trans-Atlantic slave trade has long obscured the overseas slave trade to Asia. This is not particularly surprising, for the dominant presence of African slaves in the New World has shaped much of its history from violent civil war to peaceful civil rights. The Asian slave trade has been more subtle and less conspicuous. Despite the fact that its long history reaches back into the millennia of dynastic Egypt, the reality of the modern Asian slave trade dates from the Arab conquests of the seventh century C.E. Thereafter during the next twelve centuries Africans were taken as slaves to Asia across the Sahara, the Red Sea, and the Indian Ocean. During this time, longer than a millennium, the number of Africans exported to Asia as slaves was approximately the same as the eleven million sent to the New World during the four hundred years of an intensive trans-Atlantic trade. During the last decade of the twentieth century interest has been aroused in the Indian Ocean world and particularly the relationship of Africa with the surrounding land mass of Asia beyond the Mediterranean, Red Sea, and the Indian Ocean. Led largely by scholars from India, the Middle East, Brazil, and Europe with a scattering of interest among Americans, conferences have been planned, societies and internet networks (The African Diaspora in Asia—TIDIA) organized, books published, and journals launched to redress the balance between the history of Africa and the trans-Atlantic world and the history of Africa and the Indian Ocean. Robert O. Collins argues for the recognition of this important and neglected dimension of the Asian slave trade to bring better balance and understanding to the long and tragic history of the overseas African slave trade.

African Slavery on the Upper Guinea Coast

WALTER RODNEY[1]

It has come to be widely accepted that slavery prevailed on the African continent before the arrival of the Europeans, and this indigenous slavery is said to have facilitated the rise and progress of the Atlantic slave trade. . . . The main purpose of this brief study is to test these generalizations with evidence taken from the Upper Guinea Coast—the region between the Gambia and Cape Mount.

Not only did the Upper Guinea Coast have a lengthy association with the Atlantic slave trade, beginning in the 1460s and extending over four centuries, but it is also a very useful exemplar as far as the present problem is concerned, because the so-called African "slavery" was known to be widespread in this region during the colonial period, and emancipation was eventually brought about by the intervention of the metropolitan powers involved. Sometimes, what obtained was a quasi-feudal exploitation of labour by a ruling elite, who received the greater portion of the harvest. More often than not, however, the "domestic slaves," as they have been categorized, were members of their masters' households. They could not be sold, except for serious offences; they had their own plots of land and/or rights to a proportion of the fruits of their labour; they could marry; their children had rights of inheritance, and if born of one free parent often acquired a

---

[1]Rodney, Walter, "African Slavery and Other Forms of Social Oppression on the Upper Guinea Coast in the Context of the Atlantic Slave Trade," *Journal of African History,* 2, no. 3 (Cambridge: Cambridge University Press, 1966), pp. 431–443.

Historian, educator, political activist, and scholar, Walter Rodney (1942–1980) was certainly one of the world's most renowned scholars. Rodney was born in British Guyana, educated in England, and began his teaching career in the history department at the University of the West Indies at Mona, Jamaica. Deemed subversive by the Jamaican government he was forced to leave in 1968. From 1969–1972 Rodney taught history at the University of Dar es Salaam in Tanzania before returning to his home, Guyana, to accept the chairmanship in the history department at the University of Guyana. His position was later revoked, evidently under government pressure. Later, Rodney became the leader of the Working People's Alliance, a radical political party opposed to Guyana's Prime Minister, Forbes Burnham. In 1980 Rodney was killed in a car bomb explosion. Despite his shortened career Dr. Rodney left a lasting legacy of scholarship. His Marxist writings attacked capitalism and imperialism of which his *How Europe Underdeveloped Africa* stands as a testament.

new status. Such individuals could rise to positions of great trust, including that of chief.

In seeking the roots of the indigenous slavery and serfdom of the Upper Guinea Coast, and in attempting to juxtapose these phenomena with the Atlantic slave trade, one is struck by the absence of references to local African slavery in the sixteenth or even the seventeenth century, when such evidence could reasonably be construed to mean that the institution preceded the advent of the Atlantic slave trade. Sometimes, the word "slave" was indeed used, but so loosely as to apply to all the common people. For instance, the Jesuit Alonso de Sandoval reported that, when he was in Cartagena in the early seventeenth century, a priest who came over on a slave ship told him that all the talk about the injustice of slavery was nonsense, because all the Negroes were slaves of absolute kings. Sandoval then went on to pinpoint the king of Casanga on the river Casamance as one such absolute monarch whose subjects were his slaves. In this arbitrary and figurative sense, the word "slave" is equally applicable not only to the common people of Europe at that time but also to the proletariat of the capitalist world.

Though one can identify no African slavery, serfdom or the like on the Upper Guinea Coast during the first phase of European contact, that region was one of the first sections of the West African coast from which slaves were exported; and in the sixteenth century the transfer of Africans from the Upper Guinea Coast to the Spanish Indies was already a significant undertaking. No slave-class was necessary to make this possible, because there was in existence a fundamental class contradiction between the ruling nobility and the commoners; and the ruling class joined hands with the Europeans in exploiting the African masses—a not unfamiliar situation on the African continent today.

It is a striking fact that the greatest agents of the Atlantic slave trade on the Upper Guinea Coast, the Mande and the Fulas, were the very tribes who subsequently continued to handle the internal slave trade, and whose society came to include significant numbers of disprivileged individuals labouring under coercion. The sequence of events points in the very direction in which Mungo Park had not cared to look too closely. In the first place, the political and religious dominance of the Mande and Fulas over the littoral peoples of the Upper Guinea Coast in the eighteenth century was based on a mixture of motives, among which the desire to sell more slaves to the Europeans featured prominently. Thus the Atlantic slave trade can immediately be identified as being partly responsible for the vassalage to which the coastal tribes were reduced. In the second place, the raiding of individuals for sale to the Europeans encouraged the marauding tribes to retain numbers of their captives to serve their own needs. When, for example, the Mandinga

Farim Cabo raided his neighbours to obtain captives for the slave ships, he retained a small proportion for his own needs.

One of the most direct connexions between the Atlantic slave trade and the nineteenth-century pattern of social stratification and oppression on the Upper Guinea Coast lay in the fact that numbers of Africans were captured with a view to being sold to the European slavers, but they remained for greater or lesser periods (or sometimes forever) in the service of their African captors. To begin with, there was usually a time lag between capture and the moment when a buyer presented himself. Then, there were always individuals whom the Europeans rejected for one reason or another; while the African merchants also decided against carrying through the sale under certain conditions.

While one major contribution to the rise of "domestic slavery" on the Upper Guinea Coast was made by the coastwards thrust of the interior peoples and their involvement in the slave trade, an equally great contribution was being made by the European forces acting on the littoral from the seaward side.

In the forts and factories of the Royal African Company, a distinction was made between "sale slaves" and "castle slaves" or "factory slaves." Both were acquired in the same way, but, while the former were destined to face the Middle Passage, the latter were retained around the forts and factories to help in the conduct of trade. The directors took some interest in these castle slaves. In 1702 they issued instructions that a Negro overseer should be appointed over them. They were to be converted to Christianity, given names, taught to speak English, and be allowed to have one wife (another castle slave). Perhaps the most important provision from the company's point of view was that the castle slaves should be taught skills to enhance their value and utility. Such workers were not to be sold or transported overseas except for great crimes.

Apart from the trading companies, private European traders also owned slaves on the coast, so that altogether the numbers of Africans bought by Europeans and remaining in servitude on the Upper Guinea Coast were considerable. The practice probably began with the arrival of Portuguese ships in the fifteenth century, giving rise to the term *grumete* (sailor's slave). In practice, the grumete (or *grommetto,* as the English came to use the word) was seldom a chattel. More often than not he was a wage earner, and in many cases African rulers on the Upper Guinea Coast voluntarily sent their children to live with the Europeans and to serve as auxiliaries in the coastal trade. There was a somewhat similar practice in the nineteenth century, involving the sending of children from the hinterland to the colony of Sierra Leone to learn "white man fashion." However, these children were usually only unpaid servants, and, when they grew old enough to realize that they were free, they were sold to the Mande and Fula traders.

The servitude directly introduced on to the Upper Guinea Coast by the Europeans slowly assumed an African character. The slave owners were originally white and foreigners, but the late eighteenth century saw the emergence of powerful mulatto slave-trading chiefs, who were said to own large numbers of "domestic slaves." Wadstrom explains that "if an African slave is impertinent he is sold. The children of such are occasionally sold also. But with the rich traders this is not common." The rich traders he refers to were mulattoes like the Caulkers and the Clevelands, the progeny of English slave dealers and African women. They kept "slaves" not only to serve as crews on the coastal and riverain vessels and to act as porters, but also to provide labour for the production of food and manufactures, which indirectly facilitated the Atlantic slave trade. In the latter part of the eighteenth century Chief William Cleveland (grandson of the original white Cleveland, who died in 1758) had a large "slave town" on the mainland opposite the Banana Islands. The inhabitants were employed in cultivating extensive rice fields, described as being some of the largest in Africa at the time, and equalled only by the Susu plantations which were also employing forced labour. In another smaller village, whose people were said to have been owned by Cleveland, there was a thriving mat and cotton industry.

Whether as agricultural labourers or sailing grumetes, whether as temporary members of households or as permanent residents, a large number of Africans on the Upper Guinea Coast at the end of the eighteenth century had been reduced to servile status through the agency of the Atlantic slave trade. A few quickly emerged as trusted servants and lieutenants, but the majority signalled their oppression by rebelling or escaping when the opportunity presented itself. They had every reason for so doing; because, having been spawned by the Atlantic slave trade, they in turn constituted the section of the society most liable to be exported.

The village of local slaves thus became a warren supplying the Europeans. This was the ultimate degradation to which the Atlantic slave trade had brought the African society of the Upper Guinea Coast. Without a doubt, as far as this region is concerned, to speak of African slavery as being ancient, and to suggest that this provided the initial stimulus and early recruiting ground for slaves exported to Europe and the Americas is to stand history on its head. When the European powers involved in the area (namely Britain, France and Portugal) intervened to end slavery and serfdom in their respective colonies, they were simply undoing their own handiwork.

Slavery in West African History

J. D. FAGE[2]

There have been at least three widely held and influential views about slavery and the slave trade in West Africa, and also about their relation to its society in respect both of their origins and of their effects on it.

The first is that the institution of slavery was natural and endemic in West African society, so that the coming of foreign traders with a demand for labour, whether from Muslim North Africa or from the countries of maritime Europe, led swiftly and automatically to the development by West Africans of an organized trade in slaves for export.

The second is a contrary view, that it was rather these external demands for labour which led to a great growth of both slavery and slave trading in West Africa, and so corrupted its indigenous society.

The third view, which may or may not be associated with the second, is that the external demand for West African labour, especially in the period *ca.* 1650 to *ca.* 1850, was so great that the export of slaves to meet it had a disastrous effect on the peoples of West Africa, disrupting not only their natural demographic development but their social and moral development as well.

In this paper it is proposed to examine and reassess these views in the light of recent research and thinking, and, as a result, to offer an interpretation of the roles of slavery and the slave trade in the history of West Africa which may be more in accord with its economic and social realities.

The first view, namely that the export slave trade was possible because

[2]Fage, J. D., "Slavery and the Slave Trade in the Context of West African History," *Journal of African History* 10, no. 3 (Cambridge: Cambridge University Press, 1969), pp. 393–404.

John Donnelly Fage (1921–   ) was born in Teddington, Middlesex, England, and received his D.Phil. in 1949 from Cambridge. From 1949–1955 Fage taught history at the University of Ghana, Accra, before becoming a professor of history in the School of Oriental and African Studies at the University of London. In 1963 Dr. Fage accepted a position at the University of Birmingham where he has served ever since. Fage is considered to be one of the founders of the modern study of African history who is recognized for his voluminous number of publications on an entire range of topics. But perhaps Fage is most noted for his skilled ability at writing textbooks, particularly his *Short History of Africa* (with Roland Oliver) which has gone into multiple editions.

both slavery and trading in slaves were already deeply rooted in West African society, was of course a view propagated by the European slave traders, especially perhaps when the morality of their business was being questioned. Norris's and Dalzel's books on Dahomey towards the close of the eighteenth century are developed examples of this attitude. Dalzel, for example, quite seriously argues that greater good was done by exporting slaves to American plantations than by leaving them in West Africa, where they were likely to become victims of the practice of human sacrifice. But the slave-traders' view in effect persisted into the abolitionist atmosphere of the nineteenth century and was, in fact, put forward as a principal moral justification for European colonization. To stamp out the evils of slavery and slave trading in West Africa, occupation of its territories was thought essential; indeed, it was specifically imposed as a duty on the European powers following the Brussels Act of 1890. The view that West Africans left to themselves were inherently prone to own and trade in slaves became a fact in one of the received myths of the conquering colonizers.

Analysis and criticism of this view are complicated by the problem of deciding what institution or institutions in West African societies corresponded to the European idea of slavery. Many people will be familiar with Rattray's analysis of slavery in Ashanti society, in which he defined at least five separate terms to describe the various conditions or degrees of voluntary or involuntary servitude in Ashanti. Only two of these, *odonko,* a foreigner who had been purchased with the express purpose of making him or her a slave, and *domum,* a man or woman received in tribute from a subjugated foreign state, might seem to correspond more or less to what an eighteenth-century European or white American might understand by "slave." But Rattray then goes on to consider the rights of such slaves in Ashanti society, and these were far in advance of the rights of any slaves in any colony in the Americas. He concludes that the rights of an Ashanti slave were not so very different from "the ordinary privileges of any Ashanti free man, with whom in these respects, his position did not seem to compare so unfavourably." He also states that "a condition of voluntary servitude was, in a very literal sense, the heritage of every Ashanti," and that to be masterless in that society was an open invitation to involuntary servitude. Similarly, Dalzel reports of the neighbouring, somewhat more authoritarian society of eighteenth-century Dahomey, which he knew at first hand, that its inhabitants were "*all* slaves to the king."

But it is not necessary here to enter into the arguments as to whether various forms of unfreedom in various West African societies should be called by the name of "slave," or by such other terms as "subject," "servant," "serf" or "pawn." It would seem possible to produce a straightforward definition of slavery that is perfectly adequate for the purposes of this present enquiry: namely that a slave was a man or woman who was owned by some other person, whose labour was regarded as having economic value and whose person had a commercial value.

It is obvious enough that slaves as so defined existed in many West African societies during the heyday of the Atlantic slave trade from the seventeenth to the nineteenth century, though possibly not in stateless societies or in societies that were little or not touched by the major routes of trade. The question is, then, whether such slavery existed in West African societies before the impingement on them of external trade.

In general, we can be confident that what the Portuguese sought to do in Lower Guinea from about 1480 was to profit by imposing themselves (as later they were to do in East Africa and Asia) on already existing patterns of trade, and that they found there organized kingdoms in which the idea of foreign trade, carried on under royal control and in accordance with state policy by established merchant classes or guilds, was already well established. Such a system involved the use of slaves—and an appreciation of their economic value—in a number of ways: as cultivators of crops for market on the estates of kings or nobles; as miners, or as artisans in craft workshops; as carriers on the trade roads, and even as traders themselves; as soldiers, retainers, servants, officials even, in the employ of kings or principal men in the kingdom. A similar but, one suspects, less well developed pattern was evident, as [Walter] Rodney admits, in the Senegal region on the western fringes of the Sudan, and it was undoubtedly from the Western and Central Sudan that it had spread into Lower Guinea some time before the arrival of the Portuguese. In this sense the area of Upper Guinea, where in the sixteenth and seventeenth centuries there was no organized slavery, was an economically little developed and backward region.

There seems in fact to be a close correlation in West Africa between economic development (and political development, because indigenous commercial activity was largely king- or state-directed) and the growth of the institution of slavery as here defined. This growth was already well advanced before European sea trade with West Africa began in the fifteenth century, and certainly before the main commercial demand of Europeans on West Africa was one for slaves—which was not really until the middle or the second half of the seventeenth century. Neither the first nor the second of the commonly held views about the relationship between the Atlantic slave trade and slavery and slave trading within West African society is really satisfactory. Slavery and the commercial valuation of slaves were not natural features of West African society, nor was their development and growth simply a consequence of the European demand for slaves for American plantations. This last may well have been the case in Upper Guinea, but elsewhere, e.g. in Lower Guinea, all the coming of European slave buyers meant in principle was that African kings and merchants were increasingly presented with a new element of choice—fundamentally, it would seem, an economic choice: whether it was more advantageous to them to keep their slave labourers at home, as farmers, artisans, porters, retainers, soldiers, etc., or to exchange them or some of them for other forms of wealth (or for power, e.g. guns and powder).

We arrive then at a first conclusion, that slavery and the making, buying and selling of slaves were means by which certain privileged individuals in West African society, or persons who wished to gain or to extend positions of privilege in that society, sought to mobilize the wealth inherent in the land and the people on it, and that this process had already gone some distance before the Europeans arrived. In so far as it seems to have started in the Sudan, rather than in Guinea, it is of course still possible, even perhaps likely, that the process was sparked off by the demands of visitors coming to West Africa from across the Sahara, from North Africa. On the other hand, such evidence as there is suggests that it is *un*likely that these first external demands were primarily or even essentially demands for labour. The prime North African demand was probably for gold and exotic produce, and the first basis of the trans-Saharan trade the exchange of salt for gold. It would thus be a demand for *commodities* which provoked the vital change by which some West Africans began to view some others not as kin or non-kin but as a means by which to obtain wealth and power. We are still left, however, with the questions whether, and, if so, to what extent, the external demands for West African labour, especially the great European demands for labour for the Americas, may have distorted the natural economic development of West Africa, and have produced socially, economically, and even politically disastrous consequences.

The conclusion to which one is led, therefore, is that whereas in East and Central Africa the slave trade, sometimes conducted in the interior by raiding and warring strangers, could be extremely destructive of economic, political and social life, in West Africa it was part of a sustained process of economic and political development. Probably because, by and large, in West Africa land was always more abundant than labour, the institution of slavery played an essential role in this development; without it there were really few effective means of mobilizing labour for the economic and political needs of the state. (One may recall Charles Monteil's dictum that "a Sudanic empire is in essence an association of individuals aiming to dominate the generality for profit.") But in this process the *trade* in slaves, certainly the export trade, was essentially incidental, only one of a number of ways of increasing a kingdom's wealth and power, and in the Guinea coastlands only during the eighteenth century the most important way. Whether or not to export slaves and, if so, in what quantities, seems to have been increasingly an economic choice.

Slavery in Africa
SUZANNE MEIRS AND IGOR KOPYTOFF[3]

The Outsider and his Marginality

When people were transferred from one group to another there was usually an element of compulsion, sometimes by relatives and sometimes by force of arms. Either way, the individual was wrenched from his own people, losing his social personality, his identity and status. He suffered a traumatic and sometimes violent withdrawal from kin, neighbors, and community, and often from familiar customs and language. The change was usually drastic and total—on a different order from the transfers effected as a normal part of the workings of systems of kinship and marriage already discussed. In all the various examples of "slavery" given here, the "slaves" have one thing in common: all are strangers in a new setting, be it a new kin group, community, region, or even country. The degree of trauma experienced clearly varied with the harshness of the change and the age of the victim. We have in fact scarcely any material on the psychological aspects of this experience and such material is probably almost unrecoverable now. It is, however, the structural and institutional aspects of their incorporation into the receiving group that we shall focus upon here. The condition of the person detached from his native group in this way is analogous to the situation of one who is in the midst of what anthropologists, following van Gennep, have called *rites de passage*, rituals of transition. Such rituals are widespread and accompany normal changes of status, such as the graduation from adolescence into adulthood. The person is expelled from his old social niche and put into a temporary limbo—van Gennep called it *marge*, margin. He is then in a

[3]Miers, Suzanne, and Kopytoff, Igor, "Introduction" in *Slavery in Africa: Historical and Anthropological Perspectives* (Madison: University of Wisconsin Press, 1977). Excerpted from pp. 14–21, 48–55, and 66–69.

Suzanne Miers (1921–   ) was born in Zaire and received her D.Phil. from the University of London in 1969. She has taught at the University of London, the University of Wisconsin, and Ohio University. Her many publications have brought her recognition as one of the leading authorities on slavery in Africa.

Igor Kopytoff (1930–   ) took his degree in Anthropology at Northwestern University in 1960 under Melville J. Herskovits. He taught at Brown University from 1960–1962 before going to the University of Pennsylvania where he has since been Professor of Anthropology. His most recent studies have been on gender in Africa about which he has published widely in numerous journals. His most recent work is "Leisure, Boredom and Luxury Consummerism: The Lineage Mode of Consumption in a Central African Society."

state of marginality—quite literally on the margins of society, indeed of all societies, for he has lost his old social identity and not yet acquired a new one. He is, structurally speaking, simply not a person—an ambiguous being without name, position, or status (hence, ritually, his nonexistence is often symbolized by his "playing dead").

The captive outsider, and indeed to some extent any outsider, is initially in this position vis-a-vis his new society. He is not a person in it—nor to it. In Simmel's definition of the perfect stranger, "the relation to him is a non-relation" unless, that is, there is a universalistic doctrine with a concept of a transcendent human family. If the intention is simply to resell such a captive stranger, he can remain in this marginal state and thus be literally an object or commodity. It is scarcely surprising that most reports emphasize that the "trade slave"—the one bought or captured for barter—was the worst treated of all. Victor Uchendu sums up his position among the Igbo as "no more than trade goods," and this was doubtless typical.

The outsider who is to be retained, however, cannot be left in this limbo; he must somehow be incorporated. This problem of the slave as a resident "stranger" raised by Henri Levy-Bruhl (1934) as the jural key to Roman slavery is common to all slave systems. All too often, the widespread emphasis on the disabilities of slavery makes the analysis of it one-sided by concentrating attention on how slaves are *excluded* from the host society. But the problem for the host society is really that of *including* the stranger while continuing to treat him as a stranger. As Miller put it, the problem is "how to append someone who does not belong to the local social system, who when included still remains less than fully an insider." Every society must somehow tackle this problem which, from the sociological perspective, we might call the "institutionalization of marginality" . . . [for it] shows that marginality-to-society may be institutionalized to continue over the generations, even though other marginalities, such as those of kinship, for example, may lapse. Discussions of African "slavery" often dwell on the successful integration of the "slave" into the kin group and thereby tend to assume that this must also mean integration into the society as a whole. But the two marginalities are different and the marginality-to-society has its own distinct significance. It institutionalizes a generalized social identity of "slave," which may continue even when, after abolition, there are no more specific masters left. This marginality-to-society was probably quite widespread in Africa. It was found, in addition to the Margi, at least among the Aboh, Tuareg, Vai, Fulani, Duala, and Tawana (Batawana). In the last three cases, it was also clearly reinforced by ideas about ethnic superiority of the host society.

For the stranger's marginality to be reduced and institutionalized, new bonds must be created, in the integrative sense of "bonding" him to the new society as well as in the more onerous sense of "bondage" to it. His state, of necessity, falls somewhere between two extremes. He is moving away from the condition of the trade slave—the complete outsider—and he would like to assume, but cannot, the condition of the complete insider, of the man born into the society as a full-fledged citizen. But the insider in most traditional societies of Africa was not an autonomous individual. His full citizenship derived from belonging to a kin group, usually corporate, which was the fundamental social, legal, political, and ritual protective unit.

This contrasts with the modern Western ideology of "freedom." For in the Western conception, the antithesis of "slavery" is "freedom," and "freedom" means autonomy and a lack of social bonds. However, as Simmel points out, unless a society has developed laws that specifically protect personal autonomy, such "freedom" must depend more on having the power to protect oneself than on actual autonomy; without such laws, autonomy cannot be a social value. In most African societies, "freedom" lay not in a withdrawal into a meaningless and dangerous autonomy but in attachment to a kin group, to a patron, to power—an attachment that occurred within a well-defined hierarchical framework. It was in this direction that the acquired outsider had to move if he was to reduce his initial marginality. Here, the antithesis of "slavery" is not "freedom" qua autonomy but rather "belonging." Significantly, the Giriama of the Kenya coast, when asked to name the opposite of *mutumwa* (slave), invariably replied *"Mgiriama"*, meaning simply a Giriama. Among the Suku of Zaire, a man who had quarreled with his lineage and set up his own compound with his wife and children in isolation in the countryside was compared to a *muhika*, the term for outsiders acquired by a lineage. His condition, which to a Westerner represents the height of freedom and autonomy, was considered to be analogous to that of a muhika because he had ceased to belong in, and to, a group, and thus lacked the protection enjoyed by those who really "belonged." By the same logic, the Suku, who had a king, would taunt their neighbors the Mbala, who had none, by singing that the Mbala "are the *bahika* because they have no king"—because, that is, they did not belong to and were not protected by a superior power. Here again, the greater apparent autonomy of the Mbala, living in independent villages, was irrelevant.

The process of reduction of marginality is well illustrated by Ralph Austen's description of the Duala. Here, members of the first generation of "slaves" were called *bakoni,* a term applied to all alien ethnic groups—that is, to all outsiders, whether or not they lived in Duala territory. The marginality of the bakom [sing.] in Douala was institutionalized and unalterable. However, the second generation, the *miyabedi* were in a more ambiguous position. As children of bakom, they were still outsiders and were so perceived, but since they were born locally, their marginality was reduced. They no longer "belonged" to any master, yet their status was depressed. The Germans called them "half-free." But since they had no masters and no restrictions on their movements, their disability lay in the impossibility of their acquiring full Dualahood. Instead of half-free, "half-belonging" or "half-stranger" would seem to describe their position better. Significantly, their final "freeing," or incorporation, in modern times has taken place by means of a cult that in the past was used as an instrument to exclude them from full Dualahood.

The fact that the Duala applied the same term to the first generation of acquired strangers as to "free" aliens was logical because what mattered was their common social distance from Dualahood—that is, their relative marginality and not their relative "freedom." Had the classification been concerned with "freedom," it would have lumped together the "free" Duala and the "free" alien in contrast to the "slave." Similarly, we find this principle of relative marginality among the Kerebe who classified free immigrant clients with "slaves," and the Aboh, who used the term *ndichie* to include both.

For our purpose, we shall focus upon the extreme point in this continuum of marginality: on the outsider who has involuntarily crossed the boundary of the society and is forcibly retained within it, or within a single society, one who has lost his own kin ties and has come to be under the full authority of another kin group in which he is a kind of resident alien. He is distinct from the voluntary immigrant—the alien who can choose to remain a permanent resident stranger, able to leave when he wishes. We shall call this involuntary outsider the *acquired outsider* or *acquired stranger*. The peculiarity of his condition lies in that while he is unable to leave and must have his marginality resolved, it is his acquisitors who have the power to define how his marginality is to be institutionalized. It is in this that his lack of "freedom" resides, and not necessarily in the particular institutional arrangements that follow and that may be humane or harsh, rigidly fixed or socially mobile, covering every aspect of his life or only part of it.

Dimensions of Marginality in Relation to Mobility

The institutionalization of the outsider's marginality provides him with a position in the host society. In time, this position may change, and his descendants may have a different position. These changes in degrees of marginality have to do with what has been called "social mobility." The phrase "social mobility of slaves" has been used, however, to refer to several kinds of changes, and these differences are of great importance to our discussion. It will therefore be useful to clarify them here.

The acquired outsider moves from total marginality toward greater and greater *incorporation* into the institutions of the host society. The reduction of his marginality occurs along at least three dimensions that may be usefully distinguished: the dimension of formal status, the dimension of informal

affect, and the dimension of worldly achievement and success. His movement into the society along each of these different dimensions of marginality
represents different kinds of social mobility and involves different processes
of incorporation.

The acquired outsider's *status mobility* reflects the process of his *formal
incorporation* into the new society. This means changes in his institutionalized marginality in terms of formal (usually legal) rights, duties, and privileges. For example, when the total outsider—the nonperson—becomes
someone's "slave," he moves into a definite status with defined rights and
obligations. If, in a few years, he acquires the recognized right not to be
resold, his status has changed further. If his offspring are recognized as
"free" and become incorporated as full members of the acquisitor lineage,
this represents intergenerational status mobility.

His *affective mobility* leads to a reduction in his *affective marginality* and
to his greater *affective incorporation*. This change is in the sphere of emotion
and sentiment rather than formal and legal codes. It has to do with the
esteem and affection in which he is held and the way he is treated. An
acquired outsider, for example, may be warmly accepted by his acquisitor
lineage and come to be held in high regard, yet his formal rights may remain
entirely unchanged. He may, for example, still be legally liable to be resold,
even though his masters would never consider doing it.

His *worldly success mobility* means changes toward a better style of life,
more political influence, and even control over greater wealth, all of which
reduce the marginality of his everyday existence and indicate success in the
business of living. Needless to say, this may occur with or without any
change in either his formal status or his affective incorporation. Affective
mobility and mobility in worldly success can obviously exhibit many and
subtle gradations. One's progress in these dimensions is usually gradual. By
contrast, formal statuses are clear-cut and discrete, and have definite rights
and obligations associated with them. Thus, changes in them tend to be not
a slide but a jump, even if a small one, from one constellation of precise
rights to another. It should also be emphasized that mobility in any one of
these three dimensions operates independently from mobility in each of the
others. When one speaks of the social mobility of a "slave," it is best to
specify which dimension is involved.

The status mobility of "slaves" should not be regarded as being primarily
a matter of movement out of the "slave" status. There was seldom in African
societies a single, all-embracing status of "slave" (such as existed in the early
modern Anglo-American world). Rather, a series of different statuses existed
for acquired persons and their descendants, all of which or only some of
which may be called "slavery." Much of the social mobility of acquired
persons took place within this series, and great personal success could be

achieved without ever taking the final step into the category of full-fledged citizen or complete insider.

Changes in the three dimensions—those of legal status, affective marginality, and worldly success—may occur to a single person in his lifetime. This represents his *lifetime mobility,* and it should be clearly distinguished from the changes that his offspring or descendants will experience, that is, from *intergenerational mobility.* The rather obvious distinction must be kept in mind because such statements as "The slave becomes integrated in the lineage in several generations" have sometimes been taken as showing the flexible or benign nature of a "slave" system. It should be remembered that intergenerational flexibility can coexist with rigid statuses into which each particular generation may be frozen.

Finally, we may note the fallacy of interpreting the existence of a range of "slave" statuses as showing great mobility. In the same society, acquired persons may be found in a wide range of positions, from agricultural laborers to high state officials. This need not mean that the state official began at the bottom and worked his way up, or that persons acquired by farmers have the slightest chance of becoming state ministers, as has sometimes been interpreted. All it may mean is that the acquired strangers were from the beginning marginal to quite different institutions—the peasant household in one case and the palace in the other.

All these distinct forms of mobility and varieties of status must be borne in mind when considering such phenomena as mobility, redemption, manumission, integration, and inheritance of "slave" status.

Treatment and Resistance: Some Problems of Comparative Study

The question of the treatment of "slaves" is of particular importance in Western perceptions. We have therefore taken pains to distinguish between "status mobility" and "affective" and "worldly success mobility"—a distinction between the legal position of the "slave" and the way people actually treat him as well as how he lives. This distinction is important because the modern Western view of the relationship between status and behavior has often been applied to "slavery" in general, and this has clouded the perceptions and interpretations in a way that must be understood by the historian and the social scientist. The issue has a bearing on such vital questions as reactions to enslavement, the role of coercion, the incidence of flight and rebellion, the meaning of docility—all of which have been relevant to some ideologically tinged problems of interpreting non-Western "slavery" and, by implicit contrast, Western slavery as well.

In the Western experience, the distinction between legal status and out-

ward behavior has become more and more blurred in the past century and
a half, as formal status differences between people have been crumbling
under the impact of egalitarian ideology and practice and of the ever increasing complexity and multiplicity of social structures in the West. The idea
that a noble as a noble and a peasant as a peasant (or a woman as a woman)
should enjoy different rights with legal sanction is contrary to modern ideas
of a common and uniform citizenship and of universal human rights. Differences of status persist, to be sure, but less and less as a legal matter; hence
they must often be discovered by complicated and arguable indices devised
by sociologists. In fact, these informal status differences are almost synonymous with differences in worldly success, and Westerners assume, not un-
reasonably for their own societies, that outward success or misery is a direct
clue to status. Conversely, a low status, such as that of "slave," is assumed
to carry with it relative poverty, deprivations of all kinds, and ill-treatment.

This association of the "slave" status with a deprived way of life has been
reinforced by the picture of plantation slavery, as practiced in the Anglo-
American world and as painted during the abolitionist debates of the nineteenth century. The indelible impression was created that a slave was necessarily miserable and badly treated. Moreover, in the highly specialized New
World plantation economy, the emphasis was on labor—how slaves worked,
what work they did, and how hard they worked, all in contrast to free laborers. The image of the slave as laboring under harsh conditions, exploited,
ill-treated and confined to the bottom of the social scale, has come to dominate the Western conception of the essence of slavery.

Such, then, was the yardstick against which Westerners measured an
institution in other societies to determine whether or not it was "really"
slavery. Crucial to the judgment were such questions as the individual's
worldly success, treatment, type of work, living conditions, and the differences between the lives of the "slaves" and those of the rest of the community. The assumption was that no man could *really* be a "slave" if he was
not obviously deprived in a material sense. When such deprivation was not
visible, the Western observer might never notice differences in status *per se*
and never inquire into the legal differences between the acquired stranger
and his acquisitor.

Given the evident unreliability of perceptions by European and sometimes
by African observers, historical sources have to be very carefully interpreted when they are examined for references to "slavery" in African societies. A lack of such references also calls for careful inquiry and precise
definition. Thus, we must treat with caution Rodney's argument that "slavery" and other "institutions of social oppression" (both undefined) were
absent on the upper Guinea coast and perhaps in other areas of West Africa
because there are no references to them in the early Portuguese records.
One must surely hesitate to draw conclusions from what Portuguese visitors

of the fifteenth and sixteenth centuries *failed* to report. Nonexistence is but one possible reason among many for their failure to describe the complex institutions that go under that vague umbrella term of "slavery" in Africa.

Having discussed the unreliable nature of past perceptions of "slavery" in Africa, we now come to the question of the actual treatment of "slaves." The data show very wide variation in the treatment of "slaves," just as they show wide variations in their use. As Nwachukwu-Ogedengbe emphasizes, there may be great variation in treatment within a single category of "slave" in a single society. One would expect that, in general, treatment would reflect some balance between the degree of their marginality and the kind of use to which they were put. Certainly the worst treated were those captured or bought for sale, whose position combined the greatest marginality with use only as a commodity. In this position of greatest marginality, instrumental needs dominated treatment: male captives were sometimes killed if they could not be ransomed or easily sold, and it was new outsiders who were often used for sacrifice. At the other end of the scale, the best treatment occurred with the least marginal persons, such as the descendants of "slaves," who functioned as quasi kinsmen.

The situation of most acquired outsiders usually fell between these extremes and was fraught with contradictions and ambiguities that were often unresolved. Treatment might depend on personality. Some were liked more than others; the lazy were more likely to be sold; the faithful might be kept when a real lineage member was sold. The disobedient were more likely to be sacrificed. The personal element came most often into play when the outsider served in a small household rather than on a large estate. Sometimes, however, distance had an advantage. On Hausa estates, "slave" sharecroppers were likely to merge with other tenants, but house "slaves" remained apart from the "free." Among the Sherbro, a "slave" on a farm could secretly accumulate money for redemption more easily than one living under his master's eye.

In interpreting treatment, concentration on either the legal position of the "slave" by itself, or his actual treatment by itself, can be misleading. Thomas Tlou and Nwachuku-Ogedengbe emphasize that a mere recitation of the "rights" of slaves—such as one often gets from informants in the field—ignores such crucial questions as how these rights were enforced and by whom; and if by the master alone, could the slave appeal? All too often, slaves are described as "children" of their owners. This stresses the familial side of the relationship but ignores, as we have already said, the fact that this meant that they were permanent, legal minors without rights of appeal to outside authorities. Thus, among the Aboh, Tawana, Sherbro, and Kerebe, we are specifically told that "slaves" had no access to courts that were open to the "free." However, in those societies where lineages were essentially sovereign units, neither "slave" nor "free" could appeal to outside courts or authorities, so that this fact by itself cannot be taken to show deprivation. Also, a "slave" in a small-scale society did not have very far to go to take refuge with another kin group and get beyond the reach of his masters. In this instance, knowledge of the formal legal position alone throws no light on the actual way the rules were applied and whether they could be applied at all. The discussions of the Aboh, Hausa, Kerebe, Tawana, and Sena also stress the fact that the formal rules were likely to be applied more strictly, more intransigently, and more capriciously where "slaves" were concerned.

If too great a concentration on legal rules has its dangers, so does too heavy a reliance on "what really happened." For example, among the Tuareg, in periods of adequate rainfall, differences in the way of life among the different kinds of servile dependents were scarcely apparent; but the legal distinctions were there and became very real when, with drought, access to vital resources depended upon position in the legal hierarchy. Those at the bottom were considered expendable and were forced to seek their livelihood elsewhere. Similarly, among the Sefla, whose "slavery" was among the most benign, it was in times of famine, when people had to be sold off, that the normally invisible differences in marginalities became apparent and important.

In assessing treatment and disabilities, we must distinguish between what Fortes has called the different "domains" of the social structure. For example, in the domain of kinship and familial relations, there may scarcely be any perceptible differences between "slaves" and real kinsmen, but this does not mean that there are no pronounced differences in the domain of politics or religion. The "slave" may be excluded from certain rituals or from powerful secret societies, or barred from certain public offices. Equally, special ritual and administrative positions may be reserved for "slaves" and carry considerable prestige even while publicly stamping the incumbent as a "slave." The stigma may sometimes outweigh the prestige, as in the case reported by James Vaughan when a Margi "slave" asserted his personal dignity by refusing to take a prestigious position in the king's entourage.

Resistance, flight, and rebellion give some indication of treatment. The conditions prerequisite to rebellion and their relative rarity in Africa have already been discussed. The more usual form of resistance was, of course, escape. This was simpler, usually less dangerous, and often hard to prevent. For one thing, the geographical area over which the master and his lineage, or even a state, had effective jurisdiction was usually quite small (when contrasted, for instance, with European spheres of colonial control in the Caribbean or with the southern United States). Masters were only too aware of this problem and took precautions when possible. Thus, chiefly Sherbro kin groups returned one another's fugitives, and the Tuareg used "slaves" in desert-savanna trading corridors far from the "slaves'" homeland. Masters were also selective at the outset: women and children from remote areas were preferred and adult men often had no buyers. In general, captives of war and victims of kidnapping were sold off as soon as possible to distant regions or, as among the Vai and Sherbro, into the overseas trade, or used for sacrifice locally, as among the Duala. Children were widely preferred because they could be easily acculturated, an advantage recognized by the Sena and Kerebe. Also, children were more likely to accept their servile position, a point that Carol MacCormack makes when discussing the conscious training of acquired children for their subordinate role in Sherbro homes. We have, however, all too little material on this important question of methods of socialization into servility in Africa; since the material must come from oral sources, it will all too likely soon be lost forever.

In spite of all precautions, however, escapes did occur. There is evidence of escape both from small-scale societies like that of the Giriama and some described here, and from large-scale societies. This is particularly true where there were large numbers of recently acquired, first-generation "slaves" or "slaves" used as agricultural labor on large estates, or both—in brief, where there were large numbers of highly marginal "slaves," as in parts of the Western Sudan. . . . It is apparent that, benign as many forms of African "slavery" may have seemed to Westerners, there were always some "slaves" who were dissatisfied with their lot and sought escape from it. The question that requires study, of course, is not the simplistic one of whether African "slavery" in general was benign or not, or whether African "slaves" in general sought to escape or not. Such questions are based on a false premise. They assume that these complex and extremely varied systems can be treated as a single institution—"African slavery." The relevant questions are those that accept the reality of a wide range of responses by "slaves" to their condition, and move on to ask about the variables that account for this range and for the statistical prevalence of some reactions over others in specific places and periods.

The question of treatment, it is clear, carries with it a host of implications and raises questions that are central to further serious work on African "slavery," beginning with the recognition of the immense variations in institutions covered by this name. Until recently, "slavery" was seen as relatively uniform throughout the continent, and relatively benign, and its nature was clarified by contrasting it with New World slavery. But the picture of the latter, it now appears, has not been without its own stereotypes. The dominant image of the brutal and brutalizing plantation has given way to a far more complex reality, which in turn raises a host of new questions. Similarly, the clear impossibility of maintaining a uniformly benign picture of African "slavery" should lead to the asking of complex questions that should put the analysis of African "slavery" into the same realm of discussion as other systems of servitude.

The Problem of the Origins of African "Slavery"

Anthropologists no longer look for the origins of social institutions, as if, like pottery types, they develop in one area and then diffuse to others. Questions such as "Did African slavery originate on that continent, and if so, when and where? Or did it come from outside?" are both unanswerable and meaningless. "Slavery" in Africa is simply one part of a continuum of relations, which at one end are part of the realm of kinship and at the other involve using persons as chattels. "Slavery" is a combination of elements, which if differently combined—an ingredient added here or subtracted there—might become adoption, marriage, parentage, obligations to kinsmen, clientship, and so forth. As the various elements are reshuffled under changing conditions, institutions we choose to call "slavery" can arise, disappear, and reappear, now in benign form, now as chattel servitude, and sometimes in both forms practiced side by side. It is possible to trace, as some of the studies described here do, the specific conditions that gave rise to particular combinations of these elements, but it is not possible to discuss the "origins" of "slavery" as such. For "slavery" is neither a single idea invented in some particular place from which it spread nor is it a single, clear-cut institution. It is simply an English word, a label, that we feel reasonably comfortable in applying to certain combinations of elements and feel we should not apply to other somewhat different combinations.

From this perspective, we find it impossible to join in discussions and arguments about the "origins" of African "slavery" such as those of Walter Rodney and John Fage. In their discussion, the nature of "slavery" is nowhere defined and is simply taken for granted. Our discussion in this chapter, on the other hand, makes it clear that once the problem of definition is tackled, the main question being debated—whether African "slavery" emerged in response to European or Arab or Sudanese stimuli—comes to be beside the point. We can only repeat that the emergence of the various institutions termed "slavery" must have occurred under a multitude of different conditions. To see such institutions in Africa as necessarily developing only in response to outside stimuli is to deprive the African past of internal economic dynamism, inventiveness, entrepreneurship, and, above all, of its fundamental cultural concepts of rights-in-persons. We simply cannot accept that the servile end of the kinship-to-"slavery" continuum sprang forth only under the impetus of extra-continental, and never internal, demand for people.

In this connection, a perspective beyond Africa is useful. For in every large cultural area of the world, other "bundles" containing some traits that lead us to call them "slavery" have emerged, disappeared, and reemerged. This is hardly surprising, as there is nothing unusual or particularly inventive about acquiring people by means other than marrying or begetting them, and more or less forcibly putting them to various uses. In the perspective of human history, it is not this that requires explanation but the various forms that such processes have taken. Moreover, it is the absence of such institutions rather than their presence that is unusual, and it is the claim that acquisition and use of people are absent that must bear the burden of proof.

Our analysis also makes it impossible to accept the suggestion by Claude Meillassoix that a slave is "necessarily the product of an act of violent capture" and that, therefore, "warriors or bandits are of necessity found at the origin of his economic and social existence." Our view is less dramatic and more domestic. We see the roots of these servile institutions in the need for wives and children, the wish to enlarge one's kin group, and the desire to have clients, dependents, servants, and retainers. Outsiders can fill these wants. War and brigandage can be one method of acquiring outsiders, but they are no more the mainspring of such rights-in-persons than they are of other forms of wealth. And as methods of acquisition, they could scarcely precede methods based on what Adam Smith saw as the human "propensity to truck and barter."

Finally, we must examine a set of related theories of the origins of servile institutions. In 1900, in a comparative ethnological study, Nieboer, following earlier authors, postulated that where there is a shortage of labor and a surplus of land suitable for labor-intensive farming, slavery is likely to emerge; because freemen will wish to work their own land rather than hire themselves out for wages, coerced labor becomes necessary. Where, on the other hand, the population is dense, land is scarce, and agriculture is capital intensive, hired labor is both available and preferable. In this economic argument, Nieboer assumes that slaves are primarily acquired as tillers of soil. The Russian historian Kliuchevsky, using similar economic variables, explained the emergence of a different kind of labor coercion—serfdom in the sixteenth- and seventeenth-century Russia. Kliuchevsky adds, however, the political factor as an important variable. The administration of Russia depended on the tsar's officials, who were given the right to collect rents and to demand military service from the peasants under them. As the state expanded, new territories became open for settlement and attracted the peasants away. Its administrative system threatened, the government attached the peasants to the land as serfs. The thesis points to the often critical dimension of the role of government—that is, of political factors—in distorting the working of purely economic forces and in determining the shape of the institution that emerges. Domar agrees with Nieboer that surplus land makes bound labor desirable and he adds further examples to Kliuchevsky's of the various devices used to coerce labor and prevent it from flowing into independent activity. Thus, the later Roman Empire, like sixteenth-century Russia, bound the peasants to the land by law. On the other hand, Domar points out that political factors can sometimes make this impossible. Neither the English government after the Black Death of the fourteenth century nor the northern United States in the nineteenth century could have contemplated such a solution when faced with a similar outflow of independent labor. In sum, then, Nieboer puts forward a basic premise about the economic conditions under which coerced labor might be expected to take root, whereas Kliuchevsky and, more formally, Domar indicate that political and other factors may lead to other solutions of the problem of labor shortage and unused land. Finally, Domar points out that solutions can linger on after the conditions that gave rise to them have disappeared.

What is the bearing of these theories on the African data? On the face of it, one may claim that the presence of "slavery" in Africa can thus be accounted for by the existence of surplus land and labor-intensive agriculture. However, the sparsely settled Sena, who fulfill those conditions best, have the most "social" and least labor-oriented form of "slavery," while the Aboh, Igbo, Duala, and Vai, with effectively less open land, have a more "economic" use for "slaves." The problem with these theories is, essentially, their unstated assumptions that slavery has to do primarily with labor, and that labor has to do with agriculture.

As we have seen, control over people is sought for many more reasons than that they are units of labor, in farming or elsewhere. Shortage of labor is but one kind of shortage of personnel that people may seek to remedy. As the Wolof, Hausa, Imbangala, and Duala show clearly, half the search in a society may be concerned with finding persons to fill purely social and political needs. Thus, calculation of the relative efficiencies in using "slave" or "free" persons depends on what one uses them for. In the above theories, the calculation is assumed to be only between bound labor and the hired services of the free. But as we have previously noted, when one seeks dependents and retainers, one wants whole persons and not their partial services. This is a need that hired labor cannot fill. In the broadest terms, then, we would suggest that a necessary (but far from sufficient) condition for the emergence of "slavery" is that in which one prefers to acquire men and women to be used and controlled as total persons, rather than merely to use their specific services.

As to the argument that free people will move into surplus land whenever it is available, the African data suggest that Socio-political problems of insecurity may prevent people from moving in the direction of an independent farming existence and push them toward serf-like dependence. Thus, political considerations may override economic ones not only at the level of government but also in individual decisions.

The existence of African "slavery" cannot be understood, then, in terms of the economics of the classic triad of labor, land, and capital. In the economy of living, the economics of material production is but one of a multitude of concerns, and the management of resources involves human beings as social and political resources. Hence, the roots of institutions concerned with the acquisition and use of human beings must be sought in the total social and political economy of a society.

Transformation in Slavery
PAUL LOVEJOY[4]

This book provides a thematic study of African history from the perspective of slavery. Its major thesis is that slavery was transformed, in part because of external influences and in part because of the dynamics of internal forces. On the most general level, it argues that it responded to outside influences to a greater extent than it influenced the outside world. The more important questions of how Africans shaped that response and the means through which outside influence was minimized are considered in detail. The implication of this thesis is that slavery was a central institution in many parts of Africa, and the study examines where and when this became the case.

Slavery has been an important phenomenon throughout history. It has been found in many places, from classical antiquity to very recent times. Africa has been intimately connected with this history, both as a major source of slaves for ancient civilization, the Islamic world, India, and the Americas, as one of the principal areas where slavery was common. Indeed, in Africa slavery lasted well into the present century—notably longer than in the Americas. Such antiquity and persistence require explanation, both to understand the historical development of slavery in Africa in its own right and to evaluate the relative importance of the slave trade to this development. Broadly speaking, slavery expanded in at least three stages—1350 to 1600, 1600 to 1800, and 1800 to 1900—by which time slavery had become a fundamental feature of the African political economy. This expansion occurred on two levels that were linked to the external slave trade. Firstly, slavery became more common over an increasingly greater geographical area, spreading outward from those places that participated directly in the external slave trade. Secondly, the role of slaves in the economy and society became more important, resulting in the transformation of the social, eco-

---

[4]Lovejoy, Paul, *Transformations in Slavery: A History of Slavery in Africa* (Cambridge: Cambridge Press, 1983). Excerpts from pp. xii–22.

Paul Lovejoy (1943–) was born in Girard, Pennsylvania, and received his Ph.D. under the direction of Philip Curtin at the University of Wisconsin in 1973. Since then he has been a Professor of African history at York University in Toronto. Lovejoy's voluminous writings on slavery and trade in African societies have brought him the well deserved reputation as a leading African historian.

nomic and political order. Again, the external trade was associated with this transformation.

Slavery: A Definition

Slavery was one form of exploitation. Its special characteristics included the idea that slaves were property; that they were outsiders who were alien by origin or who had been denied their heritage through judicial or other sanctions; that coercion could be used at will; that their labour power was at the complete disposal of a master; that they did not have the right to their own sexuality and, by extension, to their own reproductive capacities; and that the slave status was inherited unless provision was made to ameliorate that status. These various attributes need to be examined in greater detail to clarify the distinctions between slavery and other servile relationships.

Slavery was virtually always initiated through violence that reduced the status of a person from a condition of freedom and citizenship to a condition of slavery. The most common type of violence has been warfare, in which prisoners were enslaved. Variations in the organization of such violence— including raids whose purpose was to acquire slaves, banditry, and kidnapping—indicate that violent enslavement can be thought of as falling on a continuum from large-scale political action, in which enslavement may be only a byproduct of war and not its cause, to small-scale criminal activity, in which enslavement is the sole purpose of the action. Taken together, warfare, slave raiding, and kidnapping have accounted for the vast majority of new slaves in history. Even when the motives for war were not to acquire slaves, the link between war and slavery was often close. In societies where it was customary to enslave prisoners, the belligerents invariably took account of the possibilities of defraying the cost of war through the sale or use of slaves. When war and raids were chronic, these resulted in the continuous enslavement or reenslavement of people, and the incidence of slavery in such situations increased.

While warfare and similar violence accounted for most of the newly enslaved people in history, judicial and religious proceedings accounted for some. Slavery was a form of judicial punishment, particularly for such crimes as murder, theft, adultery, and sorcery. The methods by which suspected criminals were enslaved varied greatly, and often they were sold out of their home communities. None the less, this avenue of enslavement once again was rooted in violence, however legitimate in the eyes of the society in question. The status of a person was radically reduced: the new slave could lose his membership in the community, and his punishment could confirm a status that was passed on to his descendants.

There were instances of voluntary enslavement, particularly when the threat of starvation left the person with no other recourse. None the less, this was not a case of conscious violence by society or an enemy. There may well have been structural causes that placed people in situations where they could not be assured of survival and hence found it necessary to enslave themselves. This structural dimension may well have carried with it a dimension that was ultimately exploitative and violent. None the less, voluntary enslavement was unusual, and it probably accounted for only a small percentage of slaves in most places. Furthermore, the possibility of voluntary enslavement depended upon the existence of an institution of slavery in which violence was fundamental. If there were no such institution, a person would not become a slave but a client or some other dependant. That the status of slave was even assigned in such instances indicates that other servile statuses were not appropriate, either because they were lacking or because they were defined to exclude such cases.

The extent of coercion involved in slavery was sometimes obvious and sometimes disguised. The master could enforce his will because of his ability to punish slaves for failure to comply with his orders or to perform their tasks satisfactorily. Whipping, confinement, deprivation of food, extra hard work, and the ability to dispose of slaves through sale were common means of coercion. Physical punishment could lead to death, and even when there were legal and customary prohibitions on killing slaves, these were rarely enforceable. Often coercion was more indirect. The example of other slaves being punished or sold and the knowledge that the master could do so were usually sufficient to maintain slave discipline. Sacrifices of slaves at funerals and public ceremonies, which were common in some places, were also examples to the slaves. Such public displays were not usually a form of punishment for insubordination; in fact, they were sometimes conceived of as an honour, but most often slaves were purchased specifically for sacrifice. Since insubordination could lead to sale, the risks for the trade slave were obvious. A purchaser might well be in need of a sacrificial victim.

Slavery was fundamentally tied to labour. It was not the only form of dependent labour, but slaves could be made to perform any task in the economy. They had to do what they were told; hence they often performed the most menial and laborious tasks and sometimes undertook great risks. In the case of slaves, the concept of labour was not perceived as separate from the slave as a person. The slave was an instrument of work, and coercion could be used to force compliance with particular orders. The slave was told what to do and, if he did not do it, he was punished, often severely. Slavery could and did exist alongside other types of labour, including serfdom (in which people were tied to the land, and their obligations to the lord were fixed by custom), clientage (voluntary subordination without fixed remuneration for services), wage-labour (in which compensation for work was monetarized), pawnship (in which labour was perceived as interest on a debt and the pawn as collateral for the debt), and communal work (often based on kinship or age grades, in which work was perceived as a reciprocal activity based on past or future exchange). These other forms of labour could involve coercion, too, but usually not to the point at which they could be called slavery.

A peculiar feature of slavery was this absolute lack of choice on the part of slaves. Their total subordination to the whims of their master meant that slaves could be assigned any task in the society or economy. Hence slaves have not only performed the most menial and laborious jobs, but they have also held positions of authority and had access to considerable wealth. The plantation field hand and the slave generally had their subordination to their master in common. Both were assigned a task, but the nature of their employment was so different that they had virtually no mutual interests. The identity of the slave was through his master. Legally, the master was held responsible for the actions of the slaves, and this was the same for administrative slaves as well as common labourers. Slaves did not necessarily constitute a class, therefore. Their dependence could result in the subordination of their identity to that of their master, on whom their position depended, or it could lead to the development of a sense of comradeship with other slaves, and hence form the basis for class consciousness. Both could take place in the same society, if slaves and others recognized a clear distinction between those engaged in production and those involved in the military and administration.

Because slaves were fully subservient, their masters controlled their sexual and reproductive capacities, as well as their productive capacities. When slaves constituted a significant proportion of any population, then sexual access and reproduction were strongly controlled. Women (and men too) could be treated as sexual objects; the ability to marry could be closely administered; and males could be castrated. The significance of sex is most strikingly revealed in the market price of slaves. Eunuchs were often the most costly, with pretty women and girls close behind, their price depending upon their sexual attractiveness. These two opposites—castrated males and attractive females—demonstrate most clearly that aspect of slavery which involved the master's power over sexual and reproductive functions. Slaves lacked the right to engage in sexual relationships without the consent of their master. They could not marry without his permission and his provision of a spouse. Their children, once slaves were given an opportunity to have children, were not legally their offspring but the property of their master and often the master of the mother. Biologically, they were the offspring of the slaves, but the right to raise the children could be denied. Instead, slave children could be taken away and, even when they were not sold, they could be redistributed as part of marriage arrangements, trained for the army or administration, or adopted by the master's family.

Masters had the right of sexual access to slave women, who became concubines or wives, depending upon the society. This sexual dimension was a major reason why the price of female slaves was often higher than the price of men. Male slaves could be denied access to women, and such a dimension of slavery was a vital form of exploitation and control. The ability to acquire a spouse depended upon the willingness to accept the slave status and to work hard. Marriage or other sexual unions were a method of rewarding men. The desires of women were seldom taken into consideration. Although men could be given a wife from among the reduced pool of females available for such unions, they were not allowed effective paternity over their offspring. Actual bonds of affection and recognized biological links existed, of course, but these could be disrupted through the removal of the children if the master so wished. The master could reward the male slave, or he could deprive males of their sexuality through castration.

The slave status was inherited. This meant that the property element, the feature of being an alien, and the form of labour mobilization continued into the next generation, although in practice the slave status was often modified. The condition of slaves changed from the initial instance of enslavement through the course of the slave's life, and such an evolution continued into the next generation and beyond. The changed status varied from society to society, being more pronounced in some places than in others. The theory of the slave as an outsider became more difficult to uphold once a slave began to understand and accept his master's culture. While the theory could still define the slave as an alien, slaves were usually provided with the essentials of life, including access to land, spouses, protection, religious rites, and other attributes of citizenship. The more technical aspects of slavery, including the elements of property, labour, and alienness, could be invoked arbitrarily, but in practice these legal rights of the masters were usually not exercised fully. Usually some kind of accommodation was reached between masters and slaves. The sociological level of this relationship involved a recognition on the part of slaves that they were dependents whose position required subservience to their master, and it necessitated an acceptance on the part of the masters that there were limits on how far their slaves could be pushed.

A brief postscript is necessary to consider the special case of slavery in the Americas, because the American system was a particularly heinous development. Many features of American slavery were similar to slavery in other times and places, including the relative size of the slave population, the concentration of slaves in economic units large enough to be classified as plantations and the degree of physical violence and pyschological coercion used to keep slaves in their place. None the less, the American system of slavery was unique in two respects: the manipulation of race as a means of controlling the slave population and the extent of the system's economic rationalization. In the Americas, the primary purpose of slave labour was the production of staple commodities—sugar, coffee, tobacco, rice, cotton, gold, and silver—for sale on world markets. Furthermore, many features that were common in other slave systems were absent or relatively unimportant in the Americas. These included the use of slaves in government, the existence of eunuchs, and the sacrifice of slaves at funerals and other occasions. The similarities and differences are identified in order to counteract a tendency to perceive slavery as a peculiarly American institution. Individual slave systems had their own characteristics, but it is still possible to analyse the broader patterns that have distinguished slavery from other forms of exploitation.

Slavery in Social Formations

A "slave mode of production" existed when the social and economic structure of a particular society included an integrated system of enslavement, slave trade, and the domestic use of slaves. Slaves had to be employed in production, and hence the kind of transformation identified by Finley must have occurred. This transformation usually meant that slaves were used in agriculture and/or mining but also could refer to their use in transport as porters, stock boys, and paddlers in canoes. Slaves could still fill other functions, including concubinage, adoption into kin groups, and sacrifice, but these social and religious functions had to become secondary to productive uses. Furthermore, the maintenance of the slave population had to be guaranteed. This regeneration could occur through the birth of children into slavery (inheritance of slave status), raids, war, kidnapping, and other acts of enslavement, and the distribution of slaves through trade and tribute. Since slave populations were seldom self-sustaining through natural reproduction, enslavement and trade were usually prerequisites for the consolidation of a slave mode of production.

Slavery did not have to be the main feature of social relations in a society for a slave mode of production to exist. Other institutions could also determine the relations of production under different circumstances (kinship, pawnship, etc.). None the less, when slavery prevailed in one or more sectors of the economy, the social formation—that is, the combined social and economic structures of production—included a slave mode of production, no matter what other modes coexisted (feudalism, capitalism, etc.). This incorporation of various economic and social structures into a single system through the combination of and interaction between different modes of production could occur within the context of a single state or a wider region. Such a social formation could include peasants, for example, who were involved in a tributary relationship with a state, on the one hand, or who were autonomous and subject to raids by the state, on the other hand. The ways in which such different systems were integrated—often called their "articulation"—could be quite complex. Slavery could be linked to other modes of production through long-distance trade, tributary relationships, or raids and warfare. When the structural interaction between enslavement, trade, and domestic employment of slaves was the most important part of a social formation, it can be said that the slave mode of production was dominant. This occurred when the principal enslavers and slave merchants comprised a class of slave masters who owned a substantial number of slaves and relied on them for the maintenance of their economic and political domination. In this case, slavery became essential to the reproduction of the social formation.

The emphasis on the integration of a productive system based on slavery with the means of replenishing the supply of slaves has significance in the reconstruction of the history of slavery in its African context. This framework highlights three historical situations that were partially related and partially autonomous. Firstly, it provides a perspective for analysing the interaction between Africa and the demand for slaves in the Islamic world of North Africa and the Middle East. Secondly, it emphasizes the connection between Africa and the Americas, where African slaves were essential to plantation production and the mining sector. Thirdly, it allows for a study of the widespread productive use of slaves in Africa, particularly in the nineteenth century after the external slave trade collapsed. In all three situations, a mode of production based on slavery developed, but specific characteristics differed. The framework adopted here—the distinction between slavery as a marginal feature of production—is meant to facilitate a study of these three different situations.

The debate in the theoretical literature between Marxists and non-Marxists and among Marxists themselves has inspired this conceptual framework, but there are clear differences in my use of "mode of production" and "social formation" and their use by other scholars. I disagree emphatically with the approach of Samir Amin, Barry Hindess, Paul Q. Hirst, and others who employ a framework drawn from the interpretation of Louis Althusser, because, as these scholars readily admit, their analysis depends upon ideal constructs that are ahistorical. Rather, I follow the less dogmatic formulation of Emmanuel Terray, whose purpose is to provide an "instrument of analysis," which I assume means an "instrument of *historical* analysis." From this perspective, a "slave mode of production" is meant to be a descriptive term whose theoretical significance is not developed here. My purpose is to isolate the place of slaves in production as a first step in historical reconstruction.

The African Setting

Africa was relatively isolated in ancient and medieval times. Before the middle of the fifteenth century, virtually the only contact was along the East African coast, across the Red Sea and via the Sahara Desert. Those places bordering these frontiers were different from more isolated regions further inland. There were exceptions, depending upon natural resources, especially gold, so that five areas of gold production were drawn into the orbit of the non-African world: three in West Africa (Bure, Bambuhu, Volta basin), Ethiopia, and the Shona plateau in the interior of the Zambezi valley. In addition there was internal trade in luxuries other than gold—kola nuts between the West African forests west of the Volta River and the savanna to the north; copper, which was traded south from the Sahara into the lower Niger valley, and which was also distributed outward from the southern parts of modern Zaire; salt from many sources, including numerous sites in the Sahara Desert, the Red Sea coast of Ethiopia, local centres in the interior of Angola, many places along the Guinea coast, and other sites near the Great Lakes of east-central Africa. Despite its probable antiquity, this regional trade was relatively autonomous from the external sector. Furthermore, the other major economic developments during the millennium before the fifteenth century were also relatively isolated. The movement of Bantu-speaking farmers throughout central, eastern and southern Africa, the emergence of pastoral nomadism as a speciality in the northern savanna and down the lake corridor of East Africa, and the spread of iron working and craft production, despite occasional links to the external world, as in the case of cotton textiles, were far more influential regionally than intercontinentally.

One characteristic of regional development was a social structure based on ethnicity and kinship. Although the antiquity of kin-based societies is not known, linguistic, cultural, and economic evidence indicates that such structures were very old. The earliest references to kinship, for example, reveal that matrilineal and patrilineal distinctions were already well formed by the early sixteenth century. Much of the West African coastal region was patrilineal, except for the Akan of the Gold Coast. In west-central Africa, people followed matrilineal customs, as their descendants do today. Such continuity, which broadly speaking also matches ethnic distinctions, suggests that the interior peoples who were beyond the observations of early observers shared these structures. Thus, the coastal evidence for west-central Africa indicates the probable existence of a matrilineal belt of societies stretching across the continent to the Indian Ocean, just as it does today. Nothing in the historical record indicates that this pattern changed abruptly at any time in the past.

Those societies based on kinship have variously been described as ones characterized by a "lineage" or "domestic" mode of production. This mode of production had the following features: age and sexual distinctions were fundamental divisions in society, there being no class antagonisms. Elders controlled the means of production and access to women, and hence political power was based on gerontocracy. Since women were often the principal agricultural workers in this type of social formation, production and reproduction were closely associated. The maintenance of society depended upon the fertility of the women and the output of their labour. The crucial variables for gerontocratic domination included the number of women married to elders, the number of children born to each wife, and ability to secure cooperation from junior kin and affinal relatives, and access to the non-human resources of the lineage, including land, trees, wild products, game and water. In this situation, slavery did not alter the essential basis of the social formation. Slaves could add to the size of the population and thereby increase the number of people mobilized by the elders, but slaves performed virtually the same functions as lineage members.

Slavery was one of many types of dependency, and it was an effective means of controlling people in situations where kinship remained paramount. Slaves lacked ties into the kinship network and only had those rights that were granted on sufferance. There was no class of slaves. While they undoubtedly performed many economic functions, their presence was related to the desire of people, either individually or in small groups of related kin, to bypass the customary relationships of society in order to increase their power. Slavery was, therefore, essentially a social institution in small-scale societies where political influence depended upon the size of social groups. If they were allowed to do so, slaves could become full members of these groups, or they could be kept as voiceless dependents, but their welfare was related to the fortunes of their master and his kin. In this setting, people had slaves along with other types of dependents, but society was not organized in such a manner that slavery was a central institution. These were not slave societies.

Besides slavery, there were other categories of dependency, including pawnship, in which persons were held for security for debts, and junior age-sets, in which younger kin were not yet allowed to participate fully in the decisions of the lineage. Even marriage and concubinage were institutions of dependency.

Dependents were mobilized in the interests of the lineage as determined by the male elders. They performed cooperative work in the fields, formed hunting expeditions, defended villages against aggression, and participated in religious ceremonies. Because land was often held in common and because marriage involved payments that were too large for most youths to finance on their own, ties of kinship were strong. In times of difficulty, these connections provided insurance. Junior kin, in particular, were most vulnerable. On the one hand, they needed the family because they often were not wealthy enough or old enough to be on their own. On the other hand, they were the first to suffer in troubled times.

The emphasis on dependency could be reflected in religious practices; sacrifices, for example, were interpreted as an expression of continuity between this world and the next and the need for dependents in both. The killing of slaves and the quest for outsiders—or their heads—also emphasized dependency through the symbolism attached to such acts. These had no productive function but were indicators of social and economic standing. The demand for victims to be killed at funerals, religious rites, and political ceremonies could be haphazard and hence incidental, or it could become regularized and hence institutionalized. Funeral sites at Igbo-Ukwu suggest that the ninth-century ancestors of the Igbo had already developed a demand for sacrificial victims that could be supplied through the institution of slavery. Archaeology cannot determine the social status of those buried along with nobles—they could be free wives, children, volunteers, or others. At some point in time, none the less, slaves did become the main source for such victims.

The Islamic Factor

The existence of slaves in societies that emphasized kinship and dependency permitted their integration into a vast network of international slavery. This integration probably stretched far back into the past, but only for those areas closest to the Mediterranean basin, the Persian Gulf, and the Indian Ocean. By the eighth, ninth, and tenth centuries AD, the Islamic world had become the heir to this long tradition of slavery, continuing the pattern of incorporating black slaves from Africa into the societies north of the Sahara and along the shore of the Indian Ocean. The Muslim states of this period interpreted the ancient tradition of slavery in accordance with their new religion, but many uses for slaves were the same as before—slaves were used in the military, administration, and domestic service. The names of titles, the treatment of concubines, and other specifics of slavery were modified, but the function of slaves in politics and society was largely the same. Despite the ancient tradition, the principal concern here is with the consolidation of slavery in its Islamic context; for over seven hundred years before 1450 the Islamic world was virtually the only external influence on the political economy of Africa.

The functions performed by slaves were also different in part because the structures of Islamic societies were often on a larger scale than among kinship groups. In the large Islamic states of the Mediterranean basin, for example, slaves were used in government and the military, occupations that did not exist in stateless societies. Slave officials and soldiers often proved very loyal because of the dependency on their master for status. Eunuchs comprised a special category of slave that does not seem to have been characteristic of most non-Muslim societies based on kinship. Eunuchs, who could be used in administrative positions and as overseers of harems, were especially dependent, without even the chance of establishing interests that were independent of their master. Under the influence of Islam, this practice spread into sub-Saharan Africa, along with the employment of slaves in the army and bureaucracy.

The Islamic view of slave women was also different from one based on kinship. Islamic law limited the number of wives to four, although only material considerations and personal whim limited the number of concubines. In both Islamic and non-Islamic situations, men could have as many women as they could afford, but the legal setting was different. Islamic custom, again emphasizing a clearer line between slave and free, allowed for the emancipation of concubines who bore children by the master. Legally they became free upon the death of the master, but they could not be sold once they gave birth. In practice, the wives of slave origin in societies based on kinship were seldom sold either, and their status was closer to that of becoming a member of the kin group and hence free. The terms of reference differed, but the practice was quite similar.

In many Islamic societies, slaves also performed tasks that were more directly related to production and trade. Certainly the scale of economic activity in the Mediterranean and Indian Ocean basins involved greater exchange, a higher level of technological development, and the possibilities of more specialized exploitation of slave labour than in most of black Africa until recent times. In fact, slaves were frequently assigned tasks that were not directly productive but instead supported a political and social hierarchy that exploited a population of free peasants, craftsmen, and servile populations that were not slave. Although slaves were most often used for domestic (including sexual) purposes, or in government and the military, occasionally they were employed in production, such as in the salt mines of Arabia, Persia, and the northern Sahara. Other slaves were employed in large-scale agricultural enterprises and craft manufacturing. The frequency and scale of this labour, even though it was not the major form of production, was something quite different from the use of slaves in the less specialized economies of those African societies based on kinship.

These different uses for slaves, the more clearly defined distinction between slave and free, and the occasional employment of slaves in productive activities demonstrate a sharp distinction between the slavery of kin-based societies and the slavery of Islamic law and tradition. The most important difference was that slavery in Islamic lands had experienced a partial transformation of the kind that Finley identifies as significant in the institutionalization of slavery. A fully economic system based on slave labour had not taken place in most parts of the Islamic world between 700 and 1400, despite the importance of administrative and military slaves in the maintenance of Islamic society. Slave concubines and domestic slaves were common and indeed affected the nature of marriage as an institution and the organization of wealthy households. The adaptation of similar practices in sub-Saharan Africa involved a parallel transformation there.

The Transatlantic Trade

The rise and expansion of the European slave trade across the Atlantic Ocean had a decided impact on the evolution of slavery in Africa, particularly in those areas along the Guinea coast where the influence of Islam had been weak or nonexistent. Whereas the demand for slaves in the non-African parts of the Islamic world had a relatively gradual but steady influence on the spread of Islamic ideas and practices through parts of Africa, the impact of the European market for slaves was more intense over a much shorter period, with a correspondingly different influence. Slave exports rose gradually during the first 150 years of the Atlantic trade, amounting to 367,000 slaves from 1450 to 1600. Thereafter the trade was truly large, on a scale that dwarfed all previous exports from Africa. The total volume for the Atlantic trade reached 11,698,000 slaves, a figure derived from the pioneering census of Philip D. Curtin and the subsequent revisions of numerous scholars. The pull of the market had the effect of pushing indigenous forms of slavery further away from a social framework in which slavery was another form of dependency in societies based on kinship relationships to a system in which slaves played an increasingly important role in the economy. In short, this change also involved a transformation similar to the one that Finley has characterized as a fundamental shift in the way slavery can be embedded in a social formation.

The opening of the Atlantic to trade marked a radical break in the history of Africa, more especially because that trade involved the export of millions of slaves. Before this commercial development, the Atlantic shores of Africa had been virtually isolated from the outside world. Some salt and fish were traded into the interior in exchange for food, but by and large the coastline was a barrier. The technological breakthrough of ocean shipping had a tremendous economic impact, making available new sources of wealth for local people and facilitating political change on an unprecedented scale. Slavery here was closely associated with this transformation, not only because slaves were a major export, but also because slaves became far more common in local society than previously.

The transformation in slavery that accompanied the expansion of the European demand for slaves was largely independent of Muslim Africa. This relatively separate impact introduced a new force that modified slavery in ways different from the changes that had taken place as a result of the Islamic connection in the northern savanna and along the East African coast. There was no tradition of Islamic law, nor were there other features of Islamic slave practice, including concubinage, eunuchs, and political-military officials with Islamic titles. One important result of European trade, therefore, was the consolidation of a distinctively non-Muslim form of slavery. Slavery underwent a transformation from a marginal feature of society to an important institution, but in most places slavery continued to be interpreted in the context of lineage structures, and this is here identified as "lineage slavery."

As an institution, lineage slavery shared the same basic features as all types of slavery: the property element, the alien identity, the role of violence, and productive and sexual exploitation. The striking difference was the remarkable absence of foreign influence on the ideological plane. There was almost no internalization of European attitudes towards slavery, as Islamic theories and practices had been adopted elsewhere. The impact of the market did effect some changes that can be traced to European influence, but this factor operated more on the economic level than in the realm of ideology. Slavery continued to be conceived of in terms of kinship, even as slaves were assigned new tasks. Slaves were increasingly used in government, trade, and the military, in ways that were similar to the use of slaves in Muslim countries. The framework and titles were different, but the function was the same. The same was true in the control of women. Polygynous rules allowed men to have as many wives as they could acquire. There was no rationalization of this practice through laws governing the number of wives and the status of concubines, as there was in Islamic law. Nevertheless, the results were similar. Important men had many wives, some of whom were slaves, and this uneven distribution of women within society was an element of social control, particularly since women were often the principal agricultural workers as well as the reproducers of kin. Control of women enabled the domination of production and reproduction. This aspect of slavery had an important impact on the export trade. Europeans wanted field hands and mine workers. They did not really care about their sex, although they perhaps had a slight preference for males. Africans wanted women and children. There emerged a natural division of the slave population, with European merchants buying approximately two men for every woman, and sometimes even a greater proportion of men. The European trade was significantly different from the Muslim trade across the Sahara, Red Sea, and Indian Ocean. Muslims, too, wanted women, not men, as is evident in the higher prices for women in the Muslim trade.

The transformation of slavery in non-Muslim areas was related to the size of the export trade and the extent to which politicians and merchants catered to that trade through enslavement and commerce. As the number of slaves increased and the ability to maintain a sustained supply was established, it became possible to use slaves in new ways, not just using more slaves in the same ways. These new ways were sometimes related to increasing the scale of production, including gold, agricultural goods, craft commodities, and salt. In the nineteenth century, this productive use of slaves became important in many places. Irrespective of the difference in ideology from the European plantation economy of the Americas, slavery became firmly associated with an agricultural society that was based on large concentrations of slaves. There were many places where slavery was still conceived in terms of kinship and where slavery remained marginal to the basic organization of society. None the less, the more intensive enslavement of people and the growth in the slave trade affected the institution of slavery almost everywhere.

The interaction between the indigenous setting, Islamic influence, and the European demand for slaves provided the dynamics in the development of slavery in Africa over the past millennium, but these were not always independent variables. The indigenous setting, for example, cannot be reconstructed merely by stripping away the Islamic heritage or by temporarily ignoring the European market for slaves. That slavery probably existed in Africa before the diffusion of Islam is relatively certain, although its characteristics are not. If we mean by "slave" people who were kidnapped, seized in war, or condemned to be sold as a result of crime or in compensation for crime, then slaves there were. Structurally, however, slavery was marginal.

The influence of Islam and the European market, and indeed many other political and economic developments, has affected the course of slavery. Once such factors had an impact on particular societies, the nature of slavery changed, and the result was a different indigenous setting. In short, the history of slavery was dynamic, and the changes that took place resulted in the emergence of slave societies in places where previously there had only been a few slaves in society. That is, slavery became a central institution and not a peripheral feature. Africa could be integrated into a network of international slavery because indigenous forms of dependency allowed the transfer of people from one social group to another. When kinship links were severed, as they were in the case of slavery, then it became necessary to move people from the point of enslavement to a more distant place. The trend of this movement was towards the external slave markets, those of the Islamic world and the America's. Slaves tended to go from periphery to areas of more extensive economic and political development, both within Africa and outside Africa. Slaves were not imported into Africa; they were exported. To repeat the crucial dimension of the argument—integration of Africa into an international network of slavery occurred because Africa was an area of slave supply. In Africa, therefore, there was a structural link between this ability to supply slaves for external use and the domestic employment of slaves.

As a source for the external trade since time immemorial, Africa was a reservoir where slaves were cheap and plentiful—indeed they were there for the taking. This feature, enslavement, was another dimension of slavery in

Africa that strongly affected the history of the institution there. It is inaccurate to think that Africans enslaved their brothers—although this sometimes happened. Rather, Africans enslaved their enemies. This conception of who could be enslaved served the interests of the external market, and it enabled the political ascendency of some Africans on the continent. Warfare, kidnapping, and the manipulation of judicial and religious institutions account for the enslavement of most slaves, both those exported and those retained in Africa. Unlike other places where slavery was common, particularly the Americas and the central parts of the Islamic world, enslavement on a regular basis was one essential feature of slavery as an institution. Slave masters in the Americas and the major Islamic states relied on trade for most or all of their slaves. They were not usually responsible themselves for the direct enslavement of people. In Africa, the enslavers and the slave owners were often the same. Europe and the central Islamic lands looked to areas on their periphery as a source for slaves, and Africa was such a peripheral region—virtually the only one for the Americas and a major one for the Islamic countries. Slaves also moved within Africa, from areas that were more peripheral to places that were more central, but enslavement was usually a prominent feature everywhere. There was no separation in function between enslavement and slave use; these remained intricately associated.

This connection reveals a fundamental characteristic of slavery in Africa, and when fully articulated with the use of slaves in production slavery was transformed into a distinct mode of production. The history of slavery involved the interaction between enslavement, the slave trade, and the domestic use of slaves within Africa. An examination of this interaction demonstrates the emergence of a system of slavery that was basic to the political economy of many parts of the continent. This system expanded until the last decades of the nineteenth century. The process of enslavement increased; the trade grew in response to new and larger markets, and the use of slaves in Africa became more common. Related to the articulation of this system, with its structural links to other parts of the world, was the consolidation within Africa of a political and social structure that relied extensively on slavery. Production depended, in varying degrees, on slave labour. Political power relied on slave armies. External trade involved the sale of slaves, often as a major commodity.

Commentary on Paul Lovejoy
IGOR KOPYTOFF[5]

In his paper, Lovejoy discusses historical change. But having left the definition of what he means by "slavery" in limbo, he treats it in essentialist terms, with a leaning toward an economic, labour-use, "property" meaning. He thus tends to equate development of the institution with the rise in it of labour-use. Sometimes, however, he resorts to other criteria, with inconsistent results. For example, when slavery in western Central Africa is numerically large-scale but is not preponderantly a matter of labour-use, Lovejoy still refers to it as "slavery" but points out that it was primarily a "political institution." Yet, when Lovejoy moves into the gathering dusk of the past, the implications of the political criterion are abandoned. Since he assumes that the development of slavery must be related to the external demand, he concludes that before the Islamic and European demand appears, slavery must have been a "marginal" phenomenon—marginal in some undefined sense. The conclusion rests on the assumption that pre-Islamic and pre-European Africa had little internal economic and political dynamism—an assumption that I should like to address now.

Behind Lovejoy's historical and developmental model, there lurks the evolutionary image that things become simpler as we go back into the past and more complex as we move forward in time. But this assumption—that history expresses itself in exponential curves—is very misleading indeed when one deals with a score of centuries rather than with several millennia. For example, we know better now than to assume, because we have no written records for the West European Bronze and early Iron Ages, that the economic and political dynamism of that period must have been less impressive than it was during the Roman period. Nor is the idea tenable anymore that the later pre-history of Western Europe consists mainly of echoes of what went on in the eastern Mediterranean.

The exponential-curve view of African history sees its pre-Islamic and pre-European past as necessarily simple: dominated by small-scale societies, it could only have had minimal or marginal slavery, and developed

---

[5]Kopytoff, Igor, "Commentary on Paul Lovejoy," from Craton, Michael, ed., *Roots and Branches: Current Directions in Slave Studies* (Toronto: Pergamon Press, 1979). Excerpts from pp. 67–75. The biography of Dr. Kopytoff is listed along with that of Suzanne Miers in the third article of this problem.

slavery came only with the external slave trade. There is also a corollary to this. When Lovejoy finds numerically large-scale slavery in Central Africa after the Atlantic trade had lapsed, he attributes the high figures to the lingering impact of the Atlantic trade and not to any possible internal factors. That is, small-scale and parochial societies on their own are seen to be capable only of marginal slavery. A small exercise in figures is in order here. For matrilineal Central Africa, let us assume that a matrilineage loses one out of ten of its women members every generation through sale, debt payments, fines, compensations for homicide (real or mystical), tribute, and kidnapping, and that the matrilineage also acquires an outside woman every generation. This rate of replacement of blood members with slave members is predicated on social patterns that need have no relationship whatsoever to external trade, Islam, or the European impact: these patterns are widespread among small-scale societies around the world (though without the specific African legal definitions and sociological consequences of these transactions). Under the above assumption, and given matrilineal inheritance of slave status, the proportion of slaves in the matrilineage will rise to about forty percent in five generations—that is, in about 125 years. Even at a one-in-twenty replacement rate, the proportion will be almost twenty-five percent over the same period. This indicates that in at least some slave systems, purely internal and commonplace structural factors can result in very high proportions of slaves in the population.

Hence, structural functional models are indispensable to the historical analysis of Africa. While all history is reconstruction, African history involves a rather large amount of it. Reconstruction implies some kind of projection onto the bare bones of the pat of notions that the analyst has picked up somewhere, consciously or unconsciously. These notions are many and subtle: they include assumptions about human nature, African cultural patterns, the hierarchy of values and motives of historical actors, structural-functional relations among institutions, and the kind of process that human history is. The idea of a placid pre-sixteenth-century Central Africa, for example, exhibiting only faint "servile institutions," is a projection of a particular notion about the harmonious nature of small-scale societies and an exponential view of the development of complexity in history. The objection to this projection is not that it is a projection but that it is one based on an essentialist rather than systemic picture of historically known small-scale societies.

This also applies to warnings about the danger of projecting the condition of slaves and the statements of informants about it in colonial times into the pre-colonial past. These warnings, however, do not mean—as Klein and Lovejoy see it—that no functionalist projections can be made. On the contrary, the warning arises precisely from a functionalist understanding of variations in informants' behavior. Present-day informants are under certain constraints to present an attractive picture of slavery in the past; hence, a direct essentialist projection of what they say into the past is invalid. But his functionalist understanding of today's behavior allows us to make a more sophisticated projection into a past in which these constraints did not exist. It is not as if systemic guesses about the past do not suffuse all historical writing. The question, then is whether they are to be based on known African cultural realities or on implicit and randomly constructed social and psychological models.

I have so far dwelt on the internal systems of use of acquired persons in the African past. These internal systems, however, were connected in various ways with external systems, such as networks of trade, wider political forces, the diffusion of new weapons, the spread of new ideas, and so on. In his paper, Lovejoy makes the impingement of these external forces the main criterion for his historical periodisation of African slavery. Now, no one would argue that the external system was not important to the developments in Africa. Where I find myself uncomfortable is with the suggestion, throughout the paper, that—to quote some key statements—"slavery in Africa can only be analyzed within the context of world slave trade," that "slavery was institutionalized" when African systems were adapted to "external purposes," and that "African slavery was a response not only to European needs but to trans-Saharan and Indian Ocean demands as well," internal African conditions being of no apparent importance. For pre-contact Africa, Lovejoy recognizes only what he calls "indigenous servile institutions" but not "slavery," for a reason left unexplained.

The external perspective pre-selects for analysis certain kinds of variables over others. It focuses one's attention on certain items: slaves as commodities, salt, iron, palm oil, cloth, guns, and so on. This tends to create the impression that these items shaped the dynamics of African societies and dominated African decisions. This kind of archival selectivity is not unfamiliar: for medieval Europe, one can easily overestimate the role of beeswax in the economy by relying on the records that come preponderantly from monasteries. The stress on the external system is not likely to reveal that Africans were also ardently concerned with goats, baskets, masks, and palmwine, and made decisions not only about access to trade routes but also about hierarchy, political power, witchcraft, and marriage.

The external perspective introduces blanks not only in time but also in space. A historian necessarily focuses on what is important, and an external perspective sets up a scale of importance: things that are functionally closest to the external factors are the most important and those farthest from them the least. Thus, while focusing on the Islamic areas of the Western Sudan, Lovejoy mentions the interstitial pagan areas only as an afterthought. Yet this leaves out a sizable, probably majority, population and some important cultural norms. But since these populations are indeed marginal to Lovejoy's external perspective, their absence does not affect his analysis. What we are given, then, is something analogous to the history of a country written entirely from the perspective of its foreign relations. Once again, I must reach out for an analogy. Is Leroy Ladurie's *Montaillou* relevant to the religious and social dynamics of fourteenth century Occitania? Does it tell us something about the meaning of Catholicism and Catharism that the perspective from Toulouse and Albi does not? Lovejoy's chosen perspective on Africa inevitably makes most marginal that which is most indigenously African, be it non-Islamic Margi slavery in the Sudan or the slavery of pre-sixteenth-century Central Africa. Through this approach, both Lovejoy and we are inexorably led to the conclusion that "slavery therefore developed in conjunction with external influences from the Islamic world," and that, in western Africa, "the spread of slavery as an institution appears to have occurred along a broad frontier of extensive involvement in the external market to areas only marginally involved."

The Asian Slave Trade

ROBERT O. COLLINS[6]

Unlike the Atlantic slave trade, the transportation of slaves from Africa to Asia and the Mediterranean was thousands of years old. The first evidence was carved in stone in 2900 BCE at the second cataract depicting a boat on the Nile packed with Nubian captives for enslavement in Egypt. Thereafter, throughout the next five thousand years, African slaves captured in war, raids, or purchased in the market were marched down the Nile, across the Sahara to the Mediterranean, or transported over the Red Sea and the Indian Ocean to Asia. The dynastic Egyptians also took slaves from the Red Sea region and the Horn of Africa, which was known to them as Punt. Phoenician settlements along the North African littoral possessed African slaves from the immediate hinterland or slaves from south of the Sahara, who were forced along the established trans-Saharan trade routes to the Mediterranean markets. The Greeks and the Romans continued the ancient Egyptian raids into Nubia and sent military expeditions from their cities along the southern Mediterranean shore, where they captured slaves from the Fezzan and the highlands of the Sahara. African slaves, like those from Europe, were used in the households, fields, mines, and armies of Mediterranean and Asian empires, but Africans were only a modest portion of the Roman slave community since the abundant supply from Asia Minor and Europe was more than adequate for the economic and military needs of the empire. Not surprisingly, African slaves were more numerous in the Roman cities of the Mediterranean littoral.

There can be no reasonable estimate of the number of slaves exported from Africa to the Mediterranean basin, the Middle East, and the Indian Ocean before the arrival of the Arabs in Africa during the seventh century of the Christian era. Between 800 and 1600 the evidence for the estimated volume of slaves is more intuitive than empirical but better than none at all. One can only surmise that, given a four-thousand-year history when slaves were a common and accepted institution in most African societies, the number of slaves marched across the Sahara or transported over the Red Sea and Indian Ocean to Asia from 800 to 1600 must have been considerable. Until the seventeenth century the evidence is derived mostly from literary sources whereby maximum and minimum numbers can at best be extrapolated given the paucity of direct data. There is a considerable amount of indirect evi-

[6]Robert O. Collins, "The Asian Slave Trade," forthcoming in French in *The African Diaspora in Asia: Historical Facts*, edited by Skhan de Silva Jayasuriya and Jean-Pierre Angenot, *Cahiers des Anneaux de la Memoire-Cam-Nantes,* France, 2005.

dence from accounts of the trade, population, and the demand for black slaves for military service from which general but not unreasonable estimates of the Asian slave trade can be proposed.

When European states directly entered the world of international trade in the seventeenth century, the estimates of the number of slaves become increasingly reliable. There is a striking similarity between the total estimated number of slaves exported across the Atlantic and those sent to Asia. The trans-Atlantic trade carried an estimated 11,313,000 slaves from 1450 to 1900. The Asian trade numbered an estimated total of 12,580,000 slaves from 800 to 1900. The important difference between the Atlantic and the Asia slave trade, however, is the time span in which the exportation of slaves took place. The eleven million slaves of the Atlantic trade were exported to the Americas in only four hundred years, an intensity that had dramatic effects on the African societies engaged in the trade. The twelve and a half million slaves exported to Asia during eleven centuries obviously did not have the same traumatic impact experienced on the western African coast in just four centuries of the Atlantic trade. During three hundred years, 1600–1900, for which there is more credible evidence, the volume of the Asian trade is estimated at 5,510,000 slaves, half that of the Atlantic. At the end of the Napoleonic wars, during the first half of the nineteenth century, an extensive plantation economy was developed on the East African coast, the islands of Zanzibar, Pemba, and the Mascarenes in the Indian Ocean that required greater numbers of slaves from the interior than in the past. In a brief span of fifty years, until the European abolition movement dramatically restrained and then ended the trade to Asia after 1860, the eastern African slave trade was more reminiscent of the West African experience than any of the preceding centuries.

TABLE 1
SLAVE EXPORTS ACROSS THE SAHARA, RED SEA, AND EAST AFRICA AND THE INDIAN OCEAN, 800–1900 AND 1600–1900

Years	Trans-Saharan	Red Sea	E. Africa & Indian Ocean	All three regions combined
800–1600	4,670,000	1,600,000	800,000	
1601–1800	1,400,000	300,000	500,000	
1801–1900	1,200,000	492,000	1,618,000	
Total, 800–1900	7,270,000	2,392,000	2,918,000	
Combined total, 800–1900				12,580,000
Combined total, 1600–1900				5,510,000

Source: Paul E. Lovejoy, *Transformations in Slavery,* Tables 2.1, 2.2, 3.7, 7.1, 7.7.

Until the arrival of the Portuguese on the coasts of sub-Saharan Africa in the fifteenth century, Islam was the only ideology to introduce a more systematic regulation of slavery in Africa. By the tenth century the Arabs, who had conquered North Africa, the Middle East, and Persia, had absorbed the historic institution of slavery, but as Muslims they shaped the ancient traditions of slavery to conform to the religious laws and practices of Islam. Their legal definitions and treatment of slaves, however, constituted more of a modification in the status and function of a slave than any fundamental change in the practice of involuntary servitude. The slave remained property to be used as the master wished as an agricultural laborer, soldier, domestic, concubine, or even a high official, a *wazir*. Thousands of slaves were taken in the holy wars, *jihad*, during the expansion of the Islamic world, for their enslavement was legally and morally justified because they were not Muslims, but unbelievers (*kafirin*) were expected to abandon their traditional religions and embrace in slavery the true faith. Islam recognized that Christians, Jews, and Zoroastrians required a special status. They were "People of the Book," the Bible, the Talmud, and the Avesta (Pure Instruction), who acknowledged one supreme deity, God, Allah, or Ahura Mazda. Consequently, they were regarded as protected minorities (*dhimmis*) who were not to be enslaved; their property was safeguarded, and they were permitted to practice their religion freely as long as they paid a special tax (*jizya*). In reality, Christians, Jews, and Zoroastrians were regularly enslaved in the tumult of war, raids, or piracy where legal distinctions disappeared before passion, bigotry, and avarice.

As the Islamic empire expanded, slaves came increasingly from conquests of non-Muslim Africans on the frontiers of Islam for slave markets in the Arab Middle East, where women and children were in greater demand than men. They were more pliable and, therefore, more likely to accept Islam. Young women became domestics or concubines for the harem; young men were trained for military or administrative service. Except for the constant demand of the Moroccan sultans in the seventeenth and eighteenth centuries for slave soldiers, mature males and females were preferred to perform the menial tasks of field and household under harsh conditions and had to be continuously replaced by newly acquired slaves, preferably females.

Since the young were absorbed into Muslim society and the old perished, the need for constant replenishment of slaves was not impeded by race or color. The only criterion for the Muslim was that the slave be pagan. Since African traditional religions were unacceptable, sub-Saharan Africa became the most important source of slaves for the Muslim merchants who established elaborate commercial networks to transport them out of Africa across the Sahara, the Red Sea, and the Indian Ocean. In order to justify slavery, Europeans frequently argued that conversion to Christianity, the religion of the plantation owners, would by example bring civilization and salvation to slaves otherwise condemned to eternal damnation. Islam, however, imposed upon the Muslim master an obligation to convert non-Muslim slaves in order for them to become members of the greater Islamic society in which the beneficence of the afterlife was assumed. Indeed, the daily observance of the well-defined Islamic religious rituals was the symbolic and outward manifestation of the inward conversion without which emancipation was impossible. Unlike Christianity and African religions, Islamic legal tradition explicitly defined the act of emancipation that enabled the slave to become immediately free, in contrast with the lengthy African generational process of acceptance by social assimilation. Conversion also enabled slaves to perform different functions unknown in the slavery of the New World. The Arab conquests had produced a far-flung empire of many ethnicities, whose common denominator was Islam, administered by a vast bureaucracy that required slave officials and slave soldiers loyal to the state, for their status was dependent upon their master and his religion. These slave officials were frequently empowered to have authority over free members of the state. Often Muslim slaves became more highly specialized in commerce and industry, through the acquisition of skills in the more advanced technology of the Islamic world, than slaves in Africa or on the sugar plantations of the Americas.

Women also occupied a different status in Islamic slavery than in African or Atlantic slavery. Islamic law limited the number of legal wives to four, the sexual appetite of men being satisfied by the number of concubines they could afford. Slave women were given as concubines to other slaves, to freed slaves, or to the master's sons. The relationship between the male master and the female slave, however, was clearly defined in theory by the legal Islamic sanctions that applied to emancipation. A concubine became legally free upon the death of her owner. If she bore him children, she could not be sold and her children were free, but in practice they had a lower status than children of free wives.

Trans-Saharan Slave Trade

Although the numbers of the slave trade to North Africa and Asia are more a benchmark from which extrapolations can be disputed, there is no doubt that there was a constant demand for slaves in the Islamic world. Until the fifteenth century, the export of slaves across the Sahara, the Red Sea, and the Indian Ocean was believed to be relatively constant, numbering between 5,000 and 10,000 per year; spread throughout these many centuries, the modest numbers mitigated the impact of the loss among African societies. The estimate of the number of slaves— 4,670,000—exported across the Sahara between 800 and 1600 can only be a reasonable guess based on diffuse direct and indirect evidence. Whether more or less, there was a demonstrable demand for slaves from sub-Saharan Africa that resulted in continuous contact between the Muslim merchants who organized the trans-Saharan slave trade, and the rulers of the Sudanic states who supplied them.

The presence of Muslim traders had a profound influence at the courts of African kings. They not only conducted commerce, but also introduced literacy and Islamic law as it pertained to their transactions, principally slaves. Although the *bilad al-sudan* stretched from the Atlantic Ocean to the Red Sea, there were only six established vertical routes across the Sahara that resulted in well-defined markets at their terminals in the Sudan and North Africa. There was the Walata Road from ancient Ghana to Sijilmasa in Morocco; the Taghaza Trail from Timbuktu at the great bend of the Niger north to Taghaza and Sijilmasa or to Tuwat and Tunis; the Ghadames Road from Gao on the lower Niger to Agades, Ghat, Ghadames, and Tripoli; the Bilma Trail or the Garamantian Road that left the Hausa states at Kano and Lake Chad north to Bilma, Murzuk in the Fezzan, and on to Tripoli; the Forty Days Road or the Darb al-'Arbain from El-Fasher in Darfur north to the Nile at Asuyt; and the route furthest east that began at Suakin on the Red Sea, swung southwest to Sennar on the Blue Nile, and thence followed the Nile to Egypt. There was also a vigorous and often ignored lateral east-west trade that connected the great market towns of the sahel overland and on the Niger River, along which slaves were moved laterally for sale locally by dyula traders or to the larger markets in one of the Sudanic termini of the trans-Saharan trade.

As with the Atlantic trade, the largest number of slaves did not come from the same region throughout the millennium of the trans-Saharan trade. Although the slave trade was a very important source of revenue, the savanna states of the western and central Sudan were not dependent upon it for their rise and expansion. They were important suppliers of slaves but not at the expense of their political and cultural independence. Slaves associated with the gold and salt trade and the Ghana wars had long been taken from the headwaters of the Senegal and Niger rivers up the Walata Road to Sijilmasa in Morocco. During the reign of the Keita dynasty (1235–1492) and the expansion of the Empire of Mali, slaves were captured south of the Niger and from its headwaters to Gao, where they were exported from Timbuktu up the Taghaza Trail, or less frequently from Gao up the Ghadames Road. The Songhai Empire (1492–1599) succeeded that of Mali when Sunni Ali of the Songhai established his authority over the whole of the middle Niger River valley. His wars and those of his successors produced a substantial increase in the number of slaves exported across the Sahara in the sixteenth century, partially to offset the loss of revenue from the declining gold trade. When the Moroccan army crossed the Sahara to conquer Songhai in 1591, the large number of Songhai captured produced an ample supply of slaves in the markets of North Africa before returning to the historic pattern of the past. Further east in the central Sudan, west of Lake Chad, the Kingdom of Bornu acquired an excessive number of slaves during its wars of expansion under Idris Alawma (c.1571–1603). The slaves were exported up the Bilma Trail to Tripoli. The *mai* (kings) of Bornu utilized this historic route that had been established many centuries before by the Saifawa dynasty in Kanem. In the nineteenth century the largest number of slaves to cross the Sahara had shifted from the western and central Sudan to the two routes for the Nilotic slave trade, the Forty Days' Road (*Dar al-'Arbain*) from Darfur and the route from Sennar to Nubia and Egypt. The estimated 1,200,000 slaves exported across the Sahara in the nineteenth century, compared to 700,000 in the eighteenth, can only be explained by the increase taken from the Upper Nile basin, for the numbers exported from the states of the western and central Sudan had steadily declined.[7]

During the seventeenth and eighteenth centuries, the trans-Saharan trade steadily increased to some 700,000 in each century or 67 percent of the total exported across the Sahara in the preceding eight hundred years. This estimated average of 7,000 per year for these two centuries, based on limited evidence, may be greater than the real numbers, but the indirect evidence reasonably concludes that there was a considerable supply of slaves from the savanna and sahel because of drought and warfare. When the rains did not come, the fields were barren and the free cultivators were vulnerable to slavers when wandering the countryside in search of food. In order to survive, they often enslaved themselves voluntarily to those who could provide them with food.

These two centuries also saw the dissolution of the old Sudanic empires into petty states whose warlords carried on interminable warfare with local rivals that produced an abundance of captives who became slaves. The extent of suffering from drought or war was painfully measured by the increase in the number of slaves during these two centuries. Between 1639 and 1643 a serious drought spread from the Senegambia to the great bend of the Niger. After a period of adequate rainfall, the severe dry years returned during the last quarter of the seventeenth century. Desiccation in the *Bilad al-Sudan* proved worse in the next century. A major drought brought famine to the middle Niger valley from 1711 to 1716 and again during the early 1720s, but the great drought of the eighteenth century on the Niger and in Senegambia lasted from 1738 to 1756. Bornu in the central Sudan suffered correspondingly in the 1740s and 1750s. Thereafter sporadic and localized years of little or no rainfall were recorded from 1770 to 1771 at Timbuktu, 1786 in the Gambia, and during the 1790s in the central Sudan.

The wars that followed the fragmentation of the old empires were characterized by Islamic *jihads* led by Muslims against infidels and those whom they regarded as renegade Muslims. The historic goal of Muslims was to convert unbelievers to Islam so the enslavement of them for conversion was both legally and morally correct. These reasons, however, were often a euphemistic rationale for the warlord to resolve the problem of replacing the natural loss of slaves by exploiting new sources or by selling the slaves to gain revenue for himself and the state. The organized *razzia* became commonplace with a variety of official names, *ghazwa* or *salatiya* in Darfur and Sennar for instance, to be carried out more often than not by slave soldiers. Some of the enslaved were retained, women as concubines, men as soldiers or agricultural laborers, but a far greater number were sold, and for most warlords slaves, after direct taxes, were their greatest source of revenue. During the innumerable petty wars among the Hausa city-states, Muslim prisoners were illegally sold along with non-Muslims, to the dismay and condemnation of Islamic jurists, for the trans-Saharan trade. Further west on the middle and upper Niger and the

---

[7]Paul E. Lovejoy, *Transformations in Slavery: A History of Slavery in Africa*, second edition, Cambridge: Cambridge University Press, 2000, pp. 24–29.

plateau of the Senegambia, the distinction between Muslim and non-Muslim was more well-defined, but this did not inhibit the Muslim reformers from leading their followers, *talibes*, in holy wars against apostate Muslims who were enslaved when they refused to accept Islam as practiced by dogmatic Muslim clerics or the political authority of the theocratic Islamist states they founded.

Those who supplied slaves for the trans-Saharan trade were not always Muslims. The powerful Bambara pagan state of Segu, established on the Niger southwest of Timbuktu, was a major supplier for the trans-Saharan trade in the seventeenth and eighteenth centuries. The hunting associations of young Bambara men were easily coopted into looting for petty warlords or raiding as organized bands for panache and profit. Slave soldiers were the largest contingent in the armies of the Bambara and in the states of the Senegambia, where they collected taxes, held administrative offices, and were often the powerbrokers at the royal court.

The reduction in the number of slaves crossing the desert that accompanied the steady decline of the established trans-Saharan trade in the nineteenth century was offset by the astonishing growth of the Nilotic slave trade. In 1820 the army of the able and dynamic ruler of Egypt, Muhammad Ali, invaded the Sudan. Although nominally the viceroy of the Ottoman sultan, Muhammad Ali was in fact an independent ruler whose armies had conquered the Hijaz and its holy cities, Mecca and Medina, and advanced through Palestine to the frontiers of Syria, at great human and material expense to his army and government. He invaded the Sudan to exploit its gold to replenish his treasury and to rebuild his army with pagan Sudanese slaves. He succinctly summed up his purpose to his commander in the Sudan: "You are aware that the end of all our effort and expense is to procure Negroes. Please show zeal in carrying out our wishes in this capital matter." [8]

Hitherto the Funj Kingdom of Sennar had exported some 1,500 slaves per year to Egypt. Muhammad Ali wanted 20,000. A military training camp was constructed at Isna, and a special depot to receive slaves from the Sudan at Aswan was also constructed. From the administrative capital at Khartoum, the Egyptian governor-general organized military expeditions up the Blue and White Niles to enslave the Nilotes. Despite heavy losses from disease on the march down the Nile and across the Nubian Desert, by 1838, 10,000 to 12,000 slaves were reaching Egypt every year. Under pressure from the British government, the Ottoman sultan and the khedive of Egypt officially declared the slave trade illegal in the Commercial Convention of 1838, but on the Nile the trade shifted from the Egyptian government to an elaborate private commercial network constructed by Muslim merchants to continue and expand the trade throughout the upper Nile basin. By the 1870s, tens of thousands of slaves were exported to Egypt and to Arabia from ports on the Red Sea, and although the numbers declined dramatically during the years of the Mahdist state in the Sudan (1881–98), the Red Sea trade came to an end only after the Anglo-Egyptian conquest of the Sudan in 1898.

---

[8]Muhammad 'Ali to *sar-I 'askar* [Commander-in-Chief] of the Sudan and Kordofan [Muhammad Bey Khusraw, *Daftardar*], 23 September 1823, quoted in Richard Hill, *Egypt in the Sudan, 1820–1881*, London: Oxford University Press, 1959, p. 13.

TABLE 2
ESTIMATED SLAVE EXPORTS ACROSS THE SAHARA 1600–1900, WITH PERCENT OF THE TOTAL ASIAN TRADE 1600–1900.

Years	Number exported	Percent of total Asian trade, 1600–1900
1600–1700	700,000	12.7
1701–1800	700,000	12.7
1801–1900	1,200,000	21.7
Total, 1600–1900	2,600,000	47.1

Source: Lovejoy, *Transformations in Slavery,* Tables 3.1, 7.1.

The Red Sea Slave Trade

The Red Sea slave trade was ironically older than the trans-Saharan. The dynastic Egyptians regularly sent expeditions to the Land of Punt, the coasts of the Red Sea and northern Somalia, to return with ivory, perfumes, and slaves. Slaves were undoubtedly among the commodities exported from Africa to Arabia across the Red Sea and the Gulf of Arabia during the centuries of Greek and Roman rule in Egypt. The direct evidence is scanty, but the numbers were not large and the trade was localized rather than organized. An estimate has been 1,600,000 slaves between 800 and 1600, with an average of 2,000 slaves per year. The sources of slaves for the Red Sea trade were limited to Nubia, the Nile south of its confluence, and Ethiopia, which amounted to only 34 percent of the trans-Saharan trade during these same eight hundred years. The ports were few: Aidhab in Egypt until it was destroyed by the Ottoman Turks in 1416, Suakin in the Sudan, and Adulis (Massawa) in Ethiopia.

During the seventeenth century, the Red Sea export trade appears to have consisted of a steady but modest number of 1,000 slaves per year. The estimated number of slaves increased in the eighteenth century to some 2,000 slaves annually from Ethiopia and the Nile valley—which was, however, only a small portion of the increasing worldwide export of African slaves that continued into the nineteenth century. Throughout the eighteenth and early nineteenth centuries, Darfur, in the Nile basin, sent several thousand slaves per year to Egypt, but also to the Red Sea through Sennar on the Blue Nile and thence east along the established trade route to Suakin. The Funj Kingdom of Sennar itself exported some 1,500 slaves per year until conquered by the forces of Muhammad Ali in 1821. Thereafter, Egyptian government razzias, and later in the century powerful merchant-adventurers, organized the Nilotic trade for Egypt, but they also sent a substantial number of Sudanese slaves to Arabia through the Red Sea ports which the Egyptian government controlled. Slaves in the upper Nile basin were captured by the private armies of these merchants that raided as far as Dar Fertit in the west and southwest into the kingdoms of the Azande and Bagirmi deep in equatorial Africa.

These same centuries also saw an increase in the slave trade from the Ethiopian highlands. Slavery in Ethiopia had been an accepted institution in the long history of that Christian kingdom, and slaves had regularly been sent to Yemen and Arabia from the ancient port of Adulis that later became Massawa. Although there had been constant conflicts throughout the centuries between Christian Ethiopians in the fertile highlands and the Muslim Somalis on the arid plains below, it was not until the sixteenth century that the famous Imam of Harar, Ibrahim al-Ghazi, known as Grän the left-handed, and his Somali warriors ravaged Ethiopia, destroying churches and monasteries and enslaving Ethiopian Christians until he was killed in 1543 by Portuguese musketeers who had arrived to defend the emperor and his Christian kingdom. Thereafter, Muslim control of the Red Sea continued to ensure a dependable supply of Ethiopian slaves through Massawa during the seventeenth and eighteenth centuries when the centralized authority of imperial Ethiopia collapsed. Known as the *Masafant*, the period of judges, Ethiopia dissolved into anarchy for two hundred years during which the rival warlords of the nobility obtained many slaves in their petty wars and razzias. They retained some slaves for agriculture and domestic chores, selling the surplus captives to Muslim merchants. In the nineteenth century, strong emperors returned internal stability to Ethiopia, but they waged continuous warfare on their frontiers against the Egyptian government, whose armies raided the border hill country, while the Muslim Galla (Oromo) pillaged southwestern Ethiopia for thousands of slaves who were exported across the Gulf of Arabia from the Somali ports of Berbera and Zeila. Children, girls, and young women were particularly prized in the Ethiopian trade, outnumbering males two to one and commanding three times the price in the marketplace. During the first half of the nineteenth century, the Ethiopian Red Sea trade peaked at 6,000 to 7,000 slaves each year, with an estimated 175,000 exported in the second quarter of that century.

TABLE 3
ESTIMATED SLAVE EXPORTS FROM RED SEA, 1600–1900, WITH PERCENT OF THE TOTAL ASIAN TRADE 1600–1900

Years	Number exported	Percent of total Asian trade, 1600–1900
1600–1700	100,000	1.8
1701–1800	200,000	3.6
1801–1900	492,000	8.9
Total, 1600–1900	792,000	14.4

Source: Lovejoy, *Transformations in Slavery*, Tables 3.1, 7.l.

East Africa and the Indian Ocean Slave Trade

During the early centuries of the Christian era, Greek traders had been making their way down the coast of East Africa, where they conducted a profitable trade that included slaves. They had access to an extraordinary commercial guide to the Red Sea and the East African coast, the *Periplus of the Erythraean Sea,* probably compiled by an Alexandrian Greek shipping clerk in the second century. The *Periplus* described the ports, the articles and terms of trade, and the customs and languages of the people. The Greek mercantile presence in the Indian Ocean did not survive the dominance of Rome in the Mediterranean, but trade on the East African coast continued as in the past by merchants from Arabia, Persia, India, and China who plied the waters of the Indian Ocean on the monsoon winds of the Sabaean Lane. The Arabs brought goods from Asia—cloth, porcelains, glassware, and hardware—and, after the seventh century, Islam. They returned to Asia with ivory, gold, rhino horn, spices, and always slaves, called *Zanj* (Blacks), for fields, mines, armies, and households. The Arabs were followed by the Persians and the Chinese, who traded on the East African coast during the Sung (1127–1279) and Ming (1368–1644) dynasties for ivory, rhino horn, and tortoise shells that were highly valued in the Orient, and for a few slaves, mostly as concubines. The residents of Peking were astounded by the gift of an African giraffe.

Although there is Arabic, Persian, and Chinese documentation and there are writings of Arab geographers and travelers about East Africa and its trade, there is little direct evidence as to the number of slaves exported to Asia until the nineteenth century. By extrapolation from the slave trade in the Red Sea, an estimate of 1,000 slaves per year throughout the centuries until the eighteenth century does not appear unreasonable. At the end of the eighteenth century, there are records of the number of slaves (2,500 per year) from the mainland who passed through Kilwa to the French sugar and coffee plantations on the Mascarene Islands and records of slaves exported from Mozambique to Cape Town and Brazil, all of which add another 4,000 to 5,000 per year from the historic ports of the East African coast.[9] This was a dramatic increase from the last three decades of the eighteenth century, but only the harbinger of the massive numbers exported during the first half of the nineteenth century.

---

[9]Lovejoy, *Transformations in Slavery,* pp. 61–62.

TABLE 4
ESTIMATED SLAVE EXPORTS FROM EAST AFRICA 1600–1900, WITH THE PERCENT OF THE TOTAL ASIAN TRADE 1600–1900

Years	Number exported	Percent of total Asian trade, 1600–1900
1600–1700	100,000	1.8
1701–1800	400,000	7.3
1801–1900	1,618,000	29.4
Total, 1600–1900	2,118,000	38.4

Source: Lovejoy, *Transformations in Slavery,* Tables 3.7, 7.3.

In the first decade of the nineteenth century, 80,000 slaves are estimated to have been brought from the interior of East Africa. Over a third (30,000) were retained on the coast; the other 50,000 were shipped to the Asian mainland (Arabia, Persia, and India), the Mascarene Islands, and the Americas. During the next four decades the decline in the Mascarene trade was offset by a regular increase in the number of slaves sent to the Americas, mainly Brazil, that reached a high of 100,000 per decade during the 1830s and 1840s, thereafter to decrease drastically to a trickle by mid-century. During this same first half-century, the export trade from the East African coast to the Asian mainland experienced a modest but firm increase to a high of 65,000 per decade in the 1850s and 1860s, until 1873, when the Sultan of Zanzibar was forced by the British government and its navy to ban all trade in slaves by sea. Despite the British intervention at Zanzibar, the retention of slaves to work the growing number of plantations on the East African mainland coast rose an average 20 percent per decade, from 35,000 slaves in the first decade of the century to a high of 188,000 for the 1870s, at a time when the Indian Ocean trade was first restricted and then suppressed. When confronted by the power of British abolitionists, the slave traders brought fewer slaves to the coast—28,000 in the decade of the 1880s—but the dynamics of the slave system continued to successfully smuggle as many as 16,000 from 1890 to 1896.[10]

This spectacular increase in the nineteenth-century East African slave trade was caused by the development of plantations that required large numbers of unskilled laborers on the islands of Zanzibar and Pemba where Arab immigrants from the Hadhramaut and Oman and Swahili entrepreneurs from the mainland had planted extensive plantations of cloves, coconuts, and grain. The Swahili traffic in slaves from the mainland to the offshore islands dates from the late sixteenth century, when patrician Swahili families, the Nabhany of Pate and the Mazrui from

---

[10]Lovejoy, *Transformations in Slavery*, pp. 155–56.

Mombasa, acquired estates on Pemba and Zanzibar at the end of the sixteenth century. The fertile soils and timely rainfall of Pemba, in particular, produced sufficient rice and cereals to become the granary for the whole of the Swahili coast throughout the seventeenth and eighteenth centuries. Under the leadership of Sultan Sayyid Sa'id, who arrived in Zanzibar from Oman in the 1820s, cloves were being exported by 1827, and thereafter the island became the principal supplier to the international market. As a labor-intensive crop, the clove, like cotton, required an ever-increasing supply of slaves, and it is no coincidence that the demand for slaves was greatest during the peak of clove production in the 1860s and 1870s. Ironically, the needs of the nineteenth-century plantation economy of East Africa for slaves were similar to those in the Americas that produced the expansion of the trans-Atlantic slave trade in the eighteenth century.

During the seventeenth and eighteenth centuries, slaves for the East African coast and Asia came mainly from the hinterland of the Zambezi valley, controlled by the Portuguese. By the nineteenth century, the sources of supply had shifted to the north, where African traders, the Nyamwezi and the Yao, brought slaves to the coast from the interior of Lake Tanganyika and Lake Nyasa (Malawi). Kilwa, which had been reduced by the Portuguese to a commercial backwater, now became the principal slave entrepôt for the Zanzibar clove plantations, supplying nearly 95 percent by 1866. After the prohibition against exporting slaves across the Indian Ocean in 1873, Kilwa continued to supply slaves for the mainland plantations by marching them up the coast.[11]

During the early decades of the nineteenth century, Arab and Swahili traders from the East African coast developed a second route for slaves and ivory, using the historic road into the interior that led them to the Africans living in the vicinity of the great equatorial lakes of Tanganyika and Victoria. Their success brought them into competition with the Nyamwezi and Yao traders and precipitated hostility with the Africans of the lakes, who at first supplied slaves, only to be taken as slaves themselves by the heavily armed agents of the coastal merchants. The interior of eastern Africa erupted in raiding and petty wars. The African victims became slaves in these local struggles between rival warlords, traders, and warrior bands known as the *ruga-ruga*. The *ruga-ruga* had fled north in the 1840s and 1850s from the intense warfare of the Zulu in southern Africa in the 1830s, the years of destruction known as the *Mfecane*, to plunder, loot, and add to the insecurity of the East African interior that made slaves readily available south of the Lake Plateau of East Africa.

---

[11] Frederick Cooper, *Plantation Slavery on the East Coast of Africa*, New Haven: Yale University Press, 1977, pp. 115–30.

TABLE 5
ESTIMATED SLAVE EXPORTS FROM EAST AFRICA 1800–1900 AND PERCENT OF THE TOTAL ASIAN TRADE 1800–1900

Region	Volume	Percent East African Trade	Percent Asian Trade
Arabia, Persia, India	347,000	21.4	10.5
South-east Africa	407,000	25.1	12.3
Mascarene Islands	95,000	5.9	2.9
East African Coast	769,000	47.5	24.6
Total	1,618,000		

Source: Lovejoy, *Transformations in Slavery,* Table 7.7.

Summing Up

The history of slavery in Africa and the slave trade cannot be measured only in terms of numbers or statistics, which obscure the complexities of the system and the enormity of the misery that accompanied the institution. Yet numbers do serve their purpose, for they give a means, no matter how sterile, to understand this otherwise incomprehensible human tragedy. There are pitfalls to avoid in reading the numbers. There was, of course, no trade with the Americas until they were discovered by Europeans at the end of the fifteenth century, yet slaves had been taken out of Africa across the Sahara, the Red Sea, and East Africa for many centuries before Columbus. Their numbers can only be estimated, precariously from indirect evidence and extrapolation from 800 to the seventeenth century, at some seven million, or less than 9,000 per year. This figure is not very helpful, for the number of slaves taken to the Mediterranean and Asia varied dramatically in different times and places. Not until the seventeenth century did evidence, direct and indirect, permit greater certainty as to the estimated numbers of slaves taken out of Africa. From 1600 to 1900 the Atlantic and the Asian slave trades together systematically exported 16,414,000 slaves from Africa, 10,904,000 slaves to the Americas, 5,510,00 slaves to the Indian Ocean islands and Asia. This represents an average of 41,000 slaves per year or over 27,000 exported across the Atlantic and another 14,000 to Asia.

In Africa there are no statistics, but there are many accounts and oral traditions to confirm that the slave trade and slavery were very much a part of African life until the 1930s. Thereafter, numerous incidents of slavery have been reported to the present day, and involuntary servitude remains under new names, but after five thousand years the institution of slavery as a system has come to an end, leaving behind myths and truths. The historic obsession with the Atlantic slave trade and slavery in the Americas has often obscured the trade to Asia and slavery within Africa. Slavery was as indigenous to Africa as to Europe and Asia. Slavery was an institution in most African societies, and its abolition came later than in the Americas. The international system of slavery tied the Americas, Africa, and Asia together, and the task of emancipation was not complete until slaves were as free in Africa as in the Americas. The truths of slavery and its trade are in the statistics.

Suggestions for Further Reading

Alpers, Edward, *Ivory and Slaves: Changing Patterns of International Trade in East Central Africa to the Later Nineteenth Century* (Berkeley: University of California Press, 1975).

Beechey, R. W., *The Slave Trade of Eastern Africa* (London: Rex Collings, 1976).

Boeseken, A. J., *Slaves and Free Blacks in the Cape, 1658–1700* (Capetown: Tafelberg, 1977).

Cooper, Frederick, "The Problem of Slavery in African Studies," *Journal of African History* 20, no. 1 (Cambridge: Cambridge University Press, 1979): 103–125.

Craton, Michael, ed., *Roots and Branches: Current Directions in Slave Societies* (Toronto: Pergamon Press, 1979).

Davidson, Basil, *The African Slave Trade* (Boston: Little Brown, 1980).

Fisher, Allan G. B. and Humphrey J., *Slavery and Muslim Society in Africa* (London: C. Hurst, 1970).

Gemery, Henry, and Hogender, Jan, eds., *The Uncommon Market: Essays in the Economic History of the Atlantic Slave Trade* (New York: Academic Press, 1979).

Graham, James, "The Slave Trade, Depopulation and Human Sacrifice in Benin History," *Cahiers d'Etudes Africaines* V, Ecole Pratique des Hautes Études (Sorbonne: Mouton and Co., 1965).

Lovejoy, Paul, "The Characteristics of Plantations in Nineteenth Century Sokoto Caliphate," *American Historical Review* 74: 1267-92.

———, ed., *The Ideology of Slavery: The Womb of Iron and Gold* (London: Athlone, 1991).

Miers, Suzanne, and Igor Kopytoff, eds. *Slavery in Africa: Historical and Anthropological Perspectives* (Madison, Wis.: University of Wisconsin Press, 1977).

——— and Richard Roberts, *The End of Slavery in Africa* (Madison, Wis.: University of Wisconsin Press, 1988).

Newbury, Colin W., *The Western Slave Coast and Its Rulers* (Oxford: The Clarendon Press, 1970).

Robertson, Claire, and Klein, Martin, eds., *Women and Slavery in Africa* (Madison, Wis.: University of Wisconsin Press, 1983).

Rodney, Walter, *A History of the Upper Guinea Coast, 1545–1800* (Oxford: The Clarendon Press, 1970).

Ross, Robert, *Cape of Torments: Slavery and Resistance in South Africa* (London: Routledge and Kegan Paul, 1983).

Savage, Elizabeth, ed., special issue of the journal *Slavery and Abolition: A Journal of Comparative Studies*, "The Human Commodity: Perspectives on the Trans-Saharan Slave Trade" 13, no. 1 (London: Frank Cass, 1992).

Shell, C.-H., *Children of Bondage: A Social History of the Slave Society of the Cape of Good Hope, 1652–1838* (Hanover, N.H.: University Press of New England, 1994).

Warden, Nigel, *Slavery in Dutch South Africa* (New York: Cambridge University Press, 1985).

Watson, R. C., *The Slave Question: Liberty and Prosperity in South Africa* (Hanover: University Press of New England, 1990).

Willis, John, ed., *Slaves and Slavery in Muslim Africa* (London: Frank Cass, 1985).

Acknowledgments

The author gratefully acknowledges the following authors and publishers: Cambridge University Press for permission to reprint the following articles from *The Journal of African History:* "The Hamitic Hypothesis," by Edith Sanders, in Vol. 10, no. 4, pp. 521–532, © 1969 by Cambridge University Press; "African Slavery and Other Forms of Social Oppression on the Upper Guinea Coast in the Context of the African Slave Trade," by Walter Rodney, in Vol. 2, no. 3, pp. 431–440, © 1966 by Cambridge University Press; "Slavery and the Slave Trade in the Context of West African History," by John Fage in Vol. 10, no. 3, pp. 393–400, © 1969 by Cambridge University Press; "Some Developments in the Prehistory of the Bantu Languages," by Malcolm Guthrie, in Vol. 3, no. 2, pp. 273–282, © 1962 by Cambridge University Press.

Grateful appreciation is also expressed to Merrick Posnansky for permission to reprint "Kingship, Archaeology, and Historical Myth," Presidential address delivered on January 19, 1966, reprinted in *Uganda Journal* 30, no. 1, © 1966 by Merrick Posnansky; Lawrence Hill Books (Brooklyn, New York) for permission to reprint from *The African Origin of Civilization: Myth or Reality*, by Cheikh Anta Diop, English translation, pp. 1–7, 9, 138–139, © 1974 Lawrence Hill Books; Raymond Mauny for permission to reprint "A Review of Diop," in the *Bulletin de l'Institut Fundamental d'Afrique Noir,* XXII, Series B (1960), pp. 544–551, © 1960 by Raymond Mauny.

Also to Longman UK, Ltd., for excerpts from *Kenya's Past,* by Thomas Spear, pp. 29–33, © 1981 by Longman UK; from *The Zulu Aftermath,* by J. D. Omer-cooper, pp. 24–27, 32–37, 170–175, © 1967 by Longman UK; to the University of Chicago Press, for permission to reprint "The Languages of Africa," by Joseph H. Greenberg, in *International Journal of American Linguistics*, XXIX, no. 1, pp. 6–7, 30–33, 35–38 © 1963 by University of Chicago Press; African Studies Association for permission to reprint "the Problem of the Lwo," by C. C. Wrigley, in *History in Africa*, Vol. 8, 1981, pp. 234–241, and to reprint "Trees and Traps," by Colin Flight, in *History in Africa*, Vol. 8, 1981, pp. 43–66, both © 1981 by African Studies Association; The University of Wisconsin Press for permission to reprint from *Kingdoms of the Savanna,* by Jan Vansina, pp. 19–24, 34–6, 70–71, 81–83, 97, 245–248, © 1966 by University of Wisconsin Press; also "Sexual Demography: The Impact of the Slave Trade on Structure," by John Thornton, in *Women and Slavery in Africa*, ed. by Claire Robertson and Martin Kleine, pp. 39–45, © 1983 by University of Wisconsin Press, also "Female Slavery," by Claude Meillassoux, in *Women and Slavery in Africa*, ed. by Claire Robertson and Martin Klein, pp. 49–56 and 59–65, © 1983 by University of Wisconsin Press; also "Women in Slavery in Western Sudan," by Martin Klein, in *Women and Slavery in Africa*, ed. by Claire Robertson and Martin Klein, pp. 67–89; also the Introduction to *Slavery in Africa:*

Historical and Anthropological Perspectives, edited by Suzanne Miers and Igor Kopytoff, pp. 14–21, 48–55, 66–69, © 1977 by University of Wisconsin Press.

Also to the University of California Press for permission to reprint *Rainbow and the Kings: A History of the Luba Empire to 1891*, by Thomas Reefe, pp. 3–5, 93–97, 101, 102, 200–203, © 1981 by The Regents of The University of California Press; Holmes & Meier Publishers, Inc., for permission to reprint from *The Shona of Zimbabwe 900–1850,* by D. N. Beach, pp. 35–43, © 1980 by D. N. Beach; The International African Institute for permission to reprint *the Trading Sates of the Oil Rivers*, by G. I. Jones, pp. 5–6, 59–66, 178–181, 204, 205; also "The Jihad of Shehu dan Fodio: Some Problems," by M. G. Smith, in *Islam in Tropical Africa*, ed. by I. M. Lewis, pp. 408–419, published for the International African Institute by Oxford University Press; Oxford University Press for permission to reprint from *The Sword of Truth: The Life and Times of the Shehu Usuman dan Fodio*, by Mervyn Hiskett, pp. 3–11, © 1973 by Oxford University Press, Inc.; The Hamdard Foundation, for permission to reprint from M. O. Junaid's "19th Century Reforms in Hausaland," © by the Hamdard Foundation; The African Studies Centre for permission to reprint from "The Jihad in Hausaland as an Episode in African History" in *Kroniek Van Afrika 1975*, no. 2, pp. 141–150, © 1975, by The African Studies Centre, Leiden NL; Stanford University Press for permission to reprint from "The Signares of Saint-Louis and Goree: Women Entrepreneurs in Eighteenth Century Senegal," by George E. Brooks, Jr., pp. 19–30, 33, 38–39, and 44, also "Rebels or Status-Seekers? Women as Spirit Mediums in East Africa," by Iris Berger in *Women in Africa: Studies in Social and Economic Change*, by Nancy J. Hafkin and Edna G. Bay, © 1975, 1976 by the Board of Trustees of the Leland Stanford Junior University; The University of Chicago Press for permission to reprint from *Women, Elite, Polygyny, and Buganda State Formation*, by Nakanyike Musisi, pp. 757–86, originally published in *Signs: Journal of Women, Culture and Society*, Vol. 16, no. 4, pp. 757–86, © 1991 by The University of Chicago Press; Oyeronke Oyewumi for "Gender in Precolonial Yorubaland," © 1992 copyright by Oyeronke Oyewumi; Paul Lovejoy and Cambridge University Press for permission to reprint from "Transformations in Slavery," © 1983 by the author; Igor Kopytoff for permission to reprint from "Commentary on Paul Lovejoy," in *Roots and Branches*, ed. by Michael Craton, pp. 67–75, Pergamon Press 1979, © 1979 by Igor Kopytoff.

Finally, in this revised edition I am grateful for the permission to reprint from *Black Athena* by Free Association Books Ltd, London, U.K. © Martin Bernal 1987, pp. 17–18, 440–442, first published by Free Association Books Ltd, London, England in 1987; and for permission to reprint from *Black Athena Revisited* by Mary R. Lefkowitz and Guy M. Rogers. Copyright © 1996 by the University of North Carolina Press; used by permission of the publisher and the author. Robert O. Collins, "The Asian Slave Trade," is forthcoming in French in *The African Diaspora in Asia: Historical Facts*, edited by Skhan de Silva Jayasuriya and Jean-Pierre Angenot, *Cahiers des Anneaux de la Memoire-Cam-Nantes,* France, 2005.